Changing Regional Alliances for China and the West

Russian, Eurasian, and Eastern European Politics

Series Editor: Michael O. Slobodchikoff, Troy University

Mission Statement

Following the collapse of the Soviet Union, little attention was paid to Russia, Eastern Europe, and the former Soviet Union. The United States and many Western governments reassigned their analysts to address different threats. Scholars began to focus much less on Russia, Eastern Europe and the former Soviet Union, instead turning their attention to East Asia among other regions. With the descent of Ukraine into civil war, scholars and governments have lamented the fact that there are not enough scholars studying Russia, Eurasia, and Eastern Europe. This series focuses on the Russian, Eurasian, and Eastern European region. We invite contributions addressing problems related to the politics and relations in this region. This series is open to contributions from scholars representing comparative politics, international relations, history, literature, linguistics, religious studies, and other disciplines whose work involves this important region. Successful proposals will be accessible to a multidisciplinary audience, and advance our understanding of Russia, Eurasia, and Eastern Europe.

Advisory Board

Michael E. Aleprete, Jr
Gregory Gleason
Dmitry Gorenburg
Nicole Jackson

Matthew Rojansky
Richard Sakwa
Andrei Tsygankov
Stephen K. Wegren
Christopher Ward

Books in the Series

Understanding International Relations: Russia and the World,
edited by Natalia Tsvetkova
Geopolitical Prospects of the Russian Project of Eurasian Integration, by
Natalya A. Vasilyeva and Maria L. Lagutina
Eurasia 2.0: Russian Geopolitics in the Age of New Media, edited by Mark Bassin and
Mikhail Suslov
*Executive Politics in Semi-Presidential Regimes: Power Distribution and
Conflicts between Presidents and Prime Ministers,* by Martin Carrier
Post-Soviet Legacies and Conflicting Values in Europe: Generation Why, by
Lena M. Surzhko-Harned and Ekaterina Turkina
Through Times of Trouble: Conflict in Southeastern Ukraine Explained from Within, by
Anna Matveeva
China's Bilateral Relations with Its Principal Oil Suppliers, by George G. Eberling

Changing Regional Alliances for China and the West

Edited by
David Lane and Guichang Zhu

LEXINGTON BOOKS
Lanham • Boulder • New York • London

Published by Lexington Books
An imprint of The Rowman & Littlefield Publishing Group, Inc.
4501 Forbes Boulevard, Suite 200, Lanham, Maryland 20706
www.rowman.com

Unit A, Whitacre Mews, 26-34 Stannary Street, London SE11 4AB

British Library Cataloguing in Publication Information Available

Library of Congress Cataloging-in-Publication Data

Names: Lane, David, 1933- editor. | Zhu, Guichang, editor.
Title: Changing regional alliances for China and the West / edited by David Lane and
    Guichang Zhu.
Description: Lanham, Maryland : Lexington Books, [2017] | Series: Russian, Eurasian,
    and Eastern European politics | Includes bibliographical references and index.
Identifiers: LCCN 2017048356 (print) | LCCN 2017040475 (ebook) |
    ISBN 9781498562348 (Electronic) | ISBN 9781498562331 (cloth : alk. paper)
Subjects: LCSH: China—Foreign relations—21st century. | China—Foreign economic
    relations.—21st century. | China—Foreign relations—Western countries. |
    Western countries—Foreign relations—China.
Classification: LCC JZ1734 (print) | LCC JZ1734 .C524 2017 (ebook) |
    DDC 327.51—dc23
LC record available at https://lccn.loc.gov/2017048356

Printed in the United States of America

Contents

List of Figures

List of Tables

List of Abbreviations

ADB   Asian Development Bank
AIIB   Asian Infrastructure Investment Bank
AMF   Asian Monetary Fund
APDRO   Accelerate Power Development and Reform Program
APEC   Asia-Pacific Economic Cooperation
APR   AsiaPacific Rebalancing strategy
ARF   ASEAN Regional Forum
ARP   Agricultural Research Platform
ASEAN   Association of Southeast Asian Nations
ASEAN+3   Association of Southeast Asian Nations (Plus China, Japan, ROK)
ASPE   Association of Standardized Patient Educators
BDB   BRICS Development Bank
BNDB   BRICS-New Development Bank
B&R   Belt and Road
BRICS   Brazil, Russia,India, China and South Africa
BWI   Bretton Woods institutions
CAFTA   China and ASEAN Free Trade Area
CARECP   Central Asian Regional Economic Cooperation Programme
CASCF   China-Arab States Cooperation Forum
CDB   China Development Bank
CIC   China Investment Corporation
CIS   Commonwealth of Independent States
CMEA   Council of Mutual Economic Assistance
CPC   Communist Party of China
CPEC   China Pakistan Economic Corridor
CRA   Contingent Reserve Arrangement

CSTO	Collective Security Treaty Organization
DRCSC	Development Research Centre of the StateCouncil
EBRD	European Bank of Reconstruction and Development
EDB	Eurasian Development Bank
EEC	European Economic Community
EEU	Eurasian Economic Union
EU	European Union
FCAC	Forum on China- Africa Cooperation
FDI	Foreign direct investment
FONOP's	Freedom of Navigation Operations
FSO	Fund for Special Operations
FTA	Free Trade Area
FTAAP	Free Trade Area of the Asia-Pacific
GATS	General Agreement on Trade in Services
GATT	General Agreement on Tariffs and Trade
GDP	Gross Domestic Product
GMSR	Greater Mekong Sub-region
GSIP	Great Stone Industrial park
GTA	Global Trade Area
IADB	Inter-American Development Bank
IBRD	International Bank for Reconstruction and Development
IBSADF	IBSA (India, Brazil, South Africa) Dialogue Forum
IFC	International Finance Corporation
IIC	Inter-American Investment Corporation
IMF	International Monetary Fund
LEMOA	Logistics and Supply Memorandum of Agreement
LIBOR	London InterBank Offered Rate
LPG	Liquefied Petroleum Gas
MWO	Multipolar World Order
NAFTA	North American Free Trade Area
NATO	North Atlantic Treaty Organization
NDB	New Development Bank
NGO	Non-Governmental Organizations
NMSEU	New Member States of the European Union
OBOR	One Belt, One Road
OFDI	Outward Foreign Direct Investment
OPEC	Organization of Petroleum Exporting Countries
PCCA	Paris Climate Change Agreements
PRC	People's Republic of China
PSD	Post-Soviet Developments
RCEP	Regional Comprehensive Economic Partnership
RCTS	Regional Counter-Terrorism Structure

RICc	RIC (Russia, India, China) club
RMB	Renminbi
SCO	Shanghai Cooperation Organization
SOEs	State Owned Enterprizes
SREB	Silk Road Economic Belt
SRF	Silk road fund
Three Evils	Terrorism, Separatism and Religious extremism
TiSA	Trade in Services Agreement
TPP	Trans-Pacific Partnership
TPRM	Trade Policy Review Mechanism
TRIPS	Trade-Related Aspects of Intellectual Property Rights
TTIP	Transatlantic Trade and Investment Partnership
WTO	World Trade Organisation

Foreword

Regional Turbulence: China's Regional Landscape

The study of regions is extremely important for scholars to focus on. While much attention has been paid by scholars to global relations, the study of regions has often been done by area studies scholars. They have provided important scholarship, but much of the work has not been examined within the larger context of experts who focus on multiple regions or at the global level. Considering globalization and the interconnectedness of the world system, it becomes increasingly important to combine regional studies with a more global perspective, trying to create a meaningful dialogue between area studies experts and more general global experts. Further, regions are nested within mega regions, which in turn are nested within the global community. States must therefore act accordingly. They must be regional actors while also being cognizant of their standing in the global hierarchy of states.

This book is extremely important as it focuses on China's evolving position within its region, meta region, and the world at large, while remaining cognizant that all of these relationships are intertwined. This edited volume first examines the global system of trade that applies to all regions. Then the volume focuses on China's trade relations with its neighbors in Asia, especially focusing on such projects as the One Belt One Road project (OBOR). Part II of the book focuses on Chinese economic initiatives especially in terms of cooperation with other great powers such as Russia and the other BRICS countries. Finally, the book examines China's relations with other world powers and organizations such as the United States and the European Union. Ultimately this book is one that should be read by all regional experts, especially those who study the Asian and Eurasian regions.

Michael O. Slobodchikoff
Series Editor
Lexington Russian, Eurasian and Eastern
European Politics Book Series

Preface

The dismantling of the Soviet bloc led to a period of political and economic dominance for the United States and its allies. Predicated on neo-liberal ideas, the borders between countries became increasingly porous: de-industrialisation occurred in the dominant Western states and concurrently countries such as China became leading industrial powers. Since the beginning of the twenty-first century, a number of regional powers and associations which, while not challenging the structure of the international system, have sought greater recognition. In the coming decade regional post-socialist associations such as the Brazil, Russia, India, China and South (BRICS), the Shanghai Cooperation Organisation (SCO), the Eurasian Economic Union (EEU), the Silk Road Economic Belt and the 21st Century Maritime Silk Road ('One Belt, One Road' - OBOR) are likely to increase in economic power, strategic position and political importance. China, economically and politically, is the crucial power in these new associations. A major theme addressed in this book is the character of these new powers: Will they become complementary to the American-led economic core countries or will they evolve as countervailing powers? As a consequence of the global economic crisis of 2007, austerity programmes set against a background of de-industrialisation in the core economic economies have led to claims for greater protectionism to safeguard the interests of the economically disenfranchised sections of the population. The administration of Donald Trump in the United States seeks to assert its own form of economic sovereignty while concurrently strengthening its geo-political power.

The chapters in this collection analyse the role of China in regional organisations and the country's relations with members of other groups of states such as the BRICS, the SCO, the EEU, and the OBOR. In the introduction, authors examine the changing pattern of world trade, politics and the rise of regional institutions, by exploring China's position in the post-Soviet and more globalised and regionalized world. Distinctions are made between regionalism and regionalisation. The former is a more formal legally based set of relationships whereas the latter contains more fluid open-ended multilateral or bilateral agreements. Contributors here suggest that linkages favoured by China's regional associations are more 'network' based and informal in character. They are more in keeping with regionalisation rather than regional blocs such as the European Union which have 'locked in' members to market-driven institutions. Thus these new developments move from the neo-liberal market perspective and satisfy the needs of members to retain their economic and political sovereignty.

In Part I, authors focus on China's political and economic initiatives with respect to their implications for neighbouring Asian countries. The scope and scale of the OBOR policy initiative are outlined. The scheme is a developmental policy in some ways similar to the Marshall Plan. It envisages the setting up of enterprise zones and investment along these routes in ambitious transport projects, including road and rail links, pipelines power supplies and port along ancient trade routes. The chapters also consider the underlying motives and likely success and failure of these plans. China's intentions are questioned not only by the United States but also by many in India who see the acquisition of ports in the South China Sea as a precursor to military influence. The United States also regards India to be a balance to China.

In Part II, papers analyse China's role in wider regional initiatives. The SCO and BRICS are discussed from a comparative perspective, by exploring the energy infrastructure and the BRICS New Development Bank. The association of BRICS presents a group of countries which are geographically separate and of unequal economic and political weight. The founding of the New Development Bank (NDP) is a response by the BRICS to the Bretton Woods institutions. Its objectives are to provide an alternative source of capital for its members and other emerging and developing countries. Its current policy is to avoid the conditionality imposed by such organisations as the IMF. In character it shares a similar pluralistic goal as other institutions discussed in the collection by promoting 'financial multi-polarity'. One objective is to replace the neo-liberal emphasis on 'austerity-type' structural policy adjustment by infrastructure products.

Contributors however raise the question of whether they will perform a 'transformative' process for the international order or become an alternative—supplementary to, but not replacing the existing institutions of, the North. An important topic here is the relationship of Russia and China to the Central Asian countries of the former USSR and the interaction between the Russia-led EEU and the Chinese initiative of the Silk Road Economic Belt. Authors raise the question of the potential for the evolution of an alliance between China and Russia against the neo-liberal order led by the United States. Concurrently they bring out the possible tensions between Russia's and China's conflicting interests over influence in Central Asia.

The SCO is described as a 'partnership' not an alliance. China's increasing deployment of economic assets along the OBOR raises the issue of how it will secure them in the face of internal wars and their possible loss. While the SCO is considered on balance to further China's strategic interests it is also seen as a positive development facilitating partnership between the EEU and OBOR. Some contributors regard these new associations (OBOR and EEU) as signifying 'diversity of political systems' and importantly as both a reaction and an antidote to US policies of destabilisation through military influence and ideological intervention. Here the relationship between Russia and China is crucial and the convergence of interests and acceptance of differences are regarded as a consequence of US policies.

Part III considers China's potential role in world politics. China has moved from a trajectory of dependence on the world economic system, to a competitive regional power to its current position of a challenger to US hegemony. This was facilitated initially by access to world markets under agreements of the World Trade Organisation. Encouraged by the leadership of the United States, it was considered that China would become a 'responsible stakeholder' in the Bretton Woods' institutions and economic policies based on liberal competitive values. The optimistic view widely held in the West was that China would follow the path envisaged by S.M. Lipset—industrialisation through a socialisation process would lead to democratisation and the assumption of liberal political as well as economic principles.

However, unlike the post-socialist European countries, the Chinese Communist Party maintained its political leadership. The economic power of China has led to unexpected consequences providing a challenge to the hegemony of the United States. Such challenges give rise to an alternative interpretation of China's rise: that of a political threat. This is the position taken not only by political realists but also by some Marxist commentators. The latter emphasise that corporate capitalist interests will thwart the rise of any contending economic and political power. Until the advent of the Donald Trump administration American policy was bipartisan. Under Clinton and Obama, policy was predicated on constraining Chinese power. The Trans-Pacific Partnership (TPP) was set up to maintain US hegemony—it widened the context of trade relations to include a wider range of economic and political obligations. However, China was excluded. The US 'pivot to China' was intended to widen and deepen America's security arrangements and weaken the presence of China as a regional power. The Trump administration has adopted a hostile policy. On the one hand, the United States' commitment to the TPP has been broken, which will probably strengthen China's hand as a major player in the free trade area of Regional Comprehensive Economic Partnership. On the other hand, the Trump administration is moving from a multilateral to a bi-lateral trade policy and threatens China with discriminatory tariffs. Authors point to Trump's emphasis on military power and increasing protectionism in trade.

The contributors seek to promote a better appreciation of China's role in regional associations, and the implications of contemporary developments in economic, geo-political, and international political affairs in the 21st century.

This book originated from an international conference on regional perspective on China and its neighbours held at Leiden University in January 2017. The conference was sponsored by the Confucius Institute at Leiden University, which has been jointly established in 2006 as a non-profit institution by Shandong University in China and Leiden University in the Netherlands, with the aim of promoting Chinese language and culture and contributing to better understanding among the peoples. The editors would like to thank the Confucius Institute for the financial support for the conference. We would also like to thank Frank Pieke, Andre Gerrits, Song Xinning, and Vsevolod Samokhvalov for their support and intellectual contribution to the conference.

David Lane, Guichang Zhu
July 2017

Introduction

THE CHANGING PATTERN OF
WORLD TRADE AND POLITICS

Chapter 1

Post-Soviet Regions

From Interdependence to Countervailing Powers?

David Lane

According to Peter Katzenstein (Katzenstein, 2005), the power of the United States is derived from two sources: territorial and non-territorial power. Traditional land-based and sea-based empires are dependent on the former. The latter is a novel source of global power which has enabled the United States to penetrate foreign countries and to control foreign markets. 'World politics is now shaped by the interaction between porous regions and America's imperium' (p.42). Katzenstein's emphasis on the global non-territorial power of the United States was made in 2005. The argument in this chapter is that in a relatively short period of time the world has been transformed and the current phase of regional formation is devised as one way to limit the ubiquitous penetration of states by global processes. Regions are no longer 'organised' as part of the empire of the United States. They are not geographical shapes made 'porous by links to the American imperium and core regional states' (Katzenstein, 2005, p. 2). The 'core' of the world system is no longer uniquely formed by the dominant Western states. It is challenged by the countervailing powers of rising states.

Globalization and internationalization (processes which cross boundaries) continue, but in a context of competitive interdependency. By 'competitive interdependence' is meant processes in which economic and political blocs compete for markets one with another and which concurrently, to their mutual advantage, exchange capital, goods and services (See Sbragia, 2010). In the third and current scenario, within the core states, Europe is being challenged by Asia, and Japan has been superseded, economically and politically, by China. Regional blocs of states (dismissed by Katzenstein as 'totally misplaced' p.178) confront the American imperium. States organized in regions provide barriers to the processes of neo-liberal globalization. The rise of

China as an economic power and the political awakening of Russia presage the advent of countervailing powers to the United States.

A region is a geographical area enclosed by a boundary. Regions include a diversity of types of association with rules and formal agreements differentiated by their economic, social and political character. One might distinguish between regionalism and regionalization. Regionalism is a process by which states (usually formally) confer upon regional institutions rights over certain matters. Regionalization is the process of 'increasing economic, political, social or cultural interactions' between a group of states and societies[1]. In this sense it includes not only closer informal linkages between governments but also the growth of formal and informal networks of civil society associations on a regional scale. Regionalization can occur without any formal organization and/or can run parallel to prescribed regional agreements. Politically, the crucial component of a region is the extent to which individual states give up their sovereignty to the regional unit. The depth of integration can vary from joint coordination of activities to the complete surrender of control to a supra-national body.

FROM MULTILATERAL FREE TRADE
TO REGIONAL AGREEMENTS

A major source of ideological and non-territorial power, which goes back to Adam Smith, is the principle of multilateral free trade. Since the end of the Second World War, the international economic policies of Western industrialized countries have been guided predominantly by the logic of free trade. Orthodox economic theory has asserted that open markets and unrestricted commerce are the most efficient forms of exchange. Multilateral free trade facilitates the international division of labor and specialization by countries on products and services in which they have a comparative advantage. Such comparative advantage attracts flows of capital to places where it is most efficiently invested, thereby promoting growth and well-being. Following this logic, the policies of liberal governments are devised to eliminate protection of national companies and to minimize barriers to trade and capital flows between countries. Katzenstein's 'porous' borders are the consequence of such neo-liberal policies. Globalization has raised liberal economic practices from a national to an international level.

Behind this economic reasoning lie political interests and economic power. 'Free trade' is a non-territorial form of economic power which enables economically superior actors to exercise their power through the medium of the market. Such actors have been domiciled in, and represented by, Western capitalist states. Free trade beholds political legitimacy and is economically cheaper than administrative control through colonies. It establishes not a territorial political hegemon (as in the British Empire) but an amorphous inter-territorial power network—a 'hidden hand' driving open markets. Moreover, under globalized capitalism, international flows are combined through global and territorial processes and concurrently legitimated in terms of economic effectiveness; only the market can 'give people what they want'. Dominant states seek to formulate and to enforce rules to facilitate free trade. When ideology fails, hegemonic powers turn to the use of military force—territorial power.

Such economic principles guided the regulations incorporated into the General Agreement on Tariffs and Trade (GATT formed on January 1, 1948) and its successor, the World Trade Organization (WTO) (which operated from January 1, 1995). Policy not only included the reduction of tariffs but also sought to implement common labor standards (though not wages) and conditions of investment to allow for the effective repatriation of profits. In this way risk was diminished and an even playing field, on which the most powerful team could win, was provided. The leading Western powers prioritized multilateral agreements based on GATT/WTO rules. Under conditions of multilateralism, the United States used its hegemonic power to influence the regulations which governed trade agreements.

In the capitalist world economy, the formation of regional associations was relatively infrequent before the 1950s[2]. Many of these stemmed from newly decolonized countries in Africa, Asia and the Middle East which sought to secure and protect their newly won sovereignty against Western powers. The major regional economic area outside the influence of GATT was the Council of Mutual Economic Assistance (CMEA)—an economic and political bloc which included most of the European communist countries but not the People's Republic of China. It was an economic and political region in both a formal and informal sense though states preserved their own political identities and had separate economic plans. There was no free mobility of capital or labor and prices were fixed administratively. Its members only marginally participated in world trade (with the possible exception of Hungary and Poland in the late Soviet period); they had adopted their own planned economic systems and coexisted with the capitalist world economy. Foreign direct investment was strictly controlled and very small in volume. In the West, such regional associations were considered to be mercantilist and detrimental to world trade. While they could coexist with the capitalist powers, their economic structures, processes and ways of doing things were incompatible with the capitalist world economy. To join it they would have to be dismantled through a political and economic transformation, or sufficiently changed through market and property reforms to open their economies to outside capitalist interests.

Within the GATT/WTO context, regional trade agreements were made. While the US policy prioritized multinational trade through the GATT/WTO, the formation of the European Economic Community (from 1993, European Union) did not threaten principles of free trade, though in practice its tariff walls were discriminatory against third parties. Mansfield and Milner, writing

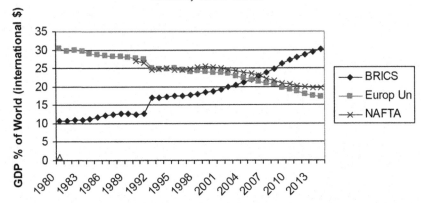

Figure 1.1   Proportion of World GDP 1980–2015: BRICS, European Union, Eurasian Economic Union and NAFTA. Created by the author from IMF World Economic Outlook Database, 2015.

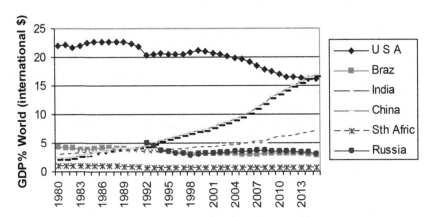

Figure 1.2   Proportion of World GDP 1980–2015: USA, Brazil, India, China, South Africa and Russia. Created by the author from IMF World Economic Outlook Database, 2015.

in 2003, contend that they promoted the liberalization of markets: 'So far, regional arrangements have seldom been used as instruments of power politics; instead, they have often been used to promote and consolidate domestic reforms that liberalise markets and foster democracy' (Mansfield and Milner 2003, p. 621). Regionalism during this period had a 'benign character' (ibid). This was because the major trading blocs at that time (the Triad of United States, European Union and Japan) all accepted the neo-liberal principles on which the WTO was founded. However, there remains an inherent tension between regional blocs and multilateral free trade. The principles of neo-liberalism require open markets, and open markets are not possible within geographically limited economic regions. The European Union, for example, has placed high tariffs on many goods as well as stringent technical conditions on their composition. Consequently, many American-sourced imports face discrimination.

POST-SOVIET DEVELOPMENTS

The ending of the bipolar structure of world politics between the NATO countries and those in the Warsaw Pact resulted in an upsurge in regional associations (Mansfield and Milner, 2012; Soderbaum, 2016, p.30). With the disintegration of the CMEA, countries of East and Central Europe sought trade relations with their preferred political and military allies. Of 200 regional trade agreements notified to GATT/WTO between 1948 and 1998, over half occurred after 1990 (Hoekman and Kostecki, 2001, see table 10.1, p. 346)[3]. Major regions were formed in the Americas, Europe and Asia[4].

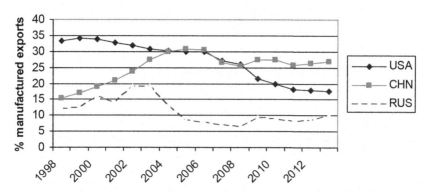

High Technology Exports: USA, China and Russia 1998 to 2014

Figure 1.3   **High-Technology Exports; USA, China and Russia 1998 to 2014.** Created by the author from World Bank Database, 2015.

David Lane

GDP (PPP) Top 11 Countries 1980 (bill int $)

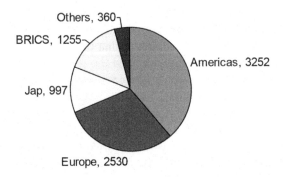

GDP (PPP) Top 11 Countries 2016 (bill int $)

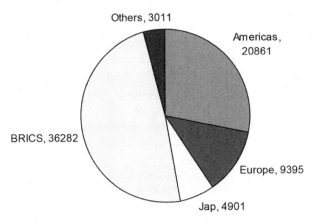

Figure 1.4   World Top Eleven Countries by GDP (PPP) 1980 and 2016, by Economic Blocs.
Created by the author from IMF, World Economic Outlook, 2015.

Decolonization in Africa and the Far East and the capitalist transformation of the post-socialist countries constitute only one part of the picture. The move to more autonomous regions may also be correlated with the waning of the United States as a world power[5] which was unable to sustain its preference for multi-lateral trade agreements (Mansfield and Milner, 2012, pp.71–73). This weakened its non-territorial power and borders became decidedly less 'porous'. The argument here is that the inability of the United States to influence countries to adopt multilateral policies based on GATT/WTO rules (which favored established developed countries) led to acceptance of a 'second best' form of regional trade agreements which brought many economies into the free market world system, albeit on a regional basis. Such a course gave some protection to companies threatened by competition consequent on the general reduction of trade barriers through agreements secured under GATT\WTO. By making preferential trade agreements on a regional basis— with a tariff against outsiders, less competitive companies were able to shield themselves from more efficient foreign firms. This is a form of territorial power exerted through and by states against globalization. Also a regional market is larger in size than a national one and thus has the advantages of economies of scale and increased consumer demand.

The formation by the United States of its own bloc (NAFTA, founded in 1994) stimulated the creation of other regional organizations[6]. The founding of NAFTA had 'struck a strong blow for economic regionalism' and presented a retreat from multilateralism (Sbragia, 2010, p.375). Peripheral dependence was maintained by the United States' influence over international organizations, and through transnational corporations domiciled in the United States as well as its military presence[7]. Territorial power is an important component of American and Western power. Later, with the dismantling of the USSR, NATO extended its borders to the Russian Federation, thus ostensibly securing Western interests through the newly formed New Member States of the European Union. Concurrently, transnational corporations extended their reach into the former socialist countries. Conditionalities required by the IMF and the World Bank (both highly under the United States' influence) were predicated on neo-liberal assumptions (Ikenberry 2001).

Political and strategic considerations influenced states forming regional blocs—governments were able to defend national companies as well as retain strategic industries. Regional organizations provide a political base for countries which have felt threatened by the forces of globalization. In the pursuit of state interests, regional power gives political parties and leaders, who are subject to periodic elections, the possibility to cultivate support from threatened political constituencies. The formation of the European Union is a major illustration of this trend. Free trade undoubtedly increased within the European Union and has led to many companies going out of business, particularly in the less economically developed economies.

Moreover, EU trade policy moved from multilateralism to a more self-centered regionalism. According to Alberta Sbragia (2010) this was because the United States under George Bush pursued free trade agreements with third parties that privileged US firms. Free trade agreements incorporated 'market-friendly business laws and regulations' which accommodated US business interests (Sbragia, 2010, p.376) quite independently of agreements made under WTO. The European Union followed the lead given by the United States. The European Union and the United States entered into a relationship of 'competitive liberalisation'. (The European Union was a customs' union with one tariff; whereas NAFTA was a free trade area allowing the United States to make its own tariffs with third parties). Borders lost their neo-liberal porousness. Thus the European Union and United States were simultaneously competitors in third party markets and economically interdependent actors. EU environmental standards also had the effect of keeping out of the European Union market many American-made products. Borders defining regions became important. Overall these developments weakened considerably the United States as an 'imperia' and shifted the balance toward competitive interdependence. American transnational businesses prospered and American consumers benefited from cheap imports. On the other hand, American workers and non-transnational companies suffered from the outsourcing of production to countries with lower labor costs. Hence the 'porousness' of borders worked in two directions. It strengthened production in the host countries of American global companies and weakened it at home. This is the process which Donald Trump's administration wishes to reverse.

The Changing Positions of the Major Powers in the World Economy

The emergence of competing regional organizations is based on the declining relative economic power of countries at the core of world capitalism. The power of a country in international affairs may be estimated on a number of criteria: its military capacity, which in turn is derived in great part, from its economic strength; its human and social capital—the quantity and quality of its population; and finally, its moral and ideological values. On all these counts (with the exception of military strength) the relative power of the United States is in decline. China in terms of population size and economic strength is rising; its human capital and moral values are catching up with the United States.

Measuring economic power is a contested academic exercise. Most writers utilize gross domestic product (GDP) as a major index[8]. The decline in the world share of GDP for the Western core states (NAFTA and the European Union) and the phenomenal rise of a new bloc of BRICS led by China is illustrated in Figure 1.1. It should be emphasized that these three groups are not comparable regional associations. The European Union is more than a customs' union having the character of a federative super state. NAFTA is a free trade area in which individual countries can fix their external tariffs independently. Whereas the BRICS are a form of regionalization—an emerging association of partners linked more by informal arrangements and mutual cooperation than formal agreements.

In Figure 1.1, we note the steady economic decline of NAFTA and the European Union against the rise of the BRICS countries. From producing only 11 percent of world GDP in 1980, the BRICS equaled the share of the

European Union in 2007, and by 2015, the BRICS accounted for 30 percent of global GDP—over 10 percent greater than NAFTA.

If we disaggregate the contribution of the component BRICS countries (as shown in Figure 1.2) we note the great disparities between them and the economic predominance of China which, in terms of national GDP, caught up with the United States in 2015. When combined, Russia, India and China have considerable manufacturing and military capacity and enormous internal markets. But, of the five countries, only three (Eurasia, India and China) share common boundaries. There are also very great differences between the economic wealth and political power of the BRICS' members. (One could, of course, say the same about the European Union (e.g., Germany, Luxembourg, Malta, Greece) though the European Union does not contain a hegemonic state similar to China; in NAFTA there is a parallel disparity between the United States on the one side and Canada and Mexico on the other).

The export of value-added manufactures is also an index of economic dynamism. The United States has experienced a steady decline in its share. As we note from Figure 1.3, US exports of high-technology products (as a proportion of all manufactured exports) declined from 2000 in the face of the rise of Chinese manufactured exports. Since the world financial crisis of 2007, China has surpassed the share of high-tech exports of the United States. One must be cautious in interpreting these data. Much of the hi-tech exports from China are the products of foreign companies located there and innovation and new product development are a different story. Nevertheless, China can certainly make the products which have displaced US as well as European manufacturing.

The balance of economic power, moreover, has shifted away from the core capitalist countries and moved to the East. Figure 1.4 illustrates the relative shares in world GDP of the top 11 countries in 1980 and 2016 by geographical areas. Not all members of the various economic blocs are shown here of course, but in combination the two figures bring out the significant change in relativities of leading countries in 1980 and 2016. The ratio of the share of world GDP of the top countries in America, Europe and Japan to other countries came to more than three quarters in 1980. By 2016 this ratio had fallen to less than half. The leading European countries share had fallen dramatically and is a potent factor underpinning the relentless enlargement policy pursued by the European Union to maintain its 'market share' (Borocz, 2014, pp. 20–34). This also spills over into the sphere of international relations: the struggle for world market share is a driving force behind the conflict between the European Union and Russia over Ukraine's proposed linkages to the European Union (at the expense of Eurasia).

One other robust measure of the declining economic power of the Western core countries is the number of companies listed in the top 2000 world companies. The Forbes List measures the strength of companies in terms of four attributes: sales, profits, assets and market value. The changing pattern of world economic power is shifting away from the Western dominant core. By 2015, in Asia were registered 691 companies, compared to Europe's 486. In this period, China with over two hundred companies has outstripped Japan, and the BRICS combined (370 companies) were just over 60 percent of the number of US companies. They included 57 Indian, 27 Russian, 24 Brazilian and 14 South African companies. The Eurasian Economic Union (EEU) (Russia, Kazakhstan and Belarus) with only 28 top companies in 2015 is a minor economic player signifying once again the unequal economic status of countries in the BRICS. Moreover, China had five companies in the top 10 and 13 in the top 100. Unlike Russia, whose major companies are predominantly in energy extraction, China has a good spread of companies across the economic sectors, including banking, materials, transportation, insurance, utilities, oil and gas, technology and hardware, consumer durables, and food and drink.

THE ASCENT OF COMPETING BLOCS

A significant rise in regionalization and the formation of regions began in the twenty-first century and should be explained in part as a reaction to failures of leadership predicated on the neo-liberal philosophy guiding policy in the core capitalist states. The United States as a hegemonic power was in decline. This is not to be explained, as suggested by Acharya, only in terms of terms of debt, health care, its 'over reach' in military and peace keeping (sic) activities in Iraq and Afghanistan[9]. There is a deeper structural realignment in the relative power of the Western hegemonic powers which are being challenged, and even displaced, by rising powers, particularly China (as noted above). The 'new economic order' promised by the Bush-Blair leadership led not to the promised globalized well-being but to endemic wars in the Middle East, a world economic crisis, domestic austerity policies and a 'war on terror'. The debacle of the international monetary system in 2007 was directly linked to the failure of neo-liberal financial policies. The populist opposition to these developments articulated by Brexit in the United Kingdom, the Front National in France, the Alternative for Germany and the election of Donald Trump in the United States is paralleled by demands for state sovereignty and growing regionalization on the part of Russia and China. Globalized neo-liberalism facilitated the transcontinental mobility of capital and thus shifted the competitive advantage of manufacture from the hegemonic core to the rising powers—particularly China.

Members of the BRICS countries are not part of the economic and political core of dominant capitalist states. The countries are spatially separated and continental in size. As Acharya (2014, pp.209–210) has pointed out, emerging powers do not form a cohesive group and this is particularly the case with the BRICS countries. Some experience internal conflict; they lack ideological convergence; their different levels of economic strength, noted above, and political power create disparities which may lead to resentment between the more powerful states and the weaker ones. The SCO 'operates a strictly state-centric, consensus-based system of decision-making offering a platform for regional cooperation' (Ritterberger and Schroeder, 2016, p.590).

What members of these associations share in common is the acceptance by their political and economic elites of private property relations and a major role for free markets. The difference with neo-liberal policy is over the extent and form of state regulation. There is also a less expansive vision for future policy. What has initially brought them together is a skepticism, which is not equally shared, of the political, military and economic policies emanating from the United States. The emphasis in this new form of regionalization is on the protection of national economic interests and developmental goals; in the Eurasian bloc on the preservation of sovereignty and re-industrialisation'. In all these countries the political class is divided over whether policy should be state coordinated rather than market led. There is an acceptance of the Westphalian concept of state sovereignty and resistance to the creation of supra-national regions such as the European Union (or earlier as the Soviet Union). Since the beginning of the world economic recession (2007) states have sought to maintain their sovereignty through alliances to form a smaller number of more powerful regions. In this way they have contained, rather than challenged, neo-liberal doctrine and policy. Certainly their borders have become less porous enabling neo-liberalism to flourish within regions rather than between regions. Consequently, social polarization within the European Union and the United States has led to opposition not from the traditional social-democratic parties, which have become cogs in the neo-liberal order, but from 'populist' parties clamoring for national protectionism.

FROM COMPETITIVE INTERDEPENDENCE TO ANTAGONISTIC BLOCS?

Against a changing background of relative Western economic decline and increasing regionalism, China and Russia are challenged in different ways by assertive policies emanating from the United States and European Union. Western critics emphasize the mischievous intentions of the Russian

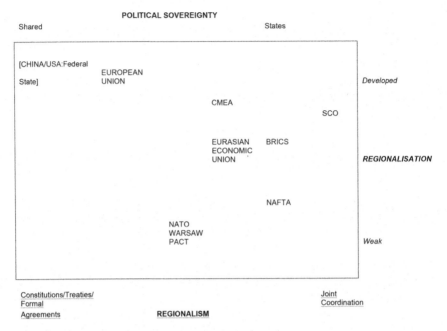

Figure 1.5   Regional Typologies of Major Political Blocs.

leadership: for them Eurasianism is a legitimation of opposition to the West (and especially the United States) and its values. They contend that it not only legitimates a false economic alternative but seeks to establish a new Russian hegemony, a geopolitical threat. A contrary interpretation is that the hidden power of globalization's non-territorial power has been exposed and the West, led by the United States, has adopted military force to secure its geopolitical goals. Evidence of this, it is argued, is the intention of America's Trump administration to increase even more the United States' military expenditure.

Russia has been confronted with enlargement of NATO. Disputes with Western powers over Yugoslavia, Eastern Ukraine, Crimea and Syria have worsened the political climate. In all these theaters (as well as Iraq and Afghanistan) the United States has resorted to 'territorial' power to maintain its political hegemony. The causes of these disagreements are claims over markets and geopolitical security. Aggressive EU trade sanctions and Russia's own counter-sanctions have had the effect of reinforcing the rise of a geopolitical bloc based on the Eurasian Union which has benefited from trade diversion from the European Union. In seeking to reassert its sovereignty, legitimated by ideas of Eurasianism, Russia is extricating itself from a period of dependence on Western powers. The consequences of Western policy push the members of the EEU to seek allies in the East, and to strengthen associations of states such as the BRICS and the SCO.

China has faced growing challenges from the United States to its security in the Pacific, where it is confronted by massive US military forces. The United States accounted for 25.8 percent of world military expenditure in 2014 (China 9.8 percent and Russia only 5.4 percent. (Military Balance 2015, p.22. Data based on PPP). The United States has reacted politically with its 'pivot to Asia' then its 'rebalance Asia' policy. Japan also regards China as a threat to its position as a Pacific leader. These conflicts are exacerbated by historically based disputes with Japan, Korea and Taiwan as well as the Philippines.

The formation of the Trans-Pacific Partnership (TPP), signed in February 2016, excludes China[10]. While lowering tariffs within the partnership, it will impose duties on China's exports. It provides a challenge to RCEP[11], which is China's preferred partner (and which excludes the United States). Further implications are that the neo-liberal ideology embodied in TPP may influence China's alternative economic and political strategy. Others in China's political class, who would benefit from further privatization, support membership as it would shift China's domestic policy more in the direction of neo-liberal practices[12]. This division is indicative of domestic policy disagreements over the extent to which China should be integrated into the dominant neo-liberal economic core and its implications for international policy. These political interests have suffered a setback with the withdrawal of the United States under the Trump administration from the TPP. Ironically, perhaps, China may benefit as a regional power though confrontation may take a military character.

The reactions of both Russia and China have been to form and strengthen their own regional associations. The BRICS, SCO, the Silk Road and the Maritime Road come into this category. Chinese leaders have emphasized cooperation between states rather than formal treaties: regionalization rather than regionalism. Such informal political associations are probably the best way to contain ambiguity and contradiction between different aspects of policy. Political leaders in Brazil, India and South Africa are subject to electoral challenge and replacement and consequently may renege on agreements. Changes of political leaders in Brazil and India could lead to more pro-US policies. Hence the BRICS should be regarded more as an association of friendly states pursuing policies of regionalization involving informal linkages than as an economic and political region rooted in treaties and formal agreements.

These organizations, however, are developing into more formally constituted groups. In 2014, the BRICS formed, under treaty, a New Development Bank, headquartered in Shanghai—potentially an alternative to the World

Bank. At the 2015 Ufa summit, the EEU has (or will) set up free trade areas with Vietnam, Egypt, India, Israel, South Korea and Chile, as well as with other countries in Latin America. In 2016 at the Goa Summit, the BRICS set up the Agricultural Research Platform, the Diplomatic Academies, the Think Tank and Academic Forum. In 2016, under the New Development Bank, has been set up the Contingent Reserve Arrangement, which operates under the 2020 Economic Partnership Strategy. While still at an early stage, regionalization involves labor and employment collaboration, education, climate change and health. Bilateral links between members (such as Russia and India) rather than regional agreements operate within the BRICS framework[13].

China has actively pursued the formation of its own reciprocal trade agreements. As of September 2016 China had 19 FTAs under construction, of which 14 had been signed and implemented[14]. None of these Agreements includes members of the EEU and they only include two former socialist states—Moldova and Georgia, both rather hostile to the Eurasian political bloc. China's existing preferential trade agreements are with Asian neighbors, including Korea, Singapore, New Zealand and Australia, as well as a growing number of rather small and marginal states (such as Iceland and Peru). China's objectives are to remain on favorable terms with the United States and concurrently to strengthen regional associations. They complement the 'competitive interdependence' we noted above. Regional policy is moving toward a stronger political and cultural dimension. For example, China has proposed the concept of the 'community of common destiny'.

However, the formation of economic and political blocs, whatever the benign intentions of their leaders, leads to competition and the infringement of rights of participants: sharing sovereignty entails the loss of sovereignty for the sharers. Economically and militarily powerful states within regions can be accused of imperialism. China's success as a world exporter is at the cost of other countries or foreign companies which lose their markets. Free trade is politically acceptable when hegemonic states can compete, when they cannot free trade is redefined as 'dumping'. India's rising business class may fear Chinese competition in a free trade area should the BRICS develop in this direction. Chinese leaders insist that China's policy is altruistic and promotes peace as well as contributing to stability in Asia. Xi Jinping in 2013 has stressed the importance of striving 'for a good surrounding environment for our country's development, to push forward the development of our country that benefits neighbouring countries more [as well as] seeding community consciousness in neighbouring countries'[15]. But China's more active role in region creation has led to suspicion from neighboring states as well as the United States. The Trump administration has indicated its intention in support of US manufacturers to weaken China's access to American markets.

China's regional policy has taken a new and distinctive style. It seeks to maintain its political sovereignty and consequently has adopted a gradualist and open form of regionalization. Bilateral, informal and inter-regional types of cooperation rather than formal binding treaties (as in the European Union) provide a platform for China's emergence as a regional power. Rather than relying on formal agreements, China has adopted a low-commitment form of cooperation which preserves state sovereignty (Chatterje-Doody, 2015). These new initiatives reflect China's increased attention to cultural and historical linkages with neighboring countries and should be contextualized in the promotion of soft power by China. Such regionalization involves a process of interaction and networking between associated states as a first step leading later to the signing of treaties.

Figure 1.5 summarizes the ways that different states relate to regional structures. Regions are differentiated on the top axis by the extent states maintain their own political sovereignty (in the sense that the state determines its own laws); on the bottom axis by how far regionalism is based on cooperative agreements or formal ties and treaties; and, finally, on the right-hand axis, whether regionalization in the form of civil society organization are highly or weakly developed. The European Union is more like a federal state, with its own courts, anthem and flag, and common external economic tariffs (similar to the United States) though the European Union's 'member states' still conduct foreign affairs and have their own armies. The SCO and BRICS rely on informal associational agreements and joint consultation.

TOWARD COUNTERVAILING POWERS?

I have argued that as a consequence of decline of the US hegemon, regions 'porous' to globalized interests have become interdependent competing blocs. The European Union, NAFTA and the emerging BRICS subscribed to a policy promoting their economic corporations to compete for profit in global markets under regulations jointly agreed. This period is coming to an end. The hegemonic blocs are becoming more confrontational in the face of the rise of developing nations such as China.

Despite historical and current economic and political differences, Russia and China face similar challenges from foreign powers which push them closer together and toward a common geopolitical interest. China, like Russia, is consolidating its regional associations and alliances. But neither Russia nor China has retreated into a mercantilist shell. Both countries maintain a positive policy toward the core economic powers and both have suggested strengthening trade links with the European Union[16]. President Putin has offered a common space running from the Atlantic to the Pacific[17]. Even an FTA between China and the United States has been suggested[18]. The underlying strategy is a geopolitical one of developing regional associations to promote their own interests without jeopardizing relationships with countries in the European Union and NAFTA. However the major component parts of the European Union and NAFTA are bound together by membership of the military alliance of NATO and by significant forms of economic, ideological, and political common ground, including allegiance to a liberal market–centered economy predicated on corporate ownership of private property, autonomous types of civil society and competitive electoral democracy.

China is facing the fundamental question of how it can be part of the global capitalist system as a major actor and concurrently maintain its sovereignty and political identity. One scenario is to strengthen its current competing interdependence with the dominant economic core states. Many in the Chinese political class, who stand to gain by liberal market policies, seek an accommodation with the core capitalist countries. To further such interests, China would complete its proposed FTAs with Korea and Japan. It would also need to improve relations with the European Union and the United States. The latter currently looks unlikely as the US policy of 'rebalance to Asia' under the Trump administration appears confrontational. Following the United States' exit from the TPP, the leadership of President Trump will weaken China's trade with the United States and the American military encirclement of China will remain and possibly be strengthened. Other factors also push China away from greater inclusion in the hegemonic core: the fear of further economic contagion following the debacle of the world economic depression of 2007, the fragmentation of the European Union, and mistrust of the US foreign policy. A move to a more countervailing power relationship will also depend on the constellation of political forces in China as well as mutual responses from possible allies such as Russia and other BRICS countries.

A more radical departure for world politics would be for China to establish its own 'counterpoint' involving the formation of a distinct bloc with its own legitimating ideology and structures. To do so, it would be necessary to strengthen links with the EEU and build up the Shanghai Cooperation Organization and the BRICS. Such a policy would involve moving from regionalization to regionalism. Whether the SCO and BRICS may deepen their forms of integration depends on the way that the members perceive external threats, the price of possible retaliation by the core states and the cost/benefit of security against sovereignty. Currently the SCO is 'state-centric'. The underlying ideology is framed in terms of countering threats posed by globalization and Western interventionism, which threatens state sovereignty.

However, there is no consensus within the political class in either China or Russia for the establishment of a 'national capitalist' type of economy challenging the neo-liberal order. Many in the political classes of both countries have profited from the transformation of state socialism to a market society which has increasingly secured access of the political and economic elites to private property. They remain skeptical not only about the Eurasian project but also about other associations formed within the framework of the BRICS. They seek a secure base for their property and prefer the neo-liberal option. Currently, the BRICS lack an alternative ideology in any way comparable to the European Union's 'basic freedoms' of movement. But neo-liberal thinking dominates public discourse and informs policy-makers, even if its virtues have been put in doubt. The strengthening of market relationships in these countries would move the regional project toward a competitive inclusion in the present global system. Regions would contain rather than replace neo-liberalism and would become complementary components in a world order. In this case, the development of an alternative geopolitical bloc would not arise (Schulz, Soderbaum and Ojendal, 2001, p.247). Such regions would become more than 'stepping-stones' to the neo-liberal world order (Hettne, 2001, pp.3–4); they would be permanent fixtures of neo-liberal competitive interdependence.

But this kind of an inclusion in the world neo-liberal economy could only be achieved if countries of the European Union and NATO would adopt more compromising policies to Russia and its allies. And for the United States, Japan and South Korea to do the same with regard to China. In this perspective, the European Union (and/or the United Kingdom) and the EEU could make an economic compromise, possibly operating under a free trade area (which would allow for certain products and services to be excluded, as in the case of Turkey). China would join the TPP even without the United States and its market-liberal principles would shift the domestic economy away from its current form of state directed capitalism. Such moves appear unlikely.

More realistic alternatives would take the shape of limited and informal patterns of regionalization and multinational agreements between Eurasia and China, and between the BRICS members. The model of the European Free Trade Area—enlarging the market while limiting regional political powers and concurrently promoting intergovernmental agreements and bilateral links with third parties—is more suited as a model for the disparate nation states constituting the BRICS. Other forms of regionalization, cultural and social in form, could be pursued along the lines of the British Commonwealth, which is even more geographically and economically diverse than the BRICS. Such a regulated regional association might develop an alternative value system with social-democratic and statist components different from market-liberal globalized capitalism.

A much more radical shift is to be found in the Beijing Consensus. This is not the policy position of the Beijing government, though some of its statements (such as support for the United Nations) are in line with it. The ideas are usually attributed to Joshua Cooper Ramo's paper, 'The Beijing Consensus' London: Foreign Policy Centre, 2004. This political orientation challenges the market-liberal outlook as well as current Russian and Chinese policy. It moves the emphasis away from measuring well-being in terms of GDP growth and puts more stress on economic improvement and social development. A greater importance is given to the provision of full employment and social equality in the distribution of income and wealth. The policy proscribes foreign military interventionalism (often disguised as democracy promotion), trade embargoes and economic sanctions which in turn are a form of economic warfare.

Internationally, if adopted, these developments would provide the basis for a more pluralist and multi-polar world. To build any significant alternative to the neo-liberal global order, it would need a combination of regional associations including the Eurasian Union, the Shanghai Cooperative Organization and other countries in the BRICS. However, there are divergent paths which bar movement in this direction. China is moving toward a form of regionalization with political and economic alignments which are informal and flexible. Whereas members of the EEU look to the European Union approach of a regionalism built on the free mobility of the factors of production which share sovereignty and weaken state power. The puzzle here for economic and political policy is to devise forms of regional association to give its members greater mobility of the factors of production while concurrently preserving political sovereignty and furthering a national developmental policy.

NOTES

1. Only the first part of this definition acknowledges Borzel and Risse (2016, p. 8), who limit regions to groups which are geographically and culturally 'contiguous'. This need not be the case, as NATO, the British Empire, Eurasia and the BRICS were (and are) not contiguous, but form regions. See also Mansfield and Milner, p. 591.

2. Between 1958 and 1994, reciprocal agreements notified to GATT/WTO averaged just under five per year. See data on agreements reported to GATT under Article XXIV in Edward D. Mansfield and E. Reinhardt (2015, see Figure 1, p. 153).

3. Data cited by B.M. Hoekman and M.M. Kostecki (2001). See table 10.1, p. 346. Here are cited figures relating only to members of the WTO, other data show a similar pattern.

4. The North American Free Trade Agreement (NAFTA composed of Canada, Mexico, United States) founded in 1994; MERCOSUR (Southern Common Market) (Argentina, Brazil, Paraguay, Uruguay, Venezuela) was founded in 1991. ASEAN was constituted as early as 1967. (Brunei, Darussalam, Myanmar/Burma, Cambodia, Indonesia, Laos, Malaysia, Philippines, Singapore, Thailand, Vietnam.) The organization of Asia-Pacific Economic Cooperation (APEC) formed in Australia in 1989 currently has 21 members, including Australia, China, United States, Russia, Japan and Singapore.

5. See discussion in Acharya (2014), chapter 2.

6. See discussion on hegemony in Mansfield and Milner (2012, pp. 71–73).

7. The United States's military spread increased significantly after the 9/11 terrorist attacks. Even in 2001, the United States already had more than a quarter of a million military personnel stationed in 153 countries (Katzenstein, 2005, p.4). Its armed forces and weapons of mass destruction not only have a global spread but (in total) are far greater than those of any other state, or group of states outside NATO.

8. There is a significant difference between the total of a country's GDP and its GDP expressed in per capita terms. Countries like China and India have large populations, making their country GDP far greater per capital GDP than that of European countries. However, population size is itself an indicator of political strength in international affairs. Both Saudi Arabia and Norway have high per capita GDP but lack international political power.

9. See Acharya (2014), chapter 2.

10. It includes the United States, Brunei, Chile, New Zealand, Singapore, Australia, Canada, Japan, Malaysia, Mexico, Peru, and Vietnam. In 2017, the participation of the United States is problematic as ratification has not been signed by the US Congress, and President Trump is opposed to the Partnership, at least in its current form.

11. Regional Comprehensive Economic Partnership. A proposed free trade association.

12. Zhang Xiaoton and Li Xiaoyue, for example, point out that regionalism is a mechanism for domestic reform. TPP, TTIP, the EU-Japan FTA, and other regional cooperation dominated by Western countries create external pressures for China to undertake domestic reforms. 'China's Regionalism in Asia'. Available at: The Asan Forum, Online ISSN 2288-5757 July–August 2016 Vol.4, No.4. http://www.theasan-forum.org/chinas-regionalism-in-asia/

13. See details in the Eighth BRICS Summit Goa Declaration, Full Text: http://indianexpress.com/article/india/india-news-india/8th-brics-summit-goa-declaration-here-is-the-full-text-adopted-by-the-member-nations/

14. As of September 2015 China's Free Trade Agreements were as follows: China-ASEAN FTA, China-Pakistan FTA, China-Chile FTA, China-New Zealand FTA, China-Singapore FTA, China-Peru FTA, Mainland and Hong Kong Closer Economic and Partnership Arrangement, Mainland and Macau, Closer Economic and Partnership Arrangement, China-Costa Rica FTA, China-Iceland FTA, China-Switzerland FTA, China-Korea FTA, China-Australia FTA.Free Trade Agreements under Negotiation: China-GCC(Gulf Cooperation Council) FTA, China-Norway FTA, China-Japan-Korea FTA, Regional Comprehensive Economic Partnership, RCEP,

China-ASEAN FTA Upgrade Negotiations, China-Sri Lanka FTA, China-Maldives FTA, China-Georgia FTA.Free Trade Agreements under Consideration: Study, China, China-Moldova FTA Joint Feasibility Study, China-Fiji FTA Joint Feasibility Study, China-Nepal FTA Joint Feasibility Study: Preferential Trade Agreement: Asia-Pacific Trade Agreement. Source: http://fta.mofcom.gov.en/En

15. See http://news.xinhuanet.com/politics/2013-10/25/c_117878944.htm. Cited by Xiaotong and Xiaoyue. 'China's Regionalism in Asia', The Asan Forum. Available online ISSN 2288-5757 July–August 2016 Vol.4, No.4. http://www.theasanforum.org/chinas-regionalism-in-asia/

16. Wen Jiabao had proposed an FTA feasibility study with the EU at the China-EU summit in 2012. See Xinhua News Agency, "Foreign Minister Yang Jiechi Briefed about Premier Wen Jiabao's Visit in Brussels for the 15th EU-China Summit," September 21 2012, http://www.gov.cn/jrzg/2012-09/21/content_2230338.htm. Cited by Xiaotong and Xiaoyue (2016).

17. Received positively by the European Bank of Reconstruction and Development (EBRD, 2012, chapter 4).

18. The Joint Statement of the fourth Annual US-China CEO and Former Senior Officials' Dialogue suggested a US-China FTA. See *China Daily*, "Fourth Annual US-China CEO and Former Senior Officials' Dialogue Concludes in Beijing," June 5, 2013, http://www.chinadaily.com.cn/china/2013-06/05/content_16571993.htm. Cited by Xiaotong and Xiaoyue (2016).

REFERENCES

Acharya, A. (2014) *The End of American World Order*. Cambridge, Polity Press.

Borocz, J. (2014) Geopolitical Scenarios for European Integration. In: Jensen J. and Miszlivetz, F. (eds), Reframing Europe's Future: Challenges and Failures of the European Construction, London, Routledge, pp. 20–34.

Borzel T.A. and Risse, T. (2016) Introduction. In: Borzel T.A. and Risse, T. (eds.), *The Oxford Handbook of Comparative Regionalism*, Oxford, Oxford University Press, pp. 3–16.

Chatterje-Doody, P.N. (2015) Roles and Realities in Russian Foreign Policy. In: Lane, D. and Samokhvalov, V. (Eds), *The Eurasian Project and Europe*, Basingstoke and New York, Palgrave, pp. 203–216.

EBRD, (2012) *Transition Report*. London, EBRD.

Hettne, B. (2001) Regionalism, Security and Development: A Comparative Perspective. In: Hettne, B., Inotai, A. and Sunkel, O. (Eds), *Comparing Regionalisms*, Basingstoke, Palgrave, pp. 1–53.

Hoekman, B.M. and Kostecki, M.M. (2001) *The Political Economy of the World Trading System*. Oxford and New York, Oxford University Press.

Ikenberry, G. J. (2001) *After Victory: Institutions, Strategic Restraint, and the Rebuilding of Order after Major Wars*. Princeton: Princeton University Press.

Katzenstein, Peter J. (2005) *A World of Regions: Asia and Europe in the American Imperium*. Ithaca: NY, Cornell University Press.

Mansfield E. D. and Milner, H.V. (2012) *Votes, Vetoes, and the Political Economy of International Trade Agreements*. Princeton and Oxford, Princeton University Press.

Mansfield, Edward D. and Reinhardt, E. (2015) Multilateral Determinants of Regionalism: the Effects of GATT/WTO on the Formation of Preferential Trading Arrangements, In: Mansfield, E.D. (ed.), *International Trade and the New Global Economy*, Cheltenham, E. Elgar, pp.150–183.

The Military Balance (2015), London: Routledge.

Mittelman, James H. and Richard Falk, (1999) Hegemony: The Relevance of Regionalism. In: Hettne B., et al. (Eds), *National Perspectives on New Regionalism in the North*, London, Macmillan.

Ritterberger, B. and P. Schroeder, 2016 The Legitimacy of Regional Institutions. In Borzel, T. and Risse, T. (eds.) *The Oxford Handbook of Comparative Regionalism*, Oxford, Oxford University Press, pp. 579–599.

Sbragia, Alberta (2010) The EU, the US, and Trade Policy: Competitive Interdependence in the Management of Globalization. *Journal of European Public Policy* 17 (3), 368–382.

Schulz, M., Soderbaum F. and Ojendal, J. (2001) Key Issues in the New Regionalism. In: Hettne, B., Inotai, A., and Sunkel O. (Eds) *Comparing Regionalisms*, London, Palgrave, pp. 234–276.

Soderbaum, F. (2016) Old, New, and Comparative Regionalism: The History and Scholarly Development of the Field. In: Borzel, T. and Risse, T. (eds.) *The Oxford Handbook of Comparative Regionalism*, Oxford, Oxford University Press, pp. 16–40.

Chapter 2

The Changing Governance and Geography of World Trade

Stefan Schmalz

In January 2017, Australian prime minister, Malcolm Turnbull, announced that Australia would be open to China joining the Trans-Pacific Partnership (TPP) agreement. The reason for this surprising statement was the decision of the new US government to withdraw from TPP (Karp, 2017). Without the US, the planned agreement of 12 nation states,[1] which represent about 40 percent of global Gross Domestic Product (GDP), would lose its anchor. The US was the largest single member state of the agreement, accounting for more than 60 percent of the GDP of the TPP members and representing a market of 318 million consumers. The Australian government therefore invoked a fallback position, with China as an alternative partner to keep the agreement alive. In fact, China is the only comparably large economy (two thirds of the US size) with a fast-growing domestic market of almost 1.4 trillion consumers.

A few months earlier, a similarly surprising event had taken place in East Asia. During his first official visit to China, recently elected Philippine president Rodrigo Duterte not only signed investment treaties worth about US$ 15 billion, but also announced his country's military and economic "separation" from the US (Paddock, 2016). In the next few months, Duterte continued his discourse. He questioned the expansion of US military bases in the Philippines; raised concern about a possible military confrontation between the US, its allies and China; and even mentioned the idea of joint Sino-Philippine exploration of oil reserves in the contested South China Sea. Only after a visit by Japanese prime minister Shinzo Abe to Duterte's private house in Davao did Duterte agree to support the expansion of US military bases, but announced only a few weeks later that he will attend a high-level "One Belt, One Road" summit in Beijing in May 2017.

Even though both announcements have yet to lead to further political action, they indicate China's new economic role in East Asia and, more generally, in global capitalism. China's rise has led to a shift in the governance and geography of world trade with important geopolitical implications, opening up new spaces of negotiation for governments in the Global South with both China and the US. In the following, the author will trace these changes by exploring China's institution building in global trade and finance. The author's main assumption will be that the American and European backed global trade regime has reached its limits, while China is now starting to experiment with new forms of network-based economic governance.

The author will elaborate this hypothesis in the following way: section 1 begins with an analysis of the global trade regime and China's integration in this system. The author describes this regime as a multilevel regime aiming at "deep integration" (Claar and Nölke, 2013), thus, not solely focusing on liberalizing trade in goods, but also on liberalizing services, investment flows, government procurement and introducing new competition rules. Section 2 will outline the development of this regime since the late 1990s. Fast economic growth in China led to a commodity boom with many countries in the Global South benefiting from this development and contributing to an increase in South-South trade. This development went along with the creation of new South-South-cooperation agreements. Section 3 will analyze how the financial crisis in 2007/08 sped up this restructuring, with China suddenly becoming the main growth center of the world economy. This is especially due to Chinese state officials' frustration with Western-dominated Bretton Woods institutions, so China started to play a more active role in South-South cooperation. Section 4 will describe the reaction of the Obama administration to the rise of China and the US attempt to contain China's influence together with its US allies in East Asia. This pivot to Asia was backed by a "T-Strategy" (Daniljuk, 2015, p. 545) in trade: The US pushed for new trade and investment agreements including the Transatlantic Trade and Investment Partnership (TTIP), the TPP Agreement, and the Trade in Services Agreement (TiSA). Section 5 maps out China's ongoing response to the T-strategy including its far-reaching plans of the "One Belt, One Road" (OBOR) initiative and the Asian Infrastructure Investment Bank (AIIB). These projects tend to establish new network-oriented governance structures, as they are mainly based on infrastructure investment and on facilitating trade. In the conclusion, the author will discuss recent events such as the election of Donald Trump and the slowdown of global trade, thus arguing that the global trade regime is in crisis and that China might be able to further influence global trade governance.

GLOBAL CAPITALISM AND THE RISE OF CHINA

The creation of the World Trade Organization (WTO) in 1994 contributed to a far-reaching change of the global trade regime (Hoekman and Kostecki, 2009). The hitherto-existing General Agreement on Tariffs and Trade (GATT) was mainly limited to the liberalization of trade in goods by reducing tariffs and non-tariff barriers in frequent rounds of trade negotiations. The WTO, in contrast, extended the range of negotiations, thus leading not only to major cuts of tariffs (about 40 percent), but also to the introduction of three new areas of liberalization. The General Agreement on Trade in Services aims at the liberalization of trade and investment in the service sector, the Agreement on Trade-Related Aspects of Intellectual Property Rights (TRIPS) comprises intellectual property right issues. And the agreement on agriculture extends the liberalization agenda to agricultural products and subsidies. These new agreements were seen as first steps to further liberalization: Since the WTO Ministerial Conference in 1996, in particular the European Union, Japan and Korea, pushed for the integration of the so-called "Singapore issues" (investment, government procurement, competition, and trade facilitation) in WTO negotiations.[2]

The creation of WTO was flanked by a new wave of regionalism (Bergsten, 1998). The official WTO website states that by June 2017 the GATT/WTO was notified of approximately 659 Regional Trade Agreements, with the majority implemented since 1990. Unlike earlier agreements of "closed regionalism" in the times of the GATT regime, these "open regionalism" treaties went far beyond the classical content of trade agreements such as the lowering of duties for industrial products. "Open regionalism" trade agreements are—similar to the WTO negotiations—aiming at "deep integration" (Claar and Nölke, 2013), thus harmonizing the business environment by deregulating competition policy, investor rights, product standards, public procurement and intellectual property rights in order to "facilitate foreign direct investment (FDI) and trade in services" (Claar and Nölke, 2013, p. 276). In many cases regional policies were barely institutionalized. NAFTA (1994)—an agreement between the US, Canada and Mexico—served as a blueprint for deep integration. Similar to other open regionalism agreements, NAFTA implies the overall liberalization of goods, capital and service markets, but comprises neither effective social and environmental clauses nor strong supranational institutions.

The global trade regime that emerged in the 1990s should be perceived as a multilevel regime with similar actors pushing at different levels for the same issues (Harmes, 2006). Even though nation states are still competing for preferential market access, trade agreements often overlap but do not contradict. For instance, Chile, Mexico, Colombia and Peru have signed agreements with a deep integration agenda with both the US and Europe. On a theoretical level, this process can be perceived as a driver of the emergence of global capitalism since the 1980s. Processes described by scholars such as Robinson (2004), Sklair (2001) and Harris (2016) such as transnational class building and the emergence of transnational state apparatuses go along with the development of transnational circuits of capital accumulation that tend to replace national processes as the main determinant of economic activities. The changing trade regime plays an important role in governing this transformation. Besides opening up new possibilities for transnational companies, exporters and investors also lock-in neoliberal policies on a supranational level. This "new constitutionalism" (Gill, 1998) separates economic and political processes from broad political responsibility in order to make governments more susceptible to the discipline of the market and, accordingly, less susceptible to popular democratic forces and processes. Taken together, the new trade regime was crucial to support the development of "global capitalism" and was designed to mainly benefit transnational capitalist groups.

However, the new trade regime is also contested. Several scholars have argued that WTO and most open regionalism agreements are backing the geopolitical interests of developed countries and, in turn, are limiting the development space of emerging and developing countries (Wade, 2003; Chang, 2007). The main argument of these skeptics is that liberalization and competitive pressures effectively hinder industrial-catch-up processes and that far-reaching regulations on intellectual property rights, government procurement and competition regulation might disable state capacities to support infant industries. Also, countries with high ratios of agricultural employment such as India saw the livelihoods of peasants at stake as small farmers feared competition from transnational agribusiness. Moreover, even success stories of dynamic exporters are often criticized as not having been sustainable, as these developments went along with increasing inequality among regions and classes. As we will see later, these critical points were present in the WTO Doha trade round (launched in 2001), when policy-makers in the Global South blocked negotiations.

However, not all countries experience negative effects. Rather, several emerging nations were able to selectively integrate into global capitalism without losing their state capabilities to push forward development and support infant industries. This observation is particularly true for several East Asian countries. In particular China was able to continue its development path of "sino-capitalism" (McNally, 2012) after its accession to the WTO in 2001. Even though WTO accession speeded up world market integration and strengthened the export- and (infrastructure) investment-driven model, China continued to limit market access and to rely on high state subsidies. For instance, China is using its 5-year plans to subsidize infant industries, spur technological development and improve infrastructure. Also, non-tariff-barriers such as censorship in the digital economy provide support to national companies (Baidu, Alibaba, etc.) (Yeo, 2016). Additionally, the close guanxi (trust relationships) between local party cadres and entrepreneurs influence government procurement (Breslin, 2007, pp. 100). In sum, the Chinese export- and investment-driven model continued to experience high GDP growth rates in the 2000s, thus contributing to the rise of China and paradoxically making China the "main beneficiary of the globalization project that the United States itself had sponsored in the 1980s and 1990s" (Arrighi, 2007, p. 295).

THE RE-EMERGENCE OF SOUTH-SOUTH COOPERATION

Since the mid-2000s, the global trade regime began to unfold a new logic. China developed as a major center of growth in East Asia and worldwide. By 2007, China contributed more than one fifth of global economic growth, and its contribution to East Asian GDP growth was also significant at about two thirds. The Chinese share in world imports had almost tripled to six percent. As China's transnationalized economic model was heavily dependent on commodity inputs, the growing importance of China in the world economy led to an increase in commodity consumption and imports (Farooki and Kaplinsky, 2012; Roache, 2012). In particular the global import shares of metals and ores, but also coal, cotton and oil, went up tremendously. For instance, between 1997 and 2007 the global import share of iron ore increased from a seventh to two-thirds, the share of copper from a seventh to almost a third and the share of bauxite from less than 5 percent to a third. As a result, the growing Chinese demand contributed to a commodity boom, with many countries in the Global South benefiting from this development. In the case of Latin America, the Chinese demand was responsible for half of the increase in commodity exports between 2003 and 2011 (Gallagher, 2016, pp. 59). The improved terms of trade for commodity exporters also led to higher earnings for exporting countries. According to the economist Rhys Jenkins (2011), higher prices led to additional export earnings of US$ 34 billion for Latin America between 2002 and 2007 alone.

The economic boom in the Global South was further pushed by new economic strategies in some emerging countries. After a series of financial crises between 1997 and 2001 in East Asia, South America, Russia and Turkey, most crisis-prone emerging countries began to embark on floating currency-regimes and export orientation (Wolf, 2008, pp. 69ff.). Given positive circumstances on the world market, emerging nations in East Asia, Latin America and Russia experienced comparatively high growth rates, thereby contributing to an accelerated increase of South-South trade. Between 1997 and 2007, trade between developing countries generally grew much faster than trade between developed countries or trade between developed and developing countries: whereas trade between developed countries had doubled, the trade between developed and developing countries had tripled, and trade between developing countries had even grown about five times (IMF, 2016). China was the most important driver of this shift, as China's trade flows to other developing countries skyrocketed by about 12 times in the period.

Moreover, the changing geography of trade also helped to improve the financial situation of several emerging countries. Most emerging countries could use their export earnings to accumulate high currency reserves. According to UNCTAD (2016), up until 2007, the currency reserves of developing countries increased to about US$ 4.5 trillion. This development helped to reduce the foreign debt of several emerging countries: for instance, after two decades of indebtedness and structural adjustment programs, two of the IMF's most important debtor nations, Argentina and Brazil, were able to pay off their IMF debt of about US$ 15.5 billion and US$ 9.8 billion respectively in late 2005. As a result, the IMF faced a crisis, because its overall credit volume fell from its peak of US$ 101.6 billion in September 2003 to around US$ 11.1 billion in April 2007.

On an institutional level, the rise of China and the commodity boom not only led to a weakening of traditional power relations in global economic governance, but also went along with the creation of new South-South-cooperation agreements. These institutions aim at both changing existing institutions and creating alternative structures in order to govern trade and investment flows. From a trade perspective, there were at least three important developments: First, there was a revival of OPEC. After years of low oil prices, in 1999 OPEC countries agreed on stronger regulation of the oil supply. New cooperation attempts with Non-OPEC members such as Russia and the (re)entry of Ecuador and Angola to OPEC in 2007 even strengthened these ties. Second, in 2003 India, Brazil and South Africa created the India-Brazil-South Africa (IBSA) dialogue forum in order to increase economic ties and political cooperation (Narlikar, 2010). Due to several agreements on trade, technology and investment the trade volume between Brazil, India and South Africa increased fourfold. Third, even before the "China boom" shaped the global economy, China, Russia and other Central Asian countries (Uzbekistan, Kazakhstan, Kyrgyzstan, Tadzhikistan) had agreed on the creation of the Shanghai Cooperation Organization (SCO). This regional institution aims at both cooperation in security and economic issues such as infrastructure, energy and trade facilitation (Yuan 2010, pp. 850ff.).

The most successful attempt to influence the operational mode of hitherto-existing economic governance institutions was the creation of the trade-G-20 (founded in 2003) of developing nations in the WTO. The G-20 was established in the run-up to the WTO ministerial meeting of Cancún in September 2003 (Narlikar and Tussie, 2004). The new group was firstly organized by the IBSA and included important emerging countries such as China, Saudi Arabia and Indonesia. The group aimed at a "soft balancing approach" (Flemes, 2009, p. 401) toward the Quad (the United States, the European Union, Japan and Canada) mainly focusing on agricultural trade, but also criticizing the inclusion of some of the Singapore issues in the negotiations. The emergence of the new group helped to change the balance of power in the WTO, thus challenging the Quad's dominant position in negotiations. It also contributed to derail the agenda of further deepening the trade regime.

Taken together, South-South cooperation began to shape the global trade regime during the 2000s. Unlike earlier attempts in the 1970s as the movement for a "New Economic Order," which was ideologically pushing forward a vision of Third-World Solidarity, current South-South cooperation is much more pragmatic and less ideological (Hudson, 1977: pp. 176ff.; Dos Santos 2011, 51f.; Gosovic, 2016). However, the economic background in the 2000s was much more favorable, as China and other emerging countries experienced fast GDP growth, and commodity prices reached new heights. However, apart from the SCO, China itself did not engage as a main actor in most of the new agreements, which were pushed forward by the Brazilian center-left-wing government and other countries. One could even argue that China's integration in the trade system during this stage was still a stabilizing element of the existing order (Hung, 2016, pp. 115ff.). China's large current account surplus was invested in US treasury bonds and other US semi-government assets, thus making China the United States' most important foreign borrower with US$ 1.2 trillion in assets in 2008. Also, the US remained China's largest export market with an export share of more than one-fifth. Consequently, at the time, China did not actively pursue an alternative agenda for a new global economic regime.

NEW DYNAMICS AFTER THE FINANCIAL CRISIS IN 2007/08

The financial crisis in 2007/08 forced China's government to rethink China's role in global economic governance. This was mainly due to the geography of the financial crisis. The crisis was a major "setback for the West" (Altman, 2009), as the US, European Union and other OECD countries were deeply affected by the crisis, while China, India and other countries managed to cope comparatively well. Their high resiliency to crisis was mainly due to a limited integration in global financial markets and a strict regulation of finance, relative to the US and European Union, so that they could prevent a major breakdown (Schmalz and Ebenau, 2012, p. 494). As a result, emerging markets that had stronger links to the US or Europe, such as Mexico or Eastern Europe, ran into great difficulties, whereas states that strengthened their ties to East Asia—for example, Brazil and sub-Saharan Africa—survived relatively unscathed. Consequently, China suddenly became the main growth center of the world economy. Between 2010 and 2013, China contributed more than one fourth to global economic growth. It also turned into the most important export market for several countries in the Global South such as Brazil, Angola and Indonesia. In sum, China seemed to emerge as a potential new "consumer of last resort" during the crisis.

The crisis was also reflected in global governance. Most importantly, the G-8 was replaced by the G-20[3] as the main forum to coordinate national crisis responses. This was a crucial change as important semi-peripheral countries like India, Brazil, Indonesia, South Africa, Saudi Arabia and China were actively involved in negotiation processes. In the course of these negotiations, G-20 countries coordinated national stimulus packages, which accounted for an overall sum of about US\$ 2 trillion (ILO, 2009). They also agreed on quota share reforms in both the IMF and the World Bank giving China and other emerging nations a greater say. Through these reforms, about 3.1 percent of the World Bank's and 5.3 percent of IMF's voting shares were planned to be redistributed to emerging countries. China's shares in the World Bank rose from 2.8 percent to 4.4 percent. Equally, China's shares in the IMF doubled to about 6.1 percent (IMF, 2010, p. S2). Regarding global trade, there was an emerging consensus between G-20 members to keep markets open. The WTO was pushed to review new protectionist measures such as import duties, non-tariff barriers and export restrictions with its Trade Policy Review Mechanism (Wolf, 2011, p. 7).

However, after the global economy had stabilized in 2010, there was a major setback to reform. Since late 2010 open conflicts about the next steps of governance reform became apparent, and the G-20 lost importance as a central coordination forum. In China, frustration with Western-dominated economic governance institutions began to grow. Even after the reforms, China's new economic role was still not reflected in global governance. China overtook Germany as the third largest shareholder in both institutions, but China's shares were still weaker than its economic position. Even worse, US congress blocked the IMF voting share reform for more than five years, effectively stalling the reform process. In addition to this representation gap, the "output legitimacy" (Scharpf, 2003) of the IMF was at a low point in the Global South. The austerity programs in the aftermath of the financial crisis of 1997/1998 still influenced the perception of the institution. Most countries in East Asia, Latin America, and Africa avoided drawing money from the institution. The IMF's comeback as a savior during the 2008 crisis granting credits worth US\$ 42 billion was therefore mainly limited to European countries (Güven, 2012, p. 891). Instead, the central banks of countries such as Brazil or Korea closely cooperated with the US Federal Reserve using swap-agreements to prevent a liquidity crisis (McDowell, 2011, pp. 164ff.). Effectively, from a geopolitical point of view, the global financial crisis turned out to be a "status quo crisis" (Helleiner, 2014), as power relationships remained largely stable: for instance, the United States still holds the veto power with more than 17 percent of voting shares in the IMF.

However, the frustration with Western-dominated institutions pushed China to establish alternative governance structures. The most important step in the aftermath of the crisis was the creation of the BRIC(S) group at the first BRIC summit in Yekaterinburg in June 2009 bringing together Brazil, Russia, India and China, with South Africa joining the group at the BRICS meeting in Sanya 2011 (Liu, 2016; Nayyar, 2016). In its first declaration, the new group identified a need for closer cooperation in key areas such as trade, technology, global economic governance reform and "a stable, predictable and more diversified international monetary system" (First BRIC Summit, 2009). In the following years, the BRICS achieved modest results of cooperation: First, the BRICS started to denominate their trade in their own currencies. For instance, Brazil and China finally began to use their own currencies for mutual trade in 2015. Second, building on the experiences of IBSA Dialogue Forum and the SCO, the BRICS were able to improve mutual trade and investment. Hence, during the last decade, intra BRICS trade increased threefold. Third, and most importantly, the BRICS started to build joint institutions. The BRICS Development Bank and the Contingent Reserve Agreement (both with US\$ 100 billion) are both attempts to create alternative financial structures to the Bretton Woods institutions (Liu, 2016). However, these institutions remain fragile, as most BRICS countries (except China) lack the financial resources to fulfill their plans (see Kasahara in this volume). Generally, China's policy-makers see the BRICS as being crucially important because, as a high Chinese trade official indicated in an interview, the BRICS group "is one of the few institutions where the US cannot exert direct influence,"[4] but the ambitious plans are proceeding rather slowly.

Chinese policy-makers also started to rethink China's role in global finance in order to challenge US financial supremacy (Liao and McDowell, 2015; Huotari and Heep, 2016). First, Chinese financial institutions began to diversify their assets. Since 2008, Chinese investors did not significantly increase their holdings of US treasury bonds. Instead, institutions such as CDB (China Development Bank), CIC (China Investment Corporation) and China Exim-Bank (Export-Import Bank of China) engaged more offensively as investors and creditors in other countries and markets. Chinese outward

FDI increased to a record level of US$ 113.6 billion (US$ 110.8 billion according to alternative calculations) in 2015 (Heritage Foundation, 2016). It went mainly to countries in the Global South, thereby internationalizing the (infrastructure) investment-driven Chinese model by providing investment for infrastructure and commodity exploration projects. For the global trade regime, these investment projects worked as a network-based approach to spur trade. This network-based approach differs from deep integration, as it prioritizes the creation of physical infrastructure of trade and investment flows over general liberalization. For instance, most of the Chinese investment projects were embedded in broader agreements with single countries such as Angola or Venezuela (on the role of the CDB: Sanderson and Forsythe, 2013). The majority of these bilateral treaties implicitly traded investments of Chinese state companies against contracts on long-term commodity supply. Moreover, they often included loans of several billion US dollars with low interest rates. Accordingly, China became a major creditor in several world regions, thereby challenging the IMF and the World Bank. For instance, between 2005 and 2015, Chinese creditors granted loans amounting to US$ 121 billion to Latin American countries, more than the World Bank or the Inter-American Development Bank (Gallagher and Myers, 2016).

Second, China started to internationalize the Renminbi in order to challenge US financial supremacy (Eichengreen and Kawai, 2014; Liao and McDowell, 2015) The Chinese approach to currency internationalization also relies on a network-based approach: Instead of floating the currency and liberalizing capital controls, the Chinese central bank signed swap-agreements with 30 single countries and the European Union amounting to more than Renminbi (RMB) 3.1 trillion. These swap-agreements aim at containing financial crises and at granting liquidity for mutual trade denominated in their own currency. With its pilot scheme of RMB trade settlement beginning in 2009, China allowed selected export-oriented cities (Shanghai and four cities in Guangdong) to settle foreign trade in Renminbi. A year later, the scheme was extended to 18 provinces and, finally, in 2011 to the entire country. China also started to build a financial infrastructure with trade financing facilities such as Renminbi offshore centers and clearing banks in cities such as Hong Kong, London, Frankfurt and Moscow. Today, the Renminbi has become an important trade currency with an overall share of more than 8 percent of global trade.

Taken together, the global economic crisis led to a speedup of the restructuring of the global trade regime. China questioned existing institutions and began to build alternative structures. China also created stronger bilateral linkages in finance and trade through swap-agreements and bilateral treaties on investment, credits and commodity supply. This network-is challenging deep integration, as it does not follow the logic of an overall liberalization of trade and investment.

OBAMA'S T-STRATEGY

The rise of China was perceived as a threat to US hegemony by most American policy-makers. The Obama administration started to react with its "pivot to Asia" strategy to challenge this policy, a security strategy aimed at containing China's influence together with US allies in East Asia (Campbell and Andrews, 2013; Ikenberry, 2015; see also Wilson in this volume). The pivot is primarily a military strategy, but also includes an important trade component. The main strategy of the US was to use its role in East Asia as a security provider to its historical (and new) allies such as Japan, Korea, Singapore, Philippines and Vietnam in order to counter growing Chinese economic influence. This strategy was possible, as East Asia is characterized by a "dual hierarchy (…) The United States still dominates the region in military capabilities and security relationships. Indeed, the rise of Chinese power has in fact increased the 'demand' for American led security assistance within the region. Yet if countries in the region look to the United States for security, they look to China for economic opportunity. China is a source of economic gain for most of East Asia." (Ikenberry, 2015, p. 21). In 2010, the US embarked on a containment strategy, thus, aiming at restructuring its military by reducing its engagement in the Middle East and increasing its presence in Southeast Asia and Oceania. The new strategy aims at situating 60 percent of the US fleet in the Pacific and increasing US troops and establishing new and growing already existing military bases in Guam, Japan, Australia, Singapore, Hawaii and the Philippines (Evans, 2013, p. 166). In practical terms, the US also actively supported their allies in the territorial disputes in the South China Sea and the East China Sea. China, in turn, also tried to engage more offensively in the region, thus, showing a stronger naval and air presence in both seas. Since 2011, conflicts between China and Vietnam, the Philippines and also Japan about the Paracel Islands, the Spratly Islands and the Senkaku/Diaoyu Islands respectively became a daily occurrence. The result of this confrontation was increasing political isolation of China in East Asia, despite its close economic ties to most East Asian countries. Similarly, conflicts between the US, European Union, and Russia about establishing an association agreement with Ukraine escalated two years later and turned into a conflict about Ukraine's geopolitical belonging (Haukkala, 2015). These growing tensions created two major fault lines and a large Eurasian geopolitical block with Russia and China at its center.

The American containment policy was also backed by a "T-Strategy" (Daniljuk, 2015) in trade: The US pushed for a new round of trade and investment agreements including the TTIP with 28 European states, the TPP Agreement with 11 Pacific states and the TiSA with 23 states in East Asia, Europe, Oceania and the Americas. The goal of these "deep integration" agreements comprised issues such as liberalization of investment, rules on competition and government procurement, which aimed at creating new business opportunities for transnational companies. However, these treaties also targeted at strengthening economic ties between the US and its allies in Europe, East Asia and Latin America and to build a power block against rising China, thus creating a large T-shaped geopolitical structure. Economically, the T-strategy would have led to closer integration between the US, European Union and some of its most reliable allies. American and European elites also hoped to spur transatlantic trade flows, which had been stagnating in the first five years after the financial crisis. Geopolitically, new economic (inter)dependencies would have emerged. For instance, TPP would have granted East Asian allies privileged not only market access to the US, but also access to strategically important American exports such as shale oil. TPP would have been built on existing bilateral treaties such as the US Vietnam Bilateral Trade Agreement (2001), which helped to increase trade more than twentyfold since its implementation.

Generally, the American T-strategy aimed at reviving the globalization project on a more limited scale thereby pushing the development of global capitalism without having to cope with the specific interests of national class fractions in the BRICS countries and other large emerging economies. Paradoxically, TPP could have led to a new round of trade liberalization in geopolitically divided East Asia. For instance, as a reaction to TPP, China and the Association of Southeast Asian Nations (ASEAN) countries pushed for the RCEP (Regional Comprehensive Economic Partnership) agreement between ASEAN and ASEAN's six Free Trade Area (FTA) partners China, India, Japan, New Zealand and Korea.[5] However, countervailing tendencies to further deepening of the WTO regime were already too strong. As we will see, both TPP and TTIP were stopped in early 2017.

EURASIAN POWER GAMES

China's reaction to the American T-strategy was targeted at creating an alternative area of integration without the US directly influencing such an agreement. The RCEP was a key component for increasing trade with East Asia and Oceania, but China also started to explore new options. In late 2013, Chinese president Xi Jinping announced the plan to push the OBOR project, comprising the land-based Silk Road Economic Belt and the ocean-going 21st century Maritime Silk Road. The aim of these ambitious projects is to link China with Europe and to contribute to a greater economic integration within Eurasia Callahan, 2016; Wang, 2016). For this goal, China plans to invest heavily in infrastructure such as railways, highways, and harbors. The primary goal of the land-based Silk Road Economic Belt is to create several economic corridors and to pursue closer economic integration. There are three major belts planned: The north belt goes through Russia, Central Asia to Eastern Europe, the Central Belt runs through Central and West Asia to the Middle East and Mediterranean and the South Belt links China with Southeast and South Asia (see Griffiths in this volume). The project is also related to additional economic corridors such as the China-Pakistan Economic Corridor and the Bangladesh-China-India-Myanmar Economic Corridor. Most of these linkages are still in planning phases, while a few components of OBOR have already been realized.

The geopolitical implications of these projects are far-reaching. Besides spurring trade flows, the strategic goal is in Xi Jinping's words to "turn China's neighborhood into a community of common destiny" (c.f. Swaine, 2015, p. 2). This means that the overall project aims at creating new production networks and trade routes, thus transforming the "Chinese dream" into an "Asian dream" (Callahan, 2016). For instance, the China-Pakistan corridor will not only connect the less developed Western Chinese Provinces such as Xinjiang with new port infrastructure in Pakistan, thereby circumventing the sea trade routes which run through the Strait of Malacca. The project will modernize important infrastructure and will change the overall structure of Pakistan's economy, thus making it more dependent on trade flows to China. The overall volume of planned investment will amount to US$ 51.5 billion, which is almost a fifth of Pakistan's GDP (see Roberts in this volume).

These large-scale projects also indicate the need for financial resources in order to finance them. China has therefore initiated the establishment of the AIIB to provide loans for the infrastructure projects (Bob et al., 2015). AIIB will have an overall capital stock of US$ 100 billion, which is equivalent to two thirds of the capital stock of the Asian Development Bank. China will pledge about US$ 30.8 billion to the capital stock. The Bank gained support from 37 regional and 20 non-regional members. Membership is a geopolitically sensitive issue, as both US and Japan are not members of the bank, whereas traditional US allies in Europe such as Germany and the United Kingdom are integrated in this project. AIIB has become an alternative source of finance, thereby challenging the role of the Asian Development Bank (ADB). Due to the high financial needs for the OBOR projects, China has also created a US$ 40 billion Silk Road fund to finance the infrastructure along land and the sea routes (Wang, 2016). Together with the US$ 10 billion China-ASEAN fund, which was established a few years earlier in 2009, there now exist several sources to finance infrastructure projects. However, as the overall planned financial volume of the OBOR projects will account for more than US$ 4 trillion and China will only partially finance them, there is still a huge financial gap to be filled.

Up to now, OBOR has the potential to become China's most successful project of trade integration. First, China has defined a continental space of economic integration without US and Japanese interference. This block building is important, as China also managed to find a common ground with Russia for this project (see Sangar in this volume). Russia is concurrently pursuing its own project of a Eurasian Economic Union, which is respected by Chinese foreign policy makers and does not contradict Chinese plans of economic integration. Also, China and Russia are pushing for an enlargement of the SCO with India and Pakistan becoming full members in 2017. Second, OBOR will mainly be financed by new Chinese-led institutions. In particular the creation of AIIB represents significant progress because of the size and diversity of the institution. With 57 shareholders, the risk of not providing enough resources as in the BRICS Development Bank with only five shareholders is much less likely, thus creating an alternative to the ADB. Third, China has found a new way of trade governance that fits China's economic model. Unlike the US and European deep integration agreements, OBOR is, up to now, mainly based on infrastructure investment and facilitating trade, thus making it possible to internationalize China's infrastructure investment–driven economic model. In this approach, the logic of integration is based not on overall liberalization but on physical infrastructure and connectivity. This type of network-based governance can be found in both the Maritime Silk Road building on a "string of pearls" of port infrastructure and the land-based Silk Road Economic Belt with its railway links between different cities throughout the Eurasian landmass.

CONCLUSION: LIMITS OF DEEP INTEGRATION

By late 2016, it was quite obvious that the WTO regime, which builds on deep integration and goes far beyond mere trade liberalization, had run into crisis (Li, 2016). There are two major signs of increasing problems in pushing the globalization project further: First, the Polanyian movement of disembedding the market from society which started with the rise of neoliberalism in the late 1970s seems to have reached its limit. The election of Donald Trump in the US and the Brexit vote in Great Britain indicates that the Polanyian pendulum seems to be swinging back with the losers of deep integration in the US rustbelt and in the north of England having voted for right-wing protectionist policies. Among the first major decisions of the Trump government was the decision to leave both the TPP and the TTIP, thus blaming these treaties on unfair trade agreements that hurt the US economy. Also, the Trump administration has vigorously criticized current account surplus countries such as Germany and China as systematically exploiting their undervalued currency.

Second, China's role in the global economy is changing. China is currently undergoing a deep transformation of its economic model, thus making domestic consumption more important. This crisis-prone transformation has led to decreasing GDP growth, stagnation in the industrial sector and a stark fall of Chinese commodity demand. As a result, commodity prices went down by about 53.7 percent between January 2014 and 2016, thus causing the end of the China boom on the commodity markets (IMF, 2016) and pushing several commodity exporters in South America, Africa and Central Asia into crisis. As a result, since 2014, global trade is stagnating. Taken together, the development in both the developing and developed world could spur new trends in global political economy as exporters are entering hard times in coping with the wave of protectionism and low commodity prices.

Moreover, the US pivot to Asia seems to have run into serious problems. Without the TPP, either the US will have to negotiate bilateral treaties with the East Asian states or China's role as a trade partner will continue to grow. Already, China has replaced the US as the main export market for all East Asian states except Vietnam. The growing economic importance of China in the long term could undermine the "dual hierarchy"-structure in East Asia with China at the center of the regional economic order and the US at the head of the security structure, thus, making it less likely that US allies continue their military alliance with the US. For instance, the improving relationship between China and the Philippines casts doubts about the sustainability of the overall US containment strategy in East Asia.

Due to this new situation, there is a historic window of opportunity for China to reshape the global economic order. For a long time, China lacked a strategy to build alternative structures. This is changing, starting with the up to now-only partially successful BRICS group and the fast internationalization of its currency, China has embarked on actively promoting alternative structures in the world economy. With its OBOR project, its strategy got much more explicit: China is now experimenting with a new form of network-governance of global trade mainly focusing on creating a physical infrastructure for trade flows (and investment) and on facilitating trade in goods and services. At the same time, China is not openly confronting the WTO regime, as China as an exporter was able to benefit from the hitherto-existing trade order. Ironically, as the last World Economic Forum in Davos indicates, key actors of the transnational capitalist class even seem to think that China shows promise to guarantee the liberal trade order (Goodman, 2017). It is therefore an open question of how the crumbling US- and EU-led multilateral trade order with its elements of deep integration, interacts with the new Chinese-led network-based trade order.

NOTES

1. TPP is an agreement between Australia, Brunei, Canada, Chile, Japan, Malaysia, New Zealand, Peru, Singapore, the United States (until January 2017), and Vietnam.
2. The US was also pushing for a further liberalization, but they preferred to do so in other institutions. After the negotiation on MAI (Multilateral Agreement on Investment) had failed in 1998, the WTO got more important in negotiations on issues such as investment or competition.
3. The G-20 and the trade G-20 are not the same institutions. The G-20 was already created after the financial crises in East Asia, Russia and Latin America and gained importance after the global financial crisis 2007/08.
4. Interview with high Chinese trade official, Beijing, February 2012.
5. Even though countries such as Japan and Korea are pushing for some far-reaching liberalization measures and intellectual property rights, RCTEP, up to now, mainly focuses on trade in goods and services and does not go as far as TPP which also includes the Singapore issues.

REFERENCES

Altman, R. C. (2009) The Great Crash, 2008: A Geopolitical Setback for the West, *Foreign Affairs*, 88(1), 2–14.
Arrighi, G. (2007) *Adam Smith in Beijing. Lineages of the Twenty-first Century*. London, Verso.
Bergsten, C. F. (1997) Open Regionalism, *The World Economy,* 20(5), pp. 551–565
Bob, D. Harris, T. Kawai, M. and Sun, Y. (2015): *Asian Infrastructure Investment Bank: China as Responsible Stakeholder?* Sasakawa Peace Foundation USA, Washington, 43–52.
Breslin, S. (2007) *China and the Global Political Economy*. Basingstoke and New York, Palgrave Macmillan.
Callahan, W. A. (2016) China's Asia Dream: The Belt Road Initiative and the new regional order, *Asian Journal of Comparative Politics,* 1(3), pp. 226–243.
Campbell, K. and Andrews, B. (2013) Explaining the US 'Pivot' to Asia, The Asia Group, Chatham House, August http://www19.iadb.org/intal/intalcdi/PE/2013/12829.pdf [Accessed 27 February 2017].
Chang, H.-J. (2007) *Kicking Away the Ladder. Development Strategy in Historical Perspective*. London, Anthem.
Claar, S. and Nölke, A. (2013) Deep Integration in North–South Relations: Compatibility Issues between the EU and South Africa, *Review of African Political Economy,* 40(2), pp. 274–289.
Daniljuk, M. (2015) America's T-Strategy. Die US-Hegemonie und die Korrektur der US-Außen- und Energiepolitik, *Prokla. Zeitschrift für kritische Sozialwissenschaften* 45(4), pp. 545–562.
Dos Santos, T. (2011) Globalization, Emerging Powers, and the Future of Capitalism, *Latin American Perspectives*, 38(1), pp. 45–57.

Eichengreen, B. J. and Kawai, M. (2014) Issues for Renminbi Internationalization: An Overview. ADBI Working Paper No. 454., de http://www.adbi.org/workingpaper/2014/01/20/6112.issues.renminbi.internationalization.overview/ [Accessed 27 February 2017].

Evans, M. (2013) American Defence Policy and the Challenge of Austerity, *Journal of Southeast Asian Economies,* 30(2), pp. 164–178.

Farooki, M. and Kaplinsky, R. (2012) *The Impact of China on Global Commodity Prices. The Global Reshaping of the Resource Sector.* London, Routledge.

First BRIC Summit (2009) Joint Statement of the BRIC Countries' Leaders. Yekaterinburg, June 16, 2009. http://www.brics.utoronto.ca/docs/ [Accessed 23 June 2014].

Flemes, D. (2009) India-Brazil-South Africa (IBSA) in the New Global Order: Interests, Strategies and Values of the Emerging Coalition, *International Studies,* 46(4), pp. 401–421.

Gallagher, K. (2016) *The China Triangle. Latin America's Boom and the Fate of the Washington Consensus.* Oxford and New York, Oxford University Press.

Gallagher, K. P. and Myers, M. (2016) China-Latin America Finance Database. Washington: Inter-American Dialogue., de http://www.bu.edu/pardeeschool/research/gegi/program-area/chinas-global-reach/china-in-latin-america/china-finance-and-investment/china-latin-america-database/ [Accessed 15 December 2016].

Gill, S. (1998) European Governance & New Constitutionalism: EMU & alternatives to disciplinary neo-liberalism in Europe, *New Political Economy,* 3(1), pp. 5–26.

Goodman, Peter S. (2017) In Era of Trump, China's President Champions Economic Globalization, *The New York Times,* January 17. 2017. https://www.nytimes.com/2017/01/17/business/dealbook/world-economic-forum-davos-china-xi-globalization.html [Accessed 27 February 2017].

Gosovic, B. (2016) The Resurgence of South–South Cooperation, *Third World Quarterly* 37(4), pp. 733—743.

Güven, A. B. (2012) The IMF, the World Bank, and the Global Economic Crisis: Exploring Paradigm Continuity, *Development and Change,* 43(4), pp. 869–898.

Harmes, A. (2006) Neoliberalism and Multilevel Governance. *Review of International Political Economy,* 13(5), pp. 725–749.

Harris, J. (2016) *Global Capitalism and the Crisis of Democracy.* Atlanta, Clarity Press.

Haukkala, H. (2015) From Cooperative to Contested Europe? The Conflict in Ukraine as a Culmination of a Long-Term Crisis in EU-Russia Relations, *Journal of Contemporary European Studies,* 23(1), pp. 25–40.

Helleiner, E. (2014) *The Status Quo Crisis. Global Financial Governance after the 2007–08 Financial Meltdown.* Oxford, Oxford University Press.

Heritage Foundation (2016) China Global Investment Tracker. Recuperado el 14 de mayo de 2016, de http://www.heritage.org/research/projects/china-global-investment-tracker-interactive-map ⌈[Accessed 15 December 2016].

Hoekman, B. and Kostecki, M. (2009) *The Political Economy of the World trading System: WTO and Beyond.* Cambridge: Cambridge University Press.

Hudson, M. (1977) *Global Fracture. The New International Economic Order.* New York, Harper&Row.

Hung, H.-F. (2016) *The China Boom: Why China Will Not Rule the World*. New York, Columbia University Press.

Huotari, M. and Heep, S. (2016) Learning geoeconomics: China's experimental financial and monetary initiatives. *Asia Europe Journal*, 14, pp. 153–171.

Ikenberry, G. J. (2015) Between the Eagle and the Dragon. America, China, and Middle State Strategies in East Asia, *Political Science Quarterly*, 131(1), pp. 9–43.

ILO (2009) *The Financial and Economic Crisis. A Decent Work Response*. Geneva, ILO.

IMF (2010) IMF Quota and Governance Reform. Elements of an Agreement. http://www.imf.org/external/np/pp/eng/2010/103110.pdf. [Accessed 23 June 2014].

IMF (2016): IMF Primary Commodity Prices. http://www.imf.org/external/np/res/commod/index.aspx. [Accessed 15 December 2016].

Jenkins, R. (2011) El 'efecto China' en los precios de los productos básicos y en el valor de las exportaciones de América Latina. *Revista CEPAL*, 103, pp. 77–93.

Karp, P. (2017) Australia open to China and Indonesia joining TPP after US pulls out. *The Guardian*, January 23, 2017, https://www.theguardian.com/australia-news/2017/jan/24/australia-open-to-china-and-indonesia-joining-tpp-after-us-pulls-out, [Accessed 27 February 2017].

Li, Eric X. (2016) The End of Globalism. *Foreign Affairs*, December 9, 2016, https://foreignaffairs.org/articles/united-states/2016–12–09/end-globalism, [Accessed 27 February 2017].

Liao, S. and McDowell, D. (2015) Redback Rising: China's Bilateral Swap Agreements and RMB Internationalization. *International Studies Quarterly*, 59(3), pp. 401–422.

Liu, M. (2016) BRICS development: a long way to a powerful economic club and new international organization, *The Pacific Review*, 29(3), pp. 443–45

McDowell, D. (2011) The US as 'Sovereign International Last-Resort Lender': The Fed's Currency Swap Programme during the Great Panic of 2007–09, *New Political Economy*, 17(2), pp. 157–178.

McNally, C. A. (2012) Sino-Capitalism: China's Reemergence and the International Political Economy, *World Politics*, 64(4), pp. 741–776.

Narlikar, A. (2010) New Powers in the Club: The Challenges of Global Trade Governance, *International Affairs*, 86(3), pp. 717–728.

Narlikar, A. and Tussie, D. (2004) The G20 at the Cancun Ministerial: Developing Countries and Their Evolving Coalitions in the WTO, *World Economy*, 27(7), pp. 947–966.

Nayyar, D. (2016) BRICS, Developing Countries and Global Governance, *Third World Quarterly*, 37(4), 575–591.

Paddock, Richard C. (2016) Rodrigo Duterte, Pushing Split With U.S., Counters Phillippines' Deep Ties. *The New York Times*, October 26, 2016, https://www.nytimes.com/2016/10/27/world/asia/philippines-duterte-united-states-alliance.html [Accessed 27 February 2017].

Roache, S. K. (2012) China's Impact on World Commodity Markets. IMF Working Paper. WP/12/115. www.imf.org/external/pubs/ft/wp/.../wp12115.pdf. [Accessed 27 February 2017].

Robinson, W. I. (2004) *A Theory of Global Capitalism. Transnational Production, Transnational Capitalists and the Transnational State.* Baltimore, Johns Hopkins University Press.

Sanderson, H. and Forsythe, M. (2013) *China's Superbank. Debt, Oil and Influence How China Development Bank Is Rewriting the Rules of Finance.* Singapore and Hoboken, Wiley and Bloomberg Press.

Scharpf, F. (2003) Problem-Solving Effectiveness and Democratic Accountability in the EU. MPIfG Working Paper 03/1, February 2003. http://www.mpifg.de/pu/workpap/wp03–1/wp03–1.html[19 June 2017].

Schmalz, S. and Ebenau, M. (2012) After Neoliberalism? Brazil, India, and China in the Global Economic Crisis, *Globalizations*, 9(4), 487–501.

Sklair, L. (2001) *The Transnational Capitalist Class.* Oxford, Wiley-Blackwell Publishing.

Swaine, M. D (2015) "Xi Jinping's Address to the Central Conference on Work Relating to Foreign Affairs: Assessing and Advancing Major-Power Diplomacy with Chinese Characteristics, *China Leadership Monitor*, 46(1), https://www.hoover.org/sites/default/files/clm46ms.pdf, [Accessed 15 December 2016].

UNCTAD (2016) UNCTADstat. http://unctadstat.unctad.org/ReportFolders/reportFolders.aspx?sCS_referer=&sCS_ChosenLang=en [15 December 2016].

Wade, R. (2003) What Strategies Are Viable for Developing Countries Today? The World Trade Organization and the Shrinking of 'Development Space', *Review of International Political Economy*, 10(4), pp. 621–644.

Wang, Y. (2016) Offensive for Defensive: The Belt and Road Initiative and China's New Grand Strategy, *The Pacific Review*, 29(3), pp. 455–463.

Wolf, M. (2008) *Fixing Global Finance.* Baltimore, Johns Hopkins University Press.

WTO Secretariat (2017) Evolution of Regional Trade Agreements in Theworld, 1948–2017. https://www.wto.org/english/tratop_e/region_e/regfac_e.htm [Accessed 1 October 2017].

Yeo, S. (2016) Geopolitics of Search: Google versus China?, *Media Culture and Society*, 38(4), pp. 591–605.

Yuan, J.-D. (2010) China's Role in Establishing and Building the Shanghai Cooperation Organization (SCO), *Journal of Contemporary China*, 19(67), pp. 855–869.

Part I

CHINA'S INITIATIVES IN ASIA

Chapter 3

'One Belt, One Road' as a Development Strategy

Richard T. Griffiths

The rise of China will be one of the defining features of the twenty-first century. For almost thirty years its unprecedented economic growth has transformed the international economy by shifting centers of production and stimulating a commodity boom that has lifted millions out of poverty in China itself and has altered the fortunes of many lesser developed countries. As China became the 'factory of the world' it has accumulated massive foreign exchange reserves with which it has fueled a boom foreign direct investment and in mergers and acquisitions. Many observers assumed that it would be only a matter of time before Beijing translated this increasing economic clout into political power. The remaining question was 'what form would it take?' The answer was not long in coming. First Beijing tried to reform existing international financial institutions. When that failed, it created new ones, better to meet the perceived needs of their clients. Then, in September 2013, President Xi Jinping launched an idea of monumental ambition and breathtaking vision—Beijing would help revive the old trade routes between China and Europe, and China and Asia, and in the process it would help transform all the economies lying in their paths. The sums involved are staggering. Already it is claimed that there are 900 projects envisaged with a combined price tag of $890 billion. Eventually China plans to invest $4 trillion in the economies involved in the project (*The Economist*, 2.7.2016). Not since the Marshall Plan has there been a scheme of such dimensions. Many Western commentators have looked for hidden motives behind the scheme. Others have highlighted the risks involved and cast doubts on its success. Few have taken the initiative at face value and analyzed it as a development project. This is a gap which this paper intends to fill.

The framing of Chinese foreign policy changed dramatically on September 7, 2013, when President Xi Jinping gave a speech to Central Asian leaders at

Nazarbayev University in Kazakhstan. He started by recalling the journeys of the imperial envoy Zhang Qian, who had retuned for Central Asia with the news that a transcontinental trade route existed that linked East and West, Asia and Europe. President Xi observed that for 2000 years the Silk Road had proved that peoples of different race, beliefs and cultures could work together for their mutual benefit and suggested that they could do so again. He listed five points for action, including the need improve transport connectivity and to improve trade facilitation (Xi, 2013). One month later, at a speech to the Indonesian Parliament, president Xi suggested reviving the old maritime highway through the South China Sea and the Indian Ocean to the Middle East and Europe, this time recalling the seven voyages made by Admiral He in the fifteenth century (Xi, 2013).The two initiatives became known as the overland 'belt' and the maritime 'road', later compressed into the acronym OBOR. However, it was to take almost a year and a half before a more detailed outline of the initiative appeared. This identified six separate corridors that would form the context for China's ambition.

Looking at the new plans, many commentators were taken aback by the breadth of vision that they represented. There seemed to be an implicit assumption that these were Chinese projections onto the rest of the Eurasian continent. However none of these ideas are new. All were already shared by other nations. All were the subject of international agreements. And herein lies part of their strength. The plans for a Trans-Asian Railway have existed since the 1950s and in 2006 eighteen Asian nations, including China, agreed to study the harmonization of transport policies to facilitate the construction of an integrated rail transport system (UN ESCAP, 1996; Kasuara, 1997; UN ECE/ESCAP, 2008). A similar project for roads started at the same time and in 2003 thirty-two countries agreed to the creation of an *Asian Highway* consisting of eight major highway networks spanning the Eurasian land-mass and a further fifty road networks of regional significance (UN ESCAP, 2003). In 2005 the signatories had committed $25 billion to the project and they later agreed to make it a priority to find an $18 billion to upgrade roads in the worst condition. Somewhat over twenty percent of the costs were carried by the Asian Development Bank (ADB) (Regmi, 2011). At a regional level the Central Asian Regional Economic Cooperation Programme was established in 1998 to promote infrastructural improvement and trade facilitation. China is a member. Since the start of operations it had helped fund projects worth $25 billion, with the ADB providing thirty-eight percent of the funding (CAREC, 2015). In South East Asia, too, there have been regional transport initiatives. In 1992 China joined with other nations to form the Great Mekong Sub-region as a forum to improve connectivity and in 2005 it specifically endorsed the construction of a Kunming-Singapore rail link, that reappears as the backbone for OBOR's South East Asian corridor (ADB, 2010; ADB, 2011a; ADB, 2011b). Six years later, in 2011, the same emphasis on rail links stretching the length of Southeast Asia and into China was adopted by ASEAN as a central feature of its connectivity plans (ASEAN, 2011; Toedoro, 2015). It is safe to conclude that many of the blueprints and studies for OBOR to succeed already existed. Moreover, individual nations and international bodies had been trying to realize them. What was missing was the impetus that Chinese leadership and funding could provide.

TRADE AND CONNECTIVITY PROBLEMS AS IDENTIFIED BY OBOR

If we are going to analyze a development strategy, we need to isolate some development problems. Indeed these were already contained in the initial OBOR proposals and in their subsequent elaboration. Basically they boil down to problems with transport and problems with international trade. The question then remains whether the problems are large or small. One global indication is provided by the World Bank and the United Nations Economic and Social Committee for Asia and the Pacific (UN, ESCAP), which presents an indication of the total costs of international trade between pairs of countries, expressed as the equivalent of a tariff levied on imports. One needs to be careful in using this indicator because it is the result of three operations. The first is an estimate of what would be the normal level of trade between pairs of countries (compensating for differences in income levels, economic structures, transport links etc.) if there were no barriers to trade (no transport costs, no frontier restrictions, no differences in laws, language and cultures, etc.). It is important to note that the exercise does not attempt to explain why trade between countries should be high or low; only the difference between the assumed trade flow without barriers and the reality. Economists often do this—they are called 'gravity models' of trade. The next step is to calculate how far the actual trade flows deviate from the predicted flows. The final step is to calculate what difference in price would be necessary to explain the difference in the size of demand for imported goods and to represent this in the form of a hypothetical import tariff (Novy, 2009). What the data suggests is that the bilateral trade between China and Russia, for example, is lower than it should be given the economic circumstances of the two countries; it is as though trade carries an import tariff of 96.5 percent. Is this high? In order to answer that question it is worth looking at the European Union, where there are no frontier barriers to trade, where single sets of rules cover product definitions and where trade is conducted in the same currency. Even so, the bilateral trade flows between France and Germany act as though they carried a tariff of thirty-four percent, those between Germany and Italy produced a result of forty-six percent (World Bank/ECSAP, International Trade Costs Dataset).

There are several reasons why countries trade less than if there were no costs at all. The most obvious one is that they do charge tariffs on imports from abroad. China, for example, charges an average of 15.6 percent on agricultural imports and 9 percent on other goods. By contrast India which has an average tariff on agriculture of 32.7 percent, and Uzbekistan charges an average of14.1 percent on non-agricultural goods. Tariffs offer part of the answer, but they do not explain the whole problem (WTO, ITC, UNCTAD, 2016). A second explanation is that governments do impose limits on certain imports, known as 'quantitative restrictions' (QRs). We lack complete information for the countries involved in OBOR but China and Kazakhstan, for example, have QRs on products covering 25–26 percent of their imports while 35 percent of Russia's imports are subject to QRs of some kind. The problem with this kind of data is that it gives no indication of the degree of restriction, whether, for example, it is one or two percent less than the previous year or whether it is an almost prohibition (Gourdon, 2014). Another problem is that the more restrictive the policy, the less it would appear in this measure, since there would be little trade. A third contributory factor in increasing the price of imported goods is the costs and time involved in obtaining the documentation and clearing customs. The World Bank has traced the costs incurred by a small trader importing a container of car parts into the country. In China (which is one of the more efficient countries, though not the cheapest) this exercise would take six and a half days and cost $360. In India it would take more than twice as long and cost twice as much. Pakistan is a little faster, but the documentation cost is a whopping $1743 (World Bank, Doing Business). A final problem is the simple act of crossing the border itself.

In 2012 the first direct freight train traveled from Chongqing in China to Duisburg in Germany. There are now fifty-one such routes carrying freight between China and Europe. The trains are all 'block trains', all arriving at the same destination and all covered by one set of documents. They are waved through as expeditiously as possible and are given priority in transferring loads when necessitated by a change in the width of the track, which takes only a couple of hours (CAREC, 2015). For trains without such privileges, the average delay in moving from China into Kazakhstan at the same border crossing is almost six days (CAREC, 2016). Borders are not the only cause of delay. Even within China it is common for freight trains to lose the battle for the track access to priority passenger trains, and the subsequent delays can take 20–30 hours each time this occurs (CAREC, 2014, 39–45).

OBOR'S DEVELOPMENT STRATEGY

Taking all the above factors into account, the decision by Beijing to join the effort to reduce costs by reducing the trade barriers and by cutting transport costs can be expected to contribute to increasing trade between nations. But the strategy implicit in the OBOR model goes much further. Much of OBOR's strategy is focused on infrastructural investment in six main areas. It is difficult to obtain an exact breakdown because, when amounts are provided at all, they are usually for an entire project, covering therefore several years.

- Railways
- Highways
- Pipelines
- Power Supplies
- Ports
- Special Enterprise Zones

Only three of these (rail, road and port development) contribute directly to furthering connectivity and trade. Pipelines also represent a form of connectivity, but the considerations here have less to do with regional development than with allaying China's concerns with energy flow security, and also those of the partner countries. The other two (power supplies and special enterprise zones) are each directed toward economic development. In the case of power supplies, however, the development impact depends on whether those supplies are intended for domestic use or for export (to China). The focus on enterprise zones of various types emulates a development strategy that lay at the center of China's own reform program, and which is still a popular strategy in China today.

In order to analyze the possible impact of these investments, it is worth borrowing a set of concepts from development economics called 'linkage effects' that measures the impact of an investment. It distinguishes between 'backward linkages' and 'forward linkages'. A backward linkage effect deals with the benefits of an investment on the supplier—labor, raw materials, finance, R&D and so forth. The forward linkage deals with the benefits for the operator or the final consumer. If it is an intermediate good the operator will employ labor and resources and hopes that these exceed costs so that he or she can benefit from the profits generated. The purchaser of such intermediate goods will hope that the reduced costs will permit increased sales and investments. The purchaser of final goods, such as food or clothing, will hope to reduce spending on such items, allowing increased demand for other products (Hirschman, 1958). In the following paragraphs, we will follow these linkages from start to finish of the process.

The process starts with China offering to finance a particular project. However, China alone cannot decide which project it will fund, but nor can the recipient country. What usually follows is a bargaining process between the two governments where project suggestions on the one side are reconciled with capacities on the other. Occasionally, a recipient government will offer a project to open tender, allowing interested parties from other countries to bid. In this process in the conditions for funding will represent an important part of the package. The fact that Beijing has chosen to implement its OBOR strategy country by country makes it difficult to make any sequential planning that will optimize the investments made. For example, if Beijing indeed intends to build a high-speed rail (HSR) route from Beijing to Europe, is the next step after the existing 3700 kms Beijing-Urumqi (Xinjiang) to be 770 kms between Moscow and Kazan? (*Russian Times*, 30.3.2015). Similarly, having constructed a 2600 kms HSR from Shanghai to Kunming is the logical next step for a Kunming-Singapore railway to build the 1900 kms between Kuala Lumpur and Singapore, always assuming that China can win the contract (*Channel News Asia*, 19.8.2016; *Asia One*, 18.10.2016)?

Chinese finance for OBOR projects usually takes the form of an interest-bearing loan. The interest charged is usually a fraction above the prevailing London Interbank Lending Rate (LIBOR) rate, which is much below what an infrastructural project in a less developed country would usually warrant. Thus the interest is lower than would have been charged if it had been determined by a commercial assessment of the risks involved. However the risk does not disappear. What follows, therefore, is a bargaining process over who should carry that risk. The lender (i.e., China) will try to tie the loan to the government, assuming that governments will offer better prospects of repayment (or some other compensatory advantage) than a commercial enterprise. The borrower will try to avoid this if possible. For example, one of the reasons why China won the contract to build a HSR line between Jakarta and Bandung was that Japan wanted a government guarantee, while China did not (*Bloomberg*, 19.5.2015, 4.9.2015; *Jakarta Post*, 30.9.2015).

A second input into the project is land. New projects often add value to land, especially if it had previously been of little value (marginal agriculture or low value housing). However the importance for economic development depends on the circumstances of acquisition. If the process is one of sequestration or forced sale with low compensation, the effects will be muted. This question is especially important for transport infrastructure where specific strips of land along the route are required for the track and large areas are desirable at the sites of major stations for commercial development. Most governments impose some price controls in attempts to curb speculation, but 'fair' compensation allows land holders of otherwise marginal land to obtain some economic benefits and thereby help raise income levels in the area. In

Chongqing, for example, there was an interesting experiment in swapping land rights and allowing negotiations over price between original 'owners' and developers (Lafarguette, 2011; Keith et al., 2014).

When it comes down to the rest of the initial project, the rule is simple: if Chinese money is involved, a Chinese firm will undertake the construction. Occasionally, a country may insist on making a choice from among several firms, all nominated by the Chinese authorities, but the effect is the same. Some countries have laws that stipulate that a foreign investor have a domestic partner, but the bulk of the work will still be undertaken by the Chinese contractor. Other countries may try to specify a minimum local content or the employment of a percentage of domestic labor, but such agreements are poorly regulated and are seldom enforced. The danger with a monopoly provider, is that there will be little incentive to reduce costs or, put another way, there will be every incentive to cost the work to match the available funding. On the other hand, Chinese firms will probably have won an open contest anyway. A World Bank survey has suggested that construction costs of HSR in China were substantially lower than those in Europe or in the United States. It ascribed this advantage to the standardization of design, and the efficient use of capital equipment (Ollivier, Sondhi and Zhou, 2014).

To sum up the argument at this stage, if one looks at the backward linkage effects in building the investment, it is difficult to avoid the conclusion that most of the linkage effects flow back to China. This would seem to reinforce the position of those who have claimed that OBOR's main purpose was to provide an outlet for China's industrial overcapacity. Of course providing market outlets for Chinese goods will increase capacity utilization, but there is a mismatch between the scale of the existing overcapacity and the scale of OBOR investment activities to date. On the other hand, there are some benefits for local recipient economies, if they can exercise sufficient leverage and if they are capable of making complementary contributions. They may supply (some) local labor, some technical expertise and possibly some of the raw materials and equipment. However, the fact must be faced that they may not be capable of supplying more than that.

Once the investment has been made, there are two possible options. There is either 'turn-key' investment, where the entire project is handed over to the recipient upon completion or there is build-operate-transfer (B-O-T) where the operational control will remain with Chinese firms for periods ranging from twenty to fifty years, after which it is handed over to the recipient. The recipient will prefer the turn-key option when there are reasonable prospects of making a profit. Remember there is still the principal of the loan and the interest to pay off, and maintenance and depreciation costs to be borne. The recipient will prefer the B-O-T option if it is uncertain of the profit or if it lacks the expertise to run the project. For many infrastructural projects uncertainty stems from the anticipated demand for the services supplied, since idle capacity will raise average production costs.

For China, the B-O-T option may also be attractive for several reasons. First, it may have the necessary management expertise to minimize the risks of making a loss. Second, the management of a project may facilitate a rationalization of the supply chain in such a way as to reduce risks. These two factors help explain China's willingness to run some of the container ports that it is building. Chinese container ports rank among the most efficient in the world, and by managing the port facilities themselves allows the port authorities more easily to form alliances with Chinese shipping companies. Finally, China may have security concerns that override commercial considerations. This is particularly the case in Liquid Natural Gas (LNG) and oil pipelines, designed primarily to enhance China's energy flow security.

Looking again at the linkage effects, at this operational stage it is difficult to judge in which direction positive linkage effects may flow. In managing projects themselves, recipient countries may reap the profits of the enterprise, but this assumes that they are capable of making profits. In many cases the provision of infrastructural services already run at a loss, whether it be the running of railways or the provision of electricity. In other cases they have no experience in managing the type of enterprise envisaged. For example, most of the sea-ports in the region are undercapitalized, over-bureaucratic and inefficiently run. The task of organizing large-scale container traffic or multi-modal 'dry ports' is simply beyond the scope of local management.

If we turn to the projects being undertaken under the OBOR umbrella, one of the most prominent items is the investment in *railways*. In particular, the public imagination has been captured by the investments in HSR which can travel at speeds of 300 km/h and can slice traveling times to fractions of what they had been. The latest HSR covering the 2252 km between Kunming and Shanghai has cut the travel time from 34 to 11 hours (*ECNS*, 28.12.2016). However, HSR will probably be the last piece of the jigsaw to be slotted into place, for several reasons. First, they are very expensive to build—costing as much as ten times the price of a conventional railway. Tickets are therefore relatively expensive. The rule of thumb is that relative advantage lies in distances between 500 and 1000 kms. Below 500 kms and conventional rail and roads offer a better alternative and above that the airlines do. All of this assumes that along the line there are sufficient people to transport. For example, on the Beijing-Duisbrug route, for the best part of 4500 kms (roughly speaking from Lanzhou to Kazan) there are on average fewer than ten inhabitants per km². The studies of the impact of HSR in China on economic development show no impact on the location of manufacturing industries, but a small effect on the concentration of service industries. The main advantage of moving passengers onto HSR is that it releases track for freight services. However, there are plenty of other ways of raising the average speed of freight than employing HSR. These include improving conventional track, increasing the power of locomotives, improving the coupling of wagons and improving logistics. While much attention was focused on China 'winning' the Jakarta-Bandung HSR contract, few noticed that Japan secured the $1.8 billion contract for upgrading the 750 km route between Jakarta and Indonesia's second largest city Surabaya (*Jakarta Post*, 28.5.2016; 8.12.2016). It is interesting that most of the passenger lines already agreed under the banner of OBOR are slower (and cheaper) than the latest Chinese HSR lines.

Although most of the OBOR focus has been on railways, there are good arguments for increasing our attention on the less glamorous alternative of *road improvements*. All transport improvements stimulate economic development by reducing costs, thereby shifting the supply curve to the right. However there is a difference between roads and rail. Since rail freight requires a minimum scale of operation, the locational advantages tend to lie in larger cities where the marshaling yards and delivery terminals are located, and from which trucks and containers leave for their final destination. Rail termini, which are the only points of access to the network, tend to reinforce the locational advantages of urban conurbations. By contrast, highways can be accessed at almost any point along their route, and improvements in local roads tend to have a demonstrable welfare effect up to two-three kms distance along the entire route, though studies are silent over whether this represents new growth, or whether the observed impact is at the costs of producers located further away (Brown, 1999; Bryceson, Bradbury, and Bradbury 2008; Lombard and Coetzer, 2006; van de Walle, 2002).

The third category of investment that we have isolated are the *pipelines*. We have suggested that these have been included in the OBOR program primarily from considerations of security of supplies. If that is indeed the case, then China has not been doing very well, and the fact it hasn't also sheds light on the limitations of China's supposed hegemonic power in an age of global interdependence. China's security problem in energy supplies lies danger posed by having to route all supplies through the 'choke point' of the Straits of Malacca. No less than seventy percent of China's energy supplies pass through the 2.8 kms wide Phillip Canal, which leaves them vulnerable to piracy and blockade (Umaña, 2012; Wheeler, 2015). As early as 2005, long before OBOR was launched, a US defense department paper ascribed China's maritime activities (described as a 'string of pearls') as motivated primarily by reasons of energy security (*Washington Post*, 7.1.2005). China has two options—secure more supplies from overland sources, or divert the energy overland before it reaches the Straits. Both options need pipelines.

In the case of Russia, the strategic advantages lie in both directions since Russia too has an interest in reducing its reliance on Western markets. In May 2014 two countries signed a deal that China would take $400 billion of gas deliveries from Russia over a thirty-year period, and pay one third the costs of a new $80 billion pipeline known as Power of Siberia-2 (Koch-Weser and Murray, 2014; *Russian Times*, 21.5.2014) However, a year later Gazprom announced that it was suspending the project indefinitely because of low energy prices and the slowdown in the Chinese economy. It did not mention that liquidity problems created by the sanctions imposed after the Ukrainian war may have contributed to the decision (Marson and Ostroukh, 2016, Henderson and Mitrova, 2016, *Russian Times*, 22.7.2015). The current oil glut has also meant that the 2230 km oil pipeline in Kazakhstan, completed in 2009 at the cost of $3.5 billion, was operating at only fifty percent capacity, because it was not worth increasing the development of it oil fields (Burkhanov and Chen, 2016; Snow, 2016). An attempt to increase supplies of gas from Uzbekistan by constructing an 850 kms pipeline to the Chinese border (passing through Kyrgyzstan and Tajikistan) collapsed when in February 2016, when Uzbekistan announced the suspension of work on its section of the pipeline for 'technical reasons', followed a few months later by Kyrgyzstan, which cited the escalating costs because of the difficult terrain (Michel 2016a; Michel 2016b, *Press Club News Agency*, 25.5.2016).

The alternative is to transfer the energy to a port before reaching the Straits. At the newly built port in Gwadar, in Pakistan, negotiations on the $2 billion pipeline to Kashgar have stalled because of delays by Pakistan in issuing the tender. Speculation has it that the Chinese loans have been spent on other projects. However, as a result China has withdrawn its B-O-T offer (*Express Tribune*, 3.5.2016; 21.10.2016). China has been more successful in a second route from the port of Kyaukpyu in Myanmar. The construction of the pipeline from there to Kunming had originally been suspended in July 2014 because of environmental objections to the proposed new railway (which helped disguise the pipeline protest) (Goldberg, 2014). The pipeline has since been built. Unfortunately, it is now at risk at what seems to be developing into a Rohingya insurgency in the coastal provinces (*Stratfor*, 21.12.2016; 22.12.2016).

Access to *cheap and reliable energy* can be expected to have strong forward linkage effects through their cost-reducing impact on all users, but especially manufacturing. For example, Pakistan is in the grip of a power crisis, with the damage caused by power shortages estimated as two percent of its GDP. The government has a crash program to increase supplies and China is committed to building projects capable in the longer term of supplying almost 20,000 MW. However, the root cause of Pakistan's problem may not be one of power generating capacity, but of pricing. By keeping prices low, the industry has become mired in debt and incapable of generating funds for expansion. If the pricing policy should remain unchanged, the fact that the new debt now front-ended (i.e., committed before capacity comes online) China's assistance may compound rather than resolve the problem (Tiezzi, 2016; Pal, 2016).

At least in Pakistan the power is intended for domestic consumption. This was not the case with the Myanmar. Under the military regime, Chinese corporations had been engaged in no less than thirty-five energy projects capable of supplying over 36,600 MW of electricity, double the country's annual consumption. Most of this output was intended for China (Kudo, 2012). In September 2011 the transitional military government abruptly suspended work on the $8 billion Myitsone dam project, which would have been one of the largest in the world, capable of supplying 6000 MW. The scheme had been the object of continuous protest by environmental groups and by the political opposition led by Suu Kyi, but whether this influenced the outgoing regime is unclear (Mon and Hammond, 2015). The project is now the subject of an environmental review with no immediate solution in sight.

As we saw earlier, China's interest in *port and harbor construction* has caused much controversy and speculation over the security threat posed. Most of the new construction is of container ports, capable of berthing large new-model container ships (and potentially also naval ships). In the Indian Ocean, and especially among Indian commentators, they are seen as a challenge to regional security (Malik, 2014). It is worth putting this into some perspective. The commercial logic is two-fold. The first is to capture more of the supply chain for Chinese concerns—large container ports serve as a hub for transhipment to ports with more limited access. The second is to shorten trade routes from inland China to the Middle East, Africa and Europe. The benefits to local economies lie in the employment generated by the port and in local firms having first access to goods and raw materials, without the cost of transhipment. If one looks at the present container port capacity in South Asia and adjust it for the equity share held by firms, then China (including Hong Kong) 'controls' 6 percent of capacity in Southeast Asia and 10 percent in South Asia (Drewry, 2016). It is true that Chinese firms are expanding in the area, but there are reasons to doubt either the commercial viability and the development impact of these investments, assuming that the plans remain unchanged.

In Malaysia, Chinese operators have been developing Port Kuantan on the East coast and they are planning a major expansion in Port Klang on the West. These developments are in addition to, and in competition with, the port of Singapore. It is true that Singapore has lost market share to Port Kuantan (Ramasamy, 2013; *New Straits Times*, 27.9.2016; 2.10.2016), but it is doubtful whether there is sufficient capacity to justify further port expansion in the area, especially since Japanese contractors are currently expanding capacity in Jakarta. A similar consideration arises in Sri Lanka, where China had already involved in the expansion of the main port Colombo, and is committed to building a new port in Hambantota. If completed, the latter would become the fifth largest container port in the world. Its location, however, is in a rural backwater of Sri Lanka, which happened to be the constituency of the former prime minister (Pattanaik, 2015). Leaving aside the question whether Sri Lanka can support two such ports, all of these planned expansions are taking place against the backdrop of a slump in container traffic and will aggravate existing overcapacity. Once again, a potential source of support for the regional economy may well become a drain on the individual participating partners.

Special Enterprise Zones (SEZ) have come to symbolize China's emergence as an economic powerhouse and new ones are still being added in China itself, as part of the OBOR strategy. In China the SEZ model obviously works partly because there is a symbiosis between strong local government, powerful local planning authorities, influential financial institution and large leading sectors all committed to (and rewarded for) following national government policies. It is doubtful whether similar conditions exist elsewhere. The Khorgos East Gate project provides a cautionary tale. Khorgos was conceived as an alternative border crossing point to the bottleneck at the main crossing point at Alashankou further north. The SEZ straddles both sides of the border with Kazakhstan. On the Chinese side there is a town of 85,000 inhabitants with broad tree-lined avenues and a buzzing commercial center. On the Kazak side there is a large yurt selling German sweets and Russian beer and a line of plastic camels for tourists to photograph. The town itself comprised a modern station, a two-lane highway, a couple of dozen old houses and a small pretty mosque (Shepard, 2016; Mações, 2016).

At the other end of the route in Belarus, the Great Stone Industrial Park opened in June 2014.By 2016, after two years of poor management and construction delays, the only firms to undertake to establish there were two fertilizer plants (the main export product to China). In 2016 Chinese technical help was enlisted called in to resolve the problems but even so, at the latest count, only eight companies finalized agreements to move there (Smok, 2015; A. Lukashenko, 2016, *Belarus Digest*, 30.8.2016). Most of the literature on special development zones emphasizes the need for clear strategic planning that takes account of local conditions and comparative advantage, and that can cope with the evolution of both the SEZ's and the country's development. There are very few places that meet such conditions (Bräutigam and Xiaoyang, 2012; Bricout 2014; Rodriguez-Pose and Hardy, 2014; UNDP, 2015).

CONCLUSION

Let us now conclude this chapter by considering the forward linkage effects of the OBOR projects. They all have the potential to benefit the recipient country—transport improvements to reduce the costs of buying raw materials and semi-manufactures and of access to markets; power plants to provide reliable energy to industry and consumers; pipelines to help exploit remote energy resources and contribute transit fees to local revenue; new container ports to cut costs and provide employment; and SEZs to offer advantages of scale and agglomeration. All of this should, in theory, promote development. So why should there be any doubts? Part of the answer is that we have been there before. Until the mid-1970s, much Western development assistance favored large-scale infrastructural and industrial projects with 'strong' linkage effects. These were rationalized by reference to 'unbalanced growth' models and 'trickle-down' effects. Most of them failed. This was because they ignored the domestic conditions of the recipient economy—projects were built ahead of a demand which failed to materialize, the per capita incomes restricted market size, the low levels of education hampered the development of human capital, rural communities remained isolated from improving conditions elsewhere, the lack of easily accessible credit stymied investment, the bureaucracy stifled entrepreneurial initiative, the legal system provided little protection levels of trust were undermined by the almost endemic corruption at all levels of society. It was partly for these reasons that Western economists (and governments and NGOs) began to emphasize the role of the good governance as a condition for successful outcomes.

With its emphasis on non-interference and national sovereignty, governance issues are precisely an area that Chinese foreign policy deliberately chooses not to address. This is not necessarily wrong since deep-seated cultural patterns are not very amenable to external pressures for change. The point, however, is that economic development is determined by a complex interaction of politics, economics and society. The infusion of one element, no matter how well-intentioned, does not change this. A second observation is that growth has to come from within if it is to be sustainable. It builds societal acceptance around the project and confers legitimacy upon it. Without such conditions, projects may be neglected or even resisted. Yet these are the very points that the Chinese policy of non-interference in the domestic affairs of other nations neglects. By avoiding the issues of governance and the question of corruption, it has no control over whether the investments it makes will be managed properly or whether the benefits flow into the pockets of the elites rather than the peoples that they are supposed to serve.

REFERENCES

ADB. (2010) *Connecting Greater Mekong Subregion Railway. A Strategic Framework.* Manilla.

ADB. (2011a) *The Greater Mekong Subregion at 20: Progress and Prospects.* Manilla.

ADB. (2011b) *Mekong Subregion: Railway Strategy Study, Final Report.* Manilla. TA-7255 (REG).*Asia One.*

Asia One

ASEAN. (2011) Master Plan on ASEAN Connectivity, Jakarta.

Belarus Digest: Bloomberg

Bräutigam D. and Xiaoyang T. (2012) Economic statecraft in China's new overseas special economic zones: soft power, business or resource security? *International Affairs.* 88 (4) 799–816.

Bricout V. (2014) *Industrial Park Governance.* Singapore.

Brown D. M. (1999) *Highway Investment and Rural Economic Development An Annotated Bibliography.* USDA, Washington.

Bryceson, D.F., A. Bradbury, and Bradbury T. (2008) Roads to Poverty Reduction? Exploring Rural Roads' Impact on Mobility in Africa and Asia. *Development Policy Review.* 26 (4) 459–82.

Burkhanov A. and Chen, Y-W. (2016) Kazakh Perspective on China, the Chinese, and Chinese Migration. *Ethnic and Racial Studies.* 1–20.

Central Asian Regional Economic Cooperation Programme (CAREC). (2014) *Development Effectiveness Review 2014, 2015; From Landlocked to Linked In.* Mandaluyong City. 3rd edition.

CAREC. (2015) *Corridor Performance Measurement and Monitoring. Annual Report, 2014.*

CAREC. (2016) *Corridor Performance Measurement and Monitoring. Annual Report, 2015.*

Channel News Asia

Drewry. (2016) *Global Container Terminal Operators. Annual Review and Forecast. Annual Report.* 167, 174.

The Economist: Express Tribune

Goldberg, J. (2014) Myanmar's Great Power Balancing Act. *The Diplomat.* 29.8.2014.

Gourdon, J. (2014) *CEPII NTM-MAP: A Tool for Assessing the Economic Impact of Non-Tariff Measures.* CEPII Working Paper 2014–24.NTM-MAP Country database. Available at: http://www.cepii.fr/CEPII/en/bdd_modele/presentation. asp?id=28 [Accessed 30 June 2017].

Griffiths, R.T. (2017) *Revitalising the Silk Road. China's Belt and Road Initiative*, Leiden.

Henderson J. and Mitrova, T. (2016) *Energy Relations between Russia and China: Playing Chess with the Dragon*. Oxford Institute for Energy Studies, Working Paper 67.

Hirschman, A.O. (1958) *The Strategy of Economic Development*. New Haven, CT.

Indian Navy. (2015) Ensuring Secure Seas: Indian Maritime Security Strategy. *Naval Strategic Publication* 1 (2).

Jakarta Post

Kasuaga, K. (1997) Trans-Asian Railway. *Japan Railway and Transport Review*. June 1997, 31–35.

Keith, M., S. Lash, J. Arnoldi and Rooker, T. (2014) *China Constructing Capitalism: Economic Life and Urban Change*. London, New York.

Koch-Weser J. and Murray, C. (2014) The China–Russia Gas Deal: Background and Implications for the Broader Relationship. *U.S.–China Economic and Security Review Commission Staff Research Backgrounder*. 9.6.2014.

Kudo, T. (2012) *China's Policy toward Myanmar: Challenges and Prospects*. IDE-JETRO Working Paper.

Lafarguette, R. (2011) Chongqing: Model for a New Economic and Social Policy? *China Perspectives*. (4) 62–4.

Lombard P. and Coetzer, L. (2006) *The Estimation Of The Impact Of Rural Road Investments On Socio-Economic Development*.

Lukashenko, A. (2016) *Обращение с ежегодным Посланием к белорусскому народу и Национальному собранию*. 21.3.2016;

Maçães, B. (2016) New Western Frontier, Conquered by China. *Politico*, 20.6.2016.

Malik M. (ed.) (2014) *Maritime Security in the Indo-Pacific: Perspectives from China, India, and the United States*. London, 2014.

Marson J. and Ostroukh, A. (2016) Gazprom Secures $2.17 Billion Loan From Bank of China. *Wall Street Journal*. 3.3.2016.

Michel C. (2016a) Can China Really Save Central Asian Economies? *The Diplomat*, 13.2.2016.

Michel C. (2016b) Line D of the Central Asia-China Gas Pipeline Delayed. *The Diplomat*. 31.5.2016.

Mon, Y. and Hammond, C. (2015) CPI Pushes for Restart of Myitsone Dam. *Myanmar Times*. 5.6.2015.

National Development and Reform Commission (NDRC). (2015) *Vision and Actions on Jointly Building the Silk Road Economic Belt and 21st Century Maritime Silk Road*, 28.3.2015.

New Straits Times

Novy, D. (2009) *Gravity redux: measuring international trade costs with panel data*. Warwick Economic Research Paper (86).

Ollivier, G., J. Sondhi and Zhou N. (2014) High Speed Railways in China: A Look at Construction Costs. *China Transport Topics.* (9) July.

Pal, S. (2016) .The China-Pakistan Corridor is All About Power. Not Electricity, but the Real Thing. *The Wire.* 3.6.2016.

Pattanaik, S.S. (2015) Controversy over Chinese Investment in Sri Lanka. *East Asia Forum.* 5.6.2015.

Press Club News Agency

Ramasamy, M. (2013) China, Malaysia Plan $3.4 Billion Industrial Park in Kuantan. *Bloomberg Business.* 5.2.2013.

Regmi, M. D. (2011) *Experience in the Development of the Asian Highway.* PowerPoint of presentation to High Level Expert Group Meeting on Trans-African Highway Addis Ababa, 19–20.9.2011.

Rodriguez-Pose A. and Hardy D. (2014) *Technology and Industrial Parks in Emerging Countries. Panacea or Pipedream?*

Russian Times

Shepard, W. (2016) Khorgos: Where East meets West. *The Diplomat.* 1.4.2016.

Smok, V. (2015) Belarus-China Relations: More Hype Than Substance? *Belarus Digest,* 22.5.2015.

Snow, S. (2016) Central Asia's Lukewarm Pivot to China. *The Diplomat.* 16.8.2016.

Stratfor

Tiezzi, S. (2016) China Powers up Pakistan: The Energy Component of the CPEC. *The Diplomat,* 13.1.2016.

Toedoro, A. (2015) *Maintaining ASEAN Centrality in Connectivity through MPAC ASEAN's Connectivity Challenge.* CIRSS Commentaries, 2 (17, June).

UN ESCAP. (1996) *Trans-Asian railway Route Requirements: Developments of the Trans-Asian Railway in the Indo-China and ASEAN sub-region.* Volume One, New York.

UN ESCAP. (2003) *Intergovernmental agreement on the Asian highway network,* s.l.

UN ECE/ESCAP (2008) *Joint Study on Developing Euro-Asian Transport Linkages.* New York.

UNDP (2015) *If Africa builds nests, will the birds come? Comparative Study on Special Economic Zones in Africa and China.* UNDP.

Umaña, F. (2012) *Transnational Security Threats in the Straits of Malacca.* Foundation for Peace, Washington.

van de Walle, D. (2002) Choosing Rural Road Investments to Help Reduce Poverty *World Development.* 30 (4) 575–89.

Washington Post

Wheeler, A. (2015) The New China Silk Road (One Belt, One Road): Changing The Face Of Oil & Gas In SE Asia. *OilPro.* 28.7.2015.

World Bank, Doing Business, Available at http://www.doingbusiness.org/data/ exploretopics/trading-across-borders (Accessed 30.6.2017).

World Bank/ECSAP, International Trade Costs Dataset. Avaliable at http://data. worldbank.org/data-catalog/trade-costs-dataset (Accessed 30.6.2017).

WTO, ITC, UNCTAD. (2016) *World Tariff Profiles*. Geneva.

Xi, J. (2013) *Promote People-to-People Friendship and Create a Better Future.* [Speech] Nazarbayev University, Kazakhstan, 11.9.2013.

Xi, J. (2013) *Speech to the Indonesian Parliament.* [Speech] 2.10.2013. Full text of speech released by ASEAN–China Centre, 2.10.2013.

Chapter 4

Donald Trump's Presidency and the Implementation of OBOR in Central Asia

Akram Umarov

INTRODUCTION

Donald Trump's accession to the governance of the United States marked significant changes in the foreign policy of Washington, DC. The election campaign of Donald Trump was rich in numerous ambiguous statements on foreign policy issues, which were primarily around reassessing the country's stance on the foreign policy in the past decades. The selection by Donald Trump of the 11 member countries but Beijing for the Agreement on the Trans-Pacific Partnership aimed at creating a free trade zone led by Washington was especially bewildering.

One of the main electoral promises of the newly elected US president was the approval of the Washington's immediate withdrawal from this agreement, which was actually realized in February 2017. This decision sparked an abundance of negative reactions and cautions about its consequences. It is generally believed that such a move leads to (1) a loss of trust in the United States among the main partners in the Pacific region and (2) a tangible increase in Beijing's influence on the historical partners of the US administration. Given the uncertainty of the further foreign policy prospects of the Trump administration in the Asia-Pacific region (APR), regional countries may express willingness to and actually attempt to upgrade their cooperation with China.

The new character of the American foreign policy under the leadership of Donald Trump has been also making an impact on Central Asia. Despite the fact that the US president practically did not mention the region in his election campaign, his recent decisions might have a direct impact on the development of events in Central Asia. The resulting "vacuum of influence" in the APR may lead to an even greater presence of China in the region and a decrease in attention to the development of the OBOR project, in which Central Asia plays one of the definitive roles.

Accounting for the aforementioned states of the world, this chapter aims to address a number of questions: What are the reasons for the promotion of OBOR project in Central Asia? How does Washington's build its new foreign policy line in the APR? What is the impact of the new foreign policy approaches of the US administration on China's presence in the APR? How will relations between the Central Asia countries, China and the United States evolve in the new international environment within the context of the implementation of OBOR?

WHY PROMOTE OBOR?

President Xi Jinping's visit to Central Asia in September 2013 was an unequivocal demonstration of the growth of the region's value for Beijing, which signaled strategic changes in China's foreign policy.

Beijing's aspiration to seize the initiative and the announcement of the strategic reorientation titled "turning to Eurasia" served as a response of China to the actions of other world powers. Having been launched in 1996, soon after founding the "Shanghai Five," the policy oriented on the cooperation with Central Asian countries was conceptually outlined and developed taking into account the long-term aims of Chinese government to create an economic belt.

The proposal of China's leader to create an economic belt along the Silk Road involves: (1) development of economic cooperation on the Eurasian continent through the construction of transport infrastructure and (2) the growth of mutual trade by removing barriers and strengthening the role of national currencies in transactions. This initiative became part of an even larger "One Belt, One Road" project with the inclusion of the marine component. Likewise, Xi Jinping suggested considering the possibility of creating a free trade zone in the region and fostering cultural and social ties, for example, scholarships for 30,000 students coming from the states in Shanghai Cooperation Organization (Xi Jinping, 2013).

The new OBOR initiative represents China's most ambitious foreign policy in recent decades reflecting Beijing's willingness to take an active and proactive position in international processes. Undoubtedly, the initiation of OBOR results from the increased influence and power of China on the world stage. More than that, this initiative is economically viable, historically justified, and has promising long-run prospects. With the rise of Xi Jinping to leadership, China's foreign policy has become more active, assertive, and global (Hong Yu, 2016).

We suppose that the initiation of the project was based on the following grounds.

The first reason is Barack Obama's declaration of the "pivot to Asia" in the USforeign policy agenda, which showed the shift of Washington's priority interests to the APR (Barack Obama, 2011).In conjunction with the gradual withdrawal of US forces from Afghanistan it laid an appropriate ground for Beijing to consolidate its presence in the strategically important Central Asia.

Interim, China precariously observed the US actions on widening its military, political, and economic presence in the APR. Further expansion of American-allied ties with Japan, the Republic of Korea, Australia and a number of states in Southeast Asia as well as the intention to establish close partnership with India, were considered by Beijing as a gradual policy of the "strategic encirclement" of China. In the future, as far as China was concerned, these steps could suppress the trade turnover of the Celestial Empire with these countries and complicate the access to vital sea transport routes.

Under these conditions, China has attempted to establish good neighborly relations with bordering countries. In particular, Beijing considers the countries of Central Asia not only as friendly neighboring countries, but also as important markets for raw materials and for promotion of Chinese produce, as well as a land transport corridor allowing access to Europe and the Middle East.

Secondly, China sought to ensure the safety and sustainable social and economic development of the Xinjiang Uygur Autonomous Region by promoting the OBOR initiative. By means of expansion of trade and economic ties with Central Asian countries, China intended to catalyze the economic development of Xinjiang. It seems indeed that Xinjiang plays an important role in relations between China and Central Asia. Transforming the western cities of China into regional trade centers, connected with Central Asia by roadways, airways, railways, and pipelines, Beijing aimed to support the creation and development of new enterprises and industries in Xinjiang.

China plausibly considers the development of the Central Asia as grounds for the stability of Xinjiang's neighbors and for the reduction of the growth of radical forms of Islam, the spread of which among the Uygur population of the autonomous region is posing serious concern to the Chinese government. This is extremely important for ensuring the security and sustainable development of the autonomous region.

Third, one of the main driving forces for the development of Beijing's relations with the Central Asian countries was to ensure its own energy security. In this regard, the supply of Central Asian energy resources to China is one of the priority areas of the Chinese strategy toward the partnership in region.

The dynamically growing economy of China demands a respective amount of energy supplies. However, the worsening tensions in the Middle East, the tension around the Iranian nuclear program and the increasing risks of delivering mineral products across the marine routes have been prompting the Chinese leadership to seek for new import markets of raw materials. One of these regions is Central Asia.

According to the General Administration of Customs of China, the country imported 381 million tons of oil by the end of 2016 (Reuters, 2017). Despite the slowdown of GDP growth, the demand for energy continues to grow steadily and so does the country's dependence on foreign energy supplies. According to the Ministry of Land and Natural Resources of China, in 2013 Chinese dependence on oil imports comprised 57 percent, by 2020 this figure could increase to 66 percent and to 72 percent by 2040 (U.S. Energy Information Agency, 2014).

In 2016, the consumption of natural gas in China increased by 7.3 percent, reaching 205 billion cubic meters (Reuters, 2016). At the same time, natural gas imports reached 66 billion cubic meters, accounting for about 32 percent of total consumption (Yinan, 2016). In this light, China has embarked on a course of gradual reduction of the share of coal in the country's energy sector in order to reduce negative environmental consequences of its usage. Hence, higher attention is devoted to increasing natural gas consumption. Forecasts project that by 2020 the share of coal in China's energy balance will decrease to 56 percent compared to 63 percent in 2015, and the share of natural gas may rise from 8 percent will to 12 percent. According to the International Energy Agency's predictions, by 2020 China will consume about 250 billion cubic meters of gas (Higashi, 2009).

The fourth reason pertains to China's concerns about Russia's attempts to form a Customs Union in the CIS countries and a deeper form of economic integration in the form of the Eurasian Economic Union. The latter actions could lead to a decreasing trend in trade between Central Asia and China due to ensuing trade barriers and limiting Beijing's opportunities to build relations in the region on a preferred bilateral basis.

The Customs Union led to the formation of unified customs tariffs for the import of Chinese products to the member states of the organization. The application of these tariffs contributed to the price surge and the decrease in the competitiveness of Chinese goods in the markets of the member states. According to the estimates of the European Bank for Reconstruction and Development, an increase in tariffs of even 2 percent will lead to a reduction in exports from China to the countries of the Customs Union by 2–3 percent (Plekhanov and Isakova, 2012).

The Customs Union has gradually tightened the terms of trade with China. For example, the supranational regulatory body of the Customs Union and the unified economic space, the Eurasian Economic Commission, launched an investigation of 5 anti-dumping and 4 special protection cases against

Chinese products in 2013 (Zykova, 2013). As a result, the Customs Union introduced duties ranging from 19 to 52 percent on certain Chinese goods (Zykova, 2013).

Interim, accounting for the high level of relations with Russia and mutual support on a number of international problems, China avoids an open political confrontation with Russia on Central Asian issues. Beijing does not demonstrate much interest in the field of security in its partnership with the Central Asian countries. This is mainly because of unwillingness to provoke discontent of Moscow, which views the region as a "sphere of privileged national interests."

Nevertheless, China's strategy was intended to demonstrate that the Customs Union is not a serious obstacle to the development of economic cooperation between the Celestial Empire and the region. In congruence with this, Beijing draw particular attention to the fact that the proposed model of cooperation is limited to economic issues (President Xi Jinping repeatedly stressed the principle of non-interference of China into the internal affairs of his international partners) and is free of any political integration in the future. This approach impressed the Central Asian states, some of which are cautions about the political component of integration projects under the aegis of Russia.

Notably, Russia is somewhat lagging behind China's pace in expanding trade and investment cooperation with the Central Asian states. The volume of China's trade with Central Asian countries reached a peak of $50.28 billion in 2013, staring with just several million dollars in 1991 (Xinhua, 2014). Chinese president Xi Jinping's visit to Central Asia resulted in a package of agreements worth about $50 billion (Kuzmina, 2013). At the same time, the volume of trade between the Russian Federation and the Central Asian states in 2013 barely exceeded $20 billion (Ministry of Foreign Affairs of the Russian Federation, 2013). The volume of Russia's investment in Central Asian countries was recorded to be around $15 billion (Ministry for Economic Development of the Russian Federation, 2013).

The OBOR initiative has not yet a detailed implementation plan, which is both advantageous and disadvantageous. The lack of a detailed plan for OBOR's implementation given the current circumstances causes uncertainty regarding the specific directions, timing, pace, and stages of the project. Politic and economic processes in Central Asia and neighboring regions are dynamically changing and delaying the details of the proposed initiative can diminish its relevance and significance. Contrary to this, the absence of the strictly outlined plan allows adjusting the project for the views and interests of the Central Asian states on the initiative. Openness to new ideas and proposals can increase further interest and support for the project in the region.

THE VIEWS OF CENTRAL ASIAN COUNTRIES ON OBOR

The promotion of China's new concept in the Eurasian region "The Economic belt of the Silk Road" initiated as part of OBOR by President Xi Jinping during the tour of the Central Asian countries, clearly demonstrates the importance of the region in implementing a large-scale project of creating a common economic space with a developed transport, energy, and other necessary infrastructure. This initiative triggered great interest among the Central Asian states, explained by the following circumstances.

Firstly, the implementation of this concept can unlock the inflow of a large amount of external financing and investments, which are necessary for the modernization of the outdated infrastructure and economic development of the region. According to the estimates of the Asian Development Bank, the Central Asian region needs investments of $565 billion in the period 2016–2030 (ADB, 2017) to maintain the pace of economic development, create necessary conditions for a dynamically increasing population, and respond to climate change challenges. However, the aggregate volume of GDP (the official exchange rate) of five Central Asian states in 2016 amounted just to 244 billion US dollars[1] (The World Factbook, 2017).

Central Asian countries are not able to implement such capital investments independently and the announcement of Xi Jinping's idea of Beijing's readiness to invest in infrastructure projects in the region is in line with the long-term interests of the Central Asian countries and is very timely for the economies of the countries. According to the World Bank (2016), the foreign direct investment (FDI) from China to other countries will increase by 5 percentage points of its GDP over the next 10 years. It is expected that Central Asia will receive a significant portion of these investments. A larger inflow of FDI will lead to an increase in fixed capital and, consequently, to the growth of the economy. This provides financing for more projects and will lead to an increase in the exchange rate, which in turn will stabilize both the trade balance and trade structure.

Secondly, the Central Asian countries need to establish trustful relations with China in the current geopolitical situation in Central Asia and the world. In the context of the growing activity of Russia in Central Asia in order to involve regional countries in its ambitious plan to expand the Eurasian Economic Union and decreasing US influence in the region, China is a valuable partner for Central Asia. Maintaining close cooperation with Beijing can deter the growth of influence by Moscow, Washington, and others.

China's positioning of OBOR as the main priority of its foreign policy determines the aspiration and perseverance of the Chinese leadership to do his best to implement the proposed projects within the initiative. One gets the impression that the leadership of China is extremely sensitive to OBOR and reacts painfully to attempts to level out the significance of the project. Central Asian states understand the context and advantages of Beijing's initiative in the region.

However, we cannot neglect a number of circumstances in the implementation of the Chinese initiative in the region, which require a deeper understanding.

First, Chinese investment can play an important role in supporting the economic development of Central Asia. However, a significant amount of investments and loans that do not correspond to the country's economy can lead to dependence on the creditor and create imbalances in certain sectors of the national economies. The main investments of China in the region are directed to the oil and gas sector and extraction of natural resources. According to some indicators, China has become the main partner of the region in this regard.

So at present, Chinese companies own almost a quarter of oil production in Kazakhstan, and in Turkmenistan more than half of gas exports fall to China (Wilson, 2016). China is the main creditor of Tajikistan and its share in the external debt structure accounts for more than half of the country's total external debt— $1.2 billion (Asia-Plus, 2017). Also, Beijing remains the main creditor of Kyrgyzstan, accounting for about 40 percent of the total external debt (CABAR—Central Asian Bureau for Analytic Reporting, 2016).

China's credit activity is the highest in Kazakhstan and Turkmenistan, which have large reserves of hydrocarbon resources. In Tajikistan and Kyrgyzstan, Chinese loans are directed to transport and energy infrastructure projects. Unlike other countries of Central Asia, Uzbekistan, as a matter of priority, directs external borrowing to finance the production sector of the economy.

Attracting large-scale investments can't always bring to improvement of the economy. The limited nature of China's investment in Central Asia can in the future lead to an unbalanced growth of individual industries against the background of stagnation or weak development in others.

Second, in Central Asia, on the other hand, there is an interpretation that China intends to invest in transferring the most polluting production enterprises into the region. In recent years, the Chinese leadership has paid close attention to the settlement of the environmental problems that have accumulated over the years of rapid economic growth, which has already caused serious damage to the country and has formed an unfavorable image of China. However, the desire of the country's leadership to develop a "green economy" may not fully extend to neighboring countries and infrastructure projects within the framework of OBOR (Tracy, Shvarts, Simonov, Babenko, 2017).

Chinese companies have not yet proven themselves as supporters of environmentally less harmful production and construction of infrastructure facilities. In recent years, Chinese companies have launched new cement plants in Kyrgyzstan and Tajikistan (Wilson, 2016), which can pollute the environment and, as a result, adversely affect the health of local residents.

The Chinese government supports its companies with regard to the relocation of excess capacity abroad and the countries of Central Asia are also considered suitable for this program. According to some estimates, the development of transport and energy in the region can pave the way for the transfer from China of labor-intensive industries that produce products with low added value (Lu, 2016). However, in the era of new technologies, development of alternative energy, environmentally friendly, and energy-efficient production, such an approach to the development of the economy in the region can give initially a certain dynamic to economic growth, but in the long term, Central Asia may be eventually at a disadvantage.

Third, the peculiarity of China's foreign economic activity is that the investment projects are implemented predominantly by Chinese companies and workforce that reduces the benefits for Central Asia of attracting Chinese capital.

In some countries of the region, there are sentiments of Sinophobia and fears about a possible flow of migrants from China. There are cases of local disturbances of the population about the presence of Chinese workers in the oil fields of Western Kazakhstan, in areas of mining in Kyrgyzstan and in the regions of Tajikistan where the road infrastructure was built (Asia-Plus, 2016). Chinese farmers also take care of agricultural land in Tajikistan, freed by local farmers, who left to find work in Russia (Hofman, 2016). In Kazakhstan, in 2016, protests took place, when rumors spread that Chinese farmers intend to rent agricultural lands in Kazakhstan (BBC, 2016).

Specific projects planned by China for implementation in the framework of the OBOR are still not completely clear. The maps showing the routes demonstrated by the Chinese government only clarify the priority transport corridors being considered by Beijing, but do not specify exactly what infrastructure initiatives in other spheres of the economy the Chinese side is willing to finance.

In general, the project of the OBOR provides new large-scale opportunities for the region to make a qualitative leap in the development of the economy, to carry out a wide modernization of the transport and energy infrastructure, and to create larger production capacities for addressing employment problems, increase exports and reduce imports. However, at the same time regional states should take into account the above mentioned unfavorable circumstances of further implementation of OBOR project.

FOREIGN POLICY PRIORITIES OF DONALD TRUMP'S ADMINISTRATION IN THE APR

The United States' rise on the international arena after the Second World War is rooted in the geographical diversification of its trading activity. The current political, economic, and military power of the United States was boosted mostly via free trade with foreign partners. Washington was one of the main supporters and engines of liberalization and simplification of international trade regimes, and this was reflected in the negotiations for the General Agreement on Tariffs and Trade in the 1940s and 1950s, which subsequently evolved into the creation of the World Trade Organization in 1995.

Meanwhile, the United States aimed to conclude trade agreements with neighboring countries and regions. Thus, the North American Free Trade Agreement was signed in 1992, allowing integration of markets in the United States, Canada, and Mexico. Subsequently, Barack Obama administration paid special attention to trade documents aimed at creating large integration blocs that significantly alleviated trade barriers.

He believed that in the light of gradual leveling of the overwhelming international domination of the United States achieved for the first time after the collapse of the USSR Washington needs to focus on bilateral and regional trade agreements. The slowdown in the development of the WTO and new negotiation processes to expand trade relations with other countries incited the US administration to seek for opportunities to conclude trade agreements with the closest political and economic partners.

Consequently, the ex-president Barack Obama proposed prioritizing the Trans-Pacific and Trans-Atlantic trade agreements, which could reemphasize the special role of the United States in the international arena, while a number of large countries have already raised the question of the need to establish a new multi-centered world order. The leitmotif of Barack Obama's second presidential term was the conclusion of the Trans Pacific Partnership (TPP). Negotiations between the parties lasted for a long time, since the TPP was intended to regulate a wide range of issues related to the legal protection of intellectual property rights, with agriculture, telecommunications, financial services, customs cooperation and tariffs, mutual investment, etc. Eventually, after exhausting negotiations between 12 participants, February 2016 marked signature of the partnership.

Obama's administration believed that the new policy in the APR would allow the United States redirect the political priorities from Europe and the Middle East to a dynamically developing region, which will be at the center of global policy in the twenty-first century (McCormick, 2016). Barack Obama team believed that this strategy might be revised by the future US presidents, yet cannot be completely abolished due to the growing importance of the APR for American foreign policy. Undoubtedly, the importance of the region for the United States further strengthens the presence of an increasing power—China. Under these conditions, it is crucial for the US administration to retain its influence in the region and to maintain close ties with strategic allies in the APR.

However, President Obama was unable to secure the support of the US Congress and the agreement remained non-ratified until the change of US leadership in November 2016. The elected president Donald Trump is known for his critical attitude to the APR. Throughout his election campaign, Donald Trump declared his denial of this document and his non-compliance with it should he be elected as a president, and in February 2017 he announced the withdrawal of the United States from the TPP.

This withdrawal might harm the US economy in the short run, and in the long run Washington may face serious political challenges in the region. Given that the other 11 participants of the agreement nurtured great hopes in this document and further improvements in relationships with the United States, the actions of the American government considerably surprised these countries, causing rejection and uncertainty in the prospects for relations with Washington (Halbert, 2016).

The TPP countries account for 44 percent of total US exports and 85 percent of total US exports in agriculture (McBride, 2017). Since traditional tariffs are already low, the TPP has focused on a number of reforms, including the liberalization of previously protected sectors of the economy, the adjustment of customs tariffs and regulations, the strengthening of intellectual property protection, the promotion of competitive and transparent business laws and enforcement of labor and environmental standards.

Given the lack of the new proposals from Donald Trump's administration on building relations with the countries in region, the above action of the United States induces closer relationships with China, which is the leading trade partner of the APR states. For example, Australia, being a strategic partner of the United States, is quite concerned about the changes in US policy and wishes to reconsider its relations (Cordesman, 2016). Also, Washington's traditional partner in Southeast Asia—the Philippines, headed by President R.Duterte— expresses a positive attitude toward developing cooperation with Beijing amid growing tensions with the United States.

Every other US president introduces new nuances to the country's foreign policy and this is a traditional notion in American political culture. The new administration has all the reasons to question certain aspects of US trade and security policy as well as maintaining an assertive position on the APR issues. However, it is important to carefully consider the views, proposals, and concerns of the countries in the region when designing an American strategy, which will maximize success of US policy in the APR.

Besides, Trump's critical attitude toward China marked a specific feature of his campaign. He accused the Chinese side of unfair trade with the United States, of the intended devaluation of the exchange rate and criticized Beijing's actions in the South China Sea. Since his presidency, he continues repeating the same accusations of China and even agreed to have a telephone conversation with Taiwan's leader Tsai Ing-wen in the status of the US president-elect, which did not conform with the established traditions and diplomatic protocol of Washington's relations with Taiwan after the recognition of the "one China" policy in 1979.

Perhaps, Trump was influenced by the fact that the American people still perceive China as a threat to the United States, and the country is often seen as one of the main rivals of the United States (Gallup, 2016). In the Pew Center studies between 1997 and 2014, many Americans considered China "a serious problem" (PollingReport.com, 2014). Generally, a significant part of the US public considers China to be the "key enemy" of the country, most consider China a "serious problem" for the United States, and the majority of the nation treats China unfavorably (McCormick, 2016).

The above diplomatic actions taken by the Donald Trump's team, given his statements that the US military assistance to the allies in the region, such as Japan and South Korea, is very expensive for the budget and these countries should consider contributing funds to financing the presence of US forces in their territories, caused a spike of negative reactions from the experts (Cordesman, 2016). Donald Trump's statement together with the decision to exit the TPP raises questions about the future role of the United States in trade and foreign investment in the APR. Outlining combating terrorism, ISIS in particular, as the main aim of its foreign policy, increased attention to the processes in the Middle East, and prioritizing internal affairs of the United States, move the APR to the far edge of Trump administration's foreign policy.

Yet, there is a noticeable lack of a long-term foreign policy planning by the United States in this region, because by subjecting to revision the policies of the previous administration Trump's team does not offer any alternative vision of the prospects for the American presence in the APR. After the announcement of the presidential election results in November 2016 and after taking office in January 2017, the new administration continues to act somewhat impulsively, actively reacting to the ongoing processes in the world, but is not offering a conceptual vision of the further development of American foreign policy.

The US internal political turmoil associated with the ongoing "war of compromising evidences" between the Democratic and Republican parties prevents the formation of a single stable team of President Donald Trump (the resignation of M. Flynn from the post of presidential adviser on national security, the exclusion of President S. Bannon's adviser from the membership in the US National Security Council, etc.). Frequent personnel changes in responsible positions pose significant barriers to the determination of priorities to ensure national security and the implementation of a well-developed, long-term, and uniform foreign policy.

During the first weeks, there was no clarity with respect to US-Chinese relationships. A US attempt to exert pressure and aggressively advance its own agenda with the Chinese government may not lead to the desired result, since China has already become an influential force on the international scene without cooperation with which it is hardly possible to solve the most important issues of sustainable development and stability in the world.

Both sides might become successful exclusively by means of negotiations and mutual compromises. Recently, one might notice certain alterations in the US approaches to relationships with China, and there has been a noticeable intensification of bilateral contacts at a highest level. US secretary of state R. Tillerson visited Beijing in March 2017, and in April 2017 Xi Jinping arrived in the United States to meet with Donald Trump and discuss the problem of the North Korean nuclear program, trade relations between the countries, Taiwan, etc.

THE IMPACT OF THE NEW US POLICY IN THE APR ON THE PRESENCE OF CHINA IN THE REGION

With the dampening world economic development, trade and the growth of services sector, China faces serious challenges and security threats. China attempts to regulate excessive indebtedness, excess production capacity, declining competitiveness, unfavorable demographics, and capital outflow. Under these circumstances, the Chinese government is taking a number of actions to improve the situation; they fall into two main priority categories: (1) the transformation of the internal financial system and (2) the implementation of the OBOR project. The success of these initiatives will be of vital importance for China's economic development, political and social stability and the growth of geopolitical influence (Dargnat, 2016).

The election of Trump depicts the dawn of an isolationist turn in US foreign policy, which already entails a reduction in security commitments in the APR. The future prospect of devoting Washington's resources and attention to domestic problems might sound optimistic to the Chinese leadership with respect to opportunities for expanding its influence in the region and on the international arena (Miura & Chen Weiss, 2016). Meanwhile, there is a growing awareness that the Donald Trump's administration will face difficulties in raising customs tariffs in trade relations with China. China is the main trading partner of most countries, including the United States. In 2016, the turnover between the United States and China amounted to more than $600 billion, whereas the trade between the former Soviet Union and the United States amounted to a maximum of only about $4 billion (Zhao, 2017). Increasingly relying on each other to ensure sustainable growth, the United States and China are becoming more interdependent.

After the US withdrawal from the TPP we can already observe to some extent the attempts of the countries in the region to establish closer contacts with Beijing. The regional states reacted promptly, and Vietnam, Malaysia, Chile, and Peru announced that they would disregard TPP initiative and would instead work on join the agreement on the trade partnership of China with 16 countries called the "Regional Comprehensive Economic Partnership."

Meanwhile, despite the promises of the Chinese leadership and ASEAN member states to strengthen bilateral cooperation, the relations remain fragile and sensitive to unexpected changes and competition (Hong, 2016). In order to settle these problems and strengthen bilateral relations with these countries, China is making attempts to implement large infrastructure projects in these countries within the framework of OBOR and to improve its image. Chinese companies and banks, including the newly created Asian Infrastructure Investment Bank, committed to invest $1.2 trillion in the construction of railway lines, oil and gas pipelines, highways, airports and large ports to improve the ties between China and Central and Southeast Asia, Russia, parts of Europe and potentially in most of Africa (60 countries) (Halbert, 2016).

In addition, after the statements of Donald Trump about the intention to withdraw from the Paris climate agreement, Xi Jinping at the economic forum in Davos, Switzerland, in January 2017, promised that China will be in front of global efforts to reduce climate change and to move to a "green" environmentally friendly energy usage. In addition, he defended economic globalization and international cooperation, and expressed his willingness to actively participate in resolution of world-threatening problems (Xi Jinping, 2017).

Nevertheless, in reality, the Chinese government faces serious internal and external challenges, which may prevent the implementation of OBOR. These challenges appear to be sufficiently intricate to slowdown the progress in the OBOR draft. The effective implementation of the OBOR initiative largely depends on the cooperativeness of Chinese neighbors. The Chinese government should engage in consultations and explain in detail the draft of the OBOR to its potential partners and reveal all potential benefits of the project (Hong, 2016).

The slowdown of Chinese economy may threaten the implementation of the OBOR project. This slowdown roots in a number of factors. The growth was funded by the accumulation of debt, which has accelerated over the past few years. Although China's public debt, which is about 55 percent of GDP, is lower than in most Western countries, China's private debt growth is a serious concern. China's total debt rose from 160 percent of GDP at the end of 2007 to 290 percent in 2015 (Christian Dargnat, 2016). There is also a financial measure of the OBOR progress as the implementation of this initiative is expected to use the Chinese national currency in financial transactions; this in turn may boost the international status of the currency (Dargnat, 2016).

The slowdown in economic growth and structural reforms in the country require a more proactive and ambitious foreign policy. To achieve the objectives set by China's president, a thoroughly thought-out and long-term foreign policy course is needed. In this context, one can even notice the similarities in the slogans of the leaders of the United States and China—"to make America great again" and "to achieve the Chinese dream."

Harvard's professor G. Allison suggest that China and the United States may fall into the "trap of Thucydides." This concept, developed almost 2500 years by the ancient Greek historian Thucydides, says that the cause of the war between Athens and Sparta was "the growth of Athenian power and the fear it caused in Sparta" (Allison, 2017). On these grounds, Allison (2017) concluded that the emergence of a growing power (China) in the presence of an already operating superpower (the United States) could lead to misunderstandings and direct clashes between the countries. However, despite Allison's pessimistic forecasts, so far the parties have managed to avoid the least pleasant scenarios in the development of relationships.

Geographically, China and the United States are on opposite sides in the APR. The problems in the region represent the greatest challenge to China's ability for peaceful development. Nonetheless, considering the experience of Moscow—Washington relationships during the Cold War, where the parties avoided a full-scale military clash, Beijing and Washington must also build a mechanism of relations that will not lead to direct wars.

Despite the decline in US interest in the APR since the presidency of Trump, it will still be relatively challenging for Beijing to occupy the niche of the "strategic partner" of the vast majority of countries in the region. Regional states might fear the steady growth of China's economic, political, and military capabilities. The Chinese leadership cannot yet convince these countries not to perceive China as one of the major security threats. The existing mistrust between the state leaders, the overhang of border disputes, and persisting Sinophobia in a number of Southeastern and East Asian countries may prevent the establishment of qualitatively new and strategic ties between China and individual countries of the region.

CURRENT STATE OF RELATIONSHIPS BETWEEN CENTRAL ASIA, CHINA, AND THE UNITED STATES WITHIN THE OBO PROJECT

With the rise of President Xi Jinping to power in China, one can notice the changes in China's approaches to Central Asia. Since 2013, one can track the marked changes in China's policy in Central Asia and Afghanistan, which is an integral part of the systemic transformation of Beijing's strategy on the international arena. China used to be committed to non-interference in the conflict settlement in neighboring countries and the rest of the world, concentrating mainly on domestic economic development. Yet, recently Beijing has embarked on an ambitious, dynamic, and long-term foreign policy aimed at preventing possible threats to the national interests, ensuring security along the entire Chinese border and the country's rapid economic development.

Since 2013, Xi Jinping's leadership opened a new page in Chinese foreign policy record. He said that, "in external affairs, the primary and most important task is to ensure and successfully use the important strategic opportunities for China" (Jinping, 2014). Speaking in Paris in March 2014, China chairman recalled Napoleon's statements about China: "Napoleon said that China is a sleeping lion, and when it wakes up, the whole world will shake." Xi Jinping assured the audience that the Chinese lion had already woken up, but this is a "peaceful, friendly, and civilized lion" (Jinping, 2013).

For the last few years, the Chinese leader has expressed himself as reformatory, aimed at transforming the entire set of domestic and foreign policy relations of the country. Xi Jinping intends to increase Chinese influence and opportunities in the international arena by pursuing a more active and assertive foreign policy, focusing on the OBOR initiative, increasing foreign trade and investment, creating new regional and international institutions, and enhancing the armed forces of the nation.

During the announcement of the OBOR initiative in 2013 with the growing US activity in the APR, China tried to seize the initiative in Central Asia and Afghanistan from the Americans. The United States previously promoted the "New Silk Road" project, which was supposed to strengthen the infrastructure links between Central and South Asia. The Beijing-led OBOR initiative will allow the implementation of large-scale infrastructure projects in the region, taking into account the Chinese interests.

If the implementation of Barack Obama "rebalancing to Asia" strategy prevented to some extent the OBOR project realization, the arrival of Donald Trump to power and his departure from the policy of the previous administration opens up new opportunities for China. Since the concept of OBOR does not apply to the Pacific Ocean, this may signal Washington that China concentrates on Central Asia and the sea coast of East Asia, East Africa and therefore does not threaten the US domination in the Pacific (Lam Peng Er, 2016).

Even so, we believe that the promotion of Barack Obama policy in the APR was one of the main motivations for the initiation of the OBOR project. The US administration's policy involving the shift of Washington's priority interests to the APR, coupled with the gradual withdrawal of US forces from Afghanistan, presented a right opportunity for Beijing to consolidate its presence in the strategically important region of Central Asia.

Along this line, China cautiously observed the US actions on building up its military, political, economic presence in the APR. Further expansion of American-allied ties with Japan, the Republic of Korea, Australia and a number of states in Southeast Asia as well as the intention to establish close partnership with India, were considered by Beijing as a gradual policy of the "strategic encirclement" of China. In the future, as far as China was concerned, these steps could suppress the trade turnover of the Celestial Empire with these countries and complicate the access to vital sea transport routes.

The announcement of the OBOR project by China was a significant event for the Eurasian continent, in particular for Central Asia. The Beijing initiative enabled many states of the continent to obtain vital investments in a number of large infrastructure projects that are difficult to implement without the support of international partners.

The arrival of Trump to the US power induces serious changes in the existing balance of forces in the APR, and these changes can have direct impact on the Central Asian region. Trump's decision to withdraw from the agreement on the Trans-Pacific Partnership and his statement on a cardinal revision of existing US trade agreements can radically change the existing nature of international relations.

In this situation, two scenarios for the development of the project of the OBOR Central Asia are possible. First, if Beijing infers from lower US cooperation with the APR that the threat of encirclement is alleviated, China's attention and determination to implement the OBOR may diminish. In turn, this could lead to a leveling of the importance of Central Asia for the Chinese leadership, which may bring a fall in investment in major projects, a decline in core economic indicators, and a wider scope for Russia and other actors in the region.

Secondly, China may perceive the willingness of Washington to prioritize internal issues as an appropriate moment for expanding its influence throughout the world, and especially in Central Asia. Greater strengthening of Beijing in the region may lead to contradictory consequences: on the one hand, it can lead to significant financial injections of China into the region and the solution of major economic problems, and on the other—the growth of China's influence can result in imbalance of powers in Central Asia and the new confrontation between the major external forces for the supremacy in the region.

To our best knowledge, China already possesses a clear long-run foreign policy agenda. The current leadership of China will not radically review its foreign policy. Stemming from the changing international environment and clarification of the priorities of Trump's foreign policy priorities, the OBOR concept can only undergo some adjustments in directions and priorities. Yet, given the long-term and fundamental stakes of Beijing in the implementation of this project, it is difficult to imagine that China will depart from the implementation of OBOR in the nearest future.

Donald Trump maintains the diminished role of Central Asia in the US foreign policy agenda, which mainly commenced after the withdrawal of most of the troops in 2014. The internal political problems of the United States together with Washington's increased attention to the Syrian conflict, the North Korean problem, relations with European countries and the development of the national economy do not allow the American leadership to pay closer attention to Central Asia. Meanwhile, the surge of the migration crisis in the European Union, Brexit, the growing influence of euro-skeptics in the member countries, and the high level of terrorist activity do not allow the proper development of EU-Central Asian relations.

CONCLUSION

China is well informed of the foreign policy state of the world's leading countries in the Central Asian region. Diminishing influence of the United States and the European Union presents China with a timely opportunity to enhance its presence in Central Asia in the long-term prospect. The current tight cooperation between Beijing and Moscow will at least initially prevent conflict of interests in Central Asia. Abundance of financial resources and technological innovations of the People's Republic of China, the declared commitment to non-interference in internal affairs of the countries of the region, as well as a decreased attention from the world's leading countries to the region can help China upgrade the level of cooperation with the Central Asian countries.

Meanwhile, internal and external forces have pressured the administration of Trump to return to the conduct of foreign policy in a way already familiar for the international community. There have been several incidents, which demonstrate Trump's deviation from the claims made on these issues earlier, for example (1) the recent missile bombing of the Syrian army's airbase by the US armed forces, (2) Xi Jinping's visit to the United States and his meeting with Donald Trump, (3) the attitude toward North Korea, (4) his statement of commitment to ensuring the security and stability of Japan and South Korea—key partners in the region.

Earlier in the course of the electoral process, Trump declared his readiness to improve relations with Russia, yet after stepping into his duties Trump's team was severely criticized for the intention to cooperate with Russia. In this light, Washington declares its commitment to supporting the territorial integrity of Ukraine and inflicted a military attack on the air base of the Syrian army, which was viewed by Moscow as anti-Russian action. In case of growing tensions in relations with the Russian Federation, one cannot exclude the greater interest of the American establishment in Central Asia, which is one of the important areas for Russia's influence.

With the growing tension between Russia and the United States in the background, China occupies the most advantageous position in Central Asia. Moderately reacting to the confrontations of US-Russian interests on various issues and striving to maintain friendly partnership relations with both sides, China is actively promoting its own foreign policy course. Contrary to Russia and the United States, China has the will, as well as financial and technological opportunities, to implement large-scale infrastructure projects in Central Asia, to invest generously and export specific production technologies from China to the region.

Given the aforementioned circumstances, Central Asian countries should avoid falling in the sphere of influence of one of these powers and strive to pursue a balanced foreign policy. When it comes to FDIs, the main policy recommendation would be to diversify their sources and not be dependent on a single country. Implementation of large-scale infrastructure projects and enhancement of production capacities are crucial for the economy. Yet they should by all means be guided by their role in developing the domestic economy, in accordance with the most up-to-date international standards for energy efficiency, safety, environmental friendliness, and productivity.

NOTE

1. Kazakhstan—$128,1 billion, Kyrgyzstan—$5,794 billion, Tajikistan—$6,612 billion, Turkmenistan—$36,57 billion, Uzbekistan—$67,22 billion.

REFERENCES

Asia-Plus (2017) Tajikistan's foreign debt nears 2.3 billion U.S. dollars. Available at https://news.tj/en/news/tajikistan/economic/20170524/240186
Asia-Plus (2016) What does China's One Belt, One Road Project mean for Central Asia? Available at https://news.tj/en/news/centralasia/20161115/233226

BBC (2016) Kazakhstan's land reform protests explained. Available at http://www. bbc.com/news/world-asia-36163103

CABAR - Central Asian Bureau for Analitical Reporting (2016) Tajikistan's External Debt: the growing risks against the backdrop of a fragile stability. Available at http://cabar.asia/en/konstantin-bondarenko-tajikistan-s-external-debt-the-growing-risks-against-the-backdrop-of-a-fragile-stability/

Cordesman, A.H., (2016) The Trump Transition and Asia: The Need for Policies and Plans. Center for Strategic and International Studies publications.

Dargnat, C., (2016) China's Shifting Geo-economic Strategy. Survival. 58 (3), pp. 63–76.

Gallup.com, (2016) "China." Available at http://www.gallup.com/1627/chin. aspx.?version=print

Graham, A., (2017) Destined for War: Can America and China Escape Thucydides's Trap? Houghton Mifflin Harcourt.

Halbert, G., (2016) End Of TPP Brings New Opportunities For China& U.S. Halbert Wealth Management publications, pp. 1–6.

Higashi, N., (2009) Natural Gas in China: Market evolution and strategy. Available at http://www.iea.org/publications/freepublications/publication/nat_gas_China.pdf

Hofman, I., (2016) Politics or profits along the "Silk Road": what drives Chinese farms in Tajikistan and helps them thrive? Eurasian Geography and Economics. 57 (3), pp. 457–481.

Hong, Y., (2016) Motivation behind China's 'One Belt, One Road' Initiatives and Establishment of the Asian Infrastructure Investment Bank. *Journal of Contemporary China*. 105 (26), pp. 353–368.

Jinping, X., (2017) Keynote at the World Economic Forum. CGT-NAmerica. Available at https://america.cgtn.com/2017/01/17/full-text-of-xi-jinping-keynote-at-the-world-economic-forum

Jinping, X. (2013) Укреплять дружбу народов, вместе открыть светлое будущее. Выступление председателя КНР Си Цзиньпина в Назарбаев университете. Available at http://kz.China-embassy.org/rus/zhgx/t1077192.htm

Jinping, X., (2014). Speech by H.E. Mr. Xi President of the People's Republic of China at the Meeting Commemorating the 50th Anniversary of the Establishment of China-France Diplomatic Relations, Paris. Available at http://www.fmChina. gov.cn/mfa_eng/wjdt_665385/zyjh_665391/t1147894.shtml

Jinping, X., (2014) The Central Conference on Work Relating to Foreign Affairs was Held in Beijing. Ministry of Foreign Affairs, the People's Republic of China. Available at http://www.fmChina.gov.cn/mfa_eng/zxxx_662805/t1215680.shtml

Kuzmina, E.M., (2013) Внешние экономические интересы как фактор экономического развития Центральной Азии. Институт экономики РАН, pp. 5–15.

Lavrov, S.V., (2013). Выступление министра иностранных дел Российской Федерации С.В.Лаврова перед студентами и профессорско-преподавательским составом Евразийского национального университета им. Л.Н. Гумилева и ответы на вопросы в ходе последовавшей дискуссии. Available at http://www. mid.ru/bdomp/brp_4.nsf/fa711a859c4b939643256999005bcbbc/704768f59bb9a0 9b44257be40058c32e!OpenDocument

Lu, Y., (2016) One Belt One Road: Breakthrough for China's Global Value Chain Upgrading. Available at http://ippreview.com/index.php/Home/Blog/single/id/113.html

McBride, J., (2017) The Trans-Pacific Partnership and U.S. Trade Policy. Available at http://www.cfr.org/trade/trans-pacific-partnership-us-trade-policy/p36422.

McCormick, J.M., (2016) Pivoting toward Asia: Comparing the Canadian and American Policy Shifts. American Review of Canadian Studies. 46(4), p. 474–495.

Miura, K. & Chen Weiss, J., (2016) Will China Test Trump? Lessons from Past Campaigns and Elections. *The Washington Quarterly*. 39 (4), 7–25.

Obama, B., (2011) Remarks By President Obama to the Australian Parliament. Available at http://www.whitehouse.gov/the-press-office/2011/11/17/remarks-president-obama-australian-parliament.

Plekhanov, A. and Isakova, A., (2012) Trade within the Russia-Kazakhstan-Belarus customs union: early evidence. European Bank for Reconstruction and Development. Available at http://www.ebrdblog.com/wordpress/2012/07/trade-within-the-russia-kazakhstan-belarus-customs-union-early-evidence/

PollingReport.com, (Eds) "China" for the summary of the Pew Research finding. Available at http://www.pollingreport.com/China.htm

Reuters (2017) China's December crude oil imports, fuel exports hit record. Available at http://in.reuters.com/article/China-economy-trade-crude-idINL4N1F31II

Reuters (2016) China oil demand to grow 4.3 percent in 2016 -CNPC research. Available at http://www.reuters.com/article/China-energy-growth-idUSL3N15A312

The Asian Development Bank (2017) Meeting Asia's Infrastructure Needs.Mandaluyong City, Philippines: Asian Development Bank.

The World Factbook (2017) Kazakhstan, Kyrgyzstan, Tajikistan, Turkmenistan, Uzbekistan. Available at https://www.cia.gov/library/publications/the-world-factbook/

Tracy, E., Shvarts, E., Simonov, E., Babenko, M., (2017) China's new Eurasian ambitions: the environmental risks of the Silk Road Economic Belt. Eurasian Geography and Economics.58 (1), pp. 56–88.

Wilson, W., (2016) China's Huge 'One Belt, One Road' Initiative Is Sweeping Central Asia. Available at http://nationalinterest.org/feature/Chinas-huge-one-belt-one-road-initiative-sweeping-central-17150

US Energy Information Administration, (2014) China. Available at http://www.eia.gov/countries/cab.cfm?fips=CH

Xinhua (2014) Внешнеторговый оборот Китая перешагнул отметку в 4 трлн. долл. США. Available at http://russian.news.cn/economic/2014–01/10/c_133034621.htm

Yinan, G., (2016) China's natural gas demand to hit 200 billion cubic meter. Available at http://usa.Chinadaily.com.cn/business/2014–02/04/content_17268125.htm

Zhao, S., (2017) American Reflections on the Engagement with China and Responses to President Xi's New Model of Major Power Relations, *Journal of Contemporary China*. 106 (26), pp. 489–503.

Zikova, T., (2013) Импорт под следствием. Российская газета. Available at http://www.rg.ru/2013/01/24/tovari.html

Chapter 5

The Rationale behind the China-Pakistan Economic Corridor

The View from Beijing

Harry Roberts

Starting in the 1960s, China and Pakistan began to forge an exceptionally close bilateral relationship. Built on mutual strategic interests, namely *realpolitik* security considerations, based on deterrence and balancing vis-à-vis India, the two nations have over the years developed high-level political, military and diplomatic relations.

However, a key component of this relationship has always been somewhat lacking, specifically, the economic aspect. However, in January 2000, President Musharraf, making his first visit to China soon after being elected in 1999, declared that both countries sought to significantly strengthen the economics of the relationship. Musharraf proposed the building of an 'energy-and-trade corridor' linking Gwadar on the Arabian Sea to Xinjiang through the development of infrastructure projects including Gwadar port, railways, roads, and oil and gas pipelines, during a visit to Beijing in February 2006.

It was not until May 2013, however, that the China-Pakistan Economic Corridor (CPEC) was announced[1]. CPEC comes at an important time for China's leaders concerned with a variety of challenges to their continued rule both domestically and from abroad. Firstly, China faces an economic slowdown in a context of sluggish global demand. While this apparent 'slowdown' started under Hu Jintao, China's current leader, Xi Jinping, has placed more emphasis China's changing economy moving away from its traditional manufacturing export-based economy and toward a greater reliance on services. In order to achieve sustained economic growth in the future, China is currently embarking on difficult economic reforms.

Furthermore, since the late 2000s, the Communist Party of China (CPC) has faced renewed challenges in the form of ethnic and religious strife in Xinjiang. Inter-ethnic tension has existed in Xinjiang for decades but violence has spiked since 2009. The linking of Uighur militants to radical Islamists in

Pakistan and Afghanistan remains a concern for Beijing, which fears that instability in these countries could blowback on China itself and directly threaten the sovereign integrity of the People's Republic of China (PRC).

Lastly, the Obama administration's 'Pivot to Asia', essentially aimed at curtailing the rise of China and particularly its growing ambitions in the South and East China Seas, has led to rising tensions between the US and China in recent years. In the light of such tensions, China is keenly aware of the vulnerability of its energy supplies and has sought to diversify the means by which it can deliver these imports to strengthen its energy security. Furthermore, India, while still a long way off in catching up to China economically, is growing rapidly and is projected to overtake China's population sometime in the 2020s, meaning India will have a larger and younger workforce in the coming years. These various developments have had a significant effect on the thinking of China's leaders and all relate to the decision to go ahead with CPEC.

THE DOMESTIC ECONOMIC DRIVERS OF CPEC

China's economic success can be traced back to the economic reforms implemented by party boss Deng Xiaoping. These reforms were effectively aimed at liberalizing the Chinese economy, transitioning it from central planning to a market-based one, while maintaining tight political control. Hence, these reforms were labeled by the party as 'reform and opening', which sort to build 'Socialism with Chinese characteristics'. Since these reforms began, China's economy has grown rapidly averaging nearly 10 percent a year, 'the fastest sustained expansion by a major economy in history—and has lifted more than 800 million people out of poverty' (The World Bank).

This traditional economic-development model has largely been characterized by an export-led manufacturing sector that relied on the low cost of land and labor available in China. The 'reform and opening' of China also paved the way for much-needed Foreign Direct Investment (FDI), with much of it going toward developing China's blossoming manufacturing sector. The introduction of limited free trade and privatization in Chinese industry and business had important and positive implications on the Chinese economy. Firstly, the establishment of Special Economic Zones (SEZ's) encouraged international investors, lured by low corporate taxes and very cheap labor, to set up shop in China's easily accessible eastern coastal regions[2].

The economic reforms inaugurated by Deng Xiaoping and carried on by consecutive CPC leaders, while underpinning the success of the Chinese economic boom over the last 30 years have given rise to an economic-development model that is no longer sustainable. While the figures and analyses regarding the overall health of the Chinese economy are disputed by economists, there is no denying that 2015 saw the weakest growth in 25 years and record net capital outflows of almost $700bn[3].

It is now a good point to explain China's economic troubles as these can be seen as deep trends in China's economic performance over the last 10 years. These trends not only underlie the CPC's quest for economic reforms but have an important correlation with China pursuing new markets through polices like CPEC and One Belt, One Road (OBOR).

China's Economic Slowdown

Firstly, doing business in China is becoming increasingly expensive making their products and services less competitive with those from emerging market powers. From 2006 to 2015 wages almost quadrupled in China and now manufactures of low-cost/low-quality manufacturers are switching their operations to still lower labor cost countries like Bangladesh and Laos[4].

It is not only labor costs that are increasing, but the price of land and electricity too. Long-term economic trends within China point at Chinese firms increasingly looking toward investing abroad to remain competitive with some manufactures employing a 'China+1strategy'. Private Chinese manufacturers are increasingly setting up factories abroad, which in fact, mirrors the advanced Asian economies like Japan, South Korea, and Taiwan, and looking to diversify their income through Outward Foreign Direct Investment (OFDI).

Secondly, government investment in industry has led to a huge debt bubble. The 2008–9 stimulus package totaled 4 trillion Yuan ($586bn) and largely went into financing the construction of mega infrastructure projects within China itself[5]. This stimulus package added to the already considerable debt levels in China. Historically, government-led investment in China has been largely inefficient and instead of channeling investment into innovative parts of the economy has in fact done the opposite, actually reinforcing inefficiency and waste. Kenneth Lieberthal, senior researcher at the Brookings Institute, highlights the necessity of the CPC to reduce 'governmental interference in the market' to build a 'development model based on efficiency' (*China Daily*, 12.08.2013).

Thirdly, there is the problem of the bloated State Owned Enterprises (SOE)'s, which have grown far too large and inefficient and have become a drain on the central governments resources, handicapping the wider economy.

Reforming the SOE's will require mass lay-offs in China. While some regional governments have started to do this, particularly in the bloated coal industry, the central government faces resistance from vested interests in the provinces. These include resistance to reform due to the decreased tax receipts this would bring to local party elites and the potential for civil unrest

among laid off workers. Although there are programs for re-training different workers to find employment in other sectors, finding meaningful work
for industrial sector employees will be a monumental task for the central and
local governments alike.

Finally, much of this inefficiency is in the industrial processing sectors such
as cement, glass and steel with SOE's being propped up by local governments
and state-owned banks. The industrial conglomerates, already bloated from
servicing the booming Chinese economy for the last 30 years were allowed
to expand with little or no oversight as regards to basic ideas of efficiency
and profitability and this was only reinforced by the 2008/9 stimulus package.

Solving these problems in China's economy has been a central theme to
Xi Jinping's leadership. Xi has publically recognized that indeed, China's
traditional economic-development model is failing and has staked his continued rule on 'rebalancing' the economy to address these problems in order to
achieve sustained and long-term economic growth. CPEC is one the initiatives chosen by the CPC to enable this outcome.

THE CPEC AND CHINA'S CHANGING DOMESTIC ECONOMY

Since the announcement of CPEC, $14bn has already been financed for
the completion of 'early-harvest' projects[6]. Moreover, these investments
are directly related to China's changing domestic economy in a number of
important ways. This section will explain how CPEC will assist in reforming
China's domestic economy.

Firstly, due to increased manufacturing costs in China, because of higher
wages, electricity and land costs, Pakistan can be seen as a favorable place
in which Chinese firms, and particularly its SOE's, can invest in starting new
operations, or at least moving some of their business there. The increased
presence of Chinese firms in Pakistan under CPEC will be able to take advantage of cheaper labor costs and unlike producers located in the interior of
China, which, although has lower wages than the coastal provinces, loses this
advantage due to poor infrastructure and long distances to the coastal ports.

However, low labor costs are just one part of the picture. There is an
increasing global trend where all types of manufacturers, especially tech
ones, are setting up shop close to their markets. For instance, North Africa
has increasingly become a hub for companies wishing to sell in Europe and
'rather than chasing low cost, tech manufacturers are thinking about operating regionally and keeping supply chains shorter'.... "Some companies call
it 'best sourcing," says North Rizza (Morris, 27.08.2015).

In part, this dimension of CPEC can be viewed as a mechanism in which
to improve the efficiency of Chinese firms across borders. The acquisition of

Gwadar port by the China Overseas Port Holding Company from the Port of Singapore Authority and CPECs proposal to establish a free trade zone and industrial parks in the vicinity of Gwadar will give China easier access the Middle Eastern, African and European markets, cutting shipping times from China's east coast significantly. This would potentially place the various industrial park projects, and particularly those at Gwadar, at the forefront of 'Contract Manufacturing', where quick turn-around times for new products is essential.

Secondly, CPEC will, to some degree, alleviate China's challenge in cutting industrial overcapacity. Now that economic growth is slower, there is significant overcapacity in heavy industry, including thousands of factories and plants, which are propped up by various local governments through loans from state banks in China. Fearing a public backlash from growing unemployment and lost tax revenues, regional leaders are reluctant to close down operations, even if those operations are surplus to requirements.

Thus, facing these entrenched interests within China from regional party elites, the central government has specially encouraged Chinese companies "to participate in infrastructure construction in other countries along the Belt and Road, and make industrial investments there" (NDRC, 2015). CPEC must be seen in the wider context of a changing Chinese economy and the realization by the leadership that Chinese firms must expand abroad if they are to continue to bring economic growth to China.

The coal industry is one such sector that has ballooned massively in recent years. With a slowing economy there is now huge overcapacity in this area to such an extent that while China has traditionally been a net importer of coal, it is expected that in the near future it could soon become a net exporter[7].

While Pakistan will not be the only recipient of China's excess coal it must be remembered that the energy component of the CPEC is by far its largest aspect. Indeed, the Pakistanis are banking on China in helping them to develop their beleaguered power industry and increase generating capacity considerably. As it stands, Pakistan's troubled economy is hampered by chronic power shortages with regular outages stopping work throughout the country, which costs its economy as much as 2 percent of Gross Domestic Product (GDP) a year[8]. One particular aspect in which a lack of reliable electricity supply hampers the Pakistani economy is in the very lucrative cotton processing and Ready Made Garment's (RMG) industry. The importance of cotton cannot be underestimated for the Pakistani economy, accounting for 55 percent of the country's export earnings and employing 40 percent of the labor force[9].

However, the potential for China to export its overcapacity in coal to Pakistan should not be over exaggerated. Pakistan itself has more than '185.5 billion tonnes of coal reserves. If half of these resources were exploited, it would be enough to generate 100,000 megawatts of electricity for 30 years'

(Climate Home, 2015). However, as it stands, much of these resources are years away from potentially being mined.

More importantly for China is the upgrading and weeding out of inefficient and excessively polluting power stations and their relocation from China to Pakistan. Following the Paris Climate Change Agreements in 2015, 'China has promised to cut emissions from its coal power plants by 60% by 2020' according to an official communiqué quoted by the New China Press Agency (Paris 2015). However, this will not stop China financing and constructing numerous coal-fired power stations in Pakistan, both in order to produce power for Pakistan's domestic needs but more importantly as a way of encouraging China's traditionally low-tech energy producers to invest in Pakistan as a way of compensating them for a reduced role in China's future energy strategy.

Given the state of the bloated Chinese coal industry, Chinese commitments to international climate change agreements and its own policy announcements on a cleaner, greener development model, CPEC provides a convenient way to reform China's SOE's and at the same time export its industrial overcapacity in various industrial and energy sectors. This is an ambitious and long-term economic strategy on the part of the CPC and the potential benefits of which will be hard to verify for years to come[10].

Thirdly, China is not only looking to establish outlets for its vast industrial overcapacity. It is also looking to establish new markets for its goods and lucrative investment opportunities for both its private and public firms. With the relatively low volume of trade that has been the hallmark of bilateral economic ties, especially when seen in the light of Sino-Indian trade, China's apparent commitment to CPEC means that this is potentially set to increase massively. Pakistan has huge potential as an under-exploited and relatively untapped market for Chinese consumer goods and other services. This is a market that includes 180 million potential customers. Currently, China is only reaching fraction of this potential, although this is rapidly changing.

One key area of Pakistan's economy provides Chinese investors with potentially a particularly lucrative opportunity: its energy market. Specific projects like the Quaid-e-Azam Solar Power Park, planned to be the world's largest and the $1.7bn Karot Hydroelectric plant in Punjab: give Chinese power companies and private investors a lot of scope to broaden their investment portfolios due to high demand for reliable energy in Pakistan and the prediction that this demand is to grow considerably in the next decade[11].

Lastly, China is partly developing CPEC due to its ongoing need for natural resources. While China can access resources from all over the world, Pakistan is abundant in many of the raw materials that continue to help drive China's economy. Furthermore, given the development aspirations of the CPC, high consumption of raw materials is only set to increase in the coming decades. While China has made huge strides in terms of development over the last 30 years[12], it is still very much a developing country where per capita income remains much below that of advanced industrial nations.

Part of the development goals, as set out by the CPC, includes the ambitious plan of 'promoting urbanization throughout the nation'.... meaning that 'villages will become township-level cities' (Xinhua News Agency, 11.12.2013). This policy alone will require the relocation of millions of people away from rural areas and into cities and will require the continuation of massive sustained capacity in heavy industry and the raw materials needed to fuel this industry will increasingly come from abroad. Furthermore, the projected consumption habits of China's growing middle class, which, according to some calculations, made up 68 percent of urban households in 2012 with expected household income predicted to at least double by 2022, will further contribute to the need to source all sorts of commodities from around the world, including Pakistan, which is a cheap source of minerals for Chinese smart phones, textiles for its garment industry and fruit for its supermarkets[13].

All in all, behind the changing Chinese economy are deep and long-term economic trends at work that lie largely out of the hands of its leaders but which, under Xi's tenure are starting to be recognized. As noted above, one area where China's economy is fundamentally changing is in the subsidence of manufacturing as the central driver of Chinese economic growth. In fact, the service sector overtook manufacturing between 2010 and 2015 as the biggest sector in the Chinese economy (Bloomberg, 29.02.2016). While this is partly down to increased manufacturing costs within China there is also a recognition that if China wants to become an advanced industrial country it should steadily phase out its manufacturing of low cost/quality goods. As China's firms increasingly produce value-added goods and services at home it can export its manufacturing know-how, gained over the last 30 years, to set up factories abroad taking advantage of lower costs thereby repatriating the profits from these operations back to China, just like the advanced economies of the west or successful 'Tiger Economies' of the east.

Despite China's continuing interest in Pakistan's natural resources, CPEC is slightly different from that of the original 'going-out' strategy or China's investment in Africa in the 2000–2010 era. China's current and projected future role in Pakistan is not solely about attaining the means to fuel China's growth. Now that its economy is slowing and Beijing is trying to move away from its traditional reliance on heavy manufacturing, there is less of a need for China to seek out such resources from Pakistan (although this will continue somewhat due to its ambitious development goals). The economics of CPEC then is also partly directed at the streamlining of its firms by encouraged them to look for investment opportunities outside of China. With CPEC, Pakistan provides a relatively easy and uncompetitive environment in which

its private firms and SOE's can operate before they attempt to directly compete with the corporations of the advanced industrial nations. Thus, CPEC is
a fundamentally important part of the China's wider economic reforms.

CPEC AND XINJIANG

Another major driver of CPEC is China's security concerns in Xinjiang. The
Chinese state has had a history of checkered relations with the native, ethnic
Uighur population of its huge, western border region of Xinjiang. Given the
poor state of relations between these actors, including attacks on representatives of the Chinese state spiking since 2008/9; CPEC (as part of OBOR) has
a strong developmental or 'state-building' aspect in relation to Xinjiang.
   Furthermore, there is also a transnational dimension to Xinjiang's internal
security. The CPC has pressing concerns over instability in Central Asia and
Pakistan that could potentially spillover and upset the already fragile relationship between Uighur's and Han Chinese, given that a number of Uighur have,
over the years, built links with trans-national Jihadi groups. The CPC faces
a difficult challenge in reconciling the opening up of Xinjiang by linking it
with the OBOR and CPEC projects while at the same time insulating it from
the political turbulence of Afghanistan and Pakistan, Central Asia and the
Middle East.

DEVELOPMENT AND 'STATE-BUILDING' IN XINJIANG

The fact that the CPEC is aimed at constructing infrastructure networks
including roads and pipelines that will link China's underdeveloped region
of Xinjiang to the Arabian Sea and beyond tells us something important
about Beijing's thinking behind the project. As Chinese economic development has traditionally been concentrated in the eastern coastal regions, due
to the fact that most people live there and its proximity to the ports and rivers, there has been a desire by the leadership to bridge the unequal development between the economically developed and prosperous coastal provinces
and the underdeveloped interior and west. This inequality, while actually
growing throughout the 1990s, was addressed in the "Xi'an Speech," where
the 'Great Western Development'/'Go West' policy was formally spelled
out in 1999.
   Moreover, Xinjiang is seen by both the leadership and elements of
China's business community as ripe with potential. Considering the
increased costs of production in the east of China, Chinese companies have
tentatively started to move parts of their operations westward. The building

of improved transportation links with the rest of Asia has the potential to make the region as competitive as the coastal regions in terms of quality infrastructure[14].

However, the CPC, in seeking to develop Xinjiang through CPEC/OBOR is in part due to their unspoken recognition that the 'Go West' campaign only had limited results. Although the regions GDP almost doubled from 2004 to 2009 and grew 12 percent to RMB753.03bn in 2012, this was essentially a case of Xinjiang piggy-backing on the wider success of China's more innovative eastern regions with much of the growth in Xinjiang economy being linked to the increase in both demand and prices of oil and gas[15].

As mentioned previously, there has been a long history of checkered relations between Xinjiang's native Uighur population and the burgeoning Han Chinese community. Furthermore, this is strongly mirrored in the anti-state sentiments within elements of the Uighur population. Unemployment and poverty are the key factors that have been highlighted by the CPC as the cause of social tensions between the Uighur and Han populations and the source of Uighur grievances with the state. Indeed, unemployment among the Uighur is startling. Whereas the Han Chinese have an unemployment rate of only about 1 percent, for the Uighur population it is 70 percent[16].

Social tensions in Xinjiang spilling over into violence have been a worrying development for the CPC, with outbreaks in modern times going back as far as the 1960s. However, since around 2008/9, there has been an increase in outbreaks of violence on representatives of the local government, security forces, industrial infrastructure and civilians. In July 2009, rioting in the regional capital Urumqi led to the deaths of at least 140 people and injuries to over 800 more[17]. In July 2014, there are disputed accounts of events that led to 96 dead in Xinjiang's Yarkant[18].

The CPC believes that the way to combat this 'civil unrest', apart from traditional law enforcement and counter-terror policies designed to break-up the organizational capacity of Uighur 'extremists', is to bring economic prosperity to the region thereby reducing the support for such activities among the wider Uighur population. OBOR/CPEC and its important link to Xinjiang is aimed at addressing the socio-economic inequalities between Uighur's and Han people within Xinjiang and between the region and more developed and prosperous Chinese provinces, thus addressing the causes of these anti-state sentiments.

The CPC has been concerned about 'separatism' in Xinjiang for a long time. Official Chinese government references to the 'Three Evils' terminology appeared as early as March 15, 2001[19]. Since this time, the CPC has put economic growth and social stability at the heart of its development strategy in Xinjiang. However, any assessment of the CPC's development model in

Xinjiang up to now must acknowledge the numerous cases of the authorities heavy-handedness which has actually added to the causes of intensified social unrest.

Under CPEC and wider OBOR initiative the CPC effectively intend to assimilate and pacify the Uighur community by creating economic opportunities and so reduce the desire for so-called 'separatism' and ensure social harmony between Han settlers and the native population. Creating job opportunities in Xinjiang would also draw young Uighur's into the cities helping "Beijing achieve its desired 'blending' of cultures in the region" by "offering a certain way of living, to make them want to be like Han people" (Patton, 2016).

Among the various development projects that are designed to bring economic prosperity to Xinjiang is the increased production and refinement of raw cotton and development of the wider textile and RMG industry. Already 60 percent of China's cotton is grown in Xinjiang, and Xi Jinping has marked the region to replace the Pearl River Delta in China's east as the center of the textile industry[20].

Furthermore, Xinjiang is expected to play a key role in CPEC/OBOR energy and pipeline sectors. By linking Xinjiang to the Arabian Sea through CPEC, it is hoped that Xinjiang's hub for oil and gas refinery will be further developed. If the hugely ambitious pipeline project, was due to start in 2017 although no work has been undertaken on this project as of yet, is able to surmount the multitude of challenges that it faces and comes into fruition, then it will not only help secure China's energy security but will provide much-needed jobs in southern Xinjiang, where most Uighur's live and where CPEC is due to terminate in the city of Kashgar.

TRANSNATIONAL THREATS AND CPEC

The CPC also has concerns regarding violence from Afghanistan and Pakistan spilling over into Xinjiang, thereby encouraging further unrest among its Muslim-Uighur population. The principal group that China identifies as posing a threat to stability in Xinjiang was the East Turkistan Islamic Movement (ETIM), now apparently augmented into the Turkistan Islamic Party (TIP), which the CPC claims has been responsible for a number of attacks within Xinjiang and across China. Furthermore, Uighur separatists have now sought to attack Chinese interests aboard[21].

Furthermore, ETIM and now TIP have at times been based in Pakistan's Federally Administered Tribal Areas, particularly in North Waziristan. While it is unclear whether groups based there were actually directly responsible for attacks carried out in China these groups have been blamed for orchestrating a wave of propaganda that helped to instigate the violence. Furthermore, Chinese officials have also publically focused on the Xinjiang-Pakistan terror link in a move that was aimed to put pressure on its ally to crackdown on its militant problem[22].

Furthermore, the CPC's concern with violence emanating from Afghanistan and Pakistan has been all the more pressing since the US withdrawal from Afghanistan in 2014. The subsequent security vacuum that now exists on the Afghanistan-Pakistan border means that, for China, economic development of Pakistan is now more pressing than ever, to bring political stability and shore up the Pakistani's states resources in its fight with various groups threatening it.

The future of CPEC as a viable project will require a vast improvement in security throughout Pakistan. Thus, if the Pakistani political elite, and this goes for civilian as well as military figures, want to reap the potential political and financial benefits of CPEC, then they will have to seriously prevent violence on Chinese interests. The CPC can use its uniquely strong political/economic leverage with Pakistan to help defeat the 'three evils' "terrorism, separatism and religious extremism" in Xinjiang and therefore shore up the sovereign integrity of the PRC. CPEC and its generous loans is one way to do this.

In short, there is a delicate balance behind the CPC's vision of developing Xinjiang. On the one hand, China seeks to take advantage of the province's geographical proximity to the hydrocarbons and resources of Central Asia and access point to the resources of the Middle East. On the other hand, China is concerned about instability emanating from these regions having an adverse impact on the security of Xinjiang and China as a whole.

Concurrently, the CPC faces a threat to the sovereign integrity of China itself in the form of Uighur separatism. It is hoped that by increasing development and economic growth in Xinjiang, Beijing can integrate Xinjiang more closely with the center and forestall separatist tendencies.

Further, considering China's fears over 'separatism' in Xinjiang, there is also an international dynamic to security in Xinjiang. Given the significant Diasporas of ethnic Uighur's in Central Asia, particularly in Kyrgyzstan and Kazakhstan, and increasingly in Pakistan, China is fearful that instability in any of these countries could spill over into Xinjiang itself. Effectively using Xinjiang as a 'land bridge' between China and its western periphery will bind China's neighbors as stakeholders in Xingjian's stability and incentivize them to aid China in its fight against Uighur 'separatism'. Indeed, by extending such lavish loans to beleaguered Pakistan under the auspices of CPEC, China hopes to secure a benign external environment for its reform, development and stability.

THE GEOPOLITICS OF CPEC

This section will explore two important geopolitical issues that have inflated the CPC's concerns regarding China's national security in recent years and will explain how CPEC, and its financial and political support for Pakistan, somewhat helps to alleviate these concerns. First is China's self-perceived vulnerability regarding its energy security and specifically what has come to be known as the 'Malacca Dilemma'. Related to this is China's concern over the US's 'Pivot to Asia', which directly effects not only its energy security but wider national security in the Asia-Pacific region. Concerned primarily with staying in power, the CPC is embarking on CPEC as one of many means to secure China's geopolitical position and thereby its own regime integrity and longevity. By developing alternatives to the Malacca Straits for its energy imports the CPC will not only help secure its position in times of regional crisis but avert potential conflict with the US in that area. Furthermore, CPEC will bolster its strategic alliance with Pakistan and therefore strengthen China's strategic position against the possibility of a long-term consolidation of the US-India strategic partnership.

CPEC and the 'Malacca Dilemma'

It is in the light of the rising tension in the South China Sea that China is seeking to develop an alternative strategy to safeguard its Sea Lines of Communications. As mentioned previously, China has built its economic success on open access to world trade and energy markets. If the access to its markets and world energy resources were to be cut in the event of a regional conflict, then this would have untold consequences for China's economy and internal stability. Among a diverse range of means that China is developing to overcome its vulnerability that the straits represent to China's energy imports, the development of CPEC is an important one that should not be overlooked.

The Malacca Straits, situated between the Malay Peninsula and the Indonesian island of Sumatra, is a major source of concern to Chinese strategic planners because it effectively acts as a 'bottleneck' through which vessels headed between China and the Indian Ocean and onwards to Africa, South Asia, Middle East and Europe have to pass. As such, the vulnerability to the shipment of goods and energy supplies through the Malacca Straits was first referred to as the 'Malacca Dilemma' by President Hu Jintao back in 2003 due to its fundamental importance to China's national security[23].

First and foremost, China is concerned about its access to Middle Eastern oil[24]. Given the predicted rise in consumption rates among China's population and particularly its growing middle class, combined with an economy that is now so large that even with reduced growth rates, the Chinese economy will still require huge amounts of energy to fuel it. Li Wei, head of the Development Research Centre of the State Council, warned recently that 'by 2030, as much as 75 percent of China's oil might be imported. The dependency on overseas natural gas will also rise rapidly, bringing with it grave energy security concerns' (*China Daily*, 17.02.2014).

China's energy security and free access to the world economy is an overarching concern of the Chinese elite and has led to a renewed emphasis on developing alternatives to the Malacca Straits. While China is developing increased storage capacity for oil as part of its 'strategic diversification', up to 550 million barrels, a target set by Beijing for 2020, is nowhere near enough to endure a prolonged interruption of energy imports, which would have a devastating impact on its economy[25].

The proposed construction of oil pipelines through Pakistan, as part of CPEC, connecting Xinjiang with the Arabian Sea will potentially allow China to bypass the Malacca Straits and ship oil directly to Pakistan and onward to China. Furthermore, as part of this project, the Chinese government has signaled that there will be a possible extension to connect Iranian oil and gas fields[26].

It comes down to one overarching point: ever since economic reforms began in the late 1970s, high and sustained economic growth and improvements in living standards have been the central points of legitimacy for the Chinese ruling elite. Without economic growth, the ruling elite fear their grip on power will slip due to the potential knock-on effects of falling employment and declining standards of living that this would cause. Such economic problems could potentially see the emergence of mass protests and calls for democratic transformation, the nightmare scenario of another "Tiananmen Square," thereby undermining the CPC's creditability domestically and risking social turmoil which China's geopolitical rivals, led by the US, could take advantage of to unseat or, at the very least, weaken the party's grip on power. Thus, for the leadership, even reduced economic growth, especially at a time of important economic reforms during a generally depressed global economy, is of paramount importance, and unhindered energy imports and access to world trade is vital. Therefore, increasing tensions in the South China Sea at a time when China is embarking on such important (and difficult) economic reforms creates uneasiness in Beijing. The potential interruption to its energy supplies passing through the Malacca Straits at this time of uncertainty is just one more incentive to develop alternatives to this route.

While few see war on the horizon, for China's strategic planners it is not outside the realm of possibility that these tensions could lead to a regional conflict sometime in the future. Furthermore, while China is increasing the capacity of the People's Liberation Army Navy (PLAN), it is still no match for the US Navy, especially in the light of an augmented US military presence in the Asia-Pacific. Most concerning from China's perspective is the strengthening of US alliances in Asia, including the stationing of US strategic bombers in Australia's Northern Territories and the permanent stationing of US Marines near Darwin. While these forces remain small and apparently on a 'rotational' basis, they are clearly intended as a show of force directed at China[27].

In the event of a regional conflict, it is feared by China's leaders that the US and its allies could effectively cut off China's access to Middle Eastern oil by easily blocking the Malacca Straits, thereby cutting off the lifeblood of China's economy. In the scenario of a blockade of the Malacca Straits, or the bigger Lombok-Makassar Straits, it is very simple: "the United States could prevent the passage of large cargo ships and tankers. In doing so, it would cripple China's export trade, which is essential to China's economy" (Davis, 2014).

In any case, the development of a pipeline from Gwadar to Kashgar should not be exaggerated. Its potential capacity to deliver oil is estimated at 200,000 bpd and the costs of constructing this proposed pipeline could potentially add $10 to every barrel due to the extreme topography of the projected route and the security implications of instability in Balochistan and elsewhere in Pakistan[28].

However, this pipeline should not be seen as the ultimate solution to China's 'Malacca Dilemma' but instead as one of many projects, including others under the auspices of the OBOR initiative as well as preceding it, that aim to diversify China's energy imports, including oil and gas pipelines from Turkmenistan, Kazakhstan and Russia that are already in operation. What the Gwadar pipeline does, along with the Myanmar–Yunnan pipeline connecting the Bay of Bengal to China's interior, is provide an alternative, should any of the larger and more important routes become jeopardized. Thus, China, just like any other modern and highly industrialized power, is hedging its bets and the best way to guarantee its energy security is by diversifying the transport means that it imports its energy. CPEC's pipeline project should thus be seen in manner.

THE 'PIVOT' AND THE US-INDIA NEXUS

CPEC should also be viewed as part of China's response to the US's eastern 'rebalancing' or 'Pivot to Asia'. While the parameters of the Obama administration's 'Pivot to Asia' was always rather unclear, one can say that there is ample evidence of increased US engagement in that region in the last few years.

Subsequently, the US 'rebalancing' has encompassed the strengthening of economic and defense ties in the Asia-Pacific region. As part of the 'Pivot', the Obama administration encouraged 11 countries[29] to join the US sponsored (now shelved under President Trump) Trans Pacific Partnership (TPP), a free trade area in the Asia-Pacific region.[30] Notably, China was not invited to join apparently due to fears that it would have too much clout in what is a US dominated entity. However, from China's perspective, such an agreement that seeks to exclude China from the potential benefits of free trade in the region not only is hypocritical but is seen effectively as a policy of 'containment' designed to curtail its growing economic and, by implication, its political influence in the region.

Furthermore, as part of the 'Pivot', the US has enthusiastically sought closer defense cooperation with a number of Asian states, with India figuring prominently in the US's strategic plans. In 2012, the Department of Defence released its new strategic guidance, which set out its expected shift toward the Asia-Pacific declaring that India would be central to the US's approach to Asia.[31] To put it in a wider context, it is feared in China that as the US moves to build closer military relationships with Japan and Australia—which are designed to hold down the Pacific, the US is simultaneously shoring up its relationship with India to safeguard its interests in the Indian Ocean. Those who support this theory point to the signing of the Logistics and Supply Memorandum of Agreement (LEMOA) signed with the United States in August 2016, and President Obama's designation of India as a "major defence partner." As a sign of India's significance in US strategic planning it is notable that India now conducts more exercises with the US than any other nation[32].

From the CPC's perspective these developments signal a growing trend in India's foreign policy thinking, moving away from half a century of strategic autonomy toward stronger defense relations with the US. The US's 'strategic bet' on India as lighted upon by former secretary of state Hillary Clinton was given further weight when she remarked on India's 'Look East' policy, a program whereby India is seeking to build extensive economic and political relations with the nations of Southeast Asia, that it was imperative for 'India not only to "Look East", but also to "Go East"[33]. Many Chinese analysts have taken this as clear evidence of US endorsement for India to actively counter China's strategic ambitions in East Asia.

Thus, CPEC should be seen in the light of the US 'Pivot' and additionally China's historic strategic competition with India. While China has little to fear from India in terms of economic or even military competition, given its ascendency and consequent ability to out produce and out buy India (Chinese economic resources being so large), there is a realization in China that India is a potential spoiler for China's geopolitical ambitions. The potential of India, encouraged by the US, to act in ways that are detrimental to China's geopolitical interests suggests that CPEC and its bolstering of economic support of Pakistan, is in part, a strategic gambit on behalf of China to balance against a growing US-Indian strategic nexus.

The development of Gwadar port, which China maintains is not for military purposes, nevertheless acts as a relatively inexpensive and effective way to keep India off-balance. Although the PLAN has up until now not used Gwadar for operations, that it not to say that it couldn't one day. The desire to have a forward naval base from which it can conduct humanitarian missions or the evacuation of its nationals may lead China's planners, at some point in the future, to see Gwadar's excellent location as a handy asset it can exploit in times of emergency[34]. Along with the construction of a military base in Djibouti, Gwadar has the potential to shore up China's naval presence in such a strategically important location, given its close proximity to Middle Eastern energy supplies. The observation by some analysts concerning the considerable depth of dredging that has taken place at Gwadar suggests that indeed the port has the potential for future use by large warships in mind. Thereby, its very development gives China a psychological advantage and is enough to keep Indian naval strategy off-balance[35].

Furthermore, in the age-old form of China-Pakistan relations, CPEC, and especially the development of Gwadar, bolsters China's geopolitical and military support of its closest ally[36]. Looking into the future of strategic developments in the Indian Ocean region, China is then able 'to leverage its relationship with Pakistan to not only frustrate Indian ambitions but also play an indirect role in frustrating and combating US interests in the Greater Central Asia region' (Clarke 2013).

For China's leaders, it is increasingly becoming clear that the US and its Asia-Pacific allies are not shying away from challenging Chinese demands to respect its claims of sovereignty over disputed islets in the South China Seas. In recent years the US has conducted numerous Freedom of Navigation Operations aimed at challenging China's territorial claims. In the light of these 'rising tensions' in the Asia-Pacific region, China has sought to develop strategies to diversify and strengthen its energy security strategy. CPEC, will not provide the sole solution to China's vulnerability regarding its energy imports, but is one of a number of alternative options being developed that will help secure against possible threats in the future.

Furthermore, with the 'Pivot to Asia', and China's territorial claims in the South China Sea, relations between the US and China are indeed becoming more 'zero-sum' as Wang Jisi (2015), an influential Chinese scholar, rightly notes. Worried about its own relative power in the world the US is strengthening its diplomatic, economic and security commitments in the Asia-Pacific region aimed at countering China's rise as a great power to 'postpone the day when China inevitably surpasses the United States to become the world's most powerful country' (Leiberthal 2011). CPEC is a project that not only is aimed at benefiting China's economy and delivering stability to its restive province of Xinjiang but also seeks to engage in an area where China has 'traditional' national security interests vis-à-vis Pakistan-India.

Such an approach would not only help prevent conflict between the US and China but simultaneously dovetail with China's burgeoning trade with Central Asia, the Middle East and Africa. As Wang Jisi suggested in 2015, 'China may decide to reduce contention with the United States and Japan in East Asia while casting an eye westward. One phrase that captures this concept is "stabilize the East, march to the West,"[37] and it could become the basic core of a "Pan-Peripheral Strategy" for China'. This is indeed China's current geopolitical strategy and CPEC could play an important part in it.

CONCLUSION

The starting premise of this paper is that the CPC is driven fundamentally by what it sees as 'defensive' motives in an uncertain global and domestic environment. The inherently 'defensive' perspective of the CPC also explains why it is embarking upon the CPEC project.

At a time of economic slowdown and the recognition that China's traditional export-led manufacturing model has run its course, CPEC is one of various strategies being proposed by the CPC to help China's economy reform. Fearful of economic stagnation that could 'see it fall into the middle-income trap that has caught so many other developing nations after eras of robust growth' China has sought to restructure its economy (Bloomberg, 29.022016). This restructuring is focused on upgrading its industry, as Premier Li Keqiang noted, from a 'manufacturer of quantity to one of quality' (Nikkei Asian Review, 2015). Moving industry and manufacturing to Pakistan (and elsewhere) is part of a larger move to restructure its economy and cut overcapacity in China and encourage opportunities (and funding) for Chinese OFDI, which CPEC will provide.

Although there are a multitude of challenges that Xi Jinping faces in the form of vested interests within China it ultimately comes down to the recognition that 'economic rebalancing and sustainability of economic growth is viewed by the leadership as critical to the health of the Communist Party and the regime' (Li, Daokui Li, Rietveld, 05.08.2015). CPEC, as part of OBOR, is one of the strands of this economic reform.

Additionally, with the increase of violence in Xinjiang from 2009 onwards, the CPC has taken the threat of 'separatist' elements within Xinjiang's Uighur population more seriously. Predominately the CPC has responded along the lines of traditional law-enforcement and counter-terror operations demonstrating that the CPC will not tolerate opposition to its rule. However, in addition to this response the CPC has concurrently strengthened the development aspect of its policy toward Xinjiang. By linking CPEC to the region (particularly to its south, where the majority of the native Uighur population live), the CPC hopes to drive economic development there and to bridge inequality between the region and the rest of China and between Han and Uighur communities within Xinjiang itself.

Furthermore, from the CPC's perspective, the linkage between extremism among ethnic Uyghur's and the influence of radical Islamism in Central, South Asia and the Middle East means that instability emanating from China's Muslim borderlands could have significant consequences for the integrity of the Chinese state, particularly with regard to Xinjiang. The development of CPEC by linking Xinjiang to Pakistan and creating strong economic interconnectedness through pipelines and road projects 'also serve as important internal balancing goals, such as contributing to security and stability in Xinjiang through bilateral cooperation on counter-terrorism and enhancing China's ability to secure energy resources and trade access to the Middle East' (Clarke, 2013 17).

Finally, CPEC can be seen as the culmination of years of close military and political cooperation between China and Pakistan. The 1960s saw China establish an exceptionally close relationship with Pakistan that has continued and actually strengthened up until the present day. The realpolitik geostrategic element of Sino-Pakistan relations is still apparent today. The CPC's realization that the US is serious about countering China, as evidenced by its view of a US military build-up in the Asia-Pacific region shows a degree of caution in the CPC's thinking. With tensions growing between the US and China, CPEC can be seen a foreign policy initiative aimed in part at avoiding conflict with the US through China pivoting to the west. By developing CPEC, there may be weight to the idea that China is seeking to avoid possible conflicts in the South China Sea which would have catastrophic implications for the CPC's regime survival through the cutting off of most of its energy supplies. While not the panacea of China's energy needs, CPEC is one of various projects aimed at securing China's future energy security.

CPEC faces innumerable challenges and whether it will be a success will be hard to judge for years to come. However, from the CPC's perspective, it has the potential to aid its policy ambitions in a number of important ways: by supporting China's future economic development, by shoring up its state-building efforts in Xinjiang, and lastly, by helping to shape a more benign geopolitical outlook for itself in the near future.

NOTES

1. Announced by Premier Li Keqiang during his visit to Pakistan in May 2013, CPEC is a multifaceted project to develop various infrastructure projects throughout Pakistan that will eventually link the Chinese owned Gwadar Port on the Arabian Sea to China's northwestern region of Xinjiang. CPEC involves projects very similar to the original proposal of an 'economic corridor', as mentioned above, but with a much more significant emphasis on power generation.

2. Often these investors were from the other East and South East Asian boom economies and bought with them cutting-edge techniques and technologies that exemplified efficiency and economies of scale, two things that would play such an important part in China's own growth over the proceeding decades.

3. BBC, "China economic growth slowest in 25 years," January 19, 2016.

4. David Morris, 27.08.2015, Will tech manufacturing stay in China?, *Fortune Magazine*, https://goo.gl/xUsw8k

5. China Seeks Stimulation, November 10, 2008, *The Economist,*https://goo.gl/Mu5wne

6. China has so far invested $14 billion in 30 CPEC projects, September 27, 2016, *Pakistan Today*.

7. According to Fitch, a credit rating agency, it is estimated that 'China's coal industry could have 3.3 billion tonnes of excess capacity within two years', and Shenhua Energy, the country's biggest coal miner, says it might export 10m tonnes soon, up from 1.2m tonnes last year. Gluts for Punishment, April 7, 2015, *The Economist*, goo.gl/ry5m6M

8. Daniel S Markey, Behind China's Gambit in Pakistan, *Council on Foreign Relations*, https://goo.gl/0blpVY

9. Country Report for Pakistan, 2013, *International Cotton Advisory Committee,* https://goo.gl/q5T95U

10. As one US analyst, Mr Shih, puts it, "When the older capacity in China is shut down, we'll have a much more modern industrial sector." "The question is," he says, "how long will this take?" The March of the Zombies, February 27, 2016, *The Economist*, https://goo.gl/3J4fzT

11. Chinese investments in Pakistan's energy producing projects have been backed by "sovereign guarantees to ensure uninterrupted payments to Chinese sponsors of CPEC energy projects" ensuring that if distribution companies default on payments the (Pakistan) government will pay up, at least 22% of the bills of customers to Chinese companies." SatyabrataPal, June 3, 2016, The China-Pakistan Corridor is All About Power. Not Electricity, but the Real Thing, *The Wire,* https://goo.gl/DTi8yE

12. China actually surpassed the US economy in value calculated in terms of Purchasing Power Parity according to IMF calculations published in 2014, Is China Economy Really the Largest in the World, December 16, 2016, *The BBC*, https://goo.gl/zHxPZt

13. Dominic Barton, Yougang Chen, and Amy Jin, June 2013, Mapping China's Middle Class, *McKinsey Quarterly*, McKinsey and Company, https://goo.gl/2kr4UB

14. The development of Khogos Eastern-Gates SEZ, which is a massive dry-port on the Kazakh-China border, means that freight can reach Europe in 15 days instead of the existing 40, which it takes by the sea route from China's eastern ports to Europe.

15. Interactive map: China Pakistan Economic Corridor, *China Dialogue*, https://goo.gl/KZ0kQn

16. World Directory of Minorities and Indigenous Peoples—China: Uyghurs, 02.11.2016, *UNHCR*, https://goo.gl/lrarQW

17. Uighur Unrest: 140 Killed in Ethnic Riots in China, 06.07.2009, *Spiegel Online* https://goo.gl/Sz4BaW

18. While state media blamed the deaths on 'rioters', 'activists say police opened fire on people protesting against a Ramadan crackdown on Muslims' (BBC, 26.09.2014, https://goo.gl/O37rLO).

19. Tenth Five Years Planning Outline of the People's Republic of China's Development on National Economy and Society.

20. As part of this plan, Xi Jinping hopes to create one million jobs in textiles by 2023, in an attempt to halt the growing trend of textile producers leaving China for cheaper countries like Vietnam where the minimum wage is around half of that in China. Dominique Patton (2016), Xinjiang Cotton at Crossroads of China's New 'Silk Road', *Reuters*.

21. Persons of Uighur origin have been convicted of the 2015 Bangkok Erawan Shrine attack, and the August 2016 bombing of the Chinese embassy in Bishkek has been linked to Syria-based Uighur militants.

22. "In August 2014, Chinese state media released a report stating that Memetuhut Memetrozi, a co-founder of ETIM who is serving a life sentence in China for his involvement in terrorist attacks, had been indoctrinated in a madrassa in Pakistan", Xu,B, Fletcher, H, Bajoria, J, September 4, 2014, The East Turkistan Islamic Movement (ETIM), *Council on Foreign Relations*, https://goo.gl/hkHcTa

23. Ian Storey, April 12, 2006, China's "Malacca Dilemma", *Jamestown Foundation*, *China Brief*, Volume: 6 Issue: 8, https://goo.gl/gNpLWU

24. It is striking how reliant China is on energy imports that have to pass through the Straits of Malacca with estimations that as much as 80 percent of China's imported energy, plus much of its trade in physical goods, passes through the straits that at its narrowest point is only 1.7 miles across. Chen Shaofeng, January 2010, China's Self-Extrication from the "Malacca Dilemma" and Implications, Vol. 1, No. 1, pp. 1-24, *International Journal of China Studies*.

25. Kalyan Kumar, January 9, 2016, China Builds More Underground Storage Tanks For Strategic Oil Reserves: Driven by Cost Savings and Security, *International Business Times*, http://goo.gl/11XHBa

26. Amid India's own pipeline projects with Iran, Iran itself is not opposed to such China-Pakistan project, "Iran never publicly articulated its opposition to the Sino-Pakistani project in Gwadar. Instead, it had aided the project by providing fresh water and fuel." While we should view such comments warily, it is true that China and Iran have increasingly close ties and a Chinese presence so close to Iran may be a favorable development for the Iranians themselves, given their concerns over the US's own presence in the Persian Gulf where the US 5th Fleet is based in Bahrain.

India's Chabahar Port Plan is to Counter Our Gwadar Port Plan: June 7, 2016, *The Hindu*.

27. US general Lori Robinson was clear in who she thought the US military buildup was intended to face, by insisting 'the US and its partners had to "maintain a credible combat power" in Asia, citing in particular "the seriousness of tone that is being set by China's militarization of the South China Sea", Peter Symonds, March 9, 2016, US Air Force to boost presence in northern Australian bases, *World Socialist Website*, https://goo.gl/WfI0Ez

28. Mathew Caesar-Gordon, M, February 26, 2016, Securing the Energy Supply: China's "Malacca Dilemma", *E-International Relations*, http://goo.gl/7ljCTw

29. TPP Members include—Japan, Malaysia, Vietnam, Singapore, Brunei, Australia, New Zealand, Canada, Mexico, Chile and Peru, US.

30. With the election of President Donald Trump, TPP is, in effect, all but dead.

31. "The United States is also investing in a long term strategic partnership with India to support its ability to serve as a regional economic anchor and provider of security in the broader Indian Ocean region" Department of Defense Strategic Guidance 2012, http://archive.defense.gov/news/Defense_Strategic_Guidance.pdf

32. This includes the annual Malabar maritime exercise, which in 2007 was broadened to include Japan, Australia and Singapore.

33. M Zhou, June 4, 2013, The Emerging Strategic Triangle in Indo-Pacific Asia, *The Diplomat*, https://goo.gl/ICJgH

34. China's successful evacuation-by-sea operation of its citizens from Yemen in April 2015 is just one example of China's increasing willingness to protect its citizens abroad.

35. In response to Gwadar, India's development of Chabahar port in Iran, located just 72 kilometers from Gwadar in Pakistan, is (perhaps rightfully) seen as a direct response and challenge to the Chinese project.

36. By developing Gwadar, China is, in effect, giving Pakistan another major deep-sea alternative to Port Qasim in Karachi. Pakistan's vulnerability in times of conflict with India was highlighted in the 1971 war, when India successfully blockaded Karachi and threatened to do again during the 1999 Kargil Crisis.

37. Wang Jisi, February 12, 2015, China in the Middle, *The American Interest*, Volume 10, Number 4, https://goo.gl/db4Zgj

REFERENCES

Barton, D Chen, Y, Jin, A, (2013), "Mapping China's Middle Class", McKinsey Quarterly, McKinsey and Company, https://goo.gl/2kr4UB

BBC, (January 2016), "China Economic Growth Slowest in 25 Years", http://goo.gl/I526X5

BBC, (December 2016), "Is China Economy Really the Largest in the World", https://goo.gl/zHxPZt

BBC, (2014), "Xinjiang unrest: China raises death toll to 50", https://goo.gl/O37rLO

Bloomberg, (2016), "Why China's Economy Will Be So Hard to Fix", Bloomberg, http://goo.gl/R5nUCr

China Daily, (2016), "China outlines strategy for energy sector", https://goo.gl/akCjB6

China Daily, (2013), "Making 'Chinese Dream' a Reality", http://goo.gl/qIvONS

China Dialogue, "Interactive map: China Pakistan Economic Corridor", https://goo.gl/KZ0kQn

Clarke, M, (2013), "China's Strategy in "Greater Central Asia: Is Afghanistan the Missing Link?," Asian Affairs: An American Review, 40:1, 1–19

Climate Home, (2015), "Pakistan shelves six coal-fired power projects", https://goo.gl/Z2Wjrr

CPEC Official Website,"China Pakistan Economic Corridor, Government of Pakistan", https://goo.gl/duWjmF

Davis, M, (2014), "China's 'Malacca Dilemma' and the Future of the PLA", China Policy Institute Blog, University of Nottingham, http://goo.gl/rSc6tc

Department of Defense Strategic Guidance, (2012), "Sustaining U.S. Global Leadership: Priorities for 21st Century Defense"

International Cotton Advisory Committee, (2013), Country Report for Pakistan, https://goo.gl/q5T95U

Jisi, W, (2015), "China in the Middle", *The American Interest*, Volume 10, Number 4, ,https://goo.gl/db4Zgj

Kumar, K, (2016), "China Builds More Underground Storage Tanks For Strategic Oil Reserves: Driven by Cost Savings and Security", *International Business Times*, http://goo.gl/11XHBa

Lieberthal, K, (2011), "The American Pivot to Asia", Foreign Policy,https://goo.gl/bE0QZb

Li, C, Daokui Li, D, and Rietveld, M, (2015), "The Big Picture: Debating China's Rebalancing," Brookings Institute, https://goo.gl/y7Poix

Markey, D, (2016), "Behind China's Gambit in Pakistan", Council on Foreign Relations, https://goo.gl/0blpVY

Morris, D, (2015), "Will Tech Manufacturing Stay in China?", Fortune, https://goo.gl/xUsw8k

Nikki Asian Review, (2015), "Manufacturers Shift Focus from Quantity to Quality", https://goo.gl/kzjnL8

Pakistan Today, (2016), "Pakistan and China are All Weather Friends: Governor", http://goo.gl/D61Sh5

Pal, S, (2016), "The China-Pakistan Corridor is All About Power. Not Electricity, but the Real Thing", https://goo.gl/DTi8yE

Patton, D, (2016), "Xinjiang cotton at crossroads of China's new Silk Road", https://goo.gl/etP7Bh

Shaofeng, C, (2010), "China's Self-Extrication from the "Malacca Dilemma" and Implications" Vol. 1, No. 1, pp. 1–24, *International Journal of China Studies*, Peking University

Spiegel Online, (2009),"Uighur Unrest: 140 Killed in Ethnic Riots in China", https://goo.gl/Sz4BaW

Storey, I, (2006),"China's "Malacca Dilemma," Jamestown Foundation, China Brief,Volume: 6 Issue: 8, https://goo.gl/gNpLWU

Symonds, P, (2016),"US Air Force to boost presence in northern Australian bases", World Socialist Website, https://goo.gl/WfI0Ez

The Economist, (2008), "China Seeks Stimulation", https://goo.gl/Mu5wne

The Economist, (April 2016), "Gluts for Punishment", goo.gl/ry5m6M

The Economist, (February 2016)"The March of the Zombies", https://goo.gl/3J4fzT

The Hindu, (2016),"India's Chabahar port plan is to counter our Gwadar port plan: Chinese media"https://goo.gl/K7DxSz

The World Bank, (2016), http://goo.gl/qKbey

UN Climate Change Conference, (2015), goo.gl/2n3XMV

UNHCR, "World Directory of Minorities and Indigenous Peoples—China :Uyghurs", https://goo.gl/lrarQW

Vision and Actions on Jointly Building Silk Road Economic Belt and 21st-Century Maritime Silk Road, (2015),(NDRC),Ministry of Foreign Affairs, and Ministry of Commerce of the People's Republic of China, with State Council Authorization, 28 March, http://goo.gl/JXkWhV

Xinhua News Agency, (2013), "Authorized Release: Communiqué of the Third Plenary Session of the 18th Central Committee of the Communist Party of China", https://goo.gl/g651Ud

Xu, B, Fletcher, H, Bajoria, J, (2014), "The East Turkistan Islamic Movement (ETIM)", Council on Foreign Relations, https://goo.gl/hkHcTa

Zhou, M, (2013), "The Emerging Strategic Triangle in Indo-Pacific Asia", The Diplomat,https://goo.gl/ICJgH

Chapter 6

India Looks East and
China Looks South

Competition, Confrontation or Balance

Xueyu Wang and Mohammad Razaul Karim

Recent Chinese and Indian diplomatic activities have attracted a lot of attention in international politics over the last three decades. Competition and sometimes confrontation between these two global powers in political, economic and diplomatic spheres has drawn scholarly and media attention (Chen, Banerjee, Toor, Downie, 2014). For over two decades India's policies in the Asia-Pacific region have led to its current Act East Policy (AEP), motivated in part by India's strategy of counter-balancing against China, while China's policy originally aimed at diplomatic and economic engagement with Southeast Asia (Rajendram, 2014). India strengthened its association with the Southeast Asian countries, signed the treaties of the Association of Southeast Asian Nations, and established free trade zones and broader security and defense ties across the whole Asia-Pacific region. Thus India signaling its willingness to play a greater role in the region (Haijun, 2012:Rajendram, 2014). Indian prime minister Narendra Modi introduced the approach as the "Act East" policy, asserting the importance of seeking deeper security ties with partners such as South Korea, Japan, Vietnam, and Australia (Rajendram, 2014). Some analysts assumed that India was trying to balance China's influence in this region by launching this policy, though India had often repeated that it was not competing with China in any way.

China is a rising power having close borders with South Asia. Its policies have great impact on the region because of its border connections. China's peaceful rise, instead of regional hegemony, is building relations with small South Asian states (Godwin, 2004). In the new century, China has placed more weight on launching the good neighboring policy, which shows the increasing significance that the Chinese leadership places on her Asian neighbors (Shulan, 2010). China and South Asian countries relationship has been significantly changed in the twenty-first century. China's South Asian policy was redefined, with China pursuing multi-dimensional cooperation with all of the South Asian countries. China is a crucial external partner of South Asia and their relationship and dependency are increasing day by day. China wishes to improve its relationship with South Asia in all fields (Baskaran&Sivakumar, 2014). China's relations with South Asian countries are based on its independent foreign policy and five principles of peaceful coexistence have always been a source of stability in this region (Saleem, 2013).

India perceives the rise of China, with which it shares a complex mix of rivalry, as a state of competition and cooperation. Beijing's increasing military engagement and growing strategic relations with South Asian smaller states have been a concern for New Delhi. Some scholars comprehend India's eastern direction as a strategy to counter-balance China's expansion with South Asian countries, which can be demonstrated by New Delhi's closer dealings with countries like Thailand, Vietnam, and Japan (Malhotra, 2015).

BACKGROUND OF INDIA'S LOOK EAST POLICY

In the beginning of 1990s, India put forward the "Look East Policy" (LEP) and it was considered as an important foreign approach of India as well as a starting point of phase I. At that time, led by Treasury Secretary Manmohan Singh, the government of Narasimha Rao began promoting economic reform, changed Indian development strategy and actively developed the economic relations with foreign countries (Haijun, 2016). Several factors have been attributed to this reorientation. In 1991, following a foreign exchange crisis, the then Indian government was forced to hasten its market reform and economic liberalization agenda, which included more open to foreign trade and investment. In addition, its relations with the South Asian countries were not emerging very intensely; that is why it was problematic to inaugurate good economic relations in the South Asia. India's chose to develop its foreign economic cooperation with East Asian countries because it has deep historical and geographical relations with this region. Moreover, East Asian countries had sound economic development. All these developments led to the formulation of the LEP (Haijun, 2016). In 1992 India officially launched the LEP that was expected to recommence political contacts with Association of Southeast Asian Nations (ASEAN) member states, enhance economic relations including investment and trade, science and technology, tourism, etc., and finally strengthen defense and strategic links with Southeast Asian countries.

In 1992, Southeast Asia's amplified importance among India's foreign policy priorities was reflected in relations with ASEAN. IK Gujral, as foreign minister and later prime minister, sought to institutionalize India's relations and maintain friendly neighborhood relations with the East Asian region. Prime Minister Atal Bihari Vajpyaee also affirmed that the Asia-Pacific region is one of the focal points of India's foreign policy, strategic concerns and economic interests (Vajpayee, 2002, Quoted Bajpaee, 2015). Phase I lasted between 1991 and 2002, when the primary thrust was toward renewed political and economic relations with ASEAN countries.

During Phase II (2003 to 2012), the opportunity of the LEP was widened to include China, Japan, South Korea, Australia, and New Zealand. India's then-external affairs minister Yashwant Sinha noted, "India's Look East' policy has now entered phase two. Phase one was focused primarily on ASEAN countries and on trade and investment linkages. Phase two is characterized by an expanded definition of East extending from Australia to China and East Asia with ASEAN as its core. Phase two marks a shift from exclusively economic issues to economic and security issues. On the economic side, Phase two is also characterized by arrangements for FTAs and establishing of institutional economic linkages between the countries of the region and India" (Sinha, 2003).

Basically the third phase (2014-present) started under the Modi government. India's LEP has transformed into a proactive Act East policy. In August 2014, Indian external affairs minister Sushma Swaraj visited several ASEAN countries. During her visit to Singapore, she articulated the necessity of an AEP persuasively: "Look East is no longer adequate; now we need Act East policy" (Ministry of External Affairs, 2014). In November 2014 Prime Minister Narendra Modi formally asserted in his speech at the annual summit of the ASEAN in Myanmar that India has turned the "Look East" policy into "Act East" policy and announced the government's intention to enthusiastically engage with its Asian neighbors (Government of India, 2014). India seeks to strengthen its relation with ASEAN through the AEP as well as the policy tries to expand the country's involvement beyond the region 'to encompass the Koreas in the North to Australia and New Zealand in the South, and from neighboring Bangladesh to Fiji and Pacific Island countries in the Far East' (Quoted from Ramabadran, 2017). Under the AEP India has broadened its economic relations with the countries including political, security, strategic, counter-terrorism realms and defense collaboration.

BACKGROUND OF CHINA LOOK AT SOUTH ASIA

Both China and South Asia share rich cultural and historical linkages (Banerjee, 2011). Before the twenty-first century, China and South Asia had no comprehensive and mutual relations and they had failed to establish sound economic relations. Even in 1962 China was involved in a border conflict with the India that caused very severe geopolitical consequences. In retrospect "China's policy towards South Asia is a collection of distinct bilateral relationships, characterized by economic opportunities, territorial disputes, and security fears and resisting US influence" (Roy, 1998).

However on China's South Asian policy, Singh, a renowned Indian expert on China and strategic affairs, argues that "beginning from early 1980s, the politico-strategic component of China's South Asian policy has been based on the mutual security and mutual benefit. This was to witness China focusing on resolving disputes and building economic engagements as its main focus" (Singh, 2003). Further elaborating the dynamics of China's South Asian policy, he says that "China's South Asian policy can be described as the reflection of China's arduous long march from ideology and revolutionary zeal to national interest and pragmatism defining core of China's national objectives. For obvious reasons, China's South Asian policy has remained Indo-centric both in its empathy and antipathy through mature and stable mutual security and mutual benefit" (Singh, 2003).

China normally looks at South Asia from five perspectives. The first perspective is the security dimension. There are several issues such as Chinese borders with four South Asian nations, its sensitivity about Tibet and Xinjiang, increasing threat of extremism in Pakistan and Afghanistan, nuclearization and political instability in South Asia, which occupy Chinese security concern on this region. Beijing thinks that the East Turkistan Islamic Movement and other anti-China rebellious groups have found shelter in the Pakistan-Afghanistan tribal regions and thousands of exiled Tibetans along with their leaders are sheltered in India and Nepal (Xinhua, 2008). Furthermore, the drug business in the Golden Crescent also poses serious threats to China (Chouvy, 2002). The second area relates to the economic prospects of the region. Access to markets in the South Asian region is an important goal for China because of its large market. In addition the potentiality of investment, energy sources, connectivity and access to sea for western China figure high in Chinese intentions. Third, political development in the South Asia is another area of interest. China closely monitors South Asian countries' political dimensions and the risks of instability, the possibility of inter-state conflict, and the progress or lack of it in bilateral and regional cooperation. The fourth perspective is strategic in nature. The rises of ferocious extremism, access to the Indian Ocean and the protection of sea lanes and access to energy are included in this list. China has to maintain the security of the energy trade and the sea lanes of communication around South Asia passing through the Indian Ocean. China uses the India Ocean to bring oil, which is imported from Africa and the Gulf region. That is why South Asian stability and good neighborly relations is one of the dominant perspectives of Chinese foreign policy. The fifth area could be labeled as diplomatic. Though China was vigorous in South Asia in the 1960s and 1970s, in recent decades China has been trying to maintain a more active relationship with the South Asia countries and stayed away from the major bilateral issues. However, it has continued to show its growing interest to remain involved in South Asia in the economic domain (Kabir, 2013).

INDIA ENGAGEMENT IN EAST ASIA

Danielle Rajendram has proclaimed that India's new Asia-Pacific strategy is partly motivated by India's aspiration for a greater global role (2014). India's LEP developed as a multi-pronged strategy connecting many institutional mechanisms at multilateral and bilateral levels, economic links, and defense engagement (Naidu, 2013).

Economic Engagement

India's trade with North and Southeast Asia now represents about a quarter of its total trade; outweighing that with the United States and the European Union (Rajendram, 2014).To strengthen economic cooperation with ASEAN countries India has commenced a number of initiatives such as the 'Trade in Goods' agreement in 2009, Agreements on Trade in Services and Investment, Free Trade agreements with Bay of Bengal Initiative for Multi-Sectoral Technical and Economic Cooperation, etc. China has become Indian's top trading partner, with bilateral trade, which was as low as US$ 7 billion in 2003–2004, reached US $ 65 billion in 2013–2014. In the same period, Indian trade with ASEAN member states has increased from approximately US$13 billion to US$74 billion, making its trade with the region as a whole even more noteworthy than with China (Rajendram, 2014). As for foreign direct investment (FDI), the inflow from India to ASEAN Member States was US$ 2.58 billion, an increase of 221.6 percent from US$811.18 million in 2009. This accounted for 3.4 percent of the total FDI into ASEAN in 2010. In 2009 India became the seventh largest trading partner and the sixth largest investor of ASEAN despite the negative effects of the global financial crisis (Government of India, 2011). As of 2015–2016, India's exports to ASEAN rise to 9.79 percent of its total exports, and its imports from the region were approximately 10.51 percent of its total imports (Kundu, 2016). India has formed a Comprehensive Economic Partnership with Singapore, South Korea, Malaysia and Thailand and is negotiating similar agreements with other East Asian countries.

Under the Comprehensive Economic Cooperation agreement between India and ASEAN which became effective in 2010, import tariffs on more than 80 percent of traded products between 2013 and 2016 will be removed. The two-way flow of investments between India and ASEAN has already reached US$43 billion by 2012 and is likely to rise to US$100 billion by 2015 (Naidu, 2013). Myanmar's opening up also promises a new land bridge between India and ASEAN. The Myanmar government has finally agreed to complete a trilateral highway project with India and Thailand by 2016 that could increase India-ASEAN trade by $100 million over five years (Nelson, 2012). According to the Ministry of Road, Transport and Highways, the India-Myanmar-Thailand Motor Vehicle Agreement will be signed soon (Sharma, 2016). Japan is also a crucial economic partner of India. Since 2005 India has been the largest recipient of Japanese Official Development Assistance (Naidu, 2013).

Security Engagement

Under the AEP, New Delhi has decisively strengthened its security engagement in the Asia-Pacific region. The United States and Japan also welcome India's role as a security provider in the region. In fact, the term "Net Security Provider" in the Indian perspective was first proposed in 2009 by the US Secretary of Defense Robert Gates, who claimed that the US looks to India "to be a partner and net provider of security in the Indian Ocean and beyond" (Mukherjee, 2014).

The economic and security linkage between India and ASEAN has been strengthened since Indian's admittance to the ASEAN Regional Forum (ARF) in 1996. The main focus of ARF is on regional security issues in the Asia-Pacific, including disarmament and non-proliferation issues. India has been an active participant in the various ARF processes and has accommodated numerous activities (Haokip, 2011). India and ASEAN have been in agreement on a number of issues, ranging from joint military exercises to high-level visits, which illustrate the increasing strength of political and military ties. India's increasing forays into South China made it an influential player in the Asia-Pacific though it is not the littoral state (Fang, 2016).

India's approach toward the South China Sea is partially motivated by the China factor, and India seeks to decrease the influence of China on this sea (Calvo, 2015). India is engaging Myanmar in various activities and with Vietnam; it has started exploration for oil and gas in the South China Sea. On the other hand China exerts much greater influence in Myanmar and in Vietnam; it has greatly opposed India's presence in waters, where it claims whole sovereignty (Lahiri). India's naval existence in the South China Sea is seen as being vital for ensuring its interests. The Indian Navy's Eastern Fleet deployed worships to South East Asia and Southern Indian Ocean, and participated in the bilateral naval exercise SIMBEX with Singapore in May 2015. The ships visited several countries such as Singapore, Malaysia, Indonesia,

Thailand, Cambodia and Australia. In May 2016, India sent another four ships of the Indian Navy's Eastern Fleet for a two-and-a-half-month operational deployment to the South China Sea and northwestern Pacific. Indian defense minister A.K. Antony in 2011 stated that India would go to the South China Sea for exercises to guard the country's interests (ANI News, October 12, 2011).

Both Japan and India rely on safe and sound sea lanes of communication for their energy supplies and economic progress. They are developing maritime capabilities to cooperate with each other and other regional powers. Both countries' navies are exercising regularly, as are their coast guards, in view of combating piracy and terrorism and cooperating during disaster relief operations. Japan thinks that the Indian Navy is merely a regional force that can be trusted to secure Indian Ocean sea lanes which are essential for Japan's energy security (Pant, 2013). During the Japanese PM Shinzo Abe's visit to Delhi in January 2015, it was followed by the India-Japan joint statement that voiced their concerns about the South China Sea issues. The statement stated that "in view of critical importance of the sea lanes of communications in the South China Sea for regional energy security and trade and commerce which underpins continued peace and prosperity of the Indo-Pacific, the two Prime Ministers ... called upon all States to avoid unilateral actions that could lead to tensions in the region" (Fang, 2016). Vietnam has assisted India's role in the South China Sea to challenge China's claims. In October 2011, India's state-owned oil company ONGC Videsh Limited signed an agreement with Vietnam to increase and uphold oil exploration in the South China Sea. Although China's protestations that the exploration of Blocks 127 and 128 is in violation of its sovereignty in the South China Sea, ONGC Videsh did not back down from the projects. India mentions that its exploration projects in the region are purely commercial. Moreover in October 2014, during Vietnamese prime minister Dung's visit to India, ONGC Videsh and Petro Vietnam signed a mutual cooperation agreement on the exploration of several South China Sea oil blocks (The Hindu, 28 October 2014).

As part of India's "Act East" policy that unites with the "U.S. rebalance" and Japan's "Proactive Contribution to Peace," India has developed coordination, both military and diplomatic, with East and Southeast nations that also see China as a threat. New Delhi is negotiating the sale of the *BrahMos* cruise missile to Vietnam and frigates and patrol craft to the Philippines, while also counterfeiting military-to-military ties and economic and trade links with Malaysia, Indonesia, Singapore and Thailand. At a time when ASEAN stands divided, India is placing itself at the center of regional relationships with Mongolia, Vietnam, the Philippines, Australia, Indonesia and Thailand as part of security architecture that would balance a rising China and enhance the safety and security of the global commons. Both the United States and India have declared in their joint statements their support for "freedom of navigation and overflight rights under UNCLOS," indicating that the Modi government is not shying away from aligning U.S. and from balancing against China (Malik, 2016).

Other Initiatives

India has also agreed to ASEAN norms of interaction, including the 'Treaty of Amity and Cooperation' in 2003, which was a prerequisite to the country being admitted as a founding member of the East Asia Summit (Mohan, 2013). In 2012, the ASEAN-India Commemorative Summit was held in India to mark the twentieth anniversary of the ASEAN-India Dialogue Relationship and the tenth anniversary of the ASEAN-India Summit. Other initiatives have sought to reinforce people-to-people, cultural and commercial contacts. These include the India-ASEAN renowned persons lecture series that was launched in 1996; the ASEAN-India Business Council that began in 2002; and India being permitted 'Observer Status' at the ASEAN Inter-Parliamentary Assembly in 2011, as well as the ASEAN-India Open Skies Regime, ASEAN-India Network on Climate Change, and ASEAN-India Healthcare Initiative (Muni, 2010). Since 2000 India had participated in a number of track-two (nongovernmental) dialogues such as the Council for Security Cooperation in the Asia-Pacific as a full member. In 2006 India also joined regional functional initiatives such as the Regional Cooperation Agreement on Combating Piracy and Armed Robbery against Ships in Asia (ReCAAP) (Bajpaee, 2015).

CHINA LOOKS SOUTH ASIA

China's growing presence in South Asia is a part of its ambition to widen its global reach. Over the two decades, China has developed a significant economic partnership through trade, diplomacy, aid and investment with the South Asian countries. Recently China's connection with South Asia is a main focus of its foreign policy and part of China's multilateral strategy intentions of raising its role at the regional as well as at the global level. Its rapport with South Asian countries extended to all fields including economic, communication, energy, cultural, tourism and the nontraditional security cooperation. (Rengma, 2012)

China's Economic Relations with South Asia

Chinese economic relations with South Asia have risen remarkably since 2003. Trade in South Asia has become lucrative because of its large population. China increased its export more than double to Bangladesh, Nepal,

Maldives, Sri Lanka and Bhutan between 2003 and 2012. Whereas in 2000 China's trade with South Asian countries was US$ 5.7 billion, in 2012 it was increased to US$ 93 billion and China's imports also increased at that period from US$1.9 billion to US$22.6 billion (Jash, 2016). China is the largest trading partner with Bangladesh and Pakistan and the second largest trading partner with Nepal and Sri Lanka. Moreover, China has offered billions of dollars in investment for big infrastructure projects, including port facilities in Pakistan, Sri Lanka, Bangladesh and Myanmar (Curtis, 2011). For economic cooperation, in September 2014, China took a plan to increase bilateral trade with South Asian nations to US$ 150 billion, to invest US$ 30 billion, and to provide US$ 20 billion as a concessional services in this region for the next five years (Liu, 2014).

China's financial assistance like trade and investment is increasing in South Asia region, consequently, the small South Asian countries made out a space to bargain with India. That is why, India is losing her dominance over this region. Some hypersensitive Indian commentators notify that China is turning the Indian Ocean into a "Chinese Lake." Shesheng mentions that 'Chinese mining companies are investing a lot in Pakistan (copper and iron), Afghanistan (copper), and Myanmar (oil and gas). China also looks forward to invest in the gas fields of Bangladesh' (2010, 292). China is mainly a manufacturing economy that requires large amounts of raw material; the stable supply of these resources is essential for the Chinese economy. Moreover, China is also investing in disputed border zones in South Asia such as it started to build dams on the rivers in Tibetan Plateau, including the upper Brahmaputra (yarlungtsangpo or Yarlung River), which could impact on populations living downstream in India and Bangladesh (Chen et al., 2014).

Beijing seeks dialogue with the South Asian government on cooperation on essential issues like countering narcotic traffic, terrorism and trafficking: dealing with the presence and activities of Tibet in the other South Asian countries. It also does its best to bring the South Asian countries on its side on the Taiwan issue; to stop Taiwan's effort to make external relationship and to ensure a South Asian positive role on the event of a US-PRC clash over Taiwan. China wants to play a role in the South Asian Association for Regional Cooperation (SAARC), where the other South Asian states will value its capacity to balance India (Garver, 2005).

Military and Security Linkage with South Asia

China is expanding its naval power projection capabilities and seeks to expand military ties with South Asian countries. Bangladesh, Pakistan, and Myanmar have been vital customers for Chinese military equipment. China has also been involved in training and maintenance with those countries. Sino-Pakistan military collaboration has also followed an upward trend, and Islamabad's missile and nuclear weapons program has been a constant security concern for India (Godwin, 2004). China helps Pakistan's missile improvement and its nuclear energy efforts. China sold to Pakistan fighter jets, 3 fire-control radar systems, 550 portable surface-to-air missiles, 24 anti-ship missiles and 8,600 anti-tank missiles (Deepak, 2005).

China has appeared as a major supplier of military hardware to Bangladesh Armed Forces. Bangladesh brought most of the tanks (T-59, T-62, T-69, and T-79), a large number of armored personnel carriers, artillery pieces and small arms and personal weapons of Army from China. Moreover, Chinese military activities have expanded in the region. In July 2010, the *People's Liberation Army daily* reported that the People's Liberation Army Air Force (PLAAF) unit was engaging in armed combat air patrols (Dengke, 2010). In this perspective it assumes that the role of PLAAF is emerging in maintaining security along the Sino-Indian border in the Tibetan area. Furthermore, China is gathering naval facilities alongside vital choke-points in the IOR for serving its economic benefits as well as to boost its strategic existence and protect energy imports whereas the country cannot depend on US Naval power for unconstrained entrance to energy (Pant, 2010). Two Gas and oil pipelines with annual capacity of 22 million tons of oil and 12 billion cubic meters of gas respectively are built by China, connecting the port of *Kyaukpyu* on the Bay of Bengal with Yunnan. None can ignore China's influence in South Asia as well as its involvement in the Indian Ocean. This has aroused mistrust and doubt about China's intentions. The country is genuinely interested in defending its trading and energy life lines, where 70 percent of its oil supplies and almost 80 percent of its total trade being shipped through the Indian Ocean region (Malik, 2014).

China has shown its power by demonstrating anti-piracy operations in the Indian Ocean since 2008 and its earliest foreign medical mission with the arrangement of hospital ship to the Indian Ocean in 2010. In February 2014 a Chinese submarine with nuclear weapon made its first declared operational arrangement into the Indian Ocean while in September 2014, a Song-class diesel-electric submarine docked at a Sri Lankan port (Bajpaee, 2015). Sri Lanka is going to be a part of Chinese Maritime Silk Road project. New Delhi is afraid of a Chinese "string of pearl" encircling India by gradually expanding deep sea port expansion. Sri Lanka allowed Chinese state-owned operating rights at Hambantola port intensified Indian concerned (Anderson, 2015).

COMPETITION, CONFRONTATION OR BALANCE

China's growing presence in the South Asian region has raised some worries in India, where this region is considered to be part of India's geopolitical backyard. India's LEP can be perceived as part of an external balancing strategy against China. Kalyani Shankar also summarizes India's LEP to engage her 'as a counterweight to China's growing influence in the region' (Shankar, 2012). According to Professor S.D. Muni, India's policy toward China rotates around the 4 'C's: containment, competition, conflict and cooperation. Different groups in India support different 'C's: the Indian business community supports competition, while part of the military supports containment, the bureaucracy calls for cooperation, and so on. (Kelegama, 2014).

Beijing is showing suspicion toward India's growing relationships with strategic partners in East and Southeast Asia, particularly with Vietnam and Japan. Though it is not in India's intentions to involve in direct rivalry with China, it can be projected that an element of competition will continue to characterize the China-India bilateral relationship (Rajendram, 2014). India accused in June 2016 China of obstructing its Nuclear Suppliers Group (NGS) membership proposal at Seoul, though China claims that it is not fair to single it out because there were some other countries which were opposed to a non-signatory of the Non-Proliferation Treaty becoming a member of NSG (Sajjanhar,August 22, 2016). However, there is a lot of issues need to be discussed to understand the dynamics of Indo-China relations.

Border Issue

There are a number of serious problems in the relations between China and India which have seriously pushed an atmosphere of mistrust. One of these is the unresolved border disputes. Both sides claim each other's territory - India, the Aksai Chin region of Kashmir and China refuses to recognize Ladakh and Arunachal Pradesh as part of India. According to the Indian side, on the eve of Xi Jinping's arrival in India September 2014, Chinese troops crossed the Line of Control (the de facto boundary) in the disputed Ladakh region and entered deep (500 meters) into Indian Territory. Indian prime minister Modi could not help avoid citing the incident to the Chinese president. Mr Modi called for an early settlement on the disputed common border between the two countries and said the "true potential of our relations" would be realized when there was "peace in our relations and in the borders" (BBC News, September 18, 2014). Among the border problems, there is also the long-lasting problem of Tibet. Back in 2003, India recognized China's sovereignty over

Tibet, but at that time China acknowledged Indian sovereignty over Sikkim only, not extracting its claim to Arunachal Pradesh, which Beijing refers to as Southern Tibet. Moreover, China's concerns about the presence of Dalai Lama and other Tibetan leaders in India, as well as India's worries about Chinese dam construction on its side of the Brahmaputra river and cyber-espionage and cyber-security threats (Chakrabarty, 2015). Chinese assertiveness on territorial disputes has given India the opportunity to increase its strategic existence in Southeast Asia, and ASEAN states are gradually expecting India to play a balancing role in the region (Rajendram, 2014).

Indian Ocean and Bay of Bengal

India is anxious of China's growing presence in the Indian Ocean and its relationships with India's South Asian neighbors. Both India and China view the Bay of Bengal as well as Indian Ocean as an important frontier in their competition over energy resources, shipping lanes, and cultural influence. The competition stemming from the two countries expanding their regional sphere of influence in each other's backyards may result in conflicts over energy, SLOCs or maritime issues (Kabir and Ahmed, 2015). India has been alert on China's actions in the Indian Ocean. Indian navy considers the Chinese Navy a threat to India in the Indian Ocean (Fang, 2016). For example, former Indian ambassador M K Bhadrakumar believed that the US's naval dominance is declining. But China's naval existence is increasing and it may have more warships than the US's in the future decade (Bhadrakumar, 2009).

Indian analysts believe such initiatives could be increased in the Indian Ocean as well as Bay of Bengal. Bangladesh wishes to build a deep sea port in Sonadia. Both India and US remain skeptical about Beijing's intention of financing and building the port. It is reported that India felt unease about Bangladesh's deal for submarines with China and sought clarification from China on the necessity of supplying submarines to Bangladesh, though India does not perceive a threat from the acquisition of submarines by Bangladesh.

Feeling threatened by China's Indian Ocean ambition, India applied its own approach to counter China's growing influence. For example, India has recently finalized the Chabahar port Agreement between India and Iran is seen as a latest initiative to mitigate Chinese influence in the Indian Ocean through the Gwadar port in Pakistan. (Gupta, 2016). Furthermore, China's growing influence in the Indian Ocean and assertiveness in maritime territorial disputes in East Asia has reinforced India's wish to upsurge its engagement with its Asia-Pacific partners (Rajendram, 2014). In response to China's rise, India also expanded its naval presence as far east as the South China Sea. Moreover, to counter Chinese presence India has instituted infrastructure development projects of her own in the Bay of Bengal countries, especially in Mayanmar and Sri Lanka (Samaranayak, 2012).

Therefore, Indian scholars think that India's naval arrangement in the East is considered" tit-for-tat" for China's forays into the India Ocean (Pant, 2016). Some Chinese scholars share similar viewpoints. Shi Hongyuan argued that 'India is likely to raise pressure on China in order to reach a China-India border solution in India's favor, to balance China-Pakistan partnership, and to repel China from the Indian Ocean' (Quoted Fang, 2016).

To conclude, we can consider that India's AEP embodies an effort to warn China away from India's neighborhood and offer confidence to other Asia-Pacific countries that want to stand up to China's assertiveness.

One Belt, One Road

One Belt, One Road, proposed by Chinese president Xi Jinping, is a dream project of China to promote regional integration as well as connectivity between China and other Asian, European and African countries. The Bangladesh-China-India-Myanmar (BCIM) Economic Corridor and the China-Pakistan Economic Corridor (CPEC) are officially categorized as "closely related to the Belt and Road Initiative" (Xinhua. March 29, 2015). Beijing visualizes that the BCIM corridor will link its southwestern Yunnan province through Myanmar to Dhaka and then on to the Indian megapolis Kolkata. This will be the key portion of the land based 'Silk Road economic belt.' It will also connect with the port city of Chennai in India, which is a midpoint of a Maritime Silk Route that starts from southeastern Fujian province of China and links littoral countries in the region. The CPEC is also a part of OBOR, passes through Pakistan-occupied Kashmir, a region that is under the control of Pakistan though India claims it as her part. India's objections are rooted on the fundamental issue of its sovereignty, and territorial integrity, which it says have been violated due to this project. Already India has boycotted the two-day Belt and Road Forum Meeting in China held on 14–15 May, 2017 saying "connectivity project must be pursued in a manner that respects sovereignty and territorial integrity."(NDTV, May 15, 2017).

Whereas India considers this project as part of its natural sphere of influence, China has sought to allay a "win-win" potential of this initiative. But China's grand plan for a network of railways, highways, pipelines and ports across central Asia, and around South Asia, is generating anxiety in New Delhi. Brahma Chellaney, professor of strategic studies at New Delhi's Centre for Policy Research, sees "The new Silk Road is just a nice new name for the strategy they've been pursuing," "They've wrapped that strategy in more benign terms. The Chinese dream is pre-eminence in Asia, and this goes to the heart of that dream." "It's not just a trade initiative," he added. "It is

China's so-called "string of pearls" strategy, which India views as an attempt to strategically encircle it" (Quoted from Kazmin, 2016).

South China Sea

China claims sovereignty almost 80 percent over the South China Sea and accused that India is fishing in trouble waters (Malik, 2016, Lahiri, n.d.). Nevertheless India's interest in the East and Southeast Asia will reduce China's regional influence because of India's ties with the US, Japan and some ASEAN states (Yinghong, 2014). Moreover India's presence in the Asia-Pacific region may also obstruct "China's peaceful rise." The Philippines filed a case in the Permanent Court of Arbitration on the South China Sea, whose judgment went completely against the positions advanced by China, including its nine-dash line and its claim to "historic rights" in this Sea. In response to this verdict India issued a statement that "India supports freedom of navigation and over flight, and unimpeded commerce, based on the principles of international law, as reflected notably in the UNCLOS," the UN Convention on the Law of the Sea. The statement further added, "Sea lanes of communication passing through the South China Sea are critical for peace, stability, prosperity and development. As a State Party to the UNCLOS, India urges all parties to show utmost respect for the UNCLOS." Noticeably, the centrality of UNCLOS in resolving the dispute was emphasized in the Indian statement (Sajjanhar, August 22, 2016).

Beijing considers India's naval presence in the South China Sea as a threatening act raising tensions. India's engagement with other countries of East Asia will generate negative impression on China's sovereignty claims over the South China Sea. Therefore India-China distrust may grow deeper (Fang, 2016). India builds up security partnership with Vietnam as well as the right to use NhaTrang port of this country. Vietnam and India have substantial stakes in safeguarding sea lanes security and avoiding sea piracy while they also share worries about Chinese access to the South China Sea and the Indian Ocean. Indian prime minister Manmohan Singh's said that "India and Vietnam are maritime neighbors. We face common security challenges from terrorism, piracy and natural disasters. We believe that it is important to ensure the safety and security of the vital sea lanes of communication. We have agreed to continue and strengthen our exchanges in these fields" (PM's statement, 2011). On the other side, China perceives India's closeness with Vietnam as a "deep political motives." New Delhi wants "to accumulate bargaining chips on other issues with China" (Global Times, October 14, 2011). Japan's uneasy relationship with China has provoked it to reach out to India as a potential strategic partner. Japan offers India significant partnership opportunities considering its naval power and as a potential source of investment.

US Policy

In strategic terms, though South Asia was never a significant region for the United States but now things have changed. Moreover, China is a competitor to USA achieving its global hegemony and contests in various sectors such as combating terrorism, non proliferation, tapping large consumers market and protects access to the riches of Gulf, Central Asia and Caspian Sea resources. In these conditions, United States finds a natural ally in India aimed at balance "the fastest growing economic entity in the world." India is observed as a "natural partner" of United States, a member of "the most populated Democracy Community." The United States and India cooperated in many areas like power security, communication, nonproliferation, etc. (Baskaran & Sivakumar, 2014). Moreover, the United States encouraged India to play a part in the East Asian affairs. As the US secretary of state Hillary Clinton said in 2011, Washington stimulated New Delhi "not just to look East, but to engage East and act East" (Fang, 2016). Washington considers India's rise as in its strategic interest and enthusiastically supports the more active role in East and Southeast Asia. As the US-India Joint Statement of 2014 points out the US is "a principal partner in the realization of India's rise as a responsible, influential world power" (The White House, September 30, 2014).

In August 29, 2016, the United States and India signed a defense agreement, 'The Logistics Exchange Memorandum of Agreement (LEMOA)', which allows the two allies to use each other's military facilities for checking China's growing influence in Asia. Thus this agreement enables US armed forces to operate out of Indian bases, and India can use US bases across the globe. *Forbes* magazine warned that "China and Pakistan beware — this week, India and US sign major war pact." Forbes noted "Having LEMOA makes it much simpler for American naval and air forces to fight there. The US does not have actual bases in India. But, it has the next best thing — a simple way to use India's bases" (*Forbes*, Aug 28, 2016). The agreement was a key part of the Obama administration's strategy to contain China, which has been increasing its influence across Asia. The media stated that the US Navy planned to deploy 60 percent of its surface ships in the Indo-Pacific very soon. They noted that 'the US would like to use the LEMOA to counter China's growing military might — particularly airbases — in the South China Sea. But the agreement would allow India and the US also to use each other's facilities against their common enemy, religious terrorism.' Thus India-China hostility will move from border disputes to economic and strategic competition for influence in this region (Dawn, August 30, 2016).

Port and Sting of Pearls

The "string of pearls" theory argues that Chinese investment in ports in South Asia is a precursor to develop overseas naval bases; India thinks that the goal of this strategy is to surround India from the sea. China has already built a port at Hambantota in Sri Lanka which directs important shipping lanes that move much of the world's oil trade and which India views as strategically vital for its own defense (Kazmin, 2016). Many Indian analysts fear that this port will be used as a naval base (Samaranyake, 2012). Moreover, Chinese submarines' visit at the Colombo port in 2014 raised worries to India that the purpose is not economic but military. China built Gwadar port at the province of Baluchistan in Pakistan, on the Arabian Sea and the government of Pakistan has handed over the control of the port to China, which is a matter of concern for India. Indian policy-makers have long been suspecting of a string of strategically located ports being built by Chinese companies in its neighborhood, as India complains up its military influence to compete with its Asian rival (Kotoky&Ananthalakshmi, 2013).

China also wishes to build new deep sea ports in Bangladesh and Myanmar, raising concerns that they may serve a dual purpose such as commercial as well as military. In the security realm, Beijing's concentration on deep sea port expansion in the Indian Ocean littoral countries, Indian and American analysts are anxious China will increase military activity in these ports as part of a larger Chinese strategy to contain India. China's response to Indian concerns over China-South Asian military cooperation has been to assert that since China does not have aggressive or malevolent intentions, China's military cooperation with India's neighbors does not threaten India. If India is concerned about China's military ties with the smaller South Asian nations, Beijing argues, the proper course is to increase mutual trust between China and India via security dialogues and other such venues (Baskaran and Sivakumar, 2014).

Therefore, we can say that India's LEP and China's look South Asia policy seems to be counter-balancing though sometimes in confrontation. In this context, some scholars attributed India's engagement with Southeast Asia as a means to counter-balance China's encroachment into India's self-perceived sphere of influence in South Asia. Though SAARC was established to develop trade and other economic cooperation among the South Asian countries. But India is unwilling to accept moving China from its observer status to a full member status, unlike the other members, especially Bangladesh, Pakistan and Nepal (Chen et al, 2014). Sridharan notes for instance that 'India has felt that by dominating Southeast Asia, China could easily challenge India's pre-eminence in South Asia' (Sridharan, 1993). Persistent concerns remain regarding China's encroachments into South Asia and the need to balance this through India's relations with Southeast Asia. Writing in 2002, Garver notes that 'New Delhi is mobilizing counter-pressure on China (via the Look East Policy) to compel Beijing to suspend, or roll back its deep and growing military involvement in the (South Asian-Indian Ocean region)' (Garver, 2002).

CONCLUSION

Although Beijing is New Delhi's top two-way trading partner, tensions along their disputed border and China's growing presence in the Indian Ocean continue to make India uneasy. India's increasing involvement in the South China Sea is also makes China uncomfortable. While India is not a direct stakeholder in the South China Sea, it tries to be a security provider and is carefully engaged in development activities with Vietnam and Philippines in the South China Sea. India has pushed this line on the South China Sea in bilateral security discussions with countries including the US, Japan and Vietnam. On the other hand, there is no sign that China will limit its scope of activities in the Indian Ocean. China will not abstain from using all its power to pressure India when its interests are perceived to be under threat (Fang, 2016).

There is no doubt that between Indian and Chinese relations manifest a trust deficit. Both countries could promote measures promoting trust; they should not be opponents but rather each other's vital partner of cooperation. Both countries should not limit their relationship in Asia; they should view in a wider context like the world at large. It is also of considerable importance to restore confidence through managing the sensitive boundary issues. In this regard, both sides should be involved in promotion of strategic mutual trust, economic and trade relations, cultural tourism and people-to-people exchange. The two countries should work together for their peaceful, cooperative development, accelerate cooperation in infrastructure, industrial production capacity and equipment to speed up the industrialization and modernization process as well as should be sincerely engaged in upholding the peace and prosperity of the region and the world at large. Furthermore, raising the bilateral relations to new upward stage will help comprehend mutual development and prosperity of both countries (Chakrabarty, 2015). In the political front it is necessary that both the sides should attempt to regular contact at the summit level and should strive for intensifying communication on major issues. Apart from that it is also high time to bestow more importance on shared cultural and spiritual past. China seems to have already taken steps to recover the spirit of that relationship. It is perhaps possible to break the ice if both the countries pursue the twin economic and cultural route.

REFERENCES

Anderson, A. & Ayres, A. (2015, Aug. 7). Expert Brief, Council on Foreign Relations, Economics of Influence: China and India in South Asia, http://www.cfr.org/economics/economics-influence-china-india-south-asia/p36862\

ANI News (2011, Oct. 12). Defense Minister Antony rules out increasing Naval presence in South China Sea. http://aninews.in/newsdetail2/story17270/defence-minister-antony-rules-out-increasing-naval-presence-in-south-china-sea.html

Bajpaee, C. (2015) The 'China factor' in India's 'Look East' policy, *FRPC Journal, Foreign Policy Research Centre, New Delhi, India*, 22(2), 66 –127.

Banerjee, D. (2011). China and South Asia in the New Era. In Zhang Yunling, (Ed.) *Making New Partnership*. UK: Paths International Ltd.

Baskaran, S. & Sivakumar, N. (2014). "China and South Asia: Issues and Future Trends," *International Journal of Liberal Arts and Social Science* 2(6):1–8.

Bhadrakumar, M. K. (2009, May 27). Asia Times, "Sri Lanka Wards Off Western Bullying," http://www.atimes.com/atimes/South_Asia/KE27Df01.html

BBC News, (2014, Sept. 18). China's Xi Jinping signs landmark deals on India visit http://www.bbc.com/news/world-asia-india-29249268

Calvo, A. (2015). "On India's 'Looking East' Policy and the South China Sea," *South China Think Tank, Issue Briefings*, no.3, p.2.

Chakrabarty, M. (2015) "2014: A Mile Stone for Paradigm Shift in India-China Relations," *FRPC Journal, Foreign Policy Research Centre, New Delhi, India*, 22(2): 40–54.

Chouvy, P.A. (2002). Drug Trade in Asia. In Levinson D. and Christensen K., (Ed.) *Encyclopedia of Modern Asia*. Vol. 2, Chicago: Scribners.

Chen, X., Banerjee, P., Toor, S.I.G. Downie, N. (2014), Pakistan Defense, China and South Asia: Contention and Cooperation Between Giant Neighbours-Analysis,http://defence.pk/threads/china-and-south-asia-contention-and-coopera-tion-between-giant-neighbours-%E2%80%93-analysis.310720/

Daily News and Analysis (2014, Aug. 24). "Time for 'Act East Policy' and not just 'Look East': SushmaSwaraj," http://www.dnaindia.com/world/report-time-for-act-east-policy-and-not-just-look-east-sushma-swaraj -2013294

Dawn, (2016, August 30), US India defense pact to impact Pakistan, China.http://www.dawn. Com/news/1280873

Deepak, B.R. (2005) *India and China 1904–2004*, New Delhi: Manak Publications.

Dengke, L.(2010) "Our Third Generation Fighters Engage in High Plateau Training for the First Time with Live Weapons," People's Liberation Army Daily, July 30, 2010 (in Chinese), [Online available] http://military.people.com.cn/GB/172467/12298463.html

Dixit, J.N. (1996) *My South Block Years: Memoirs of a Foreign Secretary*. New Delhi: UBS Publishers.

Fang, T. (2016). India's Act East Policy and Implications for China-India Relations. Conference paper, National TsingHuaUniveristy, Taiwan, http://web.isanet.org/Web/Conferences/AP%20Hong%20Kong%202016/Archive/eceba784–8da2–478d-9b07–03ad060f928a.pdf

Forbes (2016, AUG 28) China and Pakistan Should Note—This Week, India and US Sign the LEMOA Pact, http://www.forbes.com/sites/charlesti-efer/2016/08/28/china-and-pakistan-beware-this-week-india-and-us-sign-major-war-pact/#139a21f664e1

Garver, J. (2002). The Security Dilemma in Sino-Indian Relations. *India Review*, 1(4): p.34.

Garver, W.J. (2005). China's Probable Role in Central and South Asia. Asia Program Special Report, Woodrow Wilson International Centers for Scholars. Working Paper No-126.

Godwin, P.H.B. (2004) China as a Regional Hegemon? In Jim Rolfe (Ed.) *The Asia-pacific: A Region in Transition*, The Asia-Pacific Center for Security Studies: Honolulu.

Government of India (2011, Dec. 30). *Look East Policy*, Press Information Bureau.

Government of India, (2014, Nov. 13). Prime Minister's Office, Press Information Bureau, "English rendering of Prime Minister ShriNarendraModi's remarks at the East Asia Summit, Nay Pyi Taw," http://pib.nic.in/newsite/PrintRelease. aspx?relid=111346

Global Times, (2011, October 14). India-Vietnam joint work must be halted.

Gupta, S. (2016, May 25). Hindustan Times, Why the Chabahar Port agreement kills two birds with one stone, http://www.hindustantimes.com/analysis/why-the-chabahar-port-agreement-kills-two-birds-with-one-stone/story-1I2NGMuzJ-DI6GaUHjaPR7M.html

Haijun, Z. (2016, Aug 12) Peoples Daily, India's 'Look East Policy' http://www. china.org.cn/ opinion/2012–04/06/content_25075354.htm

Haokip, T. (2011) India's Look East Policy: Its Evolution and Approach, *South Asian Survey* 18(2): 239–257

Kabir, H. (2013) The Rise of China and the Future of South Asia, In Kabir, B. M. (Ed.) *Sino-South Asian Relations: Continuity and Change*, Bangladesh: Chittagong University.

Kabir, H. and Ahmad, A. (2015). The Bay of Bengal: Next theatre for strategic power play in Asia, CIRR XXI -72, Pp: 199–239

Kazmin, A. (2016, May 9). "India watches anxiously as Chinese influence grows." Financial Times, https://www.ft.com/content/e9baebee-0bd8–11e6–9456–444ab5211a2f

Kelegama, S. (2014, June 25) China's growing reach in South Asia, East Asia Forum, Institute of Policy Studies of Sri Lanka, http://www.eastasiaforum.org/2014/06/25/chinas-growing-reach-in-south-asia/

Kotoky, A. and Ananthalakshmi A. (2013, Feb. 6). Reuters, Edition: India, "India "concerned" by China role in Pakistan's Gwadar port" http://in.reuters.com/article/india-airshow-china-pakistan-antony-idINDEE91506I20130206

Kundu, S. (2016, April 08). The Diplomats, India's ASEAN Approach: Acting East http://thediplomat.com/2016/04/indias-asean-approach-acting-east/

Lahiri, I. https://www.academia.edu/4829407/EVOLUTION_AND_RATIONALE_ OF _INDIAS_LOOK_EAST_POLICY_WITH_SPECIAL_REFERENCE_TO_ BIMSTEC

Liu, S. (2014) "China Threat" in South Asia: A Perspective from China, http://www. ipcs.org/article/india/china-threat-in-south-asia-a-perspective-from-china-4695. html

Malhotra, A. (2015). India's Eastern Orientation: A case of Role Conflict, *FRPC Journal, Foreign Policy Research Centre, New Delhi, India* 22(2),151–161.

Malik, M. (2016, July 22). The American Interest, India's Response to the South China Sea Verdict (http://www.the-american-interest.com/2016/07/22/indias-response-to-the-south-china-sea-verdict/)

Malik, M. (2014) "The Indo-Pacific Maritime Domain" in *Maritime Security in the Indo-Pacific: Perspectives from China, India and the United States,* ed. MohanMalik. London: Rowman & Littlefield.

Mohan, A. (2013, Oct. 8). India and ASEAN: A Pivotal Relationship, Ministry of External Affairs: Government of India, http://mea.gov.in/in-focusarticle. htm?22297/India+ and+the+ASEAN+ A+Pivotal+Relationship

Mukherjee, A. (2014). "India as a Net Security Provider: Concept and Impediments," Policy Brief, S. Rajaratnam School of International Studies, Nanyang Technological University, p.1.https://www.rsis.edu.sg/wp-content/uploads/2014/09/ PB_140903_India-Net-Security.pdf

Muni, S.D. (2010, Aug. 30). *The Hindu,* Nalanda: A Soft Power Project.

Naidu, G.V.C., (2013). India and East Asia: The Look East Policy. *Perceptions* 18 (1):53–74.

Nelson, D. (2012, May 29). The Telegraph. India to open super highway to Burma and Thailand.http://www.telegraph.co.uk/news/worldnews/asia/india/9297354/ India-to-open-super-highway-to-Burma-and-Thailand.html

Pant, H.V. (2010). "How China Changes SAARC."[Available at: http://www.livemint.com/ 2010/04/28210010/How-China-changes-Saarc.html, April 28, 2010. Accessed on 5 August, 2016.

Pant, H.V. (2013). *China Rises, India Ponders: India's Look East Policy Gathers Momentum,* Australia India Institute, Spring, Vol.1: 1–20.

Pant, H.V. (2016, March 13). Hindustan Times. "India, US must collaborate on South China Sea,"http://www.hindustantimes.com/analysis/india-us-must-collaborate-on-south-china-sea/story-RcrRLrT1TcNqJ2jegwGCMO.html

Prime Minister of India, (2011, October 12). PM's statement at the Joint Press conference with the President of Vietnam, http://archivepmo.nic.in/drmanmohansingh/ speech-details.php?nodeid=1068

Rajendram, D. (2014, Dec.19). Author Interview: Gabriel Dominnguez,http://www. dw.com/ en/from-look-east-to-act-east-india -shifts-focus/a-18141462

Rajendram, D. (2014). India's new Asia-Pacific strategy: Modi acts East, Lowy Institute for International Policy, http://www.lowyinstitute.org/files/indias-new-asia-pacific-strategy-modi-acts-east.pdf

Rengma, K.E. (2012) "Soft Power Game: A Study of China, India and South Asian Association for Regional Cooperation (SAARC) Tripartite" [Online Available] http://indiachinainstitute.org/wp-content/uploads/2012/04/Elmie-Soft-Power-Game-A-Study-of-China-India-and-SAARC-Tripartite.pdf

Roy, D. (1998). China's Foreign Relations, London: MacMillan Press Ltd.

Sharma, R. (2016, May 22). The New Indian Express. India-Myanmar-Thailand trilateral highway agreement soon.

Sajjanhar, A. (2016, Aug. 22). The Diplomats, India and China: Asia's Uneasy Neighbors, http://thediplomat.com/2016/08/india-and-china-asias-uneasy-neighbors/

Saleem, K.B.G. (2013). "China's Policy Towards South Asia-An Appraisal." College of Defense Studies, Defense Forum Spring, NDU, PLA, [Online Available: http:// www.cdsndu.org/html_en/ to_China.articleContent_article.id=8a28e6d84ae86737 014aeb1d9b9a0105.html

Samaranayake, N., (2012), The Long Littoral Project: Bay of Bengal A Maritime Perspective on Indo-Pacific Security, Cleared for Public Release IRP-2012-U-002319, CNA.

Shesheng, H. (2010), A Chinese Perspective, in Muni, S. D. (Ed.) *The Emerging Dimensions of Saarc*. New Delhi: Cambridge University Press.

Shulan, Y. (2010). "China's Regional Policy in East Asia and its Characteristics." The University of Nottingham, China Policy Institute, Discussion Paper 66.

Singh, S. (2003). *China-South Asia: Issues, Equations, Policies*. New Delhi: Lancer Books.

Sinha, Y. (2003, Sept. 04). Remarks by External Affairs Minister at The Plenary Session Second India-ASEAN Business Summit, Ministry of External Affairs, Government of India. http://mea.gov.in/Speeches-Statements.htm?dtl/4843/ Remarks+by+Shri+Yashwant+Sinha+ External+Affairs+Minister+of+India+at+T he+Plenary+Session+Second+India++ASEAN+Business+Summit

Sridharan, K. (1993). India-ASEAN Relations: Evolution, Growth, and Prospects, in Chandran, J. (eds.), *China India Japan and the Security of South east Asia* (1st ed. pp.117–143) Regional Strategic Studies Programme, Institute of South East Asian Studies.

The Hindu (2014, Oct. 28). "ONGC Videsh to Acquire Stake in 2 Vietnamese Blocks," http://www.thehindu.com/business/Industry/ongc-videsh-toacquire-stake-in-2-vietnamese-blocks/article6541721.ece

The White House, (2014, Sept. 30). "US-India Joint Statement,"https://www.whitehouse.gov/ the-press-office/2014/09/30/us-india-joint-statement

Vajpayee, A.B. (2002, April 9). India's perspectives on ASEAN and the Asia-Pacific Region, 21st Singapore Lecture. Singapore: ISEAS.

Xinhua (2008, Oct. 21) "Eastern Turkistan Terrorists Identified." [Online available] *China Daily*: http://www.chinadaily.com.cn/china/2008–10/21/content_7126503. htm.Accessed on 6 August, 2016.

Yinghong, Y. (2014). "YinduModixinzhengfu de dui Huazhengce" ("The policy trends of India's Modinew government towards China"), YaFeizongheng (Asia & Africa Review), No.5, p.74.

Part II

CHINA'S REGIONAL INITIATIVES

Chapter 7

Russia–China Relations in Central Asia and the SCO

Mikhail A. Molchanov

Russia's fate in the Trump era of world politics will centrally depend on Moscow's relationship with Beijing, and the ability to make the best use of Russia's participation in the China-led Shanghai Cooperation Organization (SCO) and the Silk Road Economic Belt initiative. There are several important aspects to this relationship. The chapter will explore the role of Sino-Russian cooperation in the development of energy resources in Central Asia and the implicit tensions between two regional integration projects: one driven by China and another—by Russia. I argue that the potential for genuine regional cooperation exists and depends largely on role distribution in the China-Russia leadership tandem. The shape of the Eurasian region will be largely determined through evolution of the Sino-Russian relationship and the concrete shape that SCO will take in the forthcoming years.

SCO'S EMERGENCE AND GROWTH

The SCO's evolution so far has been nothing less than remarkable. The organization's immediate predecessor—the "Shanghai Five" forum—grew out of the five-party talks on confidence building measures and reduction of forces on the borders. The Sino-Soviet talks on disputed territories had started as early as the 1960s and continued on the bilateral basis until the end of 1991. With the collapse of the Soviet Union and the emergence of newly independent states, the unified post-Soviet delegation evolved to represent not one, but four of the negotiating sides: Russia, Kazakhstan, Kyrgyzstan, and Tajikistan. By 1996, demonstrable success in negotiations over the border demarcation and reduction of forces enabled formal institutionalization of the talks. The Shanghai Five forum continued as annual summits of the five countries' leaders, while its agenda progressed from confidence building in the border areas to broader cooperation in the areas of international politics and security.

Since neither China nor Central Asian states had much experience with multilateral diplomacy, it fell on Moscow's shoulders to provide the necessary know-how, thus steering group negotiations through the first phase of the forum's existence. For its own part, Beijing sensed an opportunity to wean the Central Asian states off Russia's tutelage and strike separate deals in the most crucial question of disputed territories. China had long sought a legitimate instrument of influence in Central Asia; institutionalization of the cross-border talks provided it with such an instrument.

Border delimitation talks between USSR and PRC were going on intermittently since 1960s. Both Russia, as the legal successor to the USSR, and the People's Republic of China were equally interested in bringing the newly independent Central Asian states up to speed, and Moscow diplomats in particular did a lot of coaching on behalf of their Central Asian partners. Therefore, representing the group simply as the "Chinese brainchild" (Gill and Oresman 2003: 5) does not capture all complexity of the processes that brought it into existence. Nonetheless, there is little doubt that its subsequent transformation and growth reflected a *de facto* tug-of-war between China's and Russia's leadership aspirations, as well as organizational designs and visions for the future. While China wanted to expand and solidify its presence in the region, Russia tried to contain it and manipulate the terms of China's entry. As a result, rather than providing an example of the implementation of someone's brilliant and far-reaching plan, the SCO evolution serves a textbook case of mission creep as the protracted process of negotiations spilled into new related and less related areas, and brought new institutions in its wake.

In June 2001, with the admission of Uzbekistan, Shanghai Five became the SCO. The first document it adopted was called "Shanghai Convention on Combating Terrorism, Separatism and Extremism." This happened three months before 9/11 and at the time reflected realities of the region more than anything else. In 1999–2000, both Kyrgyzstan and Uzbekistan had to fight back military incursions of the Islamic Movement of Uzbekistan (IMU)—a radical Islamist organization allied with Afghanistan's Taliban and Al-Qaida. Russia was fresh out of its second war with Chechen rebels. China was dealing with Tibetan independence movement and a protracted conflict with predominantly Muslim Uighur separatists in Xinjiang.

The SCO Charter focused primarily on international and regional security, consensus building and coordination of foreign policies of the member states; economic cooperation and cooperation in the use of natural resources appeared almost as an afterthought. Together with the Charter, the heads of state signed the agreement on the establishment of the Regional Anti-Terrorist

Structure (2002). It was not until the next year when the first comprehensive program of multilateral trade and economic cooperation was adopted. To supervise implementation of the growing portfolio of documents, the organization's Secretariat was created in 2004—the same year the SCO got its first budget. These developments opened a new phase in institutionalization of regional cooperation in Central Asia, allowed expansion into the new areas of activity and called for further building of a solid economic and financial base that would enable such expansion.

Throughout the SCO's formative period, Russia was rather cautious to endorse its functional and geographic spread. Moscow viewed proliferation of regional integration organizations in Eurasia with some annoyance, anticipating, in Foreign Minister Lavrov's (2004a) words, "the task of reducing the activities of all these structures to a common denominator which would reflect our long-term interests." A debate inside Russia's political establishment between those supporting resuscitation of the Commonwealth of Independent States and those betting on the newly formed and more dynamic organizations, such as the EurAsEC or the SCO, was not yet over.

Meanwhile, China did not waste any time and used the 2004 Tashkent summit to allocate more than $1 billion for the development of intraregional trade—$900 million in credits to the SCO member states and $350 million in grants and long-term loans to Uzbekistan in particular. The SCO created the institute of observers, admitting Mongolia in 2004, India, Pakistan and Iran in 2005, and Afghanistan in 2012. The 2005 summit of the heads of government in Moscow launched the organization's Business Council and Interbank Consortium and saw Agreement on Inter-Bank Cooperation signed. Next year, Russia had floated an idea of the SCO Energy Club. By 2008, a new institute of the SCO Dialogue Partner was created. Belarus, Sri Lanka and Turkey availed themselves of the opportunity to get affiliated. Several more countries expressed their interest to become observers. The SCO was becoming more interesting and more relevant to neighbors far and near.

In 2012–2014, general directions for development of the SCO strategy for the next decade were formulated. The 2015 Ufa summit of the organization had formally adopted the SCO Development Strategy Towards 2025. It had proclaimed that the member states had no plans of establishing a military alliance or a formal regional integration organization with a supranational organs of governance. At the same time, the SCO staked the claim toward creating a zone of peace and stability in the region, facilitating economic collaboration on the basis of China's "Silk Road Economic Belt" proposal and development of the "indivisible security space" for the member states. In a thinly veiled reference to the US international activism, the member states rejected all "unilateral forms of pressure" on sovereign states. The Ufa summit became the first one to combine the meetings of the SCO and BRICS leaders.

Although established as a security organization par excellence, SCO has since grown into a multifunctional regional club. In addition to defense and security cooperation, anti-terrorism and joint opposition to separatism and extremism, the SCO has established its Business Council, the Interbank Consortium, the Energy Club and other tools of regional economic cooperation. The SCO Charter (2002) expanded the organization's mandate to include "support for, and promotion of regional economic cooperation in various forms, fostering favorable environment for trade and investments with a view to gradually achieving free flow of goods, capitals, services and technologies."

It became a magnet for other states in the larger Eurasian region. The decision to extend the SCO membership rights to India and Pakistan, adopted in Ufa, was formalized with the signing of the accession memoranda in Tashkent during the 2016 summit. With the end of NATO's International Security Assistance Force's mission in Afghanistan, SCO is poised to become one of the key guarantors of regional security in South Asia.

Assessments given to this rapid growth by international observers varied from cautiously skeptical to enthusiastic to alarmist. While a few saw a more or less ordinary regional organization in the making, others claimed that SCO showed signs of overgrowing its purely regional phase of development and becoming a factor of global geopolitical significance. Vladimir Putin (2016) characterized the SCO "natural development" this way:

> This Organization, when it was first created, set itself quite modest goals, which I would say were important but at the same time practical. These included the settlement of various issues of cross-border cooperation, complex as well as simple ones. . . . We came to understand that such a mechanism... should not be wasted. Therefore, we actually began using the established mechanism to address other issues . . . such as political cooperation and cooperation in infrastructure development. We also launched discussions on security, on combatting the drug threat and other issues. I would not say that we have made astonishing progress . . . yet the Organization has become highly demanded and attractive in the region, and many countries of the world have expressed their willingness to join it.

THE PRESENT STAGE IN RUSSO-CHINESE RELATIONS

The Sino-Russian trade exceeded US$95 billion in 2014. China has become Russia's number one trading partner. The volume of direct trade settled in national currencies expanded from $52 million in July to $1.2 billion in November 2014 (TV Zvezda 2014). Chinese direct investment has grown, too. In its continuing expansion into Russia, CNPC bought a 20 percent stake in the $27 billion worth Yamal liquefied natural gas project and a 10 percent stake in Vankorneft, one of the most promising oil and gas fields in Eastern Siberia. An unprecedented $270 billion deal commits Russia to the sale of 365 million tons of oil to China over 25 years, in addition to the earlier negotiated 300 million tons' supply.

The Ukraine crisis and the western sanctions that followed have sped up the process of Russia's "pivoting" to its eastern neighbor. Re-orientation away from the west is most pronounced in gas trade. After the first mammoth agreement to supply 38 billion cubic meters of gas to China annually over the course of 30 years the two countries signed the second deal, which adds 30 billion cubic meters of gas a year to China's western regions. The two deals together are valued at more than $684 billion (Yep 2014). According to the Associated Press (2014), Xi Jinping "also called for an Asian security arrangement that would include Russia and Iran and exclude the United States." Whether a new Sino-Russian alliance "aimed at further hamstringing the U.S.-led neoliberal order" (Green 2014) is possible or not is a hotly debated topic. The skeptics may well be right; a growing power disparity between the two countries stands in the way (Nye 2015). Even so, the potential of Russia's bandwagoning with China should not be discounted. It is precisely in the realm of multilateral and regional politics where this potential is the greatest.

China's attention to Russia and Eurasia has been confirmed with the change from the fourth to the fifth generation of leaders in Beijing. Just like his predecessor Hu Jintao, President Xi Jinping chose Russia for his first official visit abroad. A joint statement on mutually beneficial cooperation and deepening of the comprehensive strategic partnership of cooperation was signed. It defined Sino-Russian relations as "relations of comprehensive and equal partnership, mutual trust, strategic cooperation, mutual support, common prosperity and lasting friendship" (President of Russia 2013). The two leaders expressed their support to deepening of regional cooperation and called on all major powers to "rise above thinking in terms of zero-sum games and bloc politics."

The summit pursued political, economic, and humanitarian agenda. Xi and Putin approved the action plan on implementing the friendship treaty for 2013–16 and set up new targets for the bilateral trade turnover. A decision was made to promote the use of national currencies in bilateral trade, credit and investment. The two sides designated several industrial sectors as priority areas for cooperation, and focused specifically on Russia's growing role as China's energy supplier. In leaders' presence, CNPC and Gazprom signed the $400 billion gas trade agreement. Other contracts dealt with oil supplies, cooperation in petroleum exploration, development, production and marketing, and Chinese oil majors' participation in Sakhalin-3 offshore drilling project.

In 2014, Xi Jinping has once again made Russia his first foreign destination of a year to attend the Sochi Olympic Games' opening ceremony—the first time ever China's leader would go overseas for a major sports event (*People's Daily Online* 2014). The key topics of the ensuing talks with Putin were increases in Russia's oil and gas supplies, cooperation on Syria, and Russia's participation in the construction of the Silk Road Economic Belt and the Maritime Silk Road—both initiatives aimed at the promotion of the Chinese trade interests in South and West Asia. In October 2014, China opened a $24.5 billion currency swap line with Russia to promote bilateral trade and investment. Next month, the two countries' presidents signed the second mega gas deal on the margins of the Asia-Pacific Economic Cooperation summit in Beijing.

However, the bilateral trade dropped by 27.8 percent to $64.2 billion in 2015 and rebounded only slightly, by 0.5 percent, in 2016 (TASS 2016). The downfall was caused by western sanctions, low natural resource prices, and the weak rubble. The Russian economic crisis did not help, as the demand for Chinese goods in Russia significantly lessened. The overall structure of trade remained skewed toward primary goods on the Russian side in particular, which reflected Russia's continued downslide into a less than envious role of a resource appendage for the Asian giant. Russia's high-tech exports to China consist almost exclusively of weaponry, and People's Liberation Army is a rather untrustworthy customer, working hard to reverse-engineer the military technologies and hardware it has been purchasing. Doubts as to the success of Russia's "pivot to Asia" have been raised by both domestic and international observers.

In spite of all the rhetoric of strategic partnership, bilateral relations are still contaminated with mistrust. China's enormous demographic pressure on Russia's scarcely populated Far East remains a source of concern and breeds alarmist reactions in the region. Political cooperation in the UN Security Council has not been matched by Russia's support to Beijing's territorial claims in the East China Sea. China does not recognize independence of Russia-supported enclaves of South Ossetia and Abkhazia and is ambiguous on the question of Crimea. With regard to the stalled energy deals and the continuing march of China's trade elsewhere, it appears that "rather than playing Europe by engaging with China, Russia is getting played by China" (Eder and Huotari 2016). The persistent mantra of the "relations of mutual trust" in official documents makes one wonder whether that trust is secure. All of this cannot but influence the two countries' interaction in the SCO and their implicitly competing visions of regionalism in Eurasia.

Leading the Region

The SCO's early rationale of combating terrorism, separatism, and extremism is still the basis of its foundational consensus. As NATO forces in Afghanistan assumed main responsibility for the security situation on Central Asia's borders, that rationale was somewhat weakened. This prompted China to press with speedier institutionalization of the SCO structures, while Russia responded by creating the Collective Security Treaty Organization with select post-Soviet states. The SCO attempted to reassert itself as a principal organization for collective security in the region. Joint military exercises on multilateral and bilateral bases became the norm. The Regional Anti-Terrorist Structure started functioning in 2004. The SCO Astana Declaration of July 2005 demanded a definitive timeline for the withdrawal of the US forces from military bases in Central Asia.

However, in spite of all these efforts, strong doubts remain as to the SCO's ability to stabilize the region after the NATO forces' withdrawal from Afghanistan is complete. The organization does not have a standing force. China does not want to be seen as the state leading a military build-up in Central Asia. Russia prefers to work through the organizations that it controls, and SCO is clearly not one of them. The SCO's collaboration with the Russia-led Collective Security Treaty Organization (CSTO), while potentially a solution to the problem, is not institutionalized enough to provide ready resources for sustained military engagement.

Russia and China's views on what constitutes effective regional leadership differ. From the mid-2000s on, Beijing has been emphasizing economic cooperation as the main instrument of region building. Russia, being substantially weaker economically, stressed anti-terrorist, political security and military coordination which became traditional for the organization. WenJiabao's offer of $900 million preferential credit to Central Asian states during the 2005 premiers' summit was perceived in Moscow as an attempt to "buy" allegiances of Russia's traditional allies. Russia countered by pressing for less asymmetrical forms of multilateral economic cooperation, such as creation of the SCO Development Fund and Interbank Consortium.

Beijing and Moscow differ in their assessment of the readiness of Central Asian states for more advanced forms of economic integration. The Chinese government has long been lobbying for the establishment of the SCO free trade zone, while Russia together with its Central Asian partners has long been opposed to the idea. In Russia's view, bilateral economic cooperation and cooperation on ad-hoc basis are still preferable to the full-blown economic integration, which, according to Moscow, is not yet feasible because of huge disparities between the SCO member states.

Diverging geopolitical priorities have been revealed in a debate on the SCO enlargement. While Russia supported the prospect of India's membership, China lobbied for its long-time diplomatic and trade partner Pakistan. A temporary impasse resulted in a 2006 decision to declare a moratorium on admission of new members. When, four year later, it was lifted, both India and Pakistan became front-runners for membership. By the end of 2013, Russia had no problems with the two countries joining at the same time, and in January 2015 the Russian Foreign Ministry was able to announce that all necessary decisions to make that happen were adopted.

China prefers to lead the SCO with money, while Russia—with the political-military muscle. When, in 2010, Wen Jiabao proposed to establish the SCO Development Bank, with China contributing as much as $10 billion for its start-up capital, Russia appeared cool to the proposal, arguing that each of the SCO member states should be able to contribute to the organization's joint projects. According to the Chinese plan, the bank's headquarters would be based in Beijing and the country with the largest investment share (i.e., China) would have more say in the bank's activities. Among other things, such a bank could be used to finance infrastructure projects in Central Asia, thus contributing to Russia's relative marginalization in the region. Moscow responded by promoting the Eurasian Development Bank and the Eurasian Business Council—the institutions created to service the EurAsEC, where China did not participate. Nonetheless, the demand for the SCO Development Bank from the Central Asian states kept the idea afloat, and by mid-2014 Russia itself revived the proposal, arguing that the best way to implement it would be on the basis of the already functioning Eurasian Development Bank.

At the same time, Russia jockeys for leadership of the SCO counter-terrorist activities and military exercises, where it could reasonably claim some prowess. Before the Russo-Georgian war of 2008, it looked like Moscow had made some advances in this area and might well succeed in turning the organization eventually toward the more pronounced geopolitical and security agenda. The so-called "tulip revolution" in Kyrgyzstan and the violent suppression of anti-government riots in Andijan, Uzbekistan, had brought security concerns of the authoritarian leaders of the region to the forefront. The SCO reacted by adopting the Astana 2005 summit declaration which proffered support to all efforts of the Central Asian states "aimed to guarantee peace, security and stability in their countries." The US and western criticism of the Andijan massacre resonated in the summit's request to western powers "to define the end terms of their temporary use" of military facilities in Central Asia (SCO 2005).

Uzbekistan's president-for-life Islam Karimov was pleased. Soon enough, he proceeded to cancel the American lease of the Karshi-Khanabad air base—a move that would be hardly possible without a firm backing of his SCO partners. The unilateral termination of the so-called K2 base agreement by the official Tashkent could not but be applauded by Russia and China alike. The closure of the Karshi-Khanabad had, in turn, emboldened Moscow to increase its pressure on Kyrgyzstan, which hosted Americans at the Manas air base near its capital Bishkek. When the base was finally transferred back to the Kyrgyz government in 2014, Russia stepped in to secure its own lease of the facility in exchange for writing off $500 million in Kyrgyzstan's debt.

However, Russia's leadership of security cooperation in Central Asia was put to the test in April-May 2010, when the revolution in Kyrgyzstan brought down the country's government, and then again in June 2010, when ethnic riots in and around the city of Osh displaced tens of thousands across the Kyrgyzstan-Uzbekistan border. In both cases, Kyrgyz authorities requested Russia and the CSTO to send in peacekeeping forces, yet Russia failed to deliver.

On the other hand, and in spite of many pronouncements to the effect that China relies on a "peaceful rise" strategy and is not interested in projecting military power anywhere beyond the national borders, there is little doubt that China's interest in adequate protection of its economic assets abroad grows in direct proportion to the accumulated volume of those assets. The Arab spring dealt a significant blow to the Chinese interests in North Africa. Consequently, the more Beijing invests in new oil and gas pipelines, roads and infrastructure in Central Asia, the more it is willing to safeguard its investments from any local revolution, riot or disruption that might jeopardize them. China's leading of joint anti-terrorism and military exercises with Central Asian states, with or without Russia's participation, attests to that willingness (Bin 2011).

Just as Russia prefers bilateral economic projects to the multilateral economic cooperation within the SCO framework, China is not opposed to military collaboration with individual countries of the region, but shies away from institutionalization of long-term multilateral cooperation with the Russia-led entities, such as the CSTO. Russia's idea to stage joint military exercises of CSTO and SCO in August 2007 was refuted by China. Beijing is resolutely opposed to all attempts by Moscow to transform SCO into a political-military alliance. According to China's view, SCO should be regarded as "a new model of regional cooperation, rather than an alliance" (Xinhua 2012).

By 2014, China succeeded in pushing through the agreements on the basic principles of the formation, functioning and management of the SCO Development Bank and Development Fund (Special Account), while Russia took consolation in leading institutionalization of the SCO Energy Club. However, the September 2013 Bishkek summit produced few tangible results on other issues of importance to the region: stabilization in Afghanistan, water management conflicts in Central Asia, and the organization's enlargement. On all

of these, the diverging approaches of Moscow and Beijing prevented the SCO
from moving beyond most general declarations.

Observers noted that implicit competition for leadership between Russia
and China continued with China's increasing its economic expansion in the
face of Russia's attempts to utilize the SCO as a platform for the advancement of its global agenda. Indeed, the summit's resolutions essentially backed
Russia's preferred approaches to such issues as the conflict in Syria and
international sanctions against Iran. At the same time, Xi Jinping used an
opportunity to consolidate the Chinese grip on the Central Asian economies.
The pre-summit tour of Central Asian capitals saw PRC's president offering at least US$48 billion in trade credits and investments to Kazakhstan,
Kyrgyzstan and Uzbekistan. The Silk Road Economic Belt envisions new
transportation corridors and a substantial boost in the Chinese imports of
hydrocarbons from the region. The construction of the fourth trunk of the
Central Asia-China Gas Pipeline (CAGP) will increase the volume of gas
export up to 80 billion cubic meters per year by 2020, thus accounting for
over 40 percent of China's gas imports.

The 2014 Dushanbe summit was mostly devoted to Afghanistan and
regional security. The participants have agreed on principles and procedures
for the admission of new members, which should be seen as a major achieve-
ment of the summit. Xi Jinping announced that the China-Eurasian Economic
Cooperation Fund would grow to US$5 billion. The leaders approved the
plan to prepare the SCO Development Strategy until 2025, which was to be
focused on mitigation of global and regional risks to the organization and its
members. The question of Ukraine was touched in the context of the organization's support to the peaceful resolution of the crisis.

The Ufa summit (2015) saw Russia trying to coordinate the SCO activities with those of the BRICS. The BRICS' New Development Bank was
launched and lauded as a vehicle that would correct shortcomings of existing international financial institutions. The SCO Development Strategy until
2025 rolled out a set of ambitious goals, while trying to balance between the
military-security and trade-and-development aspects of the organization's
activities. The Strategy's priorities covered just about everything from trade
and investment, infrastructure development and technical cooperation to
regional stability to social, cultural and humanitarian interactions, health and
environment. Russia's hosts clearly hoped that deeper economic cooperation
through the SCO and BRICS could be used to help alleviate the consequences
of the Western sanctions imposed in the wake of the Ukraine crisis.

The emphasis on regional integration possibilities with an eventual goal
of creating a free trade area encompassing all of the SCO member states has
been apparent in the work of the fourteenth Heads of Government Council meeting in Zhengzhou in December 2015. As the summit Declaration

proclaimed that "regional economic interaction and partnership" should be seen as the best way to "search for new models of international cooperation and global governance," all member states reaffirmed their "support for the initiative of People's Republic of China to create the Silk Road Economic Belt, which is in line with goals of development of the SCO" (Xinhua 2015). By the end of 2016 China had openly demanded creation of the SCO free trade area, to which Russia had reacted with some trepidation. The SCO current Secretary-General Rashid Alimov of Tajikistan urged caution, describing the issue as "very sensitive, because of variously scaled production potentials of the SCO members" (TopTJ.com 2016).

The question of relevance of the Russia-promoted Eurasian Union project inevitably emerges in this context. Chinese experts had argued that it is important to avoid the impression that the SCO means China, while the Eurasian Union is nothing more than Russia (Xin 2013). Beijing is interested in boosting trade and investment with all countries of the Eurasian Union on the bilateral basis, while improving multilateral channels of interaction open to the SCO and championing its own One Belt, One Road (OBOR) project. The end objective is linking the Eurasia space fully to China's sphere of economic influence, which will also affect regional geopolitics.

Russia will have to acquiesce. The initiative on regional integration has already slipped away from Moscow, and the only thing remaining is, essentially, to play into China's hands with what may appear as Russia's original proposals. Vladimir Putin's recent idea to integrate the OBOR, the Eurasian Economic Union, the SCO and Association of Southeast Asian Nations (ASEAN) into a "Big Eurasian Partnership" de-facto advances China's agenda even if its primary impetus was to delay the creation of a China-dominated free trade zone in Central Asia (cf. Romanova and Devonshire-Ellis 2016).

Meanwhile, the traditional division of responsibilities, with China leading economic development projects and Russia spearheading political and security dimensions of cooperation, also fades away as China shows increasing military prowess and capabilities. As international observers noted, it was China that led the SCO Peace Mission 2012 military exercises in Tajikistan. The emergence of Russia-India and China-Pakistan tandems within the organization may lead to further problems. Finally, the lack of a common approach to the stabilization of Afghanistan may result in the CSTO's support of the anti-Taliban forces in the north of the country, while Beijing takes a more accommodating stance and deals with the Taliban directly.

The dual leadership of the SCO is yet to be developed, and its Sino-Russian "engine" formed on the basis of mutual complementarity of the respective leadership roles and responsibilities. At this moment, and in spite of official accolades to the "unprecedented" level of bilateral relations of strategic partnership and coordination, both sides know full well that their relationship falls short of a definition of alliance or coalition. It remains a partnership based on partial overlapping of interests. The areas of tension exist not only with regard to the implicit competition of the two powers in Central Asia, but also in the continuing imbalance between the political and economic aspects of their cooperation, Chinese demographic and economic expansion in Russia's Far East, Beijing's refusal to co-sponsor state recognition of South Ossetia and Abkhazia by the SCO member states and even colder reception of Russia's annexation of Crimea. Reciprocally, Moscow is not in a hurry to lend support to the Chinese territorial claims in South and East China seas, drives a hard bargain in negotiations on the price of natural gas exports, woos Japan and Vietnam behind China's back and tries to use China as a diplomatic backup for its initiatives globally, even when Beijing has little, or no, direct interest in the subject.

All of this speaks to a relationship substantially more circumspect than its official representations. Russia's increased assertiveness in the near abroad cannot but worry Beijing. Putin's promotion of the pro-Russian separatism in the neighboring countries implicitly undermines China's efforts to contain separatists in Tibet, Xinxiang and, most importantly, Taiwan. Russia's flexing its military muscles in Transcaucasia, Ukraine and Central Asia increases business risks and may well undermine Chinese economic interests in those areas. Moreover, it contradicts the original *raison d'etre* of the SCO: to fight terrorism, separatism and extremism as not so much internal as regional and global problems.

The future development of the SCO depends on the prospects of genuine cooperation and complementarity within its leadership tandem. While China and Russia do cooperate bilaterally, they still have to find a modus vivendi for the division of responsibilities and leadership roles inside a network of bilateral, trilateral and multilateral processes that all converge on regionalist transformation of the postcommunist Eurasia. For as long as the two countries cannot agree on a meaningful division of responsibilities within the SCO and start meticulously coordinating their respective policies with respect to Central Asia and Eurasia as a whole, the SCO "engine" will continue stalling. This will undoubtedly affect not only the SCO itself, but also the Eurasian Economic Union.

IMPACT ON CENTRAL ASIA

The jockeying for leadership of the region and an implicit tug-of-war between China and Russia with respect to the SCO's role, functions and evolution profoundly influences situation in Central Asian states. According to a number of experts, Russia's influence in Central Asia is on decline (Malashenko

2013). Russia attempts to compensate by building up its military presence in the area; however, it loses strongly to China in terms of economic and financial engagement, and to Turkey—in soft power projection. The Central Asians have learned to balance between the major powers with stakes in the region, playing not only Russia against China and vice versa, but also Russia against the United States, Turkey, European Union, Saudi Arabia, India and other countries further afield. The multi-vector foreign policy that all these states embrace implies non-attachment to any single point of power in today's world and the selective engagement with all of them as necessary.

While Russia hoped for the SCO to evolve as a vehicle of managing the terms of China's entry into the region and, correspondingly, of preservation of its own influence in Central Asia, the results obtained on both accounts have been less than favorable to Moscow. Moreover, the SCO failed to bring its weight to bear on the existing problems of political development and interstate relations of its Central Asian members. The SCO was of little use in helping to resolve border delimitation and demarcation issues between Kazakhstan and Uzbekistan, Uzbekistan and Kyrgyzstan, Kyrgyzstan and Tajikistan, and Tajikistan and Uzbekistan. In the first instance, physical demarcation of the Kazakhstan-Uzbekistan border had only been completed by the end of 2013. The situation on the borders of Tajikistan remains tense, and the boundary between Uzbekistan and Kyrgyzstan has not yet been delimited in full either. Although it has grown out of confidence building measures in the border areas between China and the four post-Soviet states, the SCO's know-how in the border conflict resolution proved insufficient to address complex bilateral issues separating neighbors inside Central Asia.

The SCO did not support Russian actions in Georgia in August 2008. None of its members, save Russia itself, had recognized South Ossetia and Abkhazia as independent states. The SCO stood idly by during the "tulip" revolution in Kyrgyzstan, which led to the ouster of President Askar Akayev, and failed to intervene to stop the bloody riots in southern Kyrgyzstan in June 2010. It has not been prepared to step in as a guarantor of security in Afghanistan and adjacent areas following the withdrawal of NATO forces. Finally, the SCO has been of little use or support to Russia in the Ukrainian crisis of 2014. None of its members endorsed Russia's annexation of Crimea. The Central Asian states with significant Russian minorities, Kazakhstan in particular, have been genuinely worried by the precedent Russia's intervention in Ukraine may pose for their own countries.

The Central Asian states' membership in the SCO allows them to balance between Russia and China without throwing their lot unequivocally with one of these powers. The SCO chairmanship is rotated among its member states, thus giving the Central Asians an opportunity to preside over one of the largest regional integration entities in the world. For smaller members, the SCO serves as a school of leadership and a gateway to big international politics. The Sino-Russian competition within the SCO core opens space for genuine multivectorism in foreign policies of Kazakhstan, Kyrgyzstan, Uzbekistan and Tajikistan. Potentially, the SCO may lead in the development of mutually beneficial ties with other regional organizations. However, it is also clear that it represents an objective alternative to the Russia-centered integration projects in the region and may work at cross-purposes with the Eurasian Economic Union.

To the Central Asian states, Russia's policies in the region may appear inconsistent, if not incoherent, in comparison to the more steady approach taken by China. Russia has failed in transforming the SCO into a political-military alliance of sorts—an idea that was strongly opposed by China, Kazakhstan and Uzbekistan. Without a functioning military arm, the SCO's avowed goals of combating extremism, terrorism and separatism remain essentially unsupported. The SCO's Regional Anti-Terrorist Structure lacks necessary resources and serves at best as a coordinating mechanism for the appropriate national authorities of the member states. Russia's creation of the rapid reaction forces on the basis of the CSTO can be seen as implicitly encroaching on the SCO turf and diluting its original mandate.

At the same time, Russia does not help much in bringing out the organization's developmental potential. Moscow cannot compete with Beijing in the sheer amount of investments that China has already supplied to the region. The volume of the Chinese-accumulated investment in Kazakhstan exceeds $20 billion. In 2015–2017 alone the two countries signed investment projects worth$70 billion (Donskikh 2017). The volume of the Russian investment stock in Kazakhstan is almost three times lower, and same goes for the newly signed projects (Prime Minister of the Republic of Kazakhstan 2016). China's utilized direct investment in Uzbekistan, at $6.7 billion by the end of 2013, stood 1.5 times larger than the total investments from all of the CIS member states (Press Service of the Ministry of Foreign Affairs of the Republic of Uzbekistan 2013). In the future, the investment gap separating the two countries' footprints in Central Asia can only widen to Russia's detriment.

Same goes for trade. Russia's total trade with all of Central Asia reached $24.5 billion in 2013, while China's trade turnover with the region topped $46 billion a year earlier. Bilateral trade between China and Kazakhstan in 2013 stood at $28.6 billion, against Russia's $17.5 billion. China's trade with Uzbekistan is more than $4 billion, comparing to $2.8 billion on the Russian side (Xinhua 2014; Rosstat 2014). Beijing plans to reach a $40 billion mark in its trade with Kazakhstan by 2015 and targets $5 billion as an annual volume of trade with Uzbekistan by 2017.

It is obvious that Russia has miscalculated its ability to manage the SCO and turn it into an instrument of control over the terms of China's entry into

Central Asia. Rather than stalling the Chinese expansion, the SCO serves to promote it. China is the largest trading partner for Kazakhstan and Turkmenistan, the second largest for Uzbekistan and Kyrgyzstan, and the third largest for Tajikistan (Xinhua 2013). Xi Jinping's 2013 tour of Central Asia saw the Chinese signing $30 billion in trade and investment deals with Kazakhstan alone, and $15 billion more with Uzbekistan. Chinese premier Li Keqiang signed further $14 billion worth of accords with Kazakhstan during his December 2014 visit to Astana. Turkmenistan is already the largest natural gas supplier to PRC, and, with the opening of the Galkynysh gas field—the world's second largest—for production, is set to retain this position for the foreseeable future. The construction of the fourth strand of the CAGP from Turkmenistan to China will establish a new supply route through Kyrgyzstan and Tajikistan, to complement the already functioning Turkmenistan-Uzbekistan-Kazakhstan route.

There is no denial that China's developmental initiatives bring lots of much needed cash to its Central Asian partners. Against this background, it should have come as no surprise that all of the Central Asian states support creation of the SCO Development Bank under Chinese tutelage against Russia's long-term opposition to the idea. The China-dominated bank will supply funds for the projects that the Chinese prefer, thus translating financial might of its largest donor into political influence. Since Russia is unable to match the Chinese contributions, it will continue losing ground to China both politically and economically. As a result, the gap between Russia's rhetoric of regional leadership and its practical ability to meet the resulting expectations of its Central Asian partners will widen, and the reality of Russia's subordinate role to China in Central Asia will set in (Herd 2014: 185). It seems reasonable to conclude that whatever new institutions the SCO will be able to create in the near future they will serve Beijing's plans and visions of a desired regional order.

CONCLUSION

So far, the SCO proved rather ineffective in managing internal problems that plague bilateral relations between its member states. This relates not only to Sino-Russian jockeying for influence but also to the implicit competition between Uzbekistan and Kazakhstan, and to the more open acrimony between Tajikistan and Uzbekistan, Tajikistan and Kyrgyzstan, and Uzbekistan and Kyrgyzstan. Conversely, bilateral success stories and accomplishments, when they happen, do not happen because of the SCO mediation. Thus, neither Russia nor China demonstrates any need for the SCO institutions in building up relations with individual Central Asian states. The Central Asians' relations to each other, even when they are highly conflictual, do not benefit from the SCO good offices or conflict resolution mechanisms. As Nursultan Nazarbayev (2011b) noted, the SCO "experiences definite problems in trying to translate successful bilateral contacts into the format of multilateral cooperation."

Nonetheless, the impact of the SCO on regionalism in Eurasia is manifold and non-trivial. In spite of many a criticism levied against it, the SCO did help in resolution of China's long-standing border disputes with Russia and the Central Asian states. In less than 10 years, it had developed a geopolitical presence attractive enough to entice membership inquiries from India, Pakistan, Iran, and Turkey. In less than 15 years, it was ready to start expanding. The SCO's creation and evolution allowed advancing Russian-Chinese relations beyond mere bilateralism, and in the process brought them to a qualitatively new level of "comprehensive partnership and strategic interaction," a *de facto* political and economic, although not military, alliance. The SCO enables both China's peaceful rise and Russia's transitioning into a post-imperial phase of development. It is well positioned to facilitate interaction between the Russia-led Eurasian Economic Union and the Chinese initiative of the Silk Road Economic Belt.

Eurasian regionalism will remain dependent on the states' ability to overcome mistrust and put their common interests above the narrowly construed national priorities. This relates to Russia, China, and the Central Asian states, but equally to the European Union and states of Asia-Pacific whose interaction with the Eurasian core shapes the direction of its development. In the words of the Sino-Russian statement of May 20, 2014, it is important to think in terms of "complementarity of integration processes in Asia, the Eurasian space, and Europe" (Sovmestnoezaiavlenie 2014). If lingering tensions and mistrust will get subdued not only within the SCO or between the SCO and the Russia-oriented regional formations in Eurasia, but also between Eurasian regional integration entities and their counterparts to the west, east and south, the central Eurasia may become a place where a new political and economic hub of global significance will start growing. For that to happen, the SCO would be expected, in Nazarbayev's (2011a) words, to develop its "soft, 'smart' power," to prove itself "a potent and responsible global player" and, finally, to "convert its substantial potential into the real influence on world processes."

REFERENCES

Charter of the Shanghai Cooperation Organization (2002). Official Website of Russia's Presidency in the Shanghai Cooperation Organization 20142–015. Documents, http://en.sco-russia.ru/load/1013181846.

Donskikh, A. (2017). Genkonsul KNR v Almaty Zhang Wei: Idi s tem, s kem po puti. *Rossiiskaya gazeta*, special issue 7281 (115), May 29, https://rg.ru/2017/05/29/cumma-investicionnyh-proektov-kazahstana-i-kitaia-prevysila-70-mlrd.html

Eder, T.S., &Huotari, M. (2016:). Moscow's failed pivot to China. *Foreign Affairs*, April 17, https://www.foreignaffairs.com/articles/china/20160–41–7/moscow-s-failed-pivot-china

Herd, G. P. (2014). The "battle of ideas, concepts and geopolitical projects" in Central Asia: Implications for Russo-Chinese relations? In R.E. Kanet and R. Piet (Eds.), Shifting priorities in Russia's foreign and security policy (Burlington, VT: Ashgate), 1832–03.

Malashenko, A. (2013). The fight for influence: Russia in Central Asia. Washington, D.C.: Carnegie Endowment for International Peace.

Nazarbayev, N. (2011a). ShOS: Desiat' let istorii. *Rossiiskayagazeta*, 5495 (119), June 3, http://www.rg.ru/2011/06/03/nazarbaev.html

Nazarbayev, N. (2011b). ShOSnuzhnodokazat' svoiueffektivnost'. *Novosti-Kazakhstan*, July 14, http://www.newskaz.ru/comment/20110714/1693491.html

Press Service of the Ministry of Foreign Affairs of the Republic of Uzbekistan. (2013). Information Digest No. 182, September 17, http://www.elchixona.de/Ru/news/rpr_18091301.html

Prime Minister of the Republic of Kazakhstan (2016). Kazakhstan i Rossiya realizuyut bolee 60 proektov na 20 mlrd dollarov. October 4, 18:05, https://primeminister.kz/ru/news/mezhdunarodnie_otnosheniya/kazakhstan-i-rossiya-realizuut-bolee-60-proektov-na-20-mlrd-dollarov-13346

Putin, V.V. (2016). Interview to the Xinhua News Agency of China, June 23. President of Russia. Official Web Site, http://en.special.kremlin.ru/events/president/transcripts/52204

Romanova, M., & Devonshire-Ellis, C. (2016). China & Russia propose vast Eurasian free trade zone & SCO Development Bank. *China Briefing*, October 31, http://www.china-briefing.com/news/2016/10/31/42969.html

Rosstat (Federal State Statistics Service of the Russian Federation). (2014). Vneshniaiatorgovlia, http://www.gks.ru/wps/wcm/connect/rosstat_main/rosstat/ru/statistics/ftrade/#

Sovmestnoe zaiavlenie Rossiiskoi Federatsii i Kitaiskoi Narodnoi Respubliki o novom etape otnoshenii vseob'iemliushchego partnerstva i strategicheskogo vzaimodeistviia (2014). May 20, http://news.kremlin.ru/ref_notes/1642

TASS (2016). Russia-China trade rises by 0.5 percent in first 10 months of 2016. *Russia Beyond the Headlines*, November 8, http://rbth.com/news/2016/11/08/russia-china-trade-rises-by-05-percent-in-first-10-months-of-2016_645819

TopTJ.com (2016). Rashid Alimov: ShOS nuzhen mozgovoi tsentr po ekonomike. October 21, http://www.toptj.com/News/2016/10/21/rashid-alimov-shos-nuzhen-mozgovoy-centr-po-ekonomike

Xinhua. (2012). SCO progresses as new model of regional cooperation, not alliance. June 4, http://english.peopledaily.com.cn/90883/7835290.html

Xinhua. (2013). China-Central Asia trade accelerates. October 15, http://news.xinhuanet.com/english/china/2013–10/15/c_132801207.htm

Xinhua. (2014). China-Central Asia trade seeing fast growth. February 13, http://news.xinhuanet.com/english/china/2014–02/13/c_133112941.htm

Xinhua (2015). Full text of SCO prime ministers' statement on regional economic cooperation. Zhengzhou, Dec. 15, http://news.xinhuanet.com/english/20151–2/15/c_134920125.html

Chapter 8

Energy Infrastructure Policy and State Capacity in BRIC Countries

A Comparative Analysis

Carlos Henrique Santana

INTRODUCTION

The study of energy in BRIC countries involves not only an evaluation of the physical infrastructure but also financing and bureaucratic support as important determinants of state capacity. Infrastructure facilities demand large investments that usually exceed budget capacities and electoral cycles. Implementation depends less on the government's horizon and fundamentally more on bureaucratic structure and stable financing mechanisms. The comparative political economy literature has emphasized, in conceptual terms, the role of national finance structures and seeks to show the advantages from a system coordinated by state-owned banks' loans as a useful instrument to overcoming technology lags in production regimes (Gerschenkron 1962; Zysman 1994). Such studies have emphasized corporative governance in the institutional complementarities of domestic systems of financing, industrial and labor relations and innovation to describe certain trajectories of development. What this chapter argues is that there is certain commonalities in terms of the institutional domestic complementarities among BRIC countries and that, based on an analysis of the energy infrastructure of these countries, it is possible to observe a variety of coordinated capitalism in which the state acts prominently in at least three central aspects.

First, the pattern of financing coordinated by the credit of state-owned banks mobilized by levying either high premiums on savings and the export of energy commodities (as in the cases of Russia, China, and India) or treasury funds and para-fiscal funds (as in the case of Brazil);

Second, patterns of recruitment and career advancement in the bureaucracy. Among BRIC countries there is a tradition of governing bureaucracies.

151

However, there are important differences from the point of view of the scope and cohesion of their capacities. If based on meritocratic mechanisms, with stability and internal incentives of advancement, there is a reinforcement of the capacity in terms of pursuing long-term goals, producing corporative coherence capable of rendering high-risk and investment projects with more predictability, as in the case of infrastructure.

Third, coordination between the central government and sub-national spheres of government. The reorganization of fiscal and budget purviews among the different spheres of power implies that analyzing the institutional engineering of the relationship between the central government and the subnational levels of government is centrally important for a thorough understanding of energy management and investment policies in BRIC countries.

THE LEGACY OF MARKET-ORIENTED REFORMS AND ADOPTED REGULATORY FRAMEWORKS

Energy infrastructure was the focal point of the collapse and resumption of state capacity in Russia, heir to the soviet economic policy of gigantic monopolies controlling natural gas, coal, rail and power generation and transmission. However, in the beginning of the 1990s, the collapse of the Soviet regime led to rapid decentralization of the state's bureaucratic resources. Centralized control over territorial administration and finances became haphazard and unarticulated. Under Yeltsin [1991–1999], the central-to-regional chain of command was interrupted and bureaucratic-administrative resources were redistributed to local leaders. In contrast with other commodity exporting economies, as a result of post-Soviet economic policies, the ownership structure of the oil industry became diversified. The former ministry of oil was divided into a dozen independent companies, accentuating the intensity of political bargaining in Russia, vertically between the federal government and regional potentates, as well as horizontally, among rival companies (Ruthland 2008). The ensuing problems after the crumbling of the infrastructure were directly related to the disarray of the State. In addition to the fiscal and financial crisis, the country went through bureaucratic collapse that undermined long-term planning.

Yeltsin's privatization campaign kept in place the majority of infrastructure monopolies with a new legal status. The liberalization of prices in the Russian economy in 1992 did not affect the energy sector, whose prices remained under state control. At the same time, the electricity industry was converted into a state monopoly, the so-called Systems of Unified Energy (RAO UES). In parallel, seventy-two regional energy generation companies

(AO-Energos) were created, of which UES was the main stakeholder. The control over the price of electricity was transferred to the Regional Energy Commission (REKs), which were established in the majority of Russia's 89 federation after 1996. Gradually, however, in most regions control over decision-making of AO-Energos and the REKs by ended in the hands of regional governments.

The drastic and erratic introduction of market-oriented reform led to a dual economy: on the one hand, economic sectors with competitive market prices, and on the other, extensive sectors practicing prices regulated and controlled by the State, especially rents, transportation and energy. The government softened the impact of the transition to a market-based economy, ensuring cheap energy for industrial consumers and families. Despite the effort, by the end of the 1990s, the proportion of non-monetary commercial exchanges comprised 50 percent of all industrial transactions. However, the boom of energy commodity prices beginning in the 1990s and the regulatory and stakeholder reform structure of the gas and oil supply chain, carried out in the Putin administration [2000–2008], revived the State's fiscal capacity. Oil and gas, which together comprised 20 percent of all federal tax revenues in 2001, soared to 49 percent in 2011.[1]

In China, before the market-oriented reforms launched in 1978, the electric sector was organized as a vertically integrated State industry. In this first phase of reforms in the 1980s, the prevailing model was a bureaucratic structure embedded in a system of fragmented authority, in which bargaining, compromise and negotiation among the main ministries and provinces was fundamental for consensus and the implementation of the main policies. In 1987, the reforms to separate governmental functions from those associated with the companies were adopted after a gradual decentralization of the control exerted by the central government over the provinces, by means of a greater transfer of budget responsibility. Thus, the government was able to create a counterweight mechanism to central bureaucracy and thereby achieve market reform without changing the political system.

Decentralization and ascription to the market are typically linked to the undermining of the central government's authority to the benefit of local governments and business conglomerates in China. The restructuring of the economy in the 1980s and 1990s contributed toward a vast increase in unemployment and a drop in the state's capacity to collect tax revenues. The decline of government revenues (from 25.7 percent of the GDP in 1980 to 10.7 percent in 1995) was followed by overall growth of government expenditures. Between 1980 and 1996, the number of public servants grew from 2 to 3 percent of the population, and administrative expenditures increased from 5.5 percent to 13.1 percent of total spending.[2] At the same time, the government increased spending to coordinate decentralized governance.

It also tried to compensate the deficit reducing personnel in state enterprises. The number of jobs in these companies dropped significantly between 1993 and 1999, from 76.4 million to 47.3 million. In 1984, when the central party decided to cut personnel from the lower level of administration, the number of cadres directly controlled by the central party feel from 13,000 to 5,000, increasing the power of provinces in the administration of cadres. However, according to the literature, the capacity of the party-State to control and monitor its agents at the lowest level did not lose its momentum. The evaluation and monitoring of local leaders was reinforced in the 1990s through a system of accountability by a mechanism of rotating the bureaucracy between different administrative and geographical areas. This was reflected in the predominance of cadres from the center or other provinces in positions of party and provincial command, meaning that the central structure still coordinated centers of decision (Cheng 2004).

Despite the regionalization of economic policy implementation, the nucleus of the economic system remains socialist: state enterprises in strategic economic sectors, pyramid-shaped business groups controlled by State companies, and party committees retaining control over the commanding heights of the economy, delegating the rest to local political cadres. Despite the profound changes in the property structure, with the participation of state-owned companies in national industrial production falling from 75 percent in 1978 to 35 percent in 1995, these enterprises still have a major role as the main employer of the urban workforce and the greatest source of government revenue, as well as through the monopoly of the heavy industries that guarantee inputs for all other sectors of the economy, such as infrastructure (Huang 2008).

Market-oriented reforms in India also followed a pattern of decentralization. In 1978, the Indian economy was dominated by the public sector, which corresponded to 80 percent of all investment. Twenty years later, this sector comprised only 40 percent of total investment. Before 1991, the industry was under the supervision of the central government, through a detailed arrangement of licensing which regulated the investment of private enterprises. With the reforms initiated in 1990, India went through a deverticalization of its policy regime, through the abolition of the licensing regime known as the Raj. These changes contributed to the non-intentional decentralization of power and the increase of subnational authority, accompanied by more onerous budget demands on the states. The outcome of this process was a change in the pattern of competition among regional states: before liberalization it occurred vertically through the national State, afterward, states began competing horizontally against each other, employing party and/or bureaucratic strategy. In this context, the country's energy infrastructure was a strategic channel in shifting this pattern in policy decision-making arenas.

The fiscal crisis of the late 1980s also created political conditions for implementing electrical-sector reforms. In the course of the 1990s, central and state governments started to reorganize the sector based on the market, encouraged by a new paradigm of electricity that was oriented toward private property and the creation of competition-based markets instead of state monopolies. The reforms in India occurred in three steps: (1) the government stimulated private investment in energy generation; (2) in response to the low efficiency of the first initiative, it encouraged privatization in the distribution and formation of regulatory commissions; and (3) the enactment of Electricity Act in 2003, which reformulated the basic regulation and modified the institutional infrastructure of governance of the sector. Despite this, the electrical sector is dominated by vast state companies, both at the national and the state level: 86 percent of energy is produced by government-owned power plants (of which 60 percent belong to state governments) and the transmission grid is entirely state owned. Supplying, charging, and collecting is entirely a state responsibility, carried out through the State Electricity Boards (SEB).

The trajectory of reforms in the Brazilian electric sector is the object of intense debate in the literature (Sauer 2002; Santos et al 2006; Pires 2000). It is widely acknowledged that the public state monopoly in the energy industry was capable of expanding the energy supply more than six fold (500 percent) since 1973. Furthermore, the electric system is endowed with a complex grid that offers security and stability through various complementary matrices. In order to understand the reasons behind the reformulation of a successful model, one needs to return to the debt crisis of the late 1970s and its impact on the State's financing abilities, which became depleted. At the same time, state companies lost their capacities to expand the supply of energy, as tariffs were frozen as part of the inflation control policy of the 1980s.

The privatization of the Brazilian electrical system in the 1990s, as part of the solution to the fiscal crisis, introduced serious problems in terms of coordination within the system. The model adopted after the initial benchmark of the reform ushered in by the enactment of Law 8631 in 1993, and in 1995, year of the regulation of public service concession and the beginning of the privatization of the sector, represented an enormous impact on the electrical sector. The objectives of the reform were: 1) deverticalization of the industry, which made a distinction between certain monopolized sectors (transmission were to be regulated) and no monopolized (generation and commercialization) and 2) privatization and institution of a commercial model based on the competitive behavior of agents, in addition to 3) technical and economic regulation (independent) of the sector's activities. The creation of regulatory agencies did not guarantee a mechanism of cooperation. The first companies were privatized without specific norms on energy policy and regulation. In parallel, the state companies were kept from making new investments in generation. Agencies such as the ANEEL (National Electrical Energy Agency), the ANP (National Petroleum Agency) and the ANA (National Water Agency)—each one wielding prerogatives over crucial sources for the generation of energy, such as hydric resources and natural gas—could implement autonomous mandates that were not necessarily convergent.

The adoption of inflation stabilization plan (also known as Real Plan) put a break on the bargaining capacity of subnational spheres after 1994. During the course of the second half of the 1990s, governors lost several instruments of financial leverage, as in the case of the state banks and the energy distributors (which were privatized), while the federal government recovered its capacity to collect taxes and centralize revenues. However, this trend does not necessarily mean greater coordination capacity by Eletrobras (the major Brazilian state-owned electric energy enterprise), and neither an adequate investment policy geared toward energy infrastructure. The absence of coordination among the regulatory agencies and other decision-making arenas coupled with fiscal restrictions due to monetary policy determined a trajectory that resulted in under-investment that led to complications such as the shortages in 2001. From 1991 to 2000, energy demand grew at a pace of 4.1 percent per year, while supply only increased 3.3 percent. The Analysis Commission's own report on the Electrical Energy hydrothermal system, instituted by decree by then president Fernando Henrique Cardoso, acknowledges this deficiency of coordination in rather unequivocal terms.[3] The backdrop of these complications stemmed from the government's incapacity to organize an adequate regulatory arrangement and a reliable free market in the MAE, although it was able to thwart the coordination activities of Eletrobras. The transfer of functions from the GCOI (Group for the Coordinated Planning of the Electrical System), the creation of new rungs of decision such as the ANEEL and the ANA, in addition to the multiplication of rules and incomplete and conflicting legislation ultimately caused the Brazilian government to lose a unique interlocutor that held considerable coordination capacity (Goldenberg and Prado 2003).

BUREAUCRATIC STRUCTURE AND ITS MECHANISMS OF INTRA AND INTER GOVERNMENT COORDINATION

After the Yeltsin government [1991–1999], it was possible to observe a new shift toward centralization of the power in the policies adopted by Vladimir Putin. This policy is evident in the takeover by a state bureaucracy network over a set of companies and banks situated at the commanding heights of the Russian economy. Putin gradually tried to suppress all power contenders, concentrating all in the National State, restricting the institutional and economic capacity of regional authorities and strategic companies, especially those involved in infrastructure. To this end, Putin expanded the shareholder participation of the State in banks and companies, appointing central bureaucracy cadres to directors' boards and councils. Institutionally, Putin has centralized the federal structure of Russia, reducing the powers of regional governments through the restructuring of the upper house of the Russian parliament, assimilating political parties and factions in the Duma,[4] under the aegis of the Unity Party (created by the Kremlin), in addition to a selective campaign aimed at marginalizing oligarchs from the center of political power (Hashim 2005).

The Russian state has thus been undergoing a process of resuming its bureaucratic and fiscal capacity during the last decade. It is experimented a return of its capacities in the Putin period, benefited by the boom of oil prices. The clearest sign of this process was the increase of the number of federal public servants. During the Putin administration [2000–2010], the bureaucracy was expanded and federal employment increased up to 70 percent, reaching a total of 870 thousand employees.[5] This growth in the bureaucratic cadre has had two effects: (1) the increase of state capacity to investigate and legally persecute and (2) increasing difficulty in the control and coordination of a bureaucracy, which, by 2010, comprised 1.7 million cadres. Thus the main challenge of the regulatory system during the Putin years was not the creation of new functions, as in the 1990s, but in the rationalization, consolidation and utilization of this bureaucracy in order to increase the control over energy policies.

When Putin ascended to power he didn't have at his disposal a loyal and competent bureaucratic corpus capable of transforming his agenda into effective power, nor a system of command capable of generating the acquiescence of politicians, bureaucrats and business community. The absence of the communist party left a huge gap in the structure of command of the Russian state, which was substituted, in the Putin government, by the Federal Security Service (Федеральная служба безопасности Российской Федерации - FSB), which at the time was the most highly professional and disciplined organization left in the country. In addition to supervising governors and local offices, these cadres carried out the mission of reestablishing central power over local politics and the judicial apparatus (Reddaway and Orttung 2004). By employing the FSB's bureaucratic structure, Putin constructed a vertical chain of command (vertikal' vlasti), which, along with a parallel Executive Branch, permeates the new federal districts to a network of federal inspectors in the regions. To this end, the bureaucratic network, represented by the siloviki (servants originally from the security services) played a crucial role, occupying important posts in crucial areas of Russian infrastructure, as, for example, the energy supply complex, the military, transportation and communication (Kryshtanovskaya and White 2011).

The most recent investigations on the trajectory of veterans in the state bureaucracy between 1995 and 2004 and the biographies of the members of the council of directors and administrative groups of the twenty largest Russian companies, according to the capitalization of the market of 2009, reveal important traits. The vast majority of senior bureaucrats migrated to companies occupying the upper echelons, or the "commanding heights" of the Russian economy, in which the state placed a firm foothold during the Putin period. The most common destinations include banks and energy sector. In half of the cases, the ministries that went to the banks and to the RAO EES served as ministers in the corresponding fields, such as the Ministry of Finances for bankers or the Committee of Energy or the Ministry of Energy (Huskey 2010). This process has also been carefully detailed by the literature, which has demonstrated how the promotion of managers (menedzhery) at the expense of technical staff (energetiki) helped the Putin government to eliminate one of the main obstacles to his capacity to regulate the energy sector from the center: regional governors (Wengle 2012b).

In China, the limitation of the planned model of energy policy showed the clearest signs of exhaustion in the beginning of the 1980s, when national demand exceeded the system's supply capacity. The result was an energy shortage that lasted for years and created a serious bottleneck for economic development. The reforms of the electrical sector initiated in 1985 cleared the path to the generation of subnational investors, stimulating local governments to take credit and build their own plants. However, once again in 2002, China faced new shortages leading to rationing and blackout in 18 out of 31 provinces (Yeh and Lewis 2004). In this context, the domestic risk posed for the political system and the Chinese development model were momentous, and the need to ensure coordination among policies and institutions in charge of infrastructure became fundamental for the country's stability.

In this context, the training and formation a new generation of bureaucratic cadres played a crucial role. Until 1985, technocrats were all but absent in post within the subnational secretariat. Until 1996, twelve out of 22 members of the Politburo had engineering degrees, and by 2000 technocrats occupied up to 75 percent of the positions of command of the most important decision-making structures in China (Cheng 2000). The reconfiguration of the Chinese bureaucratic body is not unprecedented. This system has unique traits, based on the ancient tradition of the Imperial Civil Service: a civilian bureaucratic cadre premised on merit and internally competitive, capable of collecting and processing information in order to manage the economy. The party controls state company management bodies and appoints cadres for key positions. Promotions depend on balance between the performance of economic growth and loyalty to the party's hierarchy. One could assume that this configuration is fertile ground for the proliferation of corruption and economic dysfunction, dictated by rent seeking behavior (Pei 2016). However, there is also strong arguments that the systems succeed in being by and large meritocratic and that career advancements are based more on economic results than ideological loyalty (Landry 2008; Macgregor 2010).

Meanwhile, the economic bureaucracy was substantially modified, to the extent that regulatory authorities were instructed to suppress micro-managing and focus on the long term. The State Council concentrated its efforts toward constituting new administrative bodies for economic governance. In this context, the government has supervised the creation of large business conglomerates, promoting the fusion of smaller companies. The tenth Quinquenial Plan, approved by the 2001 Congress, stipulated not only that a large number of companies and business companies were to be developed, but also that they should have well-known brands, intellectual property rights and a well-defined business core. Furthermore, the plan stipulated that the three largest companies in each sector should be state-owned. The industrial companies of the most strategic sectors (as energy infrastructure) started being carefully supervised by the State Assets Supervision and Administration Commission, which became the proprietary agency (Pearson 2007; Naughton 2003).

Despite this seemingly promising scenario, the governance of the energy policy has presented a very low capacity of coordination: decentralization of the administration, production, and price-setting of energy policies in the course of reforms undermined the role of the central government in favor of local governments (Tsai 2011). Even within the powerful National Development and Reform Commission, the authority over energy policy is scattered among at least five departments, including the National Energy Administration, which, despite only being created to centralize policies, needs to bargain with all other ministry bureaucracies (Kong 2009).

Despite this scenario, China was able to reduce the intensity of energy by 19 percent between 2006 and 2010, and also became one of the countries in which there is the largest investment in the diversification of energy. This means that the country received a technological increment in energy-intensive sectors, increasing productivity. Nevertheless, it has become the largest oil importer in the world, surpassing the United States. China is currently the world's largest producer of hydroelectricity, while wind power is the second main source of renewable energy in the country. Despite these changes, problems of fragmentation still remain, as the country still does not possess a unified distribution system. This induces low cooperation among the companies, and in the absence of an integrated and secure system, as the one in place in Brazil. Although it is possible to point out that China has problems in terms of coordinating its energy policy, it was still able to implement a policy of investment and expansion of production above the average of other countries.

The Indian constitution defines electrical energy as a sector in which state and central governments have shared jurisdiction. While the central government is responsible for the sector's legislation, subnational governments are first and foremost responsible for implementation. As a result, institutions of the electrical sector get divided between the two spheres of power. Some were created by the Electricity Act of 1948, such as the SEBs and the Central Electricity Authority (CEA). The SEBs are the principal actors of the sector, responsible for the largest part of the generation and almost all the transmission and distribution. The CEA makes estimates of supply and demand at the national level and evaluates proposed energy projects. The central government later created the National Thermal Power Corporation (NTCP) and the National Hydro Power Corporation in 1975 in order to guarantee additional generation, and also became involved in transmission through the constitution of Powergrid India in 1989.

In the beginning of the 1990s, most SEBs provided heavily subsidized electrical energy for agriculture and residential consumers, and the majority of them was kept by state governments from increasing tariffs so as to compensate the elevation of production costs. While the price of coal and of transport for generating plants increased, SEB revenues remained stagnated. Considering this scenario, the deterioration of the technical and financial capacities of the SEBs become an underlying problem, accentuated by the incapacity to gage consumption and ensure final consumers were charged. During the 1990s, at the peak of the crisis losses with by distribution and transmission increased from 22.2 percent in 1996 to 29.9 percent in 2001. This has represented commercial losses that have reached 248,370 million rupees (or approximately US$ 5 billion) in 2001. At the same time, as the railway system and charcoal belonged to the central government, while generation is a state-level attribute, the costs of the SEBs incapacity to extract payment from consumers were also transferred to the central government, which began pushing for changes in the model of the electrical system in order to face the fiscal restriction the country was challenging.

The first initiative undertaken to overcome this scenario was stimulating private investors in the energy sector, through Interdependent Power Producers, with not too many substantial results. The second step of the reforms was to tackle the question of regulation, identified as the political interference of the SEBs, responsible for high subsidies and low revenues. The suggested solution was the privatization of the distribution and the creation of regulatory institutions, geared toward altering the relationship between the energy companies with consumers and among companies and state governments (Kale 2004). The objective was to subtract electoral issues from the governance of electricity. The privatization of the distribution companies occurred basically at the state level, and its scope ranged according to the relationship of power among economic and social actors in States. Some states completely privatized their distribution companies, others promoted deverticalization and divestment without the loss of control of the SEBs.

In order to "depoliticize" the SEBs the governments created autonomous tariffs institutions to regulate tariffs. The central government approved the Electricity Regulatory Commissions Act in 1998 and several states also anticipated themselves creating the State Electricity Regulatory Commissions. The critiques to the new model of regulation seem to suggest that it has not achieved its goals. The cozy relationship among the members of the Commission and the government seem to suggest that the tendency of capture for private or government interests is not completely absent (Phadke and Rajan 2003). The new electricity legislation of 2003 crowns a process of search that seeks to attract the private investor as a privileged actor in the investment agenda in the Indian electric sector (Haldea 2011). The 2003 Electricity Act maintained transmission within the scope of state companies, eliminated licensing requirements for generation, and introduced measures to face the financial and administrative problems of distribution companies by creating mechanisms to reduce energy from being stolen and the requirement that subsidies be paid from outside the state budget; it decentralized the responsibility for rural electrification; and introduced several measures to protect the consumer through the creation of grievance courts.

The self-financing capacity of the Brazilian electrical sector was intertwined with the federative dilemmas of its political system. Until the mid-1990s governors had a crucial role acting as the owners of local energy providers and stimulated not footing the bill for energy received from federal suppliers resulting in an institutional and financial crisis of the sector. In general terms, the process of democratization broadened the role of subnational spheres and its strategic actors, namely governors, in the decision-making process of the electrical energy policies: in addition to the political use of providers by governors, the reformulation of the federative pact of the 1988 Constitution extinguished the single tax, managed by Eletrobras, which was substituted by the ICMS, charged in electricity bills, administered by the states. The outcome of this process affected not only financially the companies of this sector, but also its bureaucratic structure. According to the literature, even technical groups in the sector began suffering strong political pressures and the departure of professional cadres (Rocha 2011).

Privatization opened up the infrastructure sector for private capital, but the regulatory model did not create specific mechanisms to enforce the goals and investments (Boschi and Lima 2002; Tankha 2009). The bureaucratic apparatus was substantially reduced the amount of public servants in 2010 was even lower than the number of staff in 1991. The collapse of infrastructure became evident in the energy breakdown in 2001. Infrastructure projects can face all sorts of challenges due to low bureaucratic qualification at the subnational levels (states and cities), with whom the Union must enter into agreements with in order to implement investments. This entails low capacity to elaborate projects and design plans, which associated with elevated licensing requirements, civil society participation and greater internal and external oversight, increasing substantially the cost and risk of investment and reinforcing mutual bureaucratic vetoes (Faro 2006).

FINANCIAL INVESTMENT MODEL

The trend of government centralization coincides with the strategies of development in the post-Soviet regime, which combine the planning tradition of the communist period associated with market forces. It is an agenda that seeks to integrate domestic actors and also staves off deindustrialization, unemployment and labor migration. The most recent literature emphasizes the State-business partnerships, has stressed that the important element in the trajectory of post-Soviet development and its dependence on the configuration between the State, new oligarchs, and Russian conglomerates. Unlike developing countries, highly dependent on foreign investment, in planned economies the stock markets were virtually non-existent when their economies were opened, which provided an enormous advantage. Thus the type of financial system which emerged from economies in transition is the result of path dependence, determined moreover by two factors: the chosen privatization market and the degree of bank concentration. In most post-communist countries, banks remained the most important financing resources (Popov 1999). Russian state banks expanded their market share from 30 percent to 53 percent between 2000 and 2010, increasing the degree of financial coordination of the Russian state. These institutions control the bond market for infrastructure debts, especially the three major banks: VTB, Vneshekonombank and Sberbank (Vernikov 2010). However, it is important to stress that most expenses with infrastructure financing in Russia originated from budget resources or from investments made by state-owned companies.

Considering the voucher scheme adopted in Russia did not achieve the same results as in other communist countries, as revenues collected from privatization were low, the role of banks stands out even more when compared to the stock market. It is also based on path dependence configuration that Putin is able to reorganize the alliance with the business community, championing as national promoters of development and benefiting them with all sort of state support and equipping them to compete internationally and at the same time to create jobs domestically. In other words, the centralization of the political economy has not led to the return of state property, as in the case of energy infrastructure (Wengle 2012). However, from a Polanyian perspective, the literature shows that the centralization of the Putin era and the limitation of the governors' influence over the energy sector was another key premise for the implementation of neo-liberal reform in order to create and regulate new markets. The Putin government needed to suppress its subnational competitors who, with oligarchs as allies, were the main threats to authority of the national State. It is also possible to affirm that the very takeover of the energetic infrastructure was crucial for the reestablishment of the Russian State's capacity, given that it constitutes the main source of fiscal revenue and was also where all local powers dared to challenge the sovereignty of the Russian national state.

The political economy literature on Russia fosters two kinds of narratives to explain the trajectory of post-Soviet changes: on the one hand, it classifies the national State as a predator and, on the other, as a hostage of powerful oligarchic interests. The limitations of these approaches have been gradually corrected by recent studies emphasizing that institutions in Russia are being built through mutually beneficial contracts between the government and a set of powerful economic actors, rather than simply imposed upon by a single actor. This consortium-oriented approach avoids the tendency to approach the Russian trajectory based on the polarization between predation and capture. Further literature of this intermediate approach also argues, for example, that the creation of fiscal institutions represent a negotiated arrangement between the Russian government and a more powerful set of economic actors—the oil companies (Jones Luong and Weinthal 2004).

Until 1978, the basic budget policy in China was known as *tongshon tongzhi* (in which the central government controlled all revenues and covered all costs). With the reforms on that year, this policy was dismantled, as state companies no longer had to transfer all profits to the central government, since local governments and state companies ceased to receive budget funding from the central government intended for infrastructure. After 1985, the local governments and state companies started loaning money from the central government to do so. This scenario explains the slow development of Chinese infrastructure during this period.

The reforms transferring greater budget responsibility to provinces consequently reduced the revenues of the central government, impacting on spending. Guided by a new pattern of accumulation, state companies lost investment incentives, while local governments had their tax collection and mobilization reduced with the dismantling of the popular communes. Given the scarcity of government revenue, the Chinese government chose to "confiscate" citizen savings and those of companies through financial institutions and by issuing government bonds as the main sources of public funds, channeling them through development banks to the development of infrastructure projects. Alongside the expansion of public debt, the government has opted for the broad commodification of the services infrastructure by means of the levying of user-taxer (Lin 2001; Keidel 2009). In parallel the change of perception of the Chinese regarding the reforms oriented toward the market, stimulated by the 2008 crisis, particularly benefited infrastructure. In 2009, the government announced a spending package of approximately US$ 586 billion, or 12 percent of the GDP intended for investment in the next two years.

In India, approximately, 85 percent of the exposition of the banking system for infrastructure is limited to public sector banks. Until the eleventh Quinquiennial Plan (2007–2012), while the public budget corresponded to 45 percent of the spending in infrastructure, commercial banks were the second largest source of financing for infrastructure with approximately 21 percent. Banking credit for infrastructure was at levels of approximately $72.4 billion Indian Rupees in 1999, but reached 7,860.5 billion Indian Rupees in 2012, an overwhelming high average yearly increase of 43.4 percent in the last thirteen years. For the sake of comparison, the growth of the volume of banking credit for all the Indian industry during the same period was 20.4 percent. The participation of bank funds in infrastructure in terms of overall available credit escalated from 1.63 percent in 2001 to 13.37 percent in 2013. Between 2008 and 2012 only the availability of credit for infrastructure increased more than threefold.

Besides the major share of public funds in infrastructure investment, the data of the eleventh Quinquennial Plan demonstrate an increase in the participation of private investment in infrastructure, especially in energy and telecommunications. This private investment—which doubled in relative terms—was responsible for an increase that made the figure for share of investment relative to GDP reach 8.53 percent during this period.[6] Alongside the banking sector, there are also other instruments such as the capital markets, mutual funds or non-banking-related financial companies. Between the eleventh and twelfth Quinquennial Plan, estimates concerning private sector participation in infrastructure should grow from 37 percent to approximately 48 percent. Considering all this information, one can hardly say that the lack of financing is a barrier for the development of the infrastructure sector in India (Chakrabarty 2013).

In the context of the abundant supply of financing sources, one of the instruments of coordination that the central government adopted to articulate the multiple regulatory layers was financing through banks and the budget. The scenario of financial restriction of the SEBs helps to explain how the central government exerts any degree of control over the electrical system, despite the fact the SEBs are state-level bodies. When States are in debt in relation to the central administration, article 293 of the Constitution requires that they obtain permission from the central government to borrow from the domestic market. At the same time, with the approval of the Central Electricity Regulatory Commission, the central government established goals based on a series of measurable investment results, through a new mechanism of financing: Accelerate Power Development and Reform Program (APDRP), which compensated states according to performance. The APDRP fund represented the sum of 35 billion rupees in the fiscal year 2002–3. Furthermore, the resources of public banks added another 35 billion. The resources surpassed short-term financing barriers, guaranteeing positive and negative incentives. The crucial point of the APDRP is the evaluation and classification of the performance of a series of indicators related to improvements in the distribution and transmission, installation of meters and institutional reform.

The figures relative to saving, investment and growth in Asia are distant from Brazilian reality. The rate of investment in Brazil is situated at approximately 18 percent of the GDP, while the average growth index between 1999 and 2008 stagnated at about 3.4 percent. Russia, India and China together grew approximately 6.9 percent, 7.1 percent and 10.1 percent, respectively, in the same period. In spite of this, Brazil has a developed bureaucratic structure and public banks (Loureiro; Abrucio; and Pacheco 2010; Cardoso Jr. 2011). However, since the implementation of the inflationary stabilization program (1994), the investment capacity from all levels of government was considerably limited due to the need to achieving elevated primary fiscal surpluses in order to service the public debt. This policy seriously affected not only new investment in infrastructure, but current accounts as well, which were rendered either contingent or detached.

Brazilian state-owned banks lost their shares in the total volume of credit—from 19.1 percent down to 8.6 percent of the GDP between 1995 and 2002. However, unlike all other BRIC members, the capacity of tributary extraction of the Brazilian Central State significantly increased in parallel with the control of public accounts, indicating that inter-bureaucratic fiscal coordination was sustained and perfected. This made a difference after 2006, when the fiscal restriction became more lax and Brazil stood out among the BRICs due to the scope and volume of its social expenses (Drezen and Sen 2011). Even after privatizations, the commanding heights of the economy, such as the public banks, were preserved. Although the banking system reduced credit offers from 34 to 23 percent of the GDP, between 1995 and 2003, public banks recovered credit capacity after 2003 and have resumed their role in adapting countercyclical measures, as seen in the 2008 crisis and today leads the offering of credits in the Brazilian banking system, with 21 percent of the GDP. The budgets sources, public banks and State companies are leaders in the provision of financing for the transportation, energy, sanitation, and housing in the last decade, segments that are labor and capital asset-intensive.

According to a survey, the BNDES (Brazilian Development Bank) and another public bank, Caixa Econômica, alone responded for 39 percent of the financing for infrastructure between 2010 and 2012. If we add up the contributions from other public banks, those guaranteed by the treasury, in addition to investment funds sponsored by public institutions, research estimates that the government is perhaps responsible for 65 percent of the investments made in infrastructure during the last three years (Frischtak and Davies 2014).

As the energy sector has a significant fiscal and monetary impact on public accounts, the federal government (under Rousseff's administration) has employed mechanisms of price control in order to coordinate the results of monetary policy and stimulate the cycles of investment. However, the impacts on the revenue of companies in charge of the sector, especially Petrobras and Eletrobras, have been negative, jeopardizing the long-term investments prospects. In order to maintain a trajectory of moderate tariffs that do not pressure inflation and at the same time allow the implementation of ambitious investment agenda, the National Treasury will have to make its own investment. Directly through the increase of capital or by backing debts indirectly by making loans to public banks that will flow into the system through subsidized credit (Castro et al. 2013). However, this is a model that has limits determined by the arrangement of confidence building of the monetary policy in tandem with the financial system, which has already shown alert signs relative to the level of public debt provoked by funds channeled from the treasury to public banks.[7]

Although the financial model which articulate the relations between the State and interest groups in the BRIC countries had asymmetries in terms of the coordination among strategic actors and bureaucratic cohesion, it is possible to highlight the experiences of these countries as well succeeded in terms of the role of the banking system for the transformation of the productive regime after World War II. Among these countries the prevalence of state-owned banks is absolute in the cases of India and China, while in Brazil and Russia there is greater ownership variety. The volume of resources invested by Russia, China and India in infrastructure has, on average, three times greater than in Brazil in terms of percentage of GDP. The lower dependence on the external savings has been one of the distinctive trajectories of development in Asian countries in relation to Latin America and characterize the differences in the degree of autonomy of the *policy* relative to the global restrictions experiences by national States (Kohli 2009).

CONCLUSION: THE COMPARED DIMENSION OF POLICIES

The discussion of the institutional changes related to the policies for energy infrastructure in each of the selected countries shows that there are common aspects associated with the loss of state capacity due implementing market-oriented reforms policies during the 1990s. The scale and intensity of this loss of capacity are related to the physical limitations of resources, the path dependence of the policies that preceded the market-oriented reforms, and the relationship between actors and institutions in the critical conjuncture that spurred the reforms described above in each country. In all BRIC countries, the exhaustion of the deregulation policies began in the 2000s and produced the effect of a recovery of state capacity through the return of a protagonist role for regulatory arenas of the central government in order to provide support for energy infrastructure policies.

Among the BRIC countries, Russia and Brazil, are the ones that detain the largest reserves of available energy. While Russia is one of the leading world exporters of gas and oil, it inherited a logistical infrastructure built during the Soviet period, Brazil rapidly was able and successfully achieved self-sufficiency in electric energy through investments made during the military regime in hydroelectric plants and in a distribution and transmission infrastructure nationally integrated that guaranteed a reasonable high level of security considering international standards. The legacy of these investments is what still sustains the recent trajectory of growth in the economies of both countries. The rupture of the regulatory pattern and of investment that created this model of energy infrastructure was caused by different reasons: the fiscal and inflationary crisis, as well as the debt crisis in Brazil exhausted the possibilities of State investment in the 1980s and found elective affinities with the neoliberal ideological program of deverticalization. One of the particular effects of this agenda in Brazil is that it not only elevated the costs of coordination, with the proliferation of regulatory arenas that were not capable of communicating, but also resulted in a massive elevation of energy tariffs, in a conjuncture in which no new investments were made and where the energy matrices is one of the cheapest. Unlike all the other members of the BRICs, where the energy tariff plays a complementary role to monetary and distributive policies, in Brazil this tool was cast aside in favor of permitting astronomical profits for distributing companies. In Russia, the political collapse of centralized planning system of the Soviet government, opened terrain for intergovernmental dispute. In order to overcome the resistances in the consolidated structure of the *nomenklatura*, the transition's political leadership (Yeltsin) weakened the mechanisms of inter-bureaucratic coordination and forged alliances with regional power leadership and emerging economic groups, delegating and fragmenting the authority of the central government. The impact of this process of the energy industry was decisive, not only because the State lost its regulatory capacity over the sector's policy, but also because it also resulted in a loss of tax revenues.

In the beginning of the 2000s, Brazil and Russia revised their energy policies and recovered the decision-making capacity of the central government. The Russian government carried out re-nationalization of the energy companies by converting fiscal debt into stock and reorganized the instrument of inter-bureaucratic coordination, promoting the centralization of decision-making mechanisms with immediate effects on the regulatory impacts over industry and energy. The practical effect of this process can be observed in the increase of bureaucratic cadres as well as in the expansion of the National State's tax revenue. In Brazil, the recovery of the central government's capacity of coordination over the energy infrastructure was one of the priorities in the new coalition started in 2003. The memory of the collapse of the energy supply in 2001 was still too alive, but the government did not promote a Russian-style stock restructuring in Brazil. The strategy was limited to attributing a greater role to the central administration in energy auctions and the creation of coordination arenas geared to articulate the different agencies in the sector. At the same time, the government took on the decision to stimulate the consortia that accelerated the agenda of construction of new hydroelectric power plants with the expressive influx of resources from pension funds and the BNDES. The bureaucratic obstacles that affected the implementation of this agenda were due to mutual vetoes by own Brazilian State branches particularly from judiciary system. These mutual vetoes will hardly be found in the Russian structure of government, where democracy is still affected by the high concentration of power in the Executive.

From the political point of view, India is closer to Brazil than to China. However, despite its status as a particularly dynamic democracy, the scale of social and macroeconomic dilemmas in India also serve as a comparison with China. The two countries had been going through a thirty-year long cycle of centralized organized planning and energy infrastructure was one of the crucial axes of this process. India and China are countries that depend on the import of inputs for its energy industry. India imports coal, on which the production of electrical energy relies. Although the majority of plants in China are also based on coal, the country is self-sufficient on this source, but diversified its energy matrix, becoming the world's largest oil importer. The energetic dependency of these countries is however a phenomenon occurring only in the last 30 years. The investments planned during the centralized phase of the communist period were capable of supplying the demand during this period of low economic growth in these countries. Deregulation in China stimulated mutual accountability between the central bureaucracy and provincial spheres. Decentralization's goal was to stimulate local leaderships to develop a policy of investment of their own in the construction of generating plants through the loans offered by Chinese state-owned development banks. At the same time the companies connected to the sector grew under the protection of this decentralized stimulus, the government found difficulties in establishing a coordinated structure capable of regulating the energy infrastructure. Despite the massive investments made, the country still faces energy insecurity due to problems of coordination and policy deliberation, since companies hardly become subordinated to regulatory structures formulated by government.

The decision-maker structure based on deliberation by consensus, associated with a pattern of fragmented authoritarianism, drives the economy but at the same time elevated the cost of coordination for the government. In India, the energy infrastructure is at the core of the country's federative dilemmas. Whereas the legal definition of the regulatory arrangement has been an attribution of the central government, the implementation of policies falls within subnational authority. The process of deregulation of the sector did not have the same impact on the remaining members of the BRCIs, but the legacy of the import substitution industry was sustained not only at the level of decision-making structure of the sector's policy, but also in the volume of losses that the system supports (approximately 25 percent). This is aggravated by the lack of an effective distribution grid. Although India elevated its capacity of energy production, this has not been done to the extent to compensate for the elevated demands for one of the societies with lowest per capita levels of consumption in the world. In order to overcome coordination problems, the central government has adopted credit incentives for states that meet the criteria for the formalization of the access to energy, yet successive interruptions and blackout show that there is still a long way to go.

NOTES

1. Sources: Goskomstat regarding oil export data and total export revenues and IMF and Ministry of Development for tax revenue data.
2. China Statistical Yearbook 2000, p. 255.
3. República Federativa do Brasil (2001) Relatório da Comissão de Análise do Sistema Hidrotérmico de Energia Elétrica, Brasília, Julho.
4. The Duma is the lower house of the Russian Federal Assembly. It is formed by 450 deputies, elected for four-year terms. It was created during the Russian Empire, but would be extinct in 1917. However, with the end of the Soviet Union, it was reestablished in 1993 by then president Boris Yeltsin after his political victory during the constitutional Crisis on the same year.
5. State Statistical Committe (Rosstat), considering the Executive, Legislative and Judicial branches, among which the Executive is the largest. Does not include the army and security services.
6. Deloitte/Assocham (2013) "Funding the Infrastructure Investiment Gap", March.
7. The threats to reduce risk classification of the Brazilian sovereign debt by international agencies, in addition to the critiques by multilateral organization, such as the

IMF, as well as "creative accounting" forced the former center left administration to partially realign itself with macroeconomic orthodoxy.

REFERENCES

Boschi, Renato and Maria Regina Lima (2002) O executivo e a construção do estado no Brasil—do desmonte da era Vargas ao novo intervencionismo regulatório. in *A democracia e os três poderes no Brasil*, Luiz W. Vianna (org). Rio de Janeiro/Belo Horizonte: IUPERJ/UFMG

Burns, John(2003) "Downsizing" the Chinese State: Government Retrenchment in the 1990s, *China Quarterly*, No. 175 (Sep), pp. 775–802

Cardoso Jr., José (Org) (2011) *Burocracia e Ocupação no Setor Público Brasileiro* (Vol 5 Diálogos para o Desenvolvimento), Rio de Janeiro: IPEA

Castro, Nivalde et al. (2013) "O Processo de Reestruturação do Setor Elétrico Brasileiro e os Impactos da MP 579", Texto de Discussão do Setor Elétrico nº 51 (Grupo de Estudos do Setor Elétrico IE-IFRJ)

Chakrabarty, K. C. (2013) "Infrastructure Financing by Banks in India: Myths and Realities", Reserve Bank of India (Annual Infrastruture Finance Conclave - Organised by SBI Capital Markets at Agra on August 9, 2013)

Cheng, Li (2000) Jiang Zemin Sucessors: the rise of the fourth Generation of Leaders in the PRC, *China Quarterly* Vol. 161, pp. 1–40

Cheng, Li (2004) Political Localism versus Institutional Restraints: Elite Recruitment in the Jiang Era, *Holding China Together: Diversity and Integration in the Post-Deng Era,* ed. Barry Naughton and Dali Yang, Cambridge University Press

Drezen, Jean and Armatya Sen (2011) Putting Growth In Its Place, *Outlook India*, 14 de Novembro 14, Acessado de http://www.outlookindia.com/article.aspx?278843

Faro, Luiz (2006) Adiado Amanhecer: O Brasil do Breu no Fim do Túnel, *Insight Inteligência*, n. 35, acessível em http://www.insightinteligencia.com.br/35/

Frischtak, Claudio and Katharina Davies (2014) O investimento privado em infraestrutura e seu financiamento. *Gargalos e soluções na infraestrutura de transportes*. Rio de Janeiro: Editora FGV

Gerschenkron, Alexander (1962) *Economic Backwardness in Historical Perspective*, Cambridge: Harvard University Press;

Goldenberg, José and Tadeu Prado (2003) Reforma e Crise do Setor Elétrico no Período FHC, *Tempo Social USP*, Novembro

Haldea, Gajendra (2011) *Infrastructure at Crossroads—the challenges of governance*, New Delhi: Oxford University Press

Hashim, S. Moshim (2005) Putin's etatization project and the limits of democratic reforms in Russia. *Communist and Post-Communist Studies*. Vol. 38/1, pp. 25–48

Huang, Yasheng (2008) *Capitalism with Chinese Characteristics—Entrepreneurship and the State*, New York: Cambridge University Press

Huskey, Eugene (2010) Pantouflage a la russe: The Recruitment of Russian Political and Business Elites, in Stephen Fortescue (ed.), *Russian Politics from Lenin to Putin: Essays* in Honour of T.H. Rigby, NY/London: Palgrave Macmillan

Jayme Jr, Frederico e Marco Crocco (orgs) (2010) *Bancos Públicos e Desenvolvimento*, Rio de Janeiro: IPEA

Jones Luong, Pauline and Erika Weinthal (2004) Contra coercion: Russian tax reform, exogenous shocks, and negotiated institutional change. *Am Polit Sci Rev*, Vol. 98, No.1, pp. 139–52.

Keidel, Albert (2009) China's Financial Sector: Contributions to Growth and Downside Risks, J.R. Barth et al. (eds.), *China's Emerging Financial Markets*, Santa Monica: Milken Institute.

Kong, Bo (2009) China's Energy Decision-Making: Becoming More like the United States? *Journal of Contemporary China*, Vol. 18, No. 62, pp. 789–812.

Kale, Sunila (2004) Current Reforms: The Politics of Policy Change in India's Electricity Sector, *Pacific Affairs*, Vol. 77, No. 3, pp. 467–491.

Kohli, Atul (2009) Nationalist Versus Dependent Capitalist Development: Alternate Pathways of Asia and Latin America in a Globalized World, *St Comp Int Dev*, Vol. 44, pp. 386–410

Kryshtanovskaya, Olga and Stephen White (2011) The Formation of Russia's Network Directorate, in *Russia as a Network State*, London: Palgrave Macmillan

Landry, Pierre (2008) *Decentralized Authoritarianism in China: the Communist Party's control of local elites in the post-Mao era*, Cambridge University Press

Lin, Shuangli (2001) Public Infrastructure Development in China, *Comparative Economic Studies*, Vol. XLiLL, no. 2, pp. 89–109.

Loureiro, Maria; Fernando Abrucio; and Regina Pacheco (2010) *Burocracia e Política no Brasil—desafios para o Estado Democrático no século XXI*, Rio de Janeiro: Editora FGV

Macgregor, Richard (2010) *The Party: The Secret World of China's Communist Rules,* New York: Harper-Collins.

Naughton, Barry (2003) The State Asset Commission: A Powerful New Government Body, *China Leadership Monitor*, Hoover Institution, Stanford University, No. 8

Pearson, Margaret (2007) Governing the Chinese Economy: Regulatory Reform in the Service of the State, *Public Administration Review*, July/August, pp. 718–30

Pei, Minxin (2016) *China's Crony Capitalism—The Dynamics of Regime Decay*, Cambridge, Mass. and London: Hardard University Press

Phadke, Amol and Sudhir Rajan (2003) Electricity Reforms in India- not too late to go back to the Drawing Board, *Economic and Political Weekly*, July 19.

Pires, José Cláudio (2000) Desafios da Reestruturação do Setor Elétrico Brasileiro, Textos para Discussão 76, Rio de Janeiro: BNDES.

Popov, Vladimir (1999) The Financial System in Russia Compared to Other Transition Economies: The Anglo-American Versus the German-Japanese Model, *Comparative Economic Studies*, Vol. 41, No. 1, pp. 1–42.

Reddaway Peter and Robert Orttung (eds) 2004 *The Dynamics of Russian Politics: Putin's Reform of Federal-Regional Relations* (Lanham, MD: Rowman and Littlefield)

Rocha, Thadeu (2011) Estado, Mercado e Burocracia no Setor Elétrico: trajetória e perspectivas das centrais elétricas brasileiras S/A (1954–2010), Dissertação de mestrado do programa de pós graduação em Ciência Política da UFF

Ruthland, Peter (2008) Putin's Economic Record: is the Oil Boom Sustainable? *Europe-asia Studies*, Vol. 60, No. 6, pp. 1051–1072

Santos, Gustavo et al (2006) Por que as Tarifas foram para os Céus? Propostas para o setor Elétrico Brasileiro, *Revista do BNDES*, Vol. 14, No. 29, pp. 435–74

Sauer, Ildo (2002) Um Novo Modelo para o Setor Elétrico Brasileiro, São Paulo: (Programa Interunidades de Pós-Graduação em Energia- USP);

Tankha, Sunil (2009) Lost in Translation: Interpreting the Failure of Privatisation in the Brazilian Electric Power Industry, *Journal of Latin American Studies*, Vol. 41, No. 1 (Feb., 2009), pp. 59–90

Tsai, Chung-Min (2011) The Reform Paradox and Regulatory Dilemma in China's Electricity Industry, *Asian Survey*, Vol. 51, No. 3 (May/June 2011), pp. 520–539

Vernikov, Andrei (2010) "Direct and Indirect State Ownership on Banks in Russia", MPRA Paper No. 21373, (11th International Conference of ASPE -Association for Studies in Public Economics), St.-Petersburg, March

Wengle, Susanne (2012a) Post-Soviet Developmentalism and the Political Economy of Russia's Eletricity Sector Liberalization, *St Comp Int Dev*, Vol. 47, pp. 75–114

Wengle, Susanne (2012b) Engineers versus managers: experts, market-making and state-building in Putin's Rússia, *Economy and Society*, Vol. 41, No. 3, pp. 435–467

Yeh, Emily and Joanna Lewis (2004) State Power and the Logic of Reform in China's Electricity Sector, *Pacific Affairs*, Vol. 77, No. 3, pp. 437–65

Zysman, John (1994) How Institutions Create Historically Rooted Trajectories of Growth, *Industrial and Corporate Change*, V.

Chapter 9

The BRICS' New Development Bank

Its Potential Implications to International Political Economy[1]

Shigehisa Kasahara

On July 15, 2014, a group of emerging market economies known as "BRICS"—a new multilateral financial institution created by five emerging economies (Brazil, Russia, India, China and South Africa)—signed *The Agreement of the Establishment on the New Development Bank* (NDB) for financing development projects in emerging and developing countries. This was done at the Heads of State meeting (Summit) of the BRICS members, which can be epitomized as an anti-hegemonic, Southern coalition, held in Fortaleza, Brazil. Claiming to represent the interest of the Global South, the BRICS members have been vocal about the need of reforming the existing international economic order. They have been expressing historical grievances regarding the persistent status of under-representation of the global South in general and of their own in particular, in the international policy space and decision-making (Qobo and Soko, 2015, p. 278). In this regard, the establishment of the NDB can be seen as a sign of promoting "financial multi-polarity," via decentralizing and fragmenting the existing international order (Huotari and Hanemann, 2014, p. 298). To some observers, the new institution may appear to be a harbinger of a new order where these emerging powers advance their own agenda (Griffith-Jones, 2014).

The new institution, as a supplement to the existing ones, will certainly contribute to meeting the existing need of infrastructure financing in developing countries. But we still face a political question, which have seemingly failed to draw much attention, about the BRICS members' strategic intentions. It is obviously naïve to assume that these emerging economies have created this new institution out of their humanitarian interest to meet the needs of Southern partners. We are aware that these emerging economies have long been frustrated by the slow process to raise their influence within the existing institutions and processes of global governance. But it is still unclear whether this new institution does mean that the BRICS members are interested in dismantling the existing institutions and processes altogether.

Given that its past performance is virtually non-existent and its future function hinges on many unforeseeable factors, *long-term* speculation on the NDB is an adventurous exercise, if not a hazardous conjecture. However, this does not prevent us from considering relatively *short-term*, potential implications of the NDB to international political economy, or more specifically on the governance of development cooperation. The rest of this chapter deals with three broad substantive issue areas. First, we introduce major elements embedded in the Articles of Agreement (the NDB Agreement) adopted in 2014, and then discuss immediate implications of these elements. Second, we then, as an extension of the previous section, consider scenarios of the NDB's institutional and operational evolution in the foreseeable future. Third, we contemplate potential implications of the NDB's operation to international political economy, particularly development cooperation.

THE NDB AGREEMENT: MAJOR ELEMENTS AND THEIR IMMEDIATE IMPLICATIONS

The ratification of the NDB Agreement by each of the five founding members' legislative bodies—which had occurred by March 2015—led to the eventual establishment of the new institution, in the wake of the 2015 Summit (Ufa, Russia). With the Headquarters Agreement with the Chinese government as well as the Memorandum of Understanding with the Shanghai municipal government in February 2016, the NDB became fully operational (NDB, 2016d).[2] The new institution was a clear manifestation of these emerging economies' commitment toward greater institutionalization of the BRICS process. Although the NDB started with the BRICS founders for financing their infrastructure and development projects, it is expected that its membership and financing activity will expand beyond the initial scope. Meanwhile, in public scenes, the BRICS members have been at pains to stress that the NDB is intended to "complement" rather than "supplant" existing multilateral financial institutions.

Since the adoption of the NDB Agreement, the BRICS members have worked out on many details—in numerous "policy documents" (something like bylaws) uploaded in the NDB's webpage—in order to cope with concrete operational issues. One impression we may have after reading the NDB Agreement is that the new institution resembles, rather than differs much from, many existing multilateral and regional financial institutions, particularly the World Bank. Indeed, the World Bank has presented a classic prototype template for many other institutions, including the NDB, to emulate (see Humphrey, 2014, 2015, 2016). A case in point is the structure of capital subscription, the combination of paid-in capital (20 percent) and callablecapital (80 percent) (Art.7-c).[3] (See further discussion below.) But the intra-BRICS egalitarian principle, as institutionalized throughout its governance structure, gives the NDB a "democratic flavour," and this aspect is not necessarily shared by many other multilateral and regional financial institutions (Wang, 2016, p. 8).

Purposes and Functions

The NDB Agreement states that the main purposes and functions of the new institution are: to finance infrastructure and sustainable development projects in the BRICS members and other emerging and developing economies (Art. 2) through loans, guarantees, equity participation and other financial instruments (Art. 3-b) in collaboration with international organizations and other financial entities (Art. 2-b). Thus, the NDB aims at forging partnerships with national and regional development banks as well as the World Bank group, in co-financing activities in the private and public sectors.

Some may hope that the emphasis of the NDB's financing on infrastructure projects, with direct linkages to economic development, is likely to compensate, if not to reverse, the recent general trend of multilateral and regional financial institutions that have emphasized austerity policies (structural adjustment programs) along the Washington Consensus line, at the cost of infrastructure development projects.[4] It is anticipated, therefore, the NDB will focus on microeconomic project-sustainability of individual projects whereas traditional bilateral and multilateral donors pay much greater attention to macroeconomic debt-sustainability of the borrower economies.

Membership

As mentioned earlier, the NDB began with the membership—which entails capital contribution by purchasing its shares (Art. 8-a)—of the five BRICS founders (Art. 5-a); however, its membership is open to the UN member countries. They can join the NDB as either borrowers (emerging and developing countries) or non-borrowers (developed countries) (Art. 5-b, 5-c). It is expected that some emerging economy members—most of all, the BRICS members—will be borrowers and lenders. While in principle borrowers ought to be members as a prerequisite to get access to the NDB's funding, non-members in certain situations may receive the special authorization from the NDB to get access to its funding (Art. 19-d, 19-e). While it is not totally clear, non-borrower countries without formal NDB membership can offer their capital markets for the NDB's bond-issuing activities. In this regard, the

NDB Agreement states that the NDB is empowered "to borrow funds from member countries or *elsewhere*" (Art. 26-a).

Governance Structure

The governance structure of the NDB consists of a Board of Governors, a Board of Directors, a President, Vice Presidents as decided by the Board of Governors, and other officers and staff (Art. 10). The Board of Governors, the supreme body of the NDB's governance structure (Art. 11-i), is represented by all of the member countries at Ministerial level (Art.11-a), and makes decisions on those matters that are most important to the institution, such as the admission of new members, the size of capital stock, and others (Art. 11-b), through an annual meeting and other meetings (Art. 11-c). The Board of Directors, responsible for the general conduct of the overall operation of the NDB (Art. 12-a), performs functions delegated by the Board of Governors. The Board of Directors is a non-resident body which meets quarterly, but the Board of Governors in the future may decide to make it a resident body (Art.12-g). The president, the chief manager of the NDB's daily operation (Art. 13-b) without a voting right at the Board of Governors except the casting vote (Art.13-a), is chosen from the BRICS members on a rotation basis (Art. 13-a).

At the outset, the NDB has the Board of Governors consisting of the political representatives of the five founding members, the BRICS Ministers. The Board of Directors starts with five seats, one each for the BRICS members, and the seats are allowed to be increased up to 10 as a result of new membership (Art. 12-b). The posts of four vice presidents (and possibly more in the future) are occupied by each of the BRICS members that are not represented as president (Art. 13-c). In the future, the Board of Governors may increase the number of Vice-Presidents (Art. 11-b-ix) as a result of new membership.

The concrete details of personnel matters of the NDB that have been agreed on for the initial years are as follows: the initial chair of the Board of Governors is Russian; the initial chair of the Board of Directors is Brazilian (for four years); the first president of the Bank is Indian (exceptionally for six years for the first president, or for five years for the second president and thereafter) (Art. 13-d).

Voting Power

The governing structure of the NDB has much to do with the distribution of voting power among its members. The voting power of the member countries at the Board of Governors and the Board of Directors is proportional to their subscribed capital shares (Art. 6-a). As mentioned earlier, at the time of the commencement of the NDB, the five founding members are entitled with the same voting power (20 percent each) concomitant with their subscribed capital (see the discussion on the NDB's capital below). Whereas institutional decisions normally require a simple majority of the cast votes, those of special importance require an affirmative vote of two-thirds of the total voting power of the member countries including that of four of the BRICS members (Art. 6-b).

The membership expansion beyond the BRICS founders will bear some implications for institutional governance: namely, the dilution of their voting power as a group, if not the diversion from intra-BRICS egalitarianism. The NDB Agreement contains some safeguard provisions for the BRICS members' voting power: i) the voting power of the BRICS members as a group will remain above 55 percent of the total voting power regardless of additions of new members (Art.8-c-i); ii) the voting power of the non-borrowing members, presumably developed countries, as a group cannot exceed 20 percent of the total voting power (Art. 8-c-ii); and iii) the voting power of any single non-BRICS member cannot exceed 7 percent of the total voting power (Art. 8-c-iii).

One impression on the NDB's governance structure as well as the distribution of voting power among its members is that the BRICS founders have made the new institution's structure fairly flexible to accommodate new members while firmly guarding their pivotal position. Yet, the non-borrowers will individually and collectively remain minor importance with a limited voting power. While it does not seem imminent, the following situation is a possibility. If new membership is judged to threaten the 55 percent majority threshold of the BRICS members, then the NDB will have to consider either new members' applications (including the size of their shares), or the increase of the founders' shares.

Capital

The NDB starts with an initial authorized capital of US$100 billion, of which the total subscribed capital for the BRICS members is US$50 billion (Art. 7-a, 7-c). The headspace of US$50 billion beyond the initially subscribed capital will allow the BRICS founders as well as future members (including borrower and non-borrower countries)—without obliging the Board of Governors to amend the NDB Agreement—to subscribe to additional capital shares (Art. 7-b). We understand from various writings (see, for instance, Cooper, 2016; Cooper and Farooq, 2015) that the size of the NDB's capital base was heavily debated. On the one hand, China supported the modality of capital contribution based on members' financial capacity and a large capital base for the NDB. On the other hand, India supported the modality of relatively small and equal contributions of the founding members with a capital base of a relatively modest size for the new organization (Cooper and Farooq, 2015, p.36).[5] Brazil supported India's proposal throughout, where Russia shifted its support from India's proposal to China's. At the end of negotiations, India's proposal of egalitarian division of capital contribution prevailed.

Thus, the total subscribed capital for the BRICS founders—US$50 Billion—is divided equally into five, that is, each with US$ 10 billion. Whether the individual contribution of US$10 billion is large or modest is a delicate question. Whereas US$10 billion is certainly a small amount for China that has accumulated a vast size of foreign reserves (more than US$3 trillion), it presents a serious test for South Africa, as it amounts to 2.5 percent of its GDP (Cooper, 2016, p. 74). Some observers speculate that China will eventually (and perhaps discreetly) cover, in one way or another, part of the initial and additional capital subscriptions of other members with much smaller foreign reserves (Cooper and Farooq, 2015, p. 36).[6]

Individual BRICS member's subscribed capital of US$10 billon is further divided into US$2 billion in "paid-in capital" and US$8 billion in "callable capital" (Art. 7-c). Each member is expected to make the paid-in capital (US$2 billion) in seven installments over time. The specific sizes of the installments are: US$150 million, US$250 million, US$300 million, US$300 million, US$300 million, US$350 million and US$350 million. The first payment is expected within six months after entry into force of the NDB Agreement. The second will become due 18 months from the entry into force of the NDB Agreement. Each of the remaining five will become due successively one year from the date on which the preceding one becomes due (Art. 9-a). In short, therefore, the completion of the payments of the pay-in capital will require a period of about 7 years. As shall be discussed, the total amount the NDB received from the subscribed paid-in capital does not immediately affect the amount of its lending, however.

BRICS members' callable capital (initially, US$8 billion each, and US$40 billion in total) is a sort of financial commitment, or the government guarantee that is subject to call only when the NDB must meet obligations incurred on borrowing funds for lending (Art.9-c), and thus it does not entail actual payment (Art. 9-b). The NDB Agreement stipulates that "calls on unpaid subscription," that is, the actual payment of some portion of callable capital, "will be uniform among the member countries in terms of percentage on callable capital" (Art.9-d).

The Board of Governors can decide not only to increase the authorized capital stock but also to alter the proportion between paid-in capital and callable capital; however, no member countries are obliged to subscribe to any part of such increased capital (Art. 7-c). The Board of Governors is also responsible for reviewing the NDB's authorized capital at a 5-year interval or less (Art. 7-e). As mentioned earlier, the NDB's authorized total capital at the initial stage has the headspace of US$50 billion beyond the subscribed capital of US$50 billion (that has already been allocated among the BRICS founders), the new institution can raise the capital base without amending its Agreement.

Judging from other multilateral institutions, we safely state that the paid-in capital will be used to cover the sink costs for organizational build-up and associated administrative costs of the new institution, rather than directly allocated to finance development projects. According to NDB Press Release (NDB, 2016a), each of the BRICS members made the first installment or tranche of US$150 million for paid-in capital subscription, totaling US$750 million in January 2016. And some of them have already made the second payment, as of this writing (March 2017). Clearly, the NDB will hold a relatively meager amount of cash on hand for initial organizational build-up and administrative costs. It will certainly have to wait some time before reaching the position to generate any operational profits[7] and recycle them. Of course, it is easily anticipated that China (as well as its Shanghai municipality), as the wealthy host country (city) of the new institution, will provide sizable financial contributions separately to supplement the NDB's available funds to cover organizational build-up and administrative costs.

Borrowing

The vast majority of multilateral financial institutions have raised their long-term loanable funds by borrowing from international capital markets, by issuing bonds, against the collateral of their subscribed capital stock (paid-in capital and callable capital) as well as retained profit earnings/reserves from past operational profits (Humphrey, 2014; Kapur and Raychaudhuri, 2014; Mason and Asher, 1973; Nelson, 2013).[8] In this regard, the NDB is not much different from these institutions (see Art. 26-a, b, c).The NDB Agreement states: "The total amount outstanding in respect to the ordinary operations of the Bank shall not at any time exceed the total amount of its unimpaired subscribed capital, reserves and surplus included in its ordinary capital resources" (Art. 20-a). Thus, the statutory limit on its "gearing ratio" is set at 100 percent, which means, in other words, that the maximum lending level cannot initially exceed the total subscribed capital of US$50 billion.

Let us reiterate the key point: With no capital reserves or surplus at the outset of its operation, the NDB, in theory, is authorized to borrow up to US$50 billion and lend out by the same amount. As the remaining "unsubscribed" US$50 billion of the total authorized capital becomes subscribed in due course by the BRICS founders and new members, the amount of borrowing (and thus total lending) by the NDB can rise up to US$100 billion (and possibly more, if profits should be made from past loans meanwhile) without amending its Agreement. Again, it is possible to anticipate that some of the BRICS founders (particularly China) may make miscellaneous contributions, additionally and separately from their paid-in capital subscription. On the other hand, we must also remember that NDB's paid-in capital may or may not decline as a result of its use for organizational build-up and administrative costs as well as a result of its use for portfolio investment.

Whether the NDB can borrow such large amounts at reasonably low interest rates as well as find development projects to finance, however, is another question. (See the next section for the potential loaning capacity of the NDB.) At any rate, regardless of the statutory limit, the NDB may not be driven to borrow so much of funds if not many financially viable projects are proposed.

FUTURE PROSPECTS: INSTITUTIONAL & OPERATIONAL ELEMENTS

Given the recent slowdown on the global scale (including the BRICS members), it is still not clear whether the recent emergence of the NDB and other new multilateral institutions reflects a long-term trend or an ephemeral phenomenon in the state of the world economy.[9] Let us identify and discuss some pertinent issues—which are undoubtedly inter-related—that the NDB is likely to face in the foreseeable future, namely A) membership, B) credit rating, C) lending activities, D) loans to the private sector, and E) concessional loans and grants.

Membership

The NDB began with the BRICS members, even though several countries reportedly had expressed their wish to join the new institution (Shubin, 2013, p. 42). Unlike the case of the Asian Infrastructure Investment Bank (AIIB), the five founding countries of the NDB have refrained from openly soliciting non-BRIC membership.[10] To a certain extent, the membership expansion is closely related to the performance of the NDB. The founding members have so far limited the NDB's activities in the area of co-financing with their national development banks for their own domestic infrastructure projects (see Spratt and Baron, 2015). It is anticipated that the BRICS members will in due course call for new memberships. After all, the excessive preoccupation with intra-BRICS projects will dampen potential members' enthusiasm toward the new institution. Meanwhile, the NDB must make its activities demonstratively attractive to draw new members, since no countries will be attracted to a nonstarter. The larger-scale operation resulting from the growth of membership will also make the NDB's activities more visible and possibly more effective, since larger membership makes its governance process more inclusive.

It is interesting to consider which groups of countries—non-BRICS emerging economies (as borrowers and non-borrowers), developing countries (as borrowers), and developed countries (as non-borrowers)—will be the priority candidates as new members. It could be argued that the NDB's campaign for new membership may initially target at other emerging economies and developing countries over developed countries, as the former groups will likely to consolidate its pro-South solidarity vis-à-vis traditional financial institutions. Between non-BRICS emerging economies and developing countries, the priority may lie in the former group (such as Argentina, Indonesia, Malaysia, Mexico, Turkey, etc.). This is because in comparison with others in the global South, they can provide the NDB with larger capital contributions, less risky investment opportunities and more reliable capital markets. Non-BRICS emerging economies themselves may find that membership in the NDB will raise their own investment opportunities domestically and internationally.

Many low-income developing countries can also provide investment opportunities. But the BRICS members may not share the same view regarding which countries should be accepted as new members. One observer points out that China and South Africa are particularly interested in opening up the client base to new members, whereas India and Brazil prefer a more concentrated focus within the BRICS members (Cooper, 2016, p. 76). Given the media coverage often highlighting the likelihood that the new institution will be less stringent in its loan conditionalities, potential borrower countries may find the new institution more attractive than traditional bilateral and multilateral institutions. Some observers, however, are more cautious, arguing that this may not be the case (see Bond, 2013, 2016; Taylor, 2014).

As mentioned earlier, technically speaking, non-member countries, in exceptional cases, may still obtain funding from the NDB without prior membership. Nevertheless, given that formal membership eases the project evaluation and financing process, the BRICS members are likely—again with different degrees of eagerness—to solicit new membership. In any case, the formal membership of these countries will also help them participate in the NDB's governance process as well as increase its capital base (Griffith-Jones, 2014, p.13).

Unlike the case of the AIIB, no traditional donor countries (OECD members) have openly indicated their intention to participate as non-borrower members in the NDB. The BRICS founders (and future borrower members) may feel that the participation of non-borrower countries should be welcome because it will immediately augment its capital base and raise the possibility for the NDB to improve its access to international capital markets.[11] Whereas the membership growth with non-borrower countries, even as minority stakeholders, is also likely to raise the new institution's credit rating, it will dilute the ideational foundation of the NDB as an institution of South-South cooperation. But non-borrower countries may consider that they should not harry to join the NDB, preferring to take a wait-and-see stance. Many of developed countries have already joined the newly established AIID, and they may prefer to monitor its performance to judge whether they should join another similar institution.

Credit Rating

The most critical factor that will determine the capacity of a multilateral development bank in raising loanable funds is its credit rating, which is determined by the market's perception of its creditworthiness.[12] The issue of credit rating proves to be particularly pertinent when we look at the ratings of the individual BRICS members which, except China, have not enjoyed a high rating, to say the least.[13] The NDB can improve its rating over time, but this will happen only after some good track record, at least a decade of solid operation (Humphrey, 2015, p. 18). One clear implication of a low credit rating is the relatively high funding costs, which makes it face some difficulties in attracting loan demands. This, in turn, may oblige the new institution to reduce its lending spread (i.e., the margin between the cost of funding and the terms at which it make loans) (Humphrey 2015, p. 18).

It is easy to imagine that the NDB will not be able to compete with the other long-standing multilateral financial institutions in fund-raising capacity (and thus competitive loaning) unless it takes advantage of its privileged access to financial resources other than international capital markets, such as Sovereign Wealth Funds, which may be less dependent on the rating of well-established credit rating agencies.[14] Otherwise, international investors will expect that the new institution will follow prudent operation in order to ensure sustained operation. Again, the likelihood that membership expansion—including traditional donors—will raise the NDB's credit rating is a particularly pertinent matter as long as the new institution remains too new to demonstrate a credible track record.

Lending Activities

The time-consuming process of its institutional building is likely to keep the NDB as a virtual bank for some time, that is, a network of BRICS's national development banks, which may mean that the NDB will remain an artificial figurehead for these national development banks. At any rate, the NDB will likely prioritize high-quality loans for its funding members in order to minimize the risk of default. Indeed, the BRICS members must be aware of the potential implications of their new institution's performance on its credit rating, which, in turn, will affect the costs of its borrowing and the generation of profit levels necessary to support future lending (Griffith-Jones, 2014, p. 8). Yet, excess preoccupation of this kind may seriously constrain lending particularly to poorer countries, which will add to the possibility of tension and discontents among would-be borrowers. This is the dilemma that the NDB may be confronted with.

Some developing countries may expect that in the name of South South cooperation, the NDB—as an alternative institution to the existing multilateral and regional banks—will make "faster, simpler and cheaper" disbursement of loans. In this regard, the new institution, being a small entity at the outset, is likely to impose far less bureaucratic red-tape and possibly shorter loan approval processes than many existing institutions. The NDB may also conscientiously endeavor to come up with a novel, more flexible approach to avoid the negative associations with "old" conditionalities. If it should successfully achieve this, then the new institution's popularity will surely rise among would-be borrower countries. It is expected that as the NDB expands its operation, its membership is likely to expand by attracting non-BRIC developing countries. The NDB Agreement encourages the diversification of its activities, stating, among others: "The Bank shall seek to maintain reasonable diversification in all of its investments" (Art 21-c).

The NDB's loans are purportedly free of a strong dosage of political conditions, certainly those related to institutional reforms for augmenting good governance, promoting human rights, and preventing corruption in developing countries. However, as the NDB increasingly co-finances with other institutions (beyond the BRICS's national development banks) and raises its loanable funds widely (and cheaply) from international capital markets beyond the BRICS members, it will follow conventional international banking standards, "sound banking standards principles" (Art. 21-a). Thus, even if the new institution is willing to take those "higher" risks, its loan contracts are likely to contain "prudential conditionality" provisions to ensure that loans are used purposely and rapidly. This means that the NDB will be obliged to impose similar efforts—of project-specific microeconomic conditionalities—on the part of borrower countries, just as existing multilateral and regional development banks have practiced. Let us note that the NDB has signed Memorandums of Understanding with many national and international financial institutions. These memorandums highlight potential common areas of interest, not only exploring and pursing opportunities for co-financing projects but also facilitating knowledge exchange, staff secondment and exchange (see, for example, NDB, 2016c; 2016d; 2016e, 2016g).

Griffith-Jones (2014) had ventured into estimating possible scenarios of loaning activities of the NDB. She made her estimates based on a few assumptions, such as the total *subscribed* capital of US$100 billion (consisting of 20 percent in paid-in capital and 80 percent callable capital, as done for the BRICS founders) already at the initial stage, as well as the loan-equity leverage ratio—the ratio of the outstanding loans against the total paid-in capital (US$20 billion) with retained profit earnings and other reserves—of 240 percent. These assumptions, according to Griffith-Jones, would bring forth lending (with average maturity of ten years) of about US$5 billion per year during the first 10 years, and US$7 billion annually thereafter. These figures show an extremely large size of lending by a new institution. Let us note that the total "subscribed" capital likely remaining at US$50 billion instead of reaching US$100 billion in the near future. Therefore, these figures will prove to be overestimations, unless new members (with large financial capacities) should quickly join the institutes.

Reisen (2015) estimates that how large the NDB's loan portfolio will be when the payments of BRICS members' pay-in capital are completed, that is, when the total of US$10 billion (US$2 billion x 5) is actually paid up. Given that the World Bank has the US$14 billion paid-in capital against the total loan stock of US$152 billion (as of March 2015), and assuming that the NDB can reach the World Bank's loan-capital leverage ratio of 10.9, Reisen states that the NDB after seven years of its operation will potentially have the loan portfolio of US$109 billion (US$10 billion x 10.9) against the World Bank's US$152 billion. Amazingly, this implies that the NDB's loan stock will potentially reach about two-thirds of the World Bank's. This also means that the average net accumulation of loan stock of US$14 billion per year over seven years! He optimistically—or unrealistically—concludes that the NDB could have "a discernible impact on multilateral lend, and thus on global governance" (Reisen, 2015, p. 302). This is an overly simplistic estimate because the highly leveraged loan-capital ratio of the World Bank with a well-established track record cannot be applied to the newly established institution with virtually no track record.

Humphrey (2015) presents various scenarios of the NDB's loaning activities based on more detailed and additional assumptions. All of his estimates, including the most optimistic ones, turn out to be somewhat smaller in scale than those presented by Griffith-Jones (2014) and Reisen (2015). His more realistic estimates for the NDB's cumulative loan portfolio are in the range of US$45–65 billion over the first seven years as opposed to Griffith-Jones' estimates of US$5 billion per year during the first ten years and US$7 billion per year during the second ten years, or Reisen's estimate of US$109 billion in seven years after launching operations. Humphrey thinks that the amounts of the NDB will be "relevant but fairly modest" in relations to existing multilateral development banks, and will not be a global "game-changer" (Humphrey, 2015, p. 30).

In our estimates, the new institution will probably make loans of a few US$ billion at most a year for several years. When countries (particularly non-borrower countries) line up for their membership, the NDB will determine their capital subscriptions, and review its total authorized capital (of initial US$100 billion). It is only at that occasion that the NDB will face the opportunity of raising its lending capacity substantially. According to official sources, the NDB approved its first set of loans—four projects, one each in Brazil, India, China and South Africa—totaling US$850 million for 2016, and reportedly, the NDB president hopes to raise the Bank's lending above US$2 billion in 2017. Needless to say, these actual figures announced are much smaller in scale than these estimates mentioned above.

Loans to the Private Sector

Just like some of multilateral financial institutions, the NDB's *functions* include, among others, "to support infrastructure and sustainable development projects, *public and private*, ... through the provision of loans, guarantees, equity participation and other financial instruments" (Art 3-a); and "to cooperate ... with international organizations as well as national entities whether *public or private*, in particular with international financial institutions and national development banks" (Art 3-b). Regarding its methods of operation, the NDB "may guarantee, participate in, make loans or support through any other financial instruments, *public or private projects*, including *public-private partnerships*, in any borrowing member country, as well as investment in equity, underwrite the equity issues of securities, or facilitate access to international capital markets of *any business, industrial, agricultural or service enterprises* with projects in the territories of borrowing member countries" (Art 19-a).

It is anticipated, therefore, that the NDB will be engaged, from the time of commencing its work, in public and private projects. However the NDB Agreement does not specify the different conditions of financial disbursement between public and private sector projects. It can be imagined that for private sector investment the NDB will be heavily engaged in co-financing with the IFC and other institutions that have some track record in this area. This operation would resemble the private sector–oriented financing of the European Bank for Reconstruction and Development (EBRD) established in 1991 to facilitate the market-oriented transition in East European economies, although the relative weight of private sector projects in the NDB would not be as significant as that in the EBRD.

Concessional Loans and Grants

Multilateral institutions provide their financial assistance mostly with non-concessional loans which carry interest rate and repayment requirement similar or equivalent to commercial lending. Yet, concessional loans (soft loans) at below market-based terms and grants with no repayment obligation have also occupied important components of financial assistance particularly to low-income countries. The World Bank started its operation in 1946 as an institution to provide non-concessional lending to middle-income countries and creditworthy low-income governments. Due to pressure from developing countries, however, the major Western powers agreed to create its concessional lending window, the International Development Association, for providing concessional loans and grants to low-income counties. Concessional lending resources, which are rather small relative to non-concessional counterparts, come mostly from regular replenishments by donor countries, rather than bond issuances. Similarly, major regional development banks have established soft loan window.

While details are not elaborated on, the NDB Agreement postulates that the new institution's overall loaning activities consist of "ordinary operation"—presumably non-concessional loan—which is financed from the ordinary capital resources, and "special operation"—presumably concessional loan—which is to be financed from the Special Funds resources (Art. 18-a). It is anticipated that once poorer countries, particularly those in Africa begin to join the NDB, they will ask for concessional loans. Given the fact that the BRICS members, particularly China, have increasingly been involved in concessional lending in their own bilateral South-South cooperation activities, they may not find much merit in bringing the issue of concessional lending with presumably more time-consuming negotiations to the NDB's operation. The BRICS members may prefer to use their new institution for non-concessional lending, and let concessional lending be handled on a bilateral basis.[15]

As stated above, we expect that the NDB's concessional lending window will not issue bonds and that it will instead use funds contributed directly from their member countries (replenishments), as well as retained earnings, for the operation of non-concessional lending. Needless to say, the latter option is not possible at the early stages of operation when the NDB has not generated profits. Thus, poorer countries may choose to defer their participation in the NDB until the institution becomes able to finance such preferential financing. After all, if these countries can expect concessional loans bilaterally from some BRICS members, they may continue to rely on bilateral channels of concessional loans rather than switch to multilateral channels, such as the NDB. On the other hand, low-income countries may view that the NDB can provide an institutional merit of diluting bilateral donors' political influence over recipients' decision-making.

POTENTIAL IMPLICATIONS OF THE NDB TO INTERNATIONAL POLITICAL ECONOMY

Many declaratory statements of the BRICS Summits have highlighted the legacy of collective efforts of the global South in general and the BRICS members in particular. The BRICS members are diverse in many aspects, in terms of the size of economy, population, and territory, as well as geographical location and ethnic composition. They are also diverse in national interests, political systems and the scope of development cooperation (see Cooper, 2016; Liu, 2016; Piper, 2015; Stuenkel, 2015). The BRICS process, nonetheless, has already helped its members trim their historical, "trust deficit," or at least reduced security threat to some extent. This is particularly pertinent among Russia, India and China that share borders. The inclusion of South Africa to the BRICS process may also have brought forth a political advantage to the group, that is, the creation of a more globally inclusive alliance to represent the interest of the emerging world.

We still wonder, however, whether the BRICS members are truly interested in pursuing a transformative process for the international economic order. Are the BRICS acting in the interest of the rest of the global South in the fashion similar to what we observed in the Southern attempts to create a new international economic order (NIEO) in the 1960s and 1970s? Indeed, some observers see the BRICS process as the "bridgehead for the second coming of the NIEO" (Sornarajah, 2014, p. 297). But the earlier efforts were based on the common notions among developing countries that felt that they were victims of the existing system, whereas the BRICS process has been undertaken by high performers within, or elite beneficiaries of, the existing system. Or are they simply reconfiguring themselves in an exclusive and prestigious forum, perhaps somewhat reminiscent of the Group of Seven (G7), with an emphasis on reinforcing core commonalities of perspective and downplaying points of tension and disagreement? Undoubtedly, the BRICS members seek to extend the reach of their influence through development activities (with new partners), even though they still hold diverse perspectives as bilateral aid providers (see Rowlands, 2012). In the following pages, we discuss potential implications of the NDB to international political economy.

While pursuing own domestic approaches containing a wide range of different policies, the BRICS members have come to a common understanding about potential benefits accruing from the NDB. One such benefit is purely financial, that is, high-yielding investments in the BRICS members' (and perhaps later, in others') infrastructure projects over the present practice of holding large foreign reserves with a large share invested in low-yielding financial investments in the securities of developed economies, particularly US Treasury bills. Such a shift, it may be hoped, will reduce the risk of reserve asset deflation and currency inflation, and enhance the ability of the BRICS members to deal with contagion and shocks (Tang, Yao and Huang, 2015, p. 53).

Thus, at least in their diplomatic rhetoric, these countries are strongly opposed to the heavy-handed and intrusive neoliberal conditionalities of the Bretton Woods institutions. Given that aid commitments from traditional donors have not been able to fully meet financial needs in many developing countries to overcome their infrastructure bottlenecks, the NDB's financing, as a new supplementary source, could help these countries address these bottlenecks. It could be hoped, therefore, that the NDB's financing would play an important role in reducing infrastructure deficits in many developing countries and help them tap their development potentials. The point is that the stock of infrastructure assets—particularly telecommunications, roads and electric networks (Mwase and Yang, 2012, p. 13)—has a positive impact, by reducing the domestic costs of production and increasing the productivity, on the rate of economic growth.

As pointed out earlier, however, the BRICS members do not constitute a homogenous group. Their political thoughts and orientations on specific issues differ from one another. And it is not totally clear as to how nicely their differences can be resolved, and integrated into a coherent package acceptable to them all (and other would-be members). Can we expect that there will be a greater diversion of the NDB—in the name of a South-South cooperation institution—away from the neoliberal blueprint, rejecting the Washington Consensus? It can be imagined that the principle of non-interference will become less sustainable when the BRICS members, through the NDB, establish large-scale commercial activities around the world and become concerned with the agenda of building effective states (of loan-recipient counties) as well as issues of regional security (Cary and Li, 2016, pp. 12–13).

China, India and Brazil have been among the top borrowers from the World Bank. China and India are also among the top borrowers of the AsDB. It is then wondered whether the NDB will reduce these countries' dependence on the financing from these traditional institutions. This will be plausible, but the new institution will not cause a major shift of these countries' external financial reliance. Let us recall that the NDB will supplement (particularly through co-financing) rather than replace existing institutions. Senior staff of the NDB—many of whom used to be employed by the Bretton Woods institutions and/or regional development banks—will be engaged regularly in exchanges of views on best practices with their counterparts of major multilateral financial institutions. Such exchanges will be important to avoid various risks, such as inefficiencies, occupational overlap, and perhaps most importantly the turf war. The NDB may consequently end up with the same role they have often accused the Bretton Woods institutions of playing (Van Voorhout and Wetzling, 2013, p. 6). A question, nonetheless, still remains as to how the Bretton Woods institutions' leaders will relate to the new institution.

Viewing it as a multilateralized institution of South-South cooperation activities, some observers may expect that the NDB will refrain from imposing intrusive conditionalities of political and economic nature on their member countries. They may argue that the refrainment of such conditionalities—which may cover governance, macroeconomic policy and performance, and institutional reforms—is a matter of course since these condionalities would undermine the principal of respecting national sovereignty, preserving country-ownership of reform, and forging South-South solidarity (see Mwase and Yang, 2012, pp. 4–12). However, developing countries must carefully managing their engagement with the NDB to ensure that they can sustain their debt in the long run, certainly avoiding a repeat of past debt problems. This means that potential borrowing countries need to take a prudent approach within an overall sound debt management strategy, which entails a careful evaluation of the impact of increased financing on growth and debt burden (Mwase and Yang, 2012, pp. 15–18).

As far as the NDB is concerned, the sustained banking activity requires vast human capacities and financial resources; however, neither of them will be readily available to it, particularly at its early stages of operation. In fact, the NDB is presently busy recruiting qualified professional staff, presumably from the BRICS members, but the process could be time consuming. Therefore, the membership expansion of the NDB—and thus the recruitment of capable bankers from new members—may be urged in order to make up for its initial deficiency of human and institutional resources.

Yet, as stated earlier, the expansion of the NDB's membership (particularly the admission of non-borrower countries) is likely to bring forth negative effects to developing countries. First of all, Northern membership would compromise the purported purpose of the NDB to function as a South-South institution, even though the NDB Agreement contains provisions of safeguards to reserve the influence of the BRICS members (and for that matter the developing countries in general) vis-à-vis non-borrower developed countries. There is still such a chance that the widened membership will reintroduce North-South conflict. At any rate, the realistic expectation is that the new institution will have to draw on the modus operandi and expertise of existing multilateral and regional banks.[16]

It is reasonable to expect that the establishment of the NDB, together with other alternative institutions, may act as a catalyst for reforms in the existing multilateral and regional development banks (Griffith-Jones, 2014, p. 15). It is still doubtful, however, whether these reforms are likely to take place rapidly and sufficiently for addressing the demand of the developing countries (Dix, 2015, p. 5). As stated earlier, loans without requirements, in the name of the principle of non-interference, on good governance and corruption control can be potentially problematic.

CONCLUSION

The BRICS members' advocacy of horizontal, South-South solidarity as the foundation of the new institution's operation has offered a comforting rhetoric to many developing countries (Biswa, 2015). The NDB has been institutionalized as a partnership organization of equals among its founding members, where each BRICS member initially has an equal amount of capital subscription (US$10 billion). If this equality principal should persist, the NDB's capital in the future will be heavily determined by the weakest BRICS member, that is, South Africa. Thus, unless this smallest BRICS member can manage to obtain fund—say, from other BRICS members—to cover the payment of its subscription, the new institution will remain too small—the disbursement of less than US$1 billion in 2016—to make a serious difference.

In that event, one way to make the new institution large enough to matter is to encourage the participation of non-borrowers (major Northern powers), making the NDB resemble existing multilateral financial institutions. If the NDB should decide to raise its lending but at the same time to eschew the option of extensively admitting non-borrower countries, then it would possibly have to compromise the principle of equality among the BRICS members. This is because it would mean to let China, the only one with the financial clout among the BRICS members, raise the capital base of the new institution. In that event, it is very likely that China—as the United States did for the World Bank in the 1940s and 1950s—will ask for more commensurate power in the institution's governance (Kapur and Raychaudhuri, 2014, p. 16).

Another question is whether (or to what extent) the BRICS members will be able to make the operational activities of the NDB differ from those of Western dominant multilateral financial institutions, most importantly of the World Bank. It should be reminded here that all of the BRICS members belong to the Bretton Woods institutions, which means that they are parties to the established multilateral standards of these establishments. It is then wondered how the BRICS members can refuse to use these standards for the NDB. The NDB will increasingly depend on international capital markets for sourcing loanable funds and on existing national and multilateral development organizations for co-financing. Such operational technicalities, however, will likely dampen its purported attractiveness as an alternative to the traditional financial institutions. More specifically, we wonder to what extent the NDB can do away with conventional conditionalities, when the new institution continues to rely on existing institutions for co-financing operations.

Official aids from traditional donors (bilaterally or multilaterally) have failed to meet financial needs of many developing countries to overcome their infrastructure bottlenecks. As a new supplementary source to reduce infrastructure deficits in developing countries, the NDB should expand its activities. The expansion of its activities will raise the increasing number of developing countries to tap their development potentials. In this regard, the operational scale of the new institution is expected to grow, but it will be a slow and unsteady process. If developing countries should perceive that the NDB fails in bringing in changes of wide-ranging effects in their infrastructure development as well as in the international financial architecture, they would question the merit of reinventing the wheel. Even worse, they may even regard the NDB as a smokescreen to the advantage of the BRICS members—particularly China with overwhelming foreign reserves and active construction firms—to hide their acts of exploitation in fellow developing countries. The BRICS members should be aware of this negative possibility.

NOTES

1. This paper was presented at the fourth International Conference of BICAS (BRICS Initiatives in Critical Agrarian Studies), held at China Agricultural University, Beijing, China (November 28–30, 2016). The author wishes to express his appreciation to helpful comments provided by Eri Ikeda, Benjamin Jesse Pacho, Brandon Sommer, Johan Spamer and Robert Christiaan Thomassen on earlier versions of the paper, as well as BICAS Conference participants who raised various questions to my presentation.

2. India and South Africa bargained hard for hosting the NDB's headquarters, but in the end China's insistence prevailed. Thus Shanghai, the financial center of China, won to host the headquarters. Meanwhile, South Africa got the BRICS members' consent toward the idea of establishing the African Regional Centre (Cooper and Facooq, 2015, p. 35). Interestingly, Shanghai also hosts the institution of another relatively new development initiative, namely the Shanghai Cooperative Organization (SCO), which, under the co-leadership of China and Russia, is to promote Central Asian development. The colocation of these two institutions in Shanghai has been

anticipated to promote synergies between them. Russia hosted the 2016 SCO meeting in Ufa alongside the BRICS Summit.

3. At the Bretton Woods conference in 1944, the negotiations on the Articles of Agreement on the World Bank engendered the idea of the combination of paid-in capital and callable capital (World Bank Art. 2, Sec.5-i, ii), where the founding countries were required to pay 20 percent of capital commitment in cash with the remaining 80 percent committed as a guarantee that would be called upon by the World Bank only when required to meet its obligations, that is, to pay off its creditors. Every multilateral development bank, including the NDB, has utilized the same mechanism (Humphrey, 2014, p. 618).

4. The World Bank, for instance, used to direct 70 percent of its lending to infrastructure in the 1950s and 1960s, whereas toward the end of the twentieth century the share of infrastructure in its lending declined to 19 percent (Wang, 2016, p. 3). See also Mwase and Yang (2012).

5. Seemingly, the BRICS members prioritized their equal capital subscription over the size of total capital basis of the new institution. This is because the decision of equal capital subscriptions members pre-empt difficult negotiations over the voting power allocation among them. If the BRICS members had been allowed to contribute in accordance with their financial capacity, its initial subscribed capital could have been much larger but the negotiations on the intra-BRICS division of the initial capital base would have been more time-consuming as well. Furthermore, the voting power in such an event could deviate from the egalitarian principle.

6. Possibly, non-Chinese members may recycle public funds from China for covering their capital subscriptions. This possibility may further increase when non-BRICS countries with a much meager financing capacity join the NDB.

7. How long will it take the NDB to generate the initial operational profits? Given that infrastructure projects typically carry a lending contract of about 10 years, the NDB cannot expect sizable profits from infrastructure lending for another 10 years. Thus, the earlier operational profits will be mostly from its portfolio investment using its available paid-in capital. This would not be a large amount either, because of two reasons: first, the paid-in capital will be used most of all for organizational build-up and administrative costs; and second, as discussed earlier, the paid-in capital will take another several years to complete.

8. An alternative expression is the sum of callable capital and equity, with the latter consisting of pay-in capital, retained earnings/reserves.

9. As Kahler (2016) points out, the establishment of the NDB by the BRICS members reminds us of the similar initiatives to create new institutions outside the established ones by Middle Eastern oil producers in the 1970s, such as the Arab Fund for Economic and Social Development (1974), the Islamic Development Bank (1974), the Arab Bank for Economic Development in Africa (1975), and the Organization of Petroliam Exporting Countries Fund for International Development (1976).

10. In the case of the AIIB, China, the single initiator of its establishment, was actively solicited the membership not only among Asian countries but non-Asian countries, including non-borrower developed countries. As a result, the AIIB was established in October 2014 with Asian and non-Asian founding members, including

the rest of the BRICS members as well as many traditional donors. Given its large membership (including many traditional donor countries) and China's active leadership role, the AIIB may eclipse the NDB in the long run (Humphrey, 2015).

11. Membership expansion also implies greater bureaucratization of the institution, which tends to slow down the approval process. (For an excellent comparative analysis on three multinational development banks, see Humphrey and Michaeloa, 2013).

12. The World Bank with a large number of non-borrower countries among its members has always maintained the highest credit rating (AAA) among the multilateral and regional development banks, which makes it possible to raise funds and provide its loans at the most competitive (lowest) rate. The Inter-American Development Bank (IADB) and the African Development Bank (AfDB) were created as new institutions to be controlled by borrowers, but they ended up giving non-borrowers countries greater power in order to improve their standing in the capital markets (see, for example, Humphrey, 2015 for the IADB; and Strand, 2001 for the AfDB).

13. China is rated AA-, Brazil, India and South Africa at the lowest investment grade rating, and Russia was recently downgraded to junk bond status (Humphrey, 2015, p. 17).

14. According to Liu (2014, p. 45), it can be expected that the financing for the NDB will mainly come from the members, particularly China. Let us note that, the NDB has received AAA institutional rating from China Chengxin Credit Rating Corporation and China Lianhe Credit Rating Corporation (NDB, 2016f).

15. Even if some of the BRICS members (particularly China) can secure resource supplies and market outlets for their economies through bilateral lending, they may encourage borrower countries to join the NDB. This is because, the funding through multilateral institutions, such as the NDB, enables risks to be pooled, limits reputation costs, and increases the perceived legitimacy (Dix, 2015, p. 4).

16. A sober reminder is that the BRICS members' calls for modifications of voting rights of the Bretton Woods institutions do not mean that they are willing to undermine them; instead, the countries have been instrumental in the process of keeping them alive (Stuenkel, 2015, p. 156).

REFERENCES

Ban, C., and Blyth, M. (2013). The BRICs and the Washington consensus: An introduction. *Review of International Political Economy*, 20(2), 241–255.

Biswas, R. (2015). *Reshaping the Financial Architecture for Development Finance: The new development banks*. LSE Global South Unit, Working Paper 2/2015.

Bond, P. (2013). Sub-imperialism as lubricant of neoliberalism: South African "deputy sheriff" duty within BRICS, *Third World Quarterly* 34(2) 251–270.

Bond, P. (2016). BRICS banking and the debate over sub-imperialism, *Third World Quarterly* 37(4), 611–629.

Boulle, L and Chella, J. (2014) Joining the BRICs: The case of South Africa. In Lo, VI and Hiscock, M (eds.), 99–122. Cheltenham, UK: Edward Elgar Publishing.

Bracho, G. (2015). *In Search of a Narrative for Southern Providers: The Challenge of the Emerging Economies to the Development Cooperation Agenda*. German Development Institute Discussion Paper1/2015.

BRICS (2014). Agreement *on the New Development Bank*, July 15, 2014, Fortaleza, Brazil

Carey, R. and Li, X. (2016a). The BRICS in International Development: The New Landscape, *Evidence Report No 189*. Brighton: Institute of Development Studies (IDS).

Carey, R. and Li, X. (2016b). China's Comprehensive Strategic and Cooperative Partnership with Africa. *IDS Policy Briefing 111*, Brighton: Institute of Development Studies (IDS).

Carey, R. and Li, X. (2016c). Understanding the BRICS Evolving Influence and Role in Global Governance and Development. *IDS Policy Briefing 119*. Brighton: Institute of Development Studies (IDS).

Cheng, J.Y.S. (2015) China's Approach to BRICS. *Journal of Contemporary China,* 24(92), 357–375.

Chin, G.T. (2014). The BRICS-led Development Bank: Purpose and politics beyond the G20. *Global Policy*. 5(3) 366–373.

Coleman, I. (2013). Ten Questions for the new BRICS bank. *Foreign Policy*, 4(09), 2013.

Cooper, A.F. (2016). *The BRICS: A very short introduction*. Oxford: Oxford University press.

Cooper, A. F. and Farooq, A. B. (2013). BRICS and the privileging of informality in global governance. *Global Policy*, 4(4), 428–433.

Cooper, A.F. and Farooq, A. (2015). Testing the club dynamics of the BRICS: the new development bank from conception to establishment. *International Organizations Research Journal*, 10(2), 32–44.

Cooper, A. F. and Flemes, D. (2013). Foreign policy strategies of emerging powers in a multipolar world: an introductory review. *Third World Quarterly*, 34(6), 943–962.

Deych, T. (2016) *What Does BRICS Mean for Africa?* ATINER Conference Paper Series, No. INL2016–2114.

Dixon, C. (2015). *The New BRICS Bank: Challenging the international Financial Order?* Policy Paper No. 28. The Global Policy Institute, London Metropolitan University.

Donno, D. and Rudra, N. (2014). To fear or not to fear? BRICs and the developing world. *International Studies Review*, 16(3), 447–452.

Dos Santos, R (2014) Brazil: A soft power rising with the BRICS towards a multipolar world. In Lo, VI and Hiscock, M (eds.), 67–84. Cheltenham, UK: Edward Elgar Publishing.

Flemes, D. (2009) India-Brazil-South Africa (IBSA) in the New Global Order: Interests, strategies and values of the emerging coalition, *International Studies*, 46(1), 401–421.

Ford, C. (2014). Can BRICS development bank become a rival to the World Bank? *The Christian Monitor,* July 16, 2014: 9.

Fortescue, S. (2014) The BRICS and Russia. In Lo, VI and Hiscock, M (eds.), 228–240. Cheltenham, UK: Edward Elgar Publishing.

Garcia, G. (2016). The rise of the global South, the IMF and the Future of law and development. *Third World Quarterly,* 37(2), 191–208.

Gosovics, B (2016). The resurgence of South-South cooperation, *Third World Quarterly,* 37(4), 733–743. 1

Griffith-Jones, S. (2014). *A BRICS development bank: a dream coming true?* UNCTAD Discussion Paper 215. Geneva: UNCTAD.

Hochstetler, K. (2014). *Infrastructure and sustainable Development Goals in the BRICS-led New Development Bank.* Policy Review 46. Center for International Governance Innovation (CIGI)

Hu, F. Y. (2013). The Shanghai Cooperation Organization (SCO): Prospects and problems in Russia-China relations. *Journalism and Mass Communications*, 3(2), 101–13.

Humphrey, C. (2014). The politics of loan pricing in multilateral development banks. *Review of International Political Economy.* 21(3), 611–639.

Humphrey, C. (2015). *Developmental Revolution or Bretton Woods Revisited? The prospect of the BRICS News Development Bank and the Asian Infrastructure Investment Bank.* Overseas Development Institute (ODI) Working Paper 418.

Humphrey, C. (2016). The invisible hand: Financial pressures and organisational convergence in multilateral development banks. *The Journal of Development Studies*, 52(1), 92–112.

Humphrey, C. and Michaelowa, K. (2013). Shopping for Development: Multilateral lending, shareholder composition and borrower preferences. *World Development*, 44(4), 142–155.

Huotari, M and Hanemann, T. (2014) Emerging powers and change in the global financial order. *Global Policy*, 5(3), 298–310.

Isidro Luna, V. M. (2016). BRICS' bank: Possibilities and constraints. *EconomíaInforma*, 398, 3–22.

Jha, P and Chakraborty, A. (2013). *BRICS in the Contemporary Global Economy: Prospects and challenges.* Oxfam India Working Paper Series XVIII.

John, L (2014), *The BRICS Development Bank: Why the world's newest global bank must adopt a pro-poor agenda.* Oxfam Policy Brief.

Johnson, J. and Kostem, S. (2016). Frustrated leadership: Russia's economic alternative to the West. *Global Policy*, 7(2), 207–216.

Kapur, D. and Raychaudhuri, A. (2014). *Rethinking the Financial Design of the World Bank.* Working Paper 352. Washington, DC: Center for Global Development.

Kahler, M. (2016). The global economic multilaterals: Will eighty years be enough? *Global Governance*, 22: 1–9.

Khanna, P. (2014). New BRICS bank a building block of alternative world order. *New Perspectives Quarterly*, 31(4) 46–48.

Kornegay, FA and Bohler-Muller, N. (eds.) (2013). *Laying the BRICS of a New Global Order: From Yekaterinburg 2009 to eThekwini 2013.* Pretoria: the Africa Institute of South Africa.

Laidi, Z. (2012). BRICS: Sovereignty power and weakness, *International Politics*, 49(5), 614–632.

Laryea, E.T (2014) Implications of the rise of the BRIC countries for Africa. In Lo, VI and Hiscock, M (eds.), 123–1412. Cheltenham, UK: Edward Elgar Publishing.

Li, X. and Carey, R. (2014). *The BRICS and the International Development System: Challenge and Convergence?* IDS Evidence Report No.58. Brighton: Institute of Development Studies IDS.

Liu, M. (2016). BRICS Development: a long way to a powerful economic club and new international organization. *Pacific Review*, 29(3), 443–453.

Luckhurst, J. (2013). Building cooperation between the BRICS and leading industrialized states. *Latin American Policy*, 4(2), 251–268

Lo, B (2016) *The Illusion of Convergence—Russia, China and the BRICS.* Russie. Nei. Visions No.92. ifri Russia/NIS Center.

Lo, VI and Hiscock, M (eds.). (2014). *The Rise of the BRICS in the Global Political Economy: Changing Paradigms?* Cheltenham, UK: Edward Elgar Publishing.

Mielniczuk, F. (2013). BRICS in the contemporary world: changing identities, converging interests. *Third World Quarterly*, 34(6), 1075–1090.

Mostafa, G. and Mahmood, M. (2015). The rise of the BRICS and their challenge to the G7. *International Journal of Emerging Markets*, *10*(1), 156–170.

Mwase, N and Yang, Y. (2012). *BRICs' Philosophies for Development Financing and their Implications for LICs.* IMF working Paper, WP/12/74.

Nayyar, D. (2016). BRICS, developing countries and global governance. *Third World Quarterly* 37(4) 575–591.

Nelson, RM (2013), *Multilateral Development Banks: Overviews and issues for Congress.* Congressional Research Service, R41170.

Nelson, RM (2015), *Multilateral Development Banks: U.S. contributions FY2000-FY2015.* Congressional Research Service, RS20792.

NDB (2016a). *BRICS member-states contribute first $750 million to New Development Bank*, NDB Press Release, January 14, 2016.

NDB (2016b). *CAF and New Development Bank Sign Cooperation Agreement*, NDB Press Release, September 9, 2016.

NDB (2016c). *First Set of Loans Approved by the Board of Directors of the New Development Bank*, NDB Press Release, April 15, 2016.

NDB (2016d). *New Development Bank and China Construction Bank Signed Memorandum of Understanding on Strategic Cooperation*, NDB Press Release, June 8, 2016.

NDB (2016e). *NDB, ADB Sign MOU on Cooperation for Sustainable, inclusive Growth*, NDB Press Release, July 4, 2016.

NDB (2016f). *NDB Successfully Issued First RMB-denominated Green Financial Bond.* NDB Press Release, July 19, 2016.

NDB (2016g). *World Bank group, New Development Bank Lay Ground Work for Cooperation*, NDB Press Release, September 9, 2016.

OECD (2015). *Multinational Aid 2015: Better partnership for a post-2015 world.* Paris: OECD.

Pant, H. V. (2013). The BRICS Fallacy. *The Washington Quarterly,* 36(3), 91–105.

Pickup, M. (2016) Foreign Policy of new left: Explaining Brazil's Southern Partnerships. *Contexto Internacional* 38(1), 55–93.

Piper, L. (2015), *The BRICS Phenomenon: From regional economic leaders to global political players*, BICAS Working Paper 3, BRICS Initiative for Critical Agrarian Studies (BICAS).

Qobo, M. and Soko, M. (2015). The rise of emerging powers in the global development finance architecture: The case of the BRICS and the new development bank.
South African Journal of International Affairs. 22(3), 277–288.

Reis da Silva, A.L., Spohr, A.P. and Loreto Da Silvera, I. (2016). From bandung to
Brasilia: IBSA and the political lineage of South-South cooperation, *South African
Journal of International Affairs*, 23(3), 167–184.

Reisen, H. (2015). Will the AIIB and the NDB help reform multilateral development
banking? *Global Policy*, 6(3), 297–304.

Robles, T. (2012). *A BRICS development bank: an idea whose time has come?* RSIS
Commentaries, No.210. Singapore: Nanyang Technological University.

Rowlands, D. (212) individual BRICS or a collective bloc? Convergence and divergence among 'emerging donors' nations. *Cambridge Review of International
Affairs*, 25(4) 629–649.

Sarker, R. (2016). Trends in global finance: The new development (BRICS) bank,
Loyola University Chicago International Law Review, 13(2), 89–103.

Schablitzki, J. (2014). *The BRICS Development Bank: A new tool for South-South
cooperation?*BRICS Policy Brief, V.5 N.1. Rio de Janeiro: BRICS Policy Center.

Senona, J (2010). *BRICS and IBSA Forums: Neo-liberals in disguise or Champions
of the South?* Policy Briefing 24, Emerging Powers and Global Challenges Programme (SAIIA), September.

Shield, W. (2013). The Middle Way: China and global economic governance. *Survival*, 55(6), 147–168.

Shubin, V. (2015). South Africa in the BRICS: Last But Not Least. *International
Organizations Research Journal*, 10(2), 171–183

Sidiropoulos, E. (2013). IBSA: Avoiding being BRICked up. *Strategic Analysis*,
37(3) 285–290

Sinha, D. (2015). India, BRICS and the world economy. *Indian Foreign Affairs Journal*, 10(2), 160–173.

Sornarajah, M (2014) The role of the BRICS in international law in a multipolar
world, in Vai IL and Hiscock, M. (eds), 288–307. Cheltenham, UK: Edward Elgar
Publishing.

Soule-Kohndou, F. (2013). *The India-Brazil-South Africa Forum A Decade On: Mis-
matched Partners or the Rise of the South?* GEG Working Paper 2013/88.

Sotero, P. (2013). Brazil and the BRICS: A Challenging Space for Global Relevance
and Reform of an Obsolete World Order, in Kornegay, FA and Bohler-Muller, N.
(eds.), 279–94. Pretoria: the Africa Institute of South Africa.

Spratt, S., and Barone, B. (2015). National Development Banks in the BRICS: Lessons for the Post-2015 Development Finance Framework. IDS Policy Briefing 93,
Brighton: Institute of Development Studies (IDS).

Stephen, M. D. (2012). Rising Regional Powers and International Institutions: The
foreign policy orientations of India, Brazil and South Africa. *Global Society*, 26(3),
289–309.

Stephen, M. D. (2014). Rising Powers, Global Capitalism and Liberal Global Governance: A historical materialist account of the BRICs challenge. *European Journal
of International Relations*, 20(4), 912–938.

Strand, J. R. (2001). Institutional design and power relations in the African Development Bank. *Journal of Asian and African Studies*, 36(2), 203–223.

Stuenkel, O. (2015). *THE BRICS and the Future of Global Order*. Lanham: Lexington Books.

Taylor, I. (2014). *Africa Rising? BRICS—Diversifying Dependency*. Woodbridge, UK and Rochester, New York: James Currey.

Thakur, R. (2014). *Institutionalizing BRICS: The New Development Bank and its Implications*. Delphi Policy Group (DPG) Issue Brief, August.

Thyer M.C. and Thomas, M. (2014) BRICS and morter(s): Breaking or building the global system. In Vai, IL and Hiscock (eds), 253–267. Cheltenham, UK: Edward Elgar Publishing.

Tierney, M. J. (2014). Rising powers and the regime for development finance. *International Studies Review*, 16(3), 452–455.

UNCTAD (2012). The Rise of BRICS FDI and Africa. *Global Investment Trends Monitor*, Special Edition. 25 March.

Vai, IL and iscock, M. (eds) (2014). *The Role of the BRICS in the Global Political Economy: Changing paradigms?* Cheltenham, UK: Edward Elgar.

Van Agtmael, A. (2012). Think Again: The BRICS, *Foreign Policy,* 196: 76–79.

Van Voorhout, JC andWetzling, T. (2013). The BRICS Development Bank: A partner for the post-2015 Agenda? Policy Brief 7. The Hague Institute for Global Justice.

Vickers, B. (2013). Africa and the Rising Power: bargaining for the 'marginalized many', *International Affairs,* 83(3), 673–693.

Vieira, M. A. (2013). IBSA at 10: South–South development assistance and the challenge to build international legitimacy in a changing global order. *Strategic Analysis*, 37(3), 291–298.

Vieira, M.A. and Alden, C. (2011). India, Brazil, and South Africa (IBSA): South-South cooperation and the paradox of regional leadership. *Global Governance*, 17(4), 507–528.

Vieira, P.C. and Ouriques, H.R. (2016). Brazil and the BRICS: The trap of short time, *Journal of World-Systems Research*, 22(2) 404–429.

Wang, H. (2016). *New Multilateral Development Banks: Opportunities and challenges for global governance*. New York: Council on Foreign Relations.

Watson, N., Younis, M. and Spratt, S. (2013). *What Next For the Brics Bank?* Rapid Response Briefing, Issue 03, Institute of Development Studies (IDS).

Woods, N. (2008). Whose Aid? Whose Influence? China, emerging donors and the silent revolution in international development assistance', *International Affairs*, 84(6), 1205–1221.

Wulf, H. and Debiel, T. (2015). India's 'Strategic Autonomy' and the Club Model of Global Governance: Why the Indian BRICS Engagement Warrants a Less Ambiguous Foreign Policy Doctrine. *Strategic Analysis*, 39(1), 27–43.

Xu, J. and Carey, R. (2015). China's Development Finance: Ambition, Impact and Transparency. IDS Policy Briefing 92, Brighton: Institute of Development Studies (IDS).

Chapter 10

Russia and China as the Yin-and-Yang of 21st Century Eurasia?

Kaneshko Sangar

INTRODUCTION

In 2013, president of China Xi Jinping announced plans to materialize the One Road, One Belt (OROB) project (also Belt and Road), consisting of the Silk Road Economic Belt (SREB) and the Maritime Silk Road (MSR). The primary goal of this is to integrate Eurasia by creating a new economic space, with China at its core. During the Russian-Chinese talks in Moscow on 8 May 2015, ahead of the SCO summit in Ufa, also known as Xi-Putin summit, the two Presidents Xi Jinping and Vladimir Putin agreed to coordinate the linking of the Russia-led Eurasian Economic Union (EEU) and China's Silk Road Economic Belt (SREB). These developments have led to a whirlwind of debates and disputes among academic and expert communities in Russia, China and the West. Scholars and commentators have questioned the feasibility of integrating both projects, asserting that the two were incompatible due to numerous conceptual and operational reasons (Lo, 2016; Putz, 2016; Zuenko, 2015; Remington, 2016). The two projects are entirely different in nature and are at different stages in their development. The former is an integration process, which operates through supranational and intergovernmental institutions, while the latter is Beijing's global vision backed by China's cash reserves. Hence, integration between the two is a complicated task. The second question that has been hotly debated, since the recent dynamics in Sino-Russian relations, concerns the issue of the omnipresent question of the nature of their relationship, whether it is one of rivalry or cooperation. Many experts and commentators claimed that, while Russia may benefit from the SREB's expansion in a number of ways, the entire endeavor could also result in Russia witnessing the waning remnants of its influence in Central Asia, an area considered by Kremlin as a privileged sphere of interest (Gabuev,

2015b). Some even asserted that the "SREB poses fundamental challenges to Russia's regional and global posture" and warned of "the coming battle between autocratic nations like Russia and China and the rest" (Kobrinskaya, 2016; Spanger, 2016). Others argue that although the relationship between Moscow and Beijing has never been better, Russia is becoming a "junior partner" vis-à-vis its Eastern neighbor, possibly leading to antagonism between Moscow and Beijing. Indeed, China, they claim, has occupied the USSR's role, by joining the US in the "G2." As one of the US's prominent voices on the matter, Stephen Blanc (2016) asserted when discussing the "linking" of the Russian-led EEU and China's SREB, "Russia now is merely a 'younger brother' in such endeavours."

It is important to note that due to a lack of clarity and absence of coherent road maps of the implementation of China's grand project, as well as the coordination between the SREB and EEU, most research on such questions, despite good intentions, remains speculative in nature. Interestingly, discussing the issue of implementation and realization of OROB, Chinese scholars often quote philosopher Laozi, when he said: "The highest good is like water. Water benefits all things and does not contend with them" (Shaolei, 2016; Qingsong, 2016). Hence, they see multitrillion projects as flowing water, able to "spread everywhere, avoiding conflicts with existing cooperation mechanisms and overcoming the inertia of the winner-takes-it-all mentality." The implementation, they claim, depends on specific sub-projects and their framework (e.g. signing of bilateral or multilateral agreements) (Ibid). Thus, discussing such issues is often like anticipating the direction of the unpredictable flows of water—a tricky endeavor. Furthermore, by focusing on the technicalities of the OROB's realization and SREB's integration with the EEU and the economic benefits and implications for Russia, authors and scholars (including the author of this text) have missed the political and diplomatic subtext of recent developments and their geopolitical implication for the wider Eurasia. As explored in this chapter, for Russia, the political component of the OROB and its integration with EEU is far more important than the economic and material benefits.

Therefore, this chapter shall focus on the broader picture of Sino-Russian bilateral relations since 1991 leading to the 2015 agreement to link SREB and EEU and the initiative's implication on the bilateral relations between two nations. The study shall be guided by the following research questions: (i) How has the Sino-Russian relationship developed since the conclusion of the Cold War, and why is it deemed a success? (ii) Is the Sino-Russian relationship in Central Asia one of competition or cooperation? (iii) What explains the growing wariness among some Russian scholars and commentators and Moscow's predicament with regard to the role of China's "junior partner"?

And finally, (iv) What is/are the major implication(s) of the initiative to merge the SREB and EEU?

The chapter is divided into a number of thematic sections each addressing one of the above-mentioned research questions. Section 2, following the introduction, briefly explores the evolution of Sino-Russian relations in the post-Cold War world and investigates the question of why their bilateral relations are deemed a success. The subsequent section evaluates the Sino-Russian engagement in Central Asia—a region of vital geopolitical importance for both countries. Section 4 caters an analysis of Russia's China discourse and investigates the growing skepticism in Moscow and issues concerning Russia's increasing dependency on Chinese markets and uneven trade flows between two nations, which led to claims that Russia has transformed into China's "junior partner" and raw material appendage. Finally, section 5 explores the recent developments around the two Eurasian projects: China's SREB and Russia-led EEU. Amid the 8 May 2015 agreement, both projects were to be linked, yet questions concerning the geopolitical implications of said developments on Sino-Russian relations as well as on wider Eurasia remain.

SINO-RUSSIAN RELATIONS SINCE 1991: A HISTORY OF SUCCESS AND COMPLEMENTARITY

The year 2016 was a year when China and Russia celebrated a number of milestone events: 25 years of successful post-Cold War bilateral relations, Shanghai Five's twentieth anniversary and the fifteenth anniversary of Shanghai Cooperation Organization (SCO). In addition, 2016 marked the fifteenth anniversary of the Sino-Russia Good-Neighbourly Treaty of Friendship and Cooperation and it also saw the twentieth anniversary of the two countries' forging of the "partnership of strategic coordination" by signing the Sino-Russian Joint Statement in 1996 (Xi, 2016; MOFA, 2008). Since 1991, Moscow and Beijing have steadily improved and deepened relations, achieving a stable and comprehensive strategic partnership. Both have successfully enhanced their engagement through years of trust building endeavors and Beijing's effective diplomacy. Throughout the last two decades, Moscow and Beijing also have fruitfully institutionalized their bilateral relations. Hence, their relationship currently may be seen as a textbook example of how major powers and former adversaries can engage effectively, merely by managing their numerous differences, finding some sort of consensus in their disparate foreign policy approaches and respecting each other's legitimate interests. As Russian foreign minister Sergey Lavrov noted, relations between the two "represent an example of interstate cooperation in the 21st century" (Lavrov,

2016). In contrast, as Timofey Bordachev stipulates, according to the conceptual framework of China's foreign policy, the relationship is a "new form of relations between the great powers" (Bordachev, 2016).

China and Russia have increasingly convergent interest as well as similar views on the nature of international system. Indeed, the incessantly improving relationship between Moscow and Beijing since 1991 rests on a number of issues, including opposition to the West, and particularly the US's international hegemony and protection of non-Western states' sovereignty including "the independence of national interests and the diversity of political systems" (Kim and Indeo, 2013, p. 276). Moscow and Beijing were increasingly concerned with two major issues, which they perceived as existential threats to their sovereignty and statehood. Firstly, it concerns the ever-increasing US military bases that surround both countries and the West's support for "Colored Revolution" through their NGOs. During the 2011 "Winter of Discontent"[1] in Moscow, within which protesters called for fair elections, Putin blamed the West and NGOs. The Chinese government also noted foreign influences behind the 2014 "Umbrella Revolution,"[2] described as a "Colored Revolution" by Russian and Chinese media (Trenin, 2015). Moscow and Beijing also agree that US policies have caused chaos and destruction in e.g. Libya and Syria (Ibid). Similarly, Chinese officials believe that the US aims to destabilize China's "periphery," namely Hong Kong, Tibet and Xingjian province (Trenin, 2012, p. 23). Russia and China have lucratively coordinated their efforts in the United Nations, where their representatives have numerously blocked US and European calls for alleged "humanitarian interventions" (Ibid).

Both countries have cooperated efficaciously in economic and energy spheres. Russia and China share a long border, providing a convenient hub for the transfer of natural resources and is practically impregnable for a third party to access (Trenin, 2012, p. 23). Rendering to Dmitrii Trenin, this is one of China's main rationales for considering Russia as a "genuine strategic partner," while other countries are regarded by China as "both partners and competitors" (Ibid). The Sino-Russian dialogue on cooperation and energy ignited in the 2000s, stretching far yonder than trade in oil and gas, as it embraces nuclear energy, joint promotion of renewable energy, a coordination of measures to promote energy efficiency, and collaboration and trade in electricity as well as coal (Gvosdev and Marsh, 2014, p. 134).

During Putin's Beijing visit in March 2006, the two governments engaged four energy cooperation agreements *apropos* a future cooperation in oil, gas, electricity, and nuclear energy (Weitz, 2008, p. 19). In 2009, Moscow and Beijing signed a US$100 billion oil contract. By 2011, China became Russia's largest trading partner. In the year of 2013, Chinese investments in Russia grew by a staggering 80 percent. The underpinning personal ties between Putin and Xi since 2012 have also played a very substantial role in the states' deepening of bilateral relations. Indeed, since 2013 Xi and Putin have met twelve times (Ying, 2016, p. 99). For many years, Moscow and Beijing negotiated the gas agreement, molding China into Russia's principal gas consumer. Finally, in 2014 Russia and China signed a US$400 billion gas deal and construction of a pipeline that is capable of transporting 38 billion cubic meters of Russian gas to China (Ying, 2016, p. 98).

In May 2015, Russia and China conducted a ten-day naval drill in the Mediterranean Sea, demonstrating the West their combined military abilities in locations traditionally dominated by NATO, faraway from Chinese and Russian coastlines (Inder Singh, 2015). In the same year, the Kremlin offered Beijing the occasion to purchase Russia's most advanced anti-aircraft missile, the S-400 (Ibid).

Post-Cold War Sino-Russian bilateral relations are habitually divided into evolutionary stages (Molchanov, 2015; Kaczmarski, 2015; Yunling, 2011; Gabuev, 2015a). The first phase marked the period of the normalization bilateral relations between the former foes. This stage commenced in 1991 and ended when Putin succeeded Boris El'tsin in 2000. The second phase occurred during Putin's first two presidential terms. The third phase was the period from 2008–2015, which includes the four years of Dmitrii Medvedev's presidency and the first three years of Putin's second round as president (Gabuev, 2015a, p. 2).

During the first phase, Sino-Russian relations' normalization accelerated after the failure of Andrei Kozyrev's Westernist foreign policy doctrine. Russia tightened its ties with China, among others, due to "pressures from the domestic opposition" (Tsygankov, 2009, p. 9). This stage of Sino-Russian post-Cold War relations was marked by a surge in arms trade, coordination on international issues and foreign policies (Molchanov, 2015, p. 116). Throughout this phase, ties between Moscow and Beijing bettered due to two significant factors. Firstly, economic complementarity, as Russia needed an arms export market while China had discovered a new emerging market for its consumer goods, and an opportunity to link its "depressed northeast to the needy Russian Far East" (Rozman, 2014, p. 245). During the 1990s, Russia's arms transfers to China accounted for 60 percent of the countries' foreign arms sales (Berryman, 2010, p. 128). Some of Russia's vitally important military-industrial enterprises would simply not have survived if it had not been for Chinese arms supply contracts (Ibid). The second factor that made the engagement efficacious was both countries' desire to achieve a multipolar world order. In Russia, this was a reflection of Evgenii Primakov's foreign policy. The Shanghai Five summit and the joint statement of "strategic coordination" by Boris El'tsin and Jiang Zemin, both in 1996, were perhaps the most significant achievements in Sino-Russian bilateral relations since 1989.

The 1997 UN Sino-Russian Joint Declaration on Multipolar World Order and the Establishment of a New International Order, where the two clearly stated, "no country should seek hegemony, engage in power politics or monopolize international affairs," was a clear indication that Russia and China became new partners against US unilateralism (Molchanov, 2015, p. 117). By 1998, Moscow and Beijing signed a deal whereby two Russian-made nuclear reactors were delivered to China's Lyanyungang power plant (Ibid., 116). In 1999, both denounced NATO's war on Yugoslavia, calling the West to withhold military intervention in Kosovo (Ibid., 117). Moscow and Beijing have since advocated a world where decision-making is dominated by international law and the UN, including the use of force by the members of the international community (Weitz, 2008, p. 36).

The second phase was initiated in 2001 when Russia and China headed by Presidents Putin and Jiang Zemin signed a Treaty of Friendship,[3] followed by solving the long-standing territorial disagreement, wherein Russia seceded China 337 sq.km of disputed lands, with Beijing removing its territorial claims in 2004. (Gabuev, 2015a, p. 2; Timofeev, 2014, pp. 57–60). In 2001, the Shanghai Five, which proved to be remarkably effective in issues such as resolving complex border disputes among its member states, was transformed into the Shanghai Cooperation Organization (SCO). The organization's main mission, as postulated in the 2004 Tashkent Declaration, was to promote economic development and safeguard regional peace by confronting "three evil forces" of terrorism, separatism and extremism. Between 2002 and 2008, trade between China and Russia increased by 37 percent, reaching US$55.9 billion. It should be noted that, during this period, Russia's concerns with regard to China's economic expansion into Russia, and particularly into its Far East, had also increased. This resulted in Russia planting forward informal limitations on Chinese investments in "sensitive sectors such as energy, mining, and infrastructure," pushing Chinese entrepreneurs from Russia's Far East (Gabuev, 2015a, p. 2). Nevertheless, Russian anxieties of a "Chinese threat" did not yield a negative impact on the bilateral relations' development between the two, and by 2010 China became Russia's second biggest trading partner after the EU.

During the hitherto last stage of post-Cold War Russo-Chinese rapprochement from 2008 to 2015, Russia's shift toward China had become "more pronounced," as noted by Dmitrii Trenin. The relationship had transformed into a "closer partnership that included cooperation on energy trade, infrastructure development, and defence" (Trenin, 2015). When Putin reclaimed the presidential seat in 2012, his first foreign visit was to China. During this time, Putin and Hu Jintao signed eleven major agreements on bilateral cooperation in areas such as banking, energy, nuclear power and technology, tourism, journalism, investment, insurance and industrial management

(Gvosdev and Marsh, 2014, p. 139). As Putin noted in his pre-election article on foreign policy in 2012, "Russia needs a prosperous and stable China, and I am convinced that China needs a strong and successful Russia" (Putin, 2012/2016). Xi, in a written statement issued during his first trip abroad as China's leader to Moscow in March 2013, stated, "China will make developing relations with Russia a priority in its foreign policy orientation" (Herszenhorn and Buckley, 2013). Putin noted that the strategic partnership between China and Russia "is of great importance on both a bilateral and global scale" (Timofeev, 2014, pp. 57–61). During this trip, Xi told Putin that China and Russia should "resolutely support each other in efforts to protect national sovereignty, security and development interests" (Herszenhorn and Buckley, 2013). As Alexander Lukin notes, China needs a stable Russia that, together with China, is capable of counterbalancing the West and the US, as one of the guarantors allowing China to pursue an independent (from the US) hegemony in its foreign policy (Lukin, 2015). Moreover, China also needs Russia, not only for a secure backyard, but also as a source of certain goods, which can be purchased only from Russia, such as arms, equipment for China's space program, hydrocarbons and other natural resources (Ibid). The bond between Moscow and Beijing are at their best since the long-gone days of Ivan the Terrible—and for all the elaborated reasons, including strong foundations and mutual trust, the two will continue to become intimate, as part of a long-term trajectory, with continued betterment via future initiatives of such nature.

RUSSIA AND CHINA: COMPETITION AND COOPERATION IN CENTRAL ASIA

Commentators have long argued that anticipating a Russia-China condominium in Central Asia is premature, and all one should expect is creeping competition, which "will erode the foundation of the partnership" (Cossa, 2014). Central Asia is always viewed as this "stumbling block" standing in the way of two nations becoming fully fledged allies. Others assert that China's growing regional influence has emerged on Russia's hegemonic expense. Therefore, the rivalry over Central Asia may mark the advent of conflicting Sino-Russian interests (Düben, 2015). Indeed, for the first time since the 1800s, Russia shares the region with another player. As China has replaced Russia as a key trade partner in five Central Asian states, paired with its tremendous investments, Russia's capabilities are easily exceeded. Understandably, the notion of a New Great Game, the struggle for power, influence and hegemony in Central Asia played out between Russia, China, the West and NATO (mainly USA) and the region's small and medium-sized actors e.g. Pakistan, India and Iran, have been extensively discussed in academic literature in recent decades. Marcin Kaczmarski, in his insightful and timely book, challenges the notion that Russia and China are in a fierce competition over Central Asia, asserting that a "new status quo has emerged" (Kaczmarski, 2015, p. 86, 99). Kaczmarski believes that both emerged as the regional winners. China secured access to hydrocarbons and economic expansion while Russia still holds "dominant positions in the areas of politics and security" (Ibid). Hence, the alleged tensions have been exaggerated (Indeo, 2016, p. 6).

Central Asia is significant for China's regional and global foreign policies. Chinese officials frequently recite in official documents and statements that regional peace and stability lay at the core of China's interest. China's proximity to Central Asia is an asset in itself, in terms of its access to natural resources and connections to the Muslim world, akin to the aforesaid Russian-China border where energy pipelines between Central Asia and China are unreachable to foreign actors (Peyrouse, Boonstra and Laruelle, 2012, p. 11; MacHaffie, 2010, pp. 369, 373). Furthermore, for China, the post-Soviet states are part of the Muslim world and a major element in the Beijing "strategy of building a long-term partnership with Iran, Saudi Arabia and Afghanistan" (Ibid., 10–11). Thus, the five Central Asian stats' stability and security is pivotal for the entire region's security, including China's Xinjiang province. Instability and turmoil, particularly in the Ferghana valley, encompassing Kyrgyzstan, Tajikistan, and Uzbekistan, has immediate repercussions on China. Firstly, it would disrupt trade and energy supplies. Secondly, negative cataclysms from Central Asia may flow into the Xinjiang province. At the 2012 SCO summit, the Chinese deputy minister of foreign affairs stated, "the peace and stability of Central Asia relates to the core interests of China, as well as the members of the SCO. Our determination to maintain the peace and stability of Central Asia is steadfast. We will absolutely not allow the unrest that happened in West Asia and North Africa to happen in Central Asia" (Mariani, 2013, p. 9). China's top priorities include: (i) preventing the Central Asian states from becoming the bedrock of Uyghur separatism; (ii) preventing them from becoming a "destabilizing" factor similar to Afghanistan; (iii) maintaining access to the regions' hydrocarbons and mineral resources; and (iv) using them as a corridor in its One Belt, One Road project, embodying their integration into China's global [economic] strategy.

By 2010, the trade between China and Central Asia had for the first time exceeded that of Russia and Central Asia. As a major economic partner, since more than 10 percent of China's imports of hydrocarbons originate from Kazakhstan, Turkmenistan and Kyrgyzstan (Mariani, 2013, p. 10). Due to its large reserves of hydrocarbons and geographic proximity to China, Central Asia has successfully become one of Beijing's major investment destinations. Chinese officials often state that, unlike other major players, Beijing does not require anything in return for its assistance and investments. Indeed, neither political concessions nor "additional conditions" are attached to China's generous financial programs (Ibid., 9). While Sinophobe sentiments are widespread among Central Asian civilians, the political elite seem to give preference to China over Russia as the collaboration symbolizes new energy projects, foreign investment, credits, infrastructure and funds for corruption (Luzianin, 2012). It is contentious whether these developments harm Russia's interest, as Russia is unable to compete with China in terms of investments. Seemingly, Kremlin's officials may have accepted this. Ergo, Russia is obliged to acknowledge China's investments as a "positive phenomenon" (Kim and Indeo, 2014, p. 277).

Yet, Russian regional influence sharply declined during the 1990s. As Lena Jonson (2006, pp. 1–3; 1998, p. 3) notes, Russian-Central Asian relations waned in all major fields e.g. commerce, military and security, natural resources, and in culture, the once 'brotherly nations' became estranged. On becoming prime minister, Putin recognized this and in his 1999 speech, he acknowledged Central Asia's vital place in Russia's strategic and foreign policy thinking (Ferguson, 2006, p. 206). Putin wanted to restore Russia's influence in "Central Asia and the CIS states as whole" (Duncan, 2013, p. 134). Visiting the countries topped his priority list. In the new foreign policy concept of 2000, Russia proposed to strengthen the CIS' Collective Security Treaty "in order to deal with Islamist threats in the Caucasus and Central Asia and ... declared [the] desire to regain control of the region's energy resources, particularly those in the Caspian Sea" (Laruelle, 2009, p. 5). Moscow also agreed that their national security was closely tied to the region's security (Ionova, 2014, p. 83). Ergo, the region is of great geopolitical importance for both Russia and China.

It would be misleading to argue that Russia and China did not engage in rivalry and economic competition. Rivalry over the region's energy resources was evident when, in 2002, Russia prevented the creation of the "comprehensive common market within the SCO," which was proposed by China, aimed to fill local markets with Chinese goods and services, driving "Russian enterprise away" (Weitz, 2008, pp. 63–64). Moreover, Moscow's promoted concept of organizing a regional energy club was rejected by China, as Russia could gain sway over Chinese energy strategies (Kaczmarski, 2015, p. 94). Russia opposed China's endeavors to control the region's reserves by acquiring majority shares in energy firms, coveting Russian and Central Asian companies to control natural resources (Weitz, 2008, p. 62). Moscow-Beijing rivalries were also on display when, in 2000, the Chinese Trans-Asian gas pipeline of Turkmenistan-Uzbekistan-Kazakhstan-China was established (Luzianin 2012). After the 2009 China-Turkmen gas deal, Russia accepted its third place among top Turkmen gas consumers when it was first before 2008

(Kim and Indeo, 2013, p. 277). In 2011, China signed another agreement with Turkmenistan for a gas supply of 65bn cubic meters per year. Rivalries aside, China regards its relationship with Russia as one of cooperation instead of competition, and has been very careful to avoid confrontation with its large Northern neighbor (Ibid). While both nations grasp that, economically, Russia lags far behind China in the regional arena, China has consistently recognized, and continues to do so albeit informally, Russia's political leadership and priorities (Ibid).

As Zhao Huasheng, one of China's prominent Russia and Central Asia experts, claimed the great game is played out between Russia and US, not between Russia and China. As Marcin Kaczmarski accurately notes, China and Russia found a *modus vivendi* in terms of the preservation of stability, which for them means maintaining the regional status quo. China accepts the Kremlin's claim of Central Asia as its sphere of influence, and unlike the West, has consistently recognized Russia's legitimate regional interests, and post-Soviet spaces as such. China has not revealed any apprehensions concerning Russia's military presence. *Au contraire*, Chinese officials often reiterate that Beijing is interested in Russia's support and military influence for several reasons. Assisting China to battle separatism, Wahhabism/Salafism and curbing Western influence in the region are key reasons. (Laruelle and Peyrouse, 2012, p. 42). China has thus conceded Russia's political and military primacy while Russia accepts China's economic ascendancy (Lo, 2008, p. 92). As Richard Weitz notes, expectations aside, the five "stans" have not become a platform of rivalry between Moscow and Beijing. Instead, the region embodies a "major unifying element in Chinese-Russian relations" (Weitz, 2008, p. 51). Marlène Laruelle and Sebastien Peyrouse denote the ambivalent nature of the Russian-Chinese "partnership," observing that the alliance is based on both sides' support for the status quo, and limiting Western influence in the region (Laruelle and Peyrouse, 2012, p. 42).

However, since 2001, US unilateralism and its growing regional influence have been among the foremost factors, which led to a Sino-Russian strategic convergence and growing cooperation, involving collaborations within the SCO. In the eve of September 11 2001, a level of divergence in the Sino-Russian strategic interests could be sensed (Kim and Indeo, 2013, p. 276). Putin's support of the "War on Terror" briefly transformed China's regional policy. Struck by Putin's easiness (and endorsement), Chinese officials witnessed the mushrooming of US bases in Central Asia, which had traditionally been in Russia's sphere of influence (Lo, 2008, p. 95). Certainly, the Russian-US partnership on the "War on Terror" and Moscow's "overnight" switch from a "multi-vectored approach to one unambiguously centered on comprehensive cooperation with the United States" without previous consultation with Beijing came as surprise to Chinese officials (Ibid., 96). In Bobo

Lo's assessment, this development made Chinese officials conscious of the fact that, for Russia, its Western relations will always prevail over those with China (Ibid). There is no consensus among scholars whether the chief reason behind the post-9/11 divergences was due to their imperatives of curbing terrorism, or perhaps both nations preferred the West to each other. Yet, this divergence lasted briefly and by 2004, when the Russian-US partnership on the "War on Terror" was evidently doomed to failure, the junction between Russia and China "re-emerged and was eventually strengthened by a new normative convergence" (Kim and Indeo, 2013, p. 276). As aforementioned, both states were "uneasy" with US military bases' presence and rather irked with US unilateral policies, e.g. George W. Bush's Freedom Agenda that aggressively championed democracy promotion. Additionally, since the Shanghai Five revamped itself into the SCO, the organization has served as the focal platform for Sino-Russian regional cooperation. In recent developments, both countries have agreed that SCO could serve as platform for promoting the Belt and Road initiatives, as all member states would benefit from the success of China's grand Eurasian vision.

Central Asia is evidently where Russia and China interact with their convergent and divergent interests. Aside from their rivalry over the region's natural resources, their mutual interest in a stable region continues to prevail over their desire to tighten their grasps over resources. Contrary to many anticipations and forecasts, the post-Cold War Sino-Russian engagement has broadly been that of cooperation, as opposed to competition. Both powers are likely to continue to manage their differences, respecting their legitimate interests due to their shared enthusiasm for a stable and prosperous region.

GROWING SKEPTICISM AND MOSCOW'S PREDICAMENT WITH THE ROLE OF "JUNIOR PARTNER"

As demonstrated thus far, Russia and China have gradually improved their relationship, managing their differences and clashing interests in Central Asia. It would be premature to claim that the two are on a collision course, which could pave to a major conflict. However, it should be noted that a number of issues in their bilateral relations persist, which could contribute to disagreements and divergence of interests. For instance, China's rising Eurasian influence emerges at Russian expense, Moscow's predicament concerning its position as "junior partner" in contemporary Eurasia, and Russia transmutation into a Chinese raw material appendage could become the focal source of tension between Moscow and Beijing if unaddressed. Analyzing Russia's official discourse on Sino-Russian rapprochement, an understanding of the fraternal and neighborly relationship between Moscow and Beijing arises.

As Natasha Kuhrt (2015) notes, in official discourse enforced by Kremlin, the "'China threat' has been virtually taboo" for the last decade, while "economic and trade relations have become a 'safe area' from which to criticize relations" between Moscow and Beijing. Still, discourses derived from popular talk shows, blogs, novels, and newspaper articles and interviews on Russian media demonstrate that many Russians remain uneasy concerning China. After having consulted numerous sources since 1990s (see bibliography) it may be concluded that four major concerns are always present in Russian discourse on China: a) the influx of Chinese workers and increased Chinese presence in the Far East, b) becoming China's "junior partner," c) the raw material appendage, and d) disengaging Central Asia as their sphere of privileged interests.

Some years ago, Andrei P. Tsygankov had identified two key groups when probing the China discourse in Russia, namely the Sinophiles and Sinophobes (Tsygankov, 2009). Holding high expectations concerning the Sino-Russian rapprochement, the former at times while recognizing the nature of Sino-Russian relations as strategic partnership sometimes venture to the extent where Moscow and Beijing are assumed as allies (Galenovich, 2005; Titarenko, 2014; Karaganov et al., 2015). Sinophiles also argue that China is not an expansionist country, posing no threat to any nation's statehood and sovereignty.

In contrast, Sinophobes are very suspicious of the "benign" nature of China's regional and global initiatives, e.g. the Belt and Road. In China's strategy in Eurasia and particularly in Xi Jinping's endeavors and ideas such as Belt and Road they see attempts to construct a Sino-centric regional and world order. Following the path of Africa and South America, they argue that Central Asia and Russia will simply become China's raw material appendage and a space where China dumps its excess productions (Spanger, 2016). China, they claim, is primarily interested in Russia for spatial reasons, enabling them to reach Europe. Accentuating that goods transport between Shanghai and Rotterdam a rather costly endeavor, the alternative land route to Europe via Russia would save Chinese businesses vast amounts of money and resources (Callahan, 2016, p. 235). This vision is entrenched in Russian popular discourse. Renowned writer Vladimir Sorokin has penned a novel about a dystopian Russia, where it emerges as a road from Guanzhou to Paris. In Sorokin's famed work, the road embodies the country's arteries and veins, bruised by crimes and horrors (Sorokin, 2006). Their main concern is thus that of morphing into a transit zone and a source of natural resources, effectively relegating to a Chinese-dominated periphery and (neo-colonial) subjugation.

Nevertheless, a careful analysis of Russia's China discourse[4] since 2012 reveals that a strong moderate voice has emerged. This group consists of influential Sinologists and economists whose voices cannot be ignored or simply ousted under the carpet by Russian officials. They claim that China is, understandably, self-centered and often sees other countries as instruments in achieving Beijing's global aims and objectives. While they do not fear China, these experts try to warn against rushing into China's embrace. The moderates, while pointing to the benefits of China's regional endeavors, have accentuated a series of snags in the Sino-Russian engagement. Correspondingly, the Moderates' chief concern is Russia's prospect of becoming a junior partner and/or a raw material appendage. Amid Den Xiaoping reforms, China's GDP was only 40 percent that of RSFSR. By 2016, Russia's GDP was merely 20 percent that of China. In 1990, all goods and services' output in the two countries were roughly at similar levels, and throughout the 1990s, Russia's economy shrank as that of China enjoyed "rapid but steady growth" (Tsygankov, 2009, p. 17). By 2010, China's economy had become four times larger than that of Russia (Trenin, 2012, p. 8). This trend will most likely continue. China occupies a principal place in Russia's top trading partners, whereas Russia conversely occupies a marginal place in that of China's trading partners. The dependency ratio remains uneven, 1.76 percent in 2009 and 2.15 percent in 2013 (Spanger, 2016). Lucidly, China is modernizing and diversifying its trade while Russian dependency on Chinese markets grows daily (Ibid). A structure of trade is another matter: in 1999, Russia imported a myriad of processed and unprocessed goods from China (e.g. metals, plastic, textiles, footwear, machinery) and unprocessed primary goods (e.g. wood and vegetables). In 2013, 48 percent of Russian imports were hi-tech and machinery. An alarm for Russians is the trend of trade, wherein 39 percent of Russian exports to China consisted of machinery and only six percent of imports were raw hydrocarbons in 1990, whereas by 2013, only four percent of exports were metal and machinery, yet a staggering 74 percent of its exports were energy products in raw forms (Ibid). An economist, who certainly cannot be branded as a Sinophobe, joked, "we are turning not into a petrol station for China—we are not capable of producing good quality fuel. We are turning in to an oil well where you take raw oil and gas" (Tochka Zreniia, 2015). Hundreds of trains leave Russia for China, loaded with timber, only to return with furniture manufactured with the same timber it had transported earlier (Ibid).

Finally, while Russian military industry has been shrinking for almost three decades since 1991, China's leadership has been "promoting military modernization relentlessly, and increasing its tempo in the 2000s" (Trenin 2012, p. 8). China's defense budget is the world's second largest, after the US. Russia trails on a fifth place. China has also successfully reverse-engineered a number of high-tech weaponry it had purchased from Russia since 1991. As aforementioned, while China is technologically behind the West and Japan, it overtook Russia "in many aspects of science and education" (Ibid). Within the forthcoming years, China will have three aircraft carriers whereas Russia only has one, leading to a power balance change in the oceans. The Moderates see that everything raises Russia's risks of becoming China's junior partner in a Eurasia with Beijing as its center of gravity instead of Moscow. Predictably, Russophile and Moderate groups, both of which chiefly consist of Statists, Eurasianists, Communists and other non-liberal groups, often express regret that the USSR did not embark on Deng Xiaoping-style economic reforms.

In light of Xi's two-day showcase of the OROB initiative in May 2017, precisely two years after the 8 May agreement, the growing skepticism in Russia, particularly within the Sinophobe and Moderate groups, cannot be overlooked.[5] Several factors behind this growing skepticism can be outlined. First concerns the fact that, to many commentators it remained unclear how Russia could benefit from China's initiative: it was argued that Moscow still lacked guarantees that it would benefit from the Chinese initiative and from the integration between the two projects, for Russia had hoped that the initiative would help to develop its Far East. However, it is difficult not to notice that the Chinese government has not made the infrastructure projects and maps, including Russia's Far East and Siberia, public. The Trans-Siberian Railway (TSR) and the Baikal–Amur Mainline (BAM), it seems, will remain untouched by the SREB, while the main passage shall go through Orenburg and Chelyabinsk thereby side lining Russia's Far East in China's New Silk Road. Furthermore, Russia is eager to see China invest in Russian infrastructure projects, which would help to modernize its industries while China's main concern is to sell its goods and deliver to Europe by the shortest and most convenient way (Polubota, 2017) As Gabuev has noted, by summer 2017, the only tangible result of the initiative to link the EEU with SREB were two major Silk Road Fund (SRF)-supported investments in Yamal SPG and Sibur, both organizations co-owned by Putin's close friend, the head of the Russia-China Business Council oligarch Gennadii Timchenko (Gabuev, 2017).

Another frequently mentioned issue in Russia-China discourse concerns how few of the many bilateral trade agreements are actually materialized. In 2014, when Russia and China signed the US$400bn landmark deal, the latter emphasized that large funds would find their way to Russia. Rendering to Russian officials, one main incentive for the signed agreement of the 8 May 2015 Xi-Putin summit was to integrate SREB and EEU, as part of a projected expectation rising Chinese FDI in Russia. Yet, as of the end of 2015, China failed to provide the promised payment as part of the ambitious "Power of Siberia" pipeline project originally worth US$55bn (Shtraks, 2015). The project's value was adjusted numerous times and finally China's Petrochina invested US$3.2bn in 2017 (RBK, 2017). It remains unknown whether the

Altai pipeline, designated to link Russia to China's westernmost province, after Li Keqiang asserted in November 2014 in Moscow, may ever proceed (Shtraks, 2015). Commentators and experts already overlook the planned Moscow-Kazan rail project. China has invested much less than what Russia had anticipated. An attribute is China's recent economic woes, though also unwilling to amass risks, evident in their calls for guarantees from the Russian government. Taken aback, Russian officials seem to view this relationship as that of a debtor creditor, not a partnership. Since 2015, signing new deals aside, nothing new quite happened between the two. An outspoken Russian economist noted the ratification of many agreements is imperative yet they need to be implemented. Finally, the growth of bilateral trade is far below than Russian officials' expectations. Announced on 8 May 2015, Xi and Putin's goal of raising trade to US$200bn by 2020 is unlikely to be attained. In fact, Sino-Russian trade has fallen by at least 25 percent in 2015 alone. Contrary to belief, Putin's latest meeting with Xi in June 2016 did not improve Russia's involvement in SREB and the Sino-Russian bilateral economic relations.

Due to these motives, an emergence of a rift between Moscow and Beijing due to divergent interest is also not entirely unthinkable. The two, therefore, need to source means to ensure that their relationship remains cooperative, in order to prevent divergences and aggressive competition. This is particularly imperative in the broader framework wherein the regional and global orders grow increasingly intricate and challenging. In addition to Central Asia, effective win-win diplomacy would benefit Eurasia as a whole.

THE IMPLICATIONS OF *"SOPRIAZHENIE"*

In 2013, Xi announced the One Road, One Belt (OROB) plans, consisting of the Silk Road Economic Belt (SREB) and the Maritime Silk Road (MSR) both extensively discussed in this volume. The SREB will concentrate on the continental countries of Central Asia and Eastern Europe, while the MSR will target the littoral countries of Southeast Asia, South Asia, the Middle East and East Africa. As the official Chinese blueprints suggest, the OROB vision aims to connect Asia, Europe and Africa along five major land and sea routes.[6] According to Xi, Beijing values annual trade between China and "Belt and Road" countries to "surpass 2.5 trillion U.S. dollars in a decade or so" (Tiezi, 2014). Insofar, the Asian Infrastructure Investment Bank (AIIB) has received US$100bn, with US$40bn having been allocated to the national Silk Road Fund. The China Development Bank (CDB) is planning to invest US$890bn in 900 projects by 2020 (Pantucci and Lain, 2015, p. 3).

Equally, Russian diplomats' and scholars' opinion of China and its regional initiatives, such as SREB and the integration between the two projects, remains divided between the three aforesaid groups. While most agree that China's initiatives in Central Asia serve the purpose of transforming the region according to China's geopolitical, geoeconomic and geostrategic plans, scholars have fiercely debated the initiatives' intentions and their real benefits for Russia and Central Asia. Sinophiles, while recognizing China's growing influence through OROB's increasingly secured trade corridors, new markets and sources of energy, maintain that China's endeavor will deliver everyone growth and economic prosperity along the Road. Sinophobes, conversely, argue that the controversy of developing infrastructure is a means occupying Chinese infrastructure firms, stipulating that China undergoes a phase of extreme overproduction/overcapacity—rather than as an "economic stimulant" (Cooley, 2015; Blenkinsop and Wong, 2016; Spanger, 2016). It has been contended that an important motive behind the initiative is to encourage economic development in China's Xinjiang autonomous region, as the Beijing's "Go West"-strategy of 2000 has been unsuccessful. Besides, "Silk Route(s)" through Central Asia, Iran and Russia are "an alternative to US controlled oceans" (Bordachev, 2015). China has certainly been dependent on US-dominated maritime transport routes. For instance, in ASEAN free trade zones, China's trade reached a staggering US$400bn by 2012 (China Daily, 2013). Thus, as many note, China is concerned that Washington could use this as leverage, by threatening to impose a naval blockade or block the US-controlled Strait of Malacca. Finally, the Belt and Road as many speculate, may be an effective soft power instrument to promote Chinese global interests.

Modeled on the EU, the Russia-led union "respects the free trade market principles of the WTO" (Lane, 2016, p. 51). The EEU's aims are to regulate economic activity within the territories of Russia, Kazakhstan, Belarus, Kyrgyzstan and Armenia. The project has economic and geopolitical objectives. The economic intentions are to integrate ex-Soviet countries through free movement of goods, labor, capital and services. This, many argue, is an attempt to compete with China's regional economic expansion, countering the influence of other global economic blocs, e.g. the EU. Geopolitical objectives are designated to contain US's regional presence, and thus to maintain a status quo. The West remains suspicious of the EEU. Western experts asserted that the EEU is a Muscovite attempt to "restore its influence in the post-Soviet space" (Indeo, 2016, p. 7). Others claim that, through EEU, Moscow intends to contain China's ever-growing expansion in Central Asia (Idib).

Many critics and commentators have reasoned that the EEU's has "yet to be discovered" (Kirkham, 2016, pp. 111–128). Undoubtedly, the real achievements of the Moscow-led integration project remain unclear except that citizens of all five-member states enjoy equal employment rights and a common custom space that stretches from Bishkek to Brest (Bordachev, 2015). Crucially, the EEU has recently suffered a series of significant set-back (Mankoff and Ghiasy, 2015). The Maidan Revolution was perhaps the major blow to Union, turning the prospects of Ukraine becoming a member state inconceivable. Ukraine has played a key role in the project, supposedly intended to represent one of the pillars "of a new multipolar world order, alongside the US-led West and an anticipated Chinese-dominated Asia" (Mankoff and Ghiasy, 2015). In Russia's great power mythology, Russia cannot be a great power without Ukraine in its sphere of influence. Hence, the EEU is inward-looking, operating through supranational and intergovern-mental institutions. The SREB is diametrically opposed: outward-looking and largely an abstract and ideological vision, likely to be very successful due to Beijing's colossal cash reserves.

After president Xi's announcement in 2013, it was debated that OROB initiatives pose a significant threat to Russian regional influence and the EEU would be outpaced by Beijing's proposed project. Due to China's finan-cial, business, diplomatic, academic and military resources, the OROB has been actively promoted—the vision is undoubtedly more attractive than the Russian-led EEU. Countries have established bilateral relations with China, bypassing Russia (Kobrinskaya, 2016). Many have contended that Russia is not capable of competing with China in organizing a genuine Eurasian economic community, as it is China that creates a "continental block of former Soviet republics" (Blanc, 2016). Ostensibly, Chinese officials were concerned with Moscow's reaction to the Road initiative. If Moscow views China's initiative as threatening, it would pressure the regional countries not to partake in any Chinese-led projects (Gabuev, 2015b). For Russia, reacting to China's initiative was a trial, as it has not developed a viable strategy in dealing with China's enthusiastic initiative.

Moscow reacted in a way in which it masked its concession to China. Such is the case according to influential scholar Sergey Karaganov, known for his close Kremlin ties, alleging that Russian diplomat Igor Morgulov proposed the idea of *Sopriazhenie* [7] or pairing (Karaganov, 2016). At the 2015 Boao Forum, it was announced by Russia's first deputy prime minister, Igor Shu-valov, that Moscow remains positive vis-à-vis China's regional initiatives, and as an EEU member, Russia is keen to cooperate with China (Spivak, 2016). Clearly, for Russia, it is important to convey the notion of linking the SREB and EEU as a joint initiative. As previously mentioned, on 8 May 2015 Xi and Putin signed a declaration "on cooperation in coordinating devel-opment of EEU and the Silk Road Economic Belt." According to Putin's statement, "We think that the Eurasian integration project and the Silk Road Economic Belt project complement each other very harmoniously" (Putin, 2015). Unsurprisingly, the announcement led to a whirlwind of academic and analytical articles where experts and commentators questioned the feasibility of the two projects' integration. As aforementioned, even Chinese officials and scholars failed to explain exactly how the Belt and Road would be implemented, while the signed declaration of 8 May 2015 denoted a series of vague declarations of intent and political statements. Dmitrii Medvedev in his 2016 interview with one of China's major media outlets CCTV postulated that the *Sopriazhenie* (linking) of SREB and EEU can result in the creation of a free trade zone and a fully fledged trade and economic partnership between China and the Eurasian Union (Medvedev, 2016). Regional expert Fabio Indeo also maintains that the initiative's aim was to create common economic space in Eurasia, establishing a Free Trade Agreement between China and the EEU (Indeo, 2016, p. 13).

Since 2015, numerous articles seek to explore the integration's technicalities. For example, the question of how could Moscow convince Beijing to cooperate in a multilateral framework with regional countries and other EEU member states, as opposed to China's preferred bilateral format. Though, it appears that in emphasizing the integration's technicalities has simultaneously undermined the 8 May agreement's geopolitical implications.

Alluding to one of China's leading scholars, Zhao Huasheng, the agreement to pair the SREB and EEU is political, not economic, as Russia and China have achieved a "consensus to coexist peacefully" (Huasheng and Trenin, 2016). The announcement of *Sopriazhenie* mirrors a momentous geopolitical event—namely, Russia's tacit acceptance of China's leading economic role in Eurasia, guaranteeing that neither will not enter any kind of antagonism due to clashing interests and power shifts. The *Sopriazhenie*, or the initiative to link SREB with EEU, is actually the latest transpiration of China's astutely effective win-win diplomacy.

CONCLUSION

The fruitful post-Cold War rapprochement between Moscow and Beijing, which clearly can be described as a comprehensive strategic partnership, is undoubtedly in their best interest. However, the successes in their bilateral relations thus far, combined with strong mutual trust, do not necessarily guarantee the absence of a prospective conflict. The emergence of a new, dynamic and promising economic space in Eurasia with Beijing as its center, instead of Moscow, may inevitably lead to disagreements and rivalries. As this chapter maintains, the initiative to coordinate SREB and EEU was not only a clever move by both Moscow and Beijing, but also a historical initiative where the two agree to coordinate their grand foreign policy plans in the strategically-important Central Asia and the wider Eurasia.

Following the *Sopriazhenie*—the initiative to integrate the EEU with SREB—a number of implications for the Sino-Russian bilateral relations and the wider Eurasia may be identified. Firstly, as a result, Russia's regional role is recognized by China, thereby averting a Ukraine-like scenario where China, akin to the West, steps on Russia's vital interest. Secondly, to Russia's public, Moscow appears as a key player in Eurasia, equal to Beijing, not a "junior partner." Thirdly, the agreement demonstrates that Russia—at least for the time being -- has tacitly recognized China's dominant role, coming to terms with Xi's gargantuan project and defined its own place and role within the continent's embryonic economic space. Finally, the initiative grants Russia's leadership the time and space, which it needs in order to improve and further develop its strategy of dealing with China's incessant rise. Hence, the *Sopriazhenie* is more than a mere economic or integration agreement. Besides promoting a framework for security and stability, it is an indication of a new phase in Sino-Russian bilateral relations. For both, this is ultimately an essential step in the complex and precarious road in which two nations must continuously adjust themselves to the tectonic shifts in Eurasian balance of power against the backdrop of the economic realities of the 21st century.

NOTES

1. The 2011-2012 Russian protest movement also referred as the "Snow Revolution" which began in Winter 2011 as protests against the Russian legislative election result.

2. A series of sit-in street protests in 2014 against Standing Committee of the National People's Congress (NPCSC) decision regarding a proposed reform to the Hong Kong's electoral system, which allegedly was in favor of the Chinese Communist Party.

3. The Treaty of Good-Neighborliness and Friendly Cooperation Between the People's Republic of China and the Russian Federation (FCT) signed by the Jiang Zemin and Vladimir Putin, on July 16, 2001.

4. Author had analyzed numerous academic and non-academic sources including popular political and discussion shows, and interviews (see bibliography) on Russia's mostly pro-government media such as RTR Kultura and Vesti 24, Pervyi Kanal, TVTS, Zvezda, which discuss China and the recent Sino-Russian engagement.

5. Coined by China as the event of the year in which thirty heads of states participated, the Belt and Road Forum took place on 14 May 2017.

6. The focus of the SREB will be on (i) linking China to Europe through Central Asia and Russia; (ii) connecting China with the Middle East through Central Asia; and (iii) bringing together China and Southeast Asia, South Asia and the Indian Ocean. The Maritime Silk Road will focus on using Chinese coastal ports to: (iv) link China with Europe through the South China Sea and the Indian Ocean; and (v)

connect China with the South Pacific Ocean through the South China Sea (Belt and Road, 2015).

7. From verb *sopryach'/sopriagat'* meaning to mate, combine, associate. According to dictionary *Sopriazhenie* is a method to compound and bond portions and parts in wooden structures; relationship of anything with anything, an indispensable concomitant, the combination of several objects or phenomena.

REFERENCES

Aleksei Maslov and Irina Sorokina (2016) Aktual'naia zagranitsa: Rossiia i Kitai: v poiskakh sopriazheniia [online], available: http://radio.mediametrics.ru/actual_zagraniza/1427/ [accessed 12 October 2016].

Berryman, J. (2010) Russia and China in Eurasia: The Wary Partnership. In Freire, M. R. and Kanet, R. E. (eds) *Key Players and Regional Dynamics in Eurasia: The Return of the 'Great Game'*, Basingstoke and New York: Palgrave Macmillan.

Belt and Road (2015) What is Belt and Road Initiative [online], available: http://belt-android.hktdc.com/en/about-the-belt-and-road-initiative/about-the-belt-and-road-initiative.aspx [accessed 18 April 2016].

Blanc, S. (2016) Russian Writers on the Decline of Russia in the Far East and the Rise of China [online], available: https://jamestown.org/program/stephen-blank-russian-writers-on-the-decline-of-russia-in-the-far-east-and-the-rise-of-china/#sthash.38auEFdW.dpuf [accessed 22 September 2016].

Blenkinsop, P. and Wong, S.-L. (2016) As global steel crisis grips, China says March output was a record [online], available: http://www.reuters.com/article/us-china-steel-overcapacity-idUSKCN0XF2LI [accessed 19 April 2016].

Bol'shenstvo. PMF-2016: udastsia li nam priblizit' Dal'nii Vostok? (2016) [online], available: http://www.ntv.ru/peredacha/Bolshinstvo/m49747/o397896/video/ [accessed 10 October 2016].

Bol'shenstvo. Rossiia—Kitai: partnery ili konkurenty? (2016) [online], available: http://www.ntv.ru/peredacha/Bolshinstvo/m49747/o398559/video/ [accessed 19 September 2016].

Bordachev, T. (2015) V Kitaiskom iazyke net slova brat [online], available: https://lenta.ru/articles/2015/09/30/sopr/ [accessed 30 September 2015].

Bordachev, T. (2016) The Great Win-Win Game [online], available: http://eng.globalaffairs.ru/number/The-Great-Win-Win-Game-18395 [accessed 3 November 2016].

Business Insider (2016) Xi Jinping and Vladimir Putin meet in Beijing, vow to deepen their 'strategic partnership [online], available: http://uk.businessinsider.com/xi-jinping-and-vladimir-putin-meet-in-beijing-vow-to-deepen-their-strategic-partnership-2016-6 [accessed 25 June 2016].

Callahan, W. A. (2016) China's "Asia Dream": The Belt Road Initiative and the new regional order, *Asian Journal of Comparative Politics*, 1(3), pp. 226–243.

Chas istiny—Rossiia i Kitai. Istoriia otnoshenii (2015) [online], available: http://www.365days.ru/news/15392 [accessed 22 July 2016].

China playing a rising role in ASEAN business (2013) [online], available: http://usa.chinadaily.com.cn/business/2013–10/11/content_17023601.htm [accessed 2 February 2014].

Chto Delat'? Kak Kitai otnositsia k svoei i k nashei istorii? (2016) [online], available: http://tvkultura.ru/video/show/brand_id/20917/episode_id/1267557/video_id/1439945/ [accessed 23 September 2016].

Chto Delat'? Kto budet kontrolirovat' TSentral'nuiu Aziiu? [online], available: https://www.youtube.com/watch?v=QIqsMZRrku0 [accessed 24 September 2016].

Cooley, A. (2015) Novyi shelkovyi put' ili klassicheskii variant tupikovogo razvitiia [online], available: [accessed 12 December 2015].

Cooley: China's Silk Road initiative is "conceptually incompatible" with Russia's EEU (2016) [online], available: http://www.ponarseurasia.org/article/china-silk-road-initiative-conceptually-incompatible-russia-eeu [accessed 9 March 2016].

Cossa, R. A. (2014) China and Russia's Great Game in Central Asia [online], available: http://nationalinterest.org/blog/the-buzz/china-russias-great-game-central-asia-11385 [accessed 6 October].

Duncan, P. J. S. (2013) Russia, NATO and the 'War on Terror': Competition and Co-operation in Central Asia after 11 September 2001. In Tanrisever, O. F. (ed) *Afghanistan and Central Asia: NATO's Role in Regional Security Since 9/11*, Amsterdam: IOS Press, pp. 120–142.

Düben, B. A. (2015) Can the China-Russia Warmth Last? [online], available: http://thediplomat.com/2015/05/can-the-china-russia-warmth-last/ [accessed 12 May 2015].

Ekspert: Kitai sozdaet finansovuiu strukturu v protivoves MVF (2015) [online], available: http://www.tvc.ru/news/show/id/64985 [accessed 12 September 2016].

Ferguson, J. P. (2006) Russian Strategic Thinking Towards Central , South, and Southeast Asia. In Rozman, G., Togo, K. and Ferguson, J. P. (eds) *Russian Strategic Thought Towards Asia*, Basingstoke and New York: Palgrave, pp. 2015–228.

Ying, F. (January/February 2016) How China sees Russia: Beijing and Moscow are close, but not allies, *Foreign Affairs*, 95(1), pp. 96–105.

Gabuev, A. (2015a) *A Soft Alliance"? Russia-China Relations After Ukraine Crisis*, London: European Council on Foreign Relations.

Gabuev, A. (2015b) China's Silk Road Challenge [online], available: http://carnegie.ru/commentary/2015/11/12/china-s-silk-road-challenge/ilrk [accessed 17 February 2016].

Gabuev, A. (2017) The Silk Road to Nowhere [online], available: http://carnegie.ru/commentary/?fa=70061 [accessed 25 May 2017].

Galenovich, I. M. (2005) K voprosu o rossiisko-kitaiskom global'nom partnerstve. In Titarenko, M. L. (ed) *Rossia i Kitai: sotrudnichestvo v usloviiakh globalizatsii*, Moscow: RAN, pp. 2–24.

Gvosdev, N. K. and Marsh, C. (2014) *Russian Foreign Policy: Interests, Vectors and Sectors*, Los Angeles-Washington, DC: Sage.

Herszenhorn, D. M. and Buckley, C. (2013) China's New Leader, Visiting Russia, Promotes Nations' Economic and Military Ties [online], available: http://www.nytimes.com/2013/03/23/world/asia/xi-jinping-visits-russia-on-first-trip-abroad.html?_r=0 [accessed 2 April 2014].

Huasheng, Z. and Trenin, D. (2016) Rossiia i Kitai v TSentral'noi Azii: sotrudnich-estvo ili sopernichestvo? [podcast], available: https://soundcloud.com/carnegie-endowment/jckajn7fov8m?in=carnegie-endowment/sets/hv3mtanq7ac8 [accessed 18 July 2016].

Indeo, F. (2016) The Eurasian Economic Union and the Silk Road Economic Belt: the impact of the Sino-Russian geopolitical strategies in the Eurasia region, Maastricht, The Maastricht School of Management.

Interv'iu Dmitriia Medvedeva Rossiiskim telekanalom (2008) [online], available: http://kremlin.ru/events/president/news/1276 [accessed 27 September 2016].

Ionova, E. (2014) Aktivizatsiia Rossii v TSentral'noi Azii i rossiisko-kirgizskikh otnosheniia, *Rossiia i Musul'manskii Mir*, 2(260), 81–86.

Jeffrey, Mankoff and Ghiasy, R. (2015) Central Asia's Future: Three Powers, Three Visions [online], available: http://thediplomat.com/2015/05/central-asias-future-three-powers-three-visions/ [accessed 11 June 2015].

Jonson, L. (1998) *Russia and Central Asia: A New Web of Relations*, London: Royal Institute of International Affairs.

Jonson, L. (2006) V*ladimir Putin and Central Asia: The Shaping of Russian Foreign Policy*, London-New York: I.B. Tauris.

Kaczmarski, M. (2015) *Russia-China Relations in the Post-Crisis International Order*, New York: Routledge.

Karaganov, S. ed. (2015) *Toward the Great Ocean-3: Creating Central Eurasia*, Moscow: Valdai Forum.

Karagonov, S. (2016) From East to West, or Greater Eurasia [online], available: http://eng.globalaffairs.ru/pubcol/From-East-to-West-or-Greater-Eurasia-18440 [accessed 3 November 2016].

Kim, Y. and Indeo, F. (2013) The new great game in Central Asia post 2014: The US "New Silk Road" strategy and Sino-Russian rivalry, *Communist and Post-Communist Studies*, 46(2), 275–286.

Kirkham, K. (July 2016) The formation of the Eurasian Economic Union: How success-ful is the Russian regional hegemony?, *Journal of Eurasian Studies*, 7(2), 111–28.

Kitai postroit Novyi Shelkovyi put' (2014) [online], available: http://www.vesti.ru/videos/show/vid/606820/www.m24.ru/videos/61628 [accessed 1 July 2016].

Kobrinskaya, I. (2016) Is Russia Coming to Terms with China's "Silk Road"? [online], available: http://eng.globalaffairs.ru/PONARS-Eurasia/Is-Russia-Com-ing-to-Terms-with-Chinas-Silk-Road-18526 [accessed 30 December 2016].

Kuhrt, N. (2015) Russian and China: Competing or Complementary Priorities [online], available: https://cpianalysis.org/2016/04/14/russia-and-china-compet-ing-or-complementary-priorities/ [accessed 1 December 2016].

Lane, D. (2016) Going Forward: The Eurasian Economic Union, the European Union and the Others. In Nitoiu, C. (ed) *Avoiding a New 'Cold War': The Future of EU-Russia Relations in the Context of the Ukraine Crisis*, London: LSE Ideas, pp. 50–56.

Laruelle, M. (2009) Russia in Central Asia: Old History, New Challenges?, EUCAM Working Paper 3 [online], available: http://www.eucentralasia.eu/publications/eucam-publications/working-papersreports/2009.html [accessed 13 January 2013].

Laruelle, M. and Peyrouse, S. (2012) Regional Organisations in Central Asia: Patterns of Interaction, Dilemmas of Efficiency, UCA Working Paper 10 [online], available: http://www.ponarseurasia.org/article/regional-organisations-central-asia-patterns-interaction-dilemmas-efficiency [accessed 3 November 2013].

Lavrov, S. (2016) Vystuplenie ministra inostrannykh del Rossii S.V. Lavrova [online], available: http://www.mid.ru/vistupleniya_ministra/-/asset_publisher/MCZ7HQuMdqBY/content/id/2297742 [accessed 22 July 22].

Lo, B. (2008) *Axis of Convenience: Moscow, Beijing, and the New Geopolitics*, London and Baltimore, Brookings Institute Press.

Lo, B. (2016) The Illusion of Convergence—Russia, China, and the BRICS, *Russie. Nei.Visions* 92 [online], available: https://www.ifri.org/en/publications/enotes/russieneivisions/illusion-convergence-russia-china-and-brics [accessed 7 June 2016].

Lukin, A. (2015) Russia, China and the Emerging Greater Eurasia [online], available: http://old.mgimo.ru/news/experts/document276496.phtml [accessed 18 August 2015].

Luzianin, S. G. (2012) Tsentral'naia Aziia: izmereniia bezopasnosti i sotrudnichestvo [online], available: http://www.perspektivy.info/table/centralnaja_azija_izmerenija_bezopasnosti_i_sotrudnichestva_2012–02–06.htm [accessed 26 January 2013].

MacHaffie, J. (2010) China's Role in Central Asia: Security Implications for Russia and the United States, *Comparative Strategy*, 29(4), 368–380.

Mariani, B. (2013) China's role and interests in Central Asia, London, Saferworld.

Medvedev, D. (2016) Sopriazhenie 'Poiasa i puti' I EAES mozhet zavershit'sia sozdaniem zony svobodnoi torgovli [online], available: http://newscontent.cctv.com/NewJsp/news.jsp?fileId=381776 [accessed 2 December 2016].

MOFA (2008) China and Russia: partnership of strategic coordination [online], available: http://www.fmprc.gov.cn/mfa_eng/ziliao_665539/3602_665543/3604_665547/t18028.shtml [accessed 16 March 2015].

Molchanov, M. A. (2015) *Eurasian Regionalism and Russian Foreign Policy*, Farnham and Burlington: Ashgate.

Pantucci, R. and Lain, S. (2015) *The Economics of the Silk Road Economic Belt*, London: RUSI.

Peyrouse, S., Boonstra, J. and Laruelle, M. (2012) Security and development approaches to Central Asia: The EU compared to China and Russia, EUCAM Working Paper 3 [online], available: http://www.eucentralasia.eu/uploads/tx_icticontent/WP11.pdf [accessed 2 February 2013].

Pravo Golosa. Rossiia—Kitai: Brak po raschetu? (2016) [online], available: http://www.tvc.ru:8020/channel/brand/id/36/show/episodes/episode_id/27331/ [accessed 1 October 2016].

Press statements following Russian-Chinese talks (2015) [online], available: http://en.kremlin.ru/events/president/transcripts/49433 [accessed 15 August 2016].

Prognozy: Vypusk 4 (2016) [online], available: http://tvzvezda.ru/schedule/programs/content/201604261008–5ean.htm/201605311500-xdni.htm [accessed 11 September 2016].

Polubota, A. (2017) Rossiia okazalos' na obochine Novogo shelkovogo puti [online], available: http://svpressa.ru/economy/article/172322/ [accessed 25 May 2017].

Putin, V. Russia and the changing world [online], available: https://www.rt.com/ politics/official-word/putin-russia-changing-world-263/ [accessed 22 March 2012].

Putz, C. (2016) China's Silk Road Belt Outpaces Russia's Economic Union [online], available: http://thediplomat.com/2016/03/chinas-silk-road-belt-outpaces-russias-economic-union/ [accessed 27 March 2016].

Put'. Doroga, kotoruiu my poteriali (2015) [online], available: http://www.vesti.ru/ videos/show/vid/654608/# [accessed 16 June 2016].

Qingsong, W. (2016) The Highest Good Is Like Water [online], available: http:// eng.globalaffairs.ru/number/The-Highest-Good-Is-Like-Water-17985 [accessed 22 May 2016].

RBK. (2016) Kitaiskaia Petrochina investiruet v "Silu Sibirii" do 3,2 mlrd [online], available: http://www.rbc.ru/rbcfreenews/58dd3ee89a7947676d5d610d [accessed 2 April 2017].

Remington, T. F. (2016) One Belt, one road, one Eurasia [online], available: https:// blogs.nottingham.ac.uk/chinapolicyinstitute/2016/04/06/one-belt-one-road-one-eurasia/ [accessed 6 April 2016].

Rozman, G. (2014) The Sino - Russian Challenge to the World Order: National Identities, Bilateral Relations, and East versus West in the 2000s, Washington, DC and Stanford, Woodrow Wilson Center Press and Stanford University Press.

Shaolei, F. (2016) Odin put' mnogo vozmozhnostei [online], available: http:// www.globalaffairs.ru/number/Odin-put--mnogo-vozmozhnostei-18151 [accessed 12 August 2016].

Shelkovyi put' kak evraziiskaia VTO. Replika Georgiia Bovta (2015) [online], available: http://www.vesti.ru/doc.html?id=2656311&cid=6 [accessed 1 September 2016].

Shtraks, G. (2015) A Cold Summer for China and Russia? [online], available: http:// thediplomat.com/2015/09/a-cold-summer-for-china-and-russia/ [accessed 12 September 2015].

Singh, A. I. (2015) Unequal Partners: China and Russia and Eurasia [online], available: http://thediplomat.com/2015/06/unequal-partners-china-and-russia-in-eurasia/ [accessed 15 June 2015].

Sorokin, V. (2009) *Den' Oprichnika*, Moscow: Zakharov.

Spanger, H. J. (2016) Russia's Turn Eastward [online], available: http://eng.globalaffairs.ru/number/Russias-Turn-Eastward-Chinas-Turn-Westward-18251 [accessed 22 July 2016].

Spivak, V. (2016) A New Great Game in Russia's Backyard [online], available: http://carnegie.ru/2016/09/10/new-great-game-in-russia-s-backyard-pub-64542 [accessed 19 September 2016].

Tiezi, S. (2014) China's 'New Silk Road' Vision Revealed [online], available: http:// thediplomat.com/2014/05/chinas-new-silk-road-vision-revealed/ [accessed 4 February 2016].

Timofeev, O. A. (2014) Rossiisko-kitaiskie otnosheniia na sovremennom etape i perspektivy ikh razvitiia, *Vestnik Amurskogo gosudartstvennogo universiteta*, 64, pp. 57–61.

Titarenko, M. L. (2014) *Rossiia i Kitai: strategicheskoe sotrudnichestvo i vyzovy vremeni*, Moscow: ID Forum.

Tochka Zreniia: Kiati v Ob"iatiiakh Rossii (2015) [online], available: http://www.rline.tv/programs/tochka-zreniya/video-59442/ [accessed 22 November 2016].

Trenin, D. (2012) *True partners? How Russia and China see each other*, London: Centre for European Reforms.

Trenin, D. (2015) From Greater Europe to Greater Asia? The Sino-Russian Entente [online], available: http://carnegie.ru/2015/04/09/from-greater-europe-to-greater-asia-sino-russian-entente-pub-59728 [accessed 14 April 2015].

Tsygankov, A. P. (2009) What Is China to Us? Westernizers and Sinophiles in Russian Foreign Policy, *Russie.Nei.Visions* 45 [online], available: https://www.ifri.org/sites/default/files/atoms/files/ifritsygankovengrussiachinanov2009_1.pdf [accessed 12 January 2012].

Weitz, R. (2008) China - Russia Security Relations: Strategic Parallelism without Partnership or Passion?, Carlisle, Strategic Studies Institute, U.S. Army War College.

Yunling, Z. (2011) China's Relations with Its Neighbours after Reform and Opening up. In Yizhou, W. (ed) *Transformation of Foreign Affairs and International Relations in China*, 1978, Leiden: Brill.

Xi, J. (2016) Zaiavlenie dlia pressy po itogam rossiisko-kitaiskikh peregovorov [online], available: http://kremlin.ru/events/president/news/52273 [accessed 1 July 2016].

Zuenko, I. (2015) Connecting the Eurasian Economic Union and the Silk Road Economic Belt: Current Problems and Challenges for Russia [online], available: http://chinaincentralasia.com/2015/10/30/connecting-the-eurasian-economic-union-and-the-silk-road-economic-belt-current-problems-and-challenges-for-russia/ [accessed 25 November 2015].

Part III

CHINA AND WORLD POLITICS

Chapter 11

Strong as Silk

China in the Liberal Order

Michael O. Slobodchikoff

In 1986, China joined the General Agreement on Tariffs and Trade (GATT), signaling its intent to fully join the liberal international order led by the United States. What followed were fifteen years of intense efforts to meet the conditions of joining the World Trade Organization (WTO). As Zhu Rongji, China's former prime minister famously stated, it was long enough to "turn black hair white."[1]

Foreign policy makers in the United States and Western Europe welcomed China's membership and viewed the actions as evidence that as China joined the liberal world order, the Soviet Union would become more isolated, and that it would eventually lead to the defeat of the Soviet Union. Just five years later, the Soviet Union indeed collapsed, leading many observers to declare the end of history and the triumph of the liberal order (Fukuyama, 1989; Ikenberry, 2008; Legro, 2007). Communism had been defeated, showing that there could be only one global order, the liberal order established by the United States.

Prior to the collapse of the Soviet Union, Moscow had pursued a policy of both economic and political reform. While Moscow hadn't embraced the liberal order, it had slowly started moving in that direction through *perestroika*, while at the same time tackling political reform the *glasnost'*. Mikhail Sergeevich Gorbachev, the last president of the Soviet Union, truly believed that the Soviet Union needed massive reform to survive. However, ultimately, these reforms led to the collapse of the Soviet Union.

In contrast to the Soviet Union, China had moved to accept the liberal order much earlier, but carefully chose how to accept the liberal order. China determined that Moscow had made an enormous mistake by taking on both political and economic reforms at the same time. Beijing decided that it would be more practical to reform the economy, but not to undertake any political reforms. Thus, China decided to develop a unique strategy of accepting the liberal economic order, but not undertaking political reforms. The first step in that strategy was to join the WTO.

China's gamble to join the WTO has paid big dividends. China's economy has boomed, and consumers have benefited from an influx of Chinese goods. China has not only worked within the WTO framework, but has also worked closely with the European Union (EU) through the EU-China Strategic Partnership. Moreover, China has worked to develop bilateral treaties with many states further expanding and cementing its role within the liberal economic order.

In fact, China has been so successful, that some international relations theorists have stated that China's growth will eventually lead to direct conflict with the United States (Glaser, 2011; Kirshner, 2012; Mearsheimer, 2006, 2014). This group of scholars is made up of mostly realist theorists. In contrast, other international relations scholars have viewed China's economic success and acceptance of the WTO as evidence that China fully accepts the liberal economic and political order, and that the more it is integrated into these international governmental organizations (IGOs), the more likely China will undergo liberal democratic transition (Ikenberry, 2008; Legro, 2007). This group of scholars is made up of liberal scholars. Despite China's openness to joining the liberal economic order, China has been very resistant to any organizations requiring political change. The Western liberal order not only values liberal economics, but also stresses liberal freedoms and democracy. For example, the EU's Copenhagen Criteria specifically state which democratic norms must be internalized by candidate states prior to becoming members. Similarly, the International Monetary Fund (IMF) often attaches conditions about liberal values and democracy prior to loaning money. While China has been very open to joining liberal institutions, it has balked at joining institutions that work to spread liberal democratic values. Instead, it has worked to develop its own alternatives to such institutions. For example, in response to the Trans-Pacific Partnership (TPP), China developed the Regional Comprehensive Economic Partnership (RCEP) which includes ASEAN member states, China, Japan, Korea, Australian, and India. In contrast to many of the Western liberal institutions, RCEP will not focus on any politically sensitive topics, instead merely focusing on economic cooperation. Similarly, China has used both the Shanghai Cooperation Organization (SCO) and BRICS organizations to create institutions that foster trade yet do not mix trade and politics. In the SCO, all of the member states agree to cooperate in both security and economics, yet put no pressure on any member states to accept certain political behavioral norms. Similarly, the new BRICS Development Bank is similar to the IMF in many ways except that it provides loans without certain political preconditions having to be met.

In this chapter, I first examine the claims from realist international relations scholars about the rise of China leading to conflict between the United States and China. Next, I examine the contrary claim by liberal scholars that China's relations with international relations will lead to China's full integration into the global order, which will in turn lead to democratic transition within China itself. Third, I use network analysis to examine China's relations with the European Union (EU). In examining China's relations with the EU, it becomes apparent that China's dual approach to the global liberal order is extremely important. On the one hand it is very accepting of the liberal economy and economic cooperation; on the other hand it is very resistant to political pressure being a part of that liberal order. Further, it is only very accepting of economic cooperation. It is extremely reluctant to engage liberal organizations in many security issues. In contrast to Russia, which is in stark opposition to all aspects of the liberal order, China offers a different approach. China's approach cleanly separates economics from politics and security and thus provides an attractive alternative to the global liberal order pushed by the United States. Ultimately, I find that neither the realist scholars nor the liberal scholars are correct in their assessment of China. China is too big and powerful a state to be forced to change its approach to liberal institutions, and will ultimately have a profound impact on the future of the global liberal order. Yet it also does not want to directly challenge the global order. Instead, the global order will adapt to China as opposed to China having to adapt to maintain its place in the global order.

REALIST APPROACH TO THE RISE OF CHINA

While China joined GATT in 1986, it took 15 years for the Chinese government to institute the necessary reforms for China to fully meet the conditions to join the World Trade Organization (WTO). China's GDP growth rate went from 5 percent in 1981 to close to a 15 percent growth rate in 1984. Following its agreement to join the GATT in 1986, China spent four years with variable GDP growth rates ranging from approximately a 9 percent GDP growth rate in 1986 to only a 4 percent GDP growth rate in 1990. However, following 1990, China's GDP growth rate continued to increase yearly never falling before a 7 percent growth rate between 1990 and 2015.[2] This economic growth allowed China to become the second largest economy in the world, second only to the United States.

According to power transition theory, there will be major conflict between a global hegemon and a rising state if the rising state's power capabilities are relatively equal to that of the global hegemon and if the state is dissatisfied with the global order established by the global hegemon (DiCicco and Levy,

1999; Kim, 2002; Kugler and Organski, 1989; Lemke and Werner, 1996; Levy, 1998; Tammen and Kugler, 2006). While China's economy has grown to be second only to that of the United States, its power capabilities are still quite a bit less than those of the United States. Nevertheless, China's growth relative to that of the United States made it such that in the not so distant future, China would overtake the United States as the most powerful state in the global system. When that transition will occur, according to power transition theory, war would break out between China and the United States (Brzezinski et al., 2005; Glaser, 2011; Kirshner, 2012; Mearsheimer, 2003, 2006, 2014).

One of the major proponents of such a view of China's growth is John Mearsheimer. Mearsheimer (2014, 2006, 2003) strongly believes that China's incredible growth will absolutely lead to conflict with the United States. He believes that while Beijing has been cooperating with Moscow, it will only do so as long as the power remains in favor of Washington. Once Beijing accumulates enough power, it would be able to challenge the global order established by the United States. Given the vast number of people and resources that China would be able to muster, any war between the United States and China would be devastating. Scholars who fear China's rise believe that the United States has committed several missteps by focusing on the Global War on Terror and the War in Iraq rather than paying attention to China. They argue that China has now effectively gained control over the South China Sea and is close to being able to challenge the United States for regional dominance in Asia. Despite Washington's pivot to Asia, the scholars argue that China has still outplayed the United States, and that more attention needs to be paid to the growth of China. In contrast to international scholars who view China as a future threat to US hegemony, many liberal scholars view the rise of China as an opportunity to integrate China into the current global order and thus bring about internal political change within China itself. I now turn to a discussion about the liberal perspective of the growth of China.

LIBERAL APPROACH TO THE RISE OF CHINA

In 1959, Seymour Martin Lipset identified that democracy and economic modernization were closely tied together. He argued that economic modernization was a prerequisite to democracy, and that democratization would occur because economic modernization led to a wealthy middle class which would in turn demand political change and a voice in governing their country, which in turn would lead to democracy (Lipset, 1959). While the causal relationship between modernization and democracy has been challenged, nevertheless, economic wealth and democracy are closely intertwined concepts

(Almond, 1991; Arat, 1988; Heo and Tan, 2001). Many scholars believe that the two concepts become reinforcing concepts and that is why most of the wealthy states are democracies.

The end of the Cold War heralded a new era in international relations theory. Theorists were convinced that the end of the Cold War was evidence of the triumph of liberal values. The global liberal order established by the United States was the only one left standing and thus, all other states in the system would fully adopt the liberal order (Fukuyama, 1989). This was especially true for neoliberal institutionalists who believed that the more interconnected a state became with international governmental organizations, the more likely that state was to have peaceful relations with other states (Doyle, 1983, 1986; Russett et al., 1998). Further, neoliberal institutionalists argued that as states became interconnected to each other through international governmental organizations that it would have a democratic effect in that it would make a state wealthier, lead to an increased middle class, and thus have a democratizing effect (Bearce and Bondanella, 2007; Huntington, 1993; Ingram et al., 2005). Finally, it has been noted that membership in international organizations leads to a synchronization of member states' preferences, meaning that as new states join IGOs, they go through a period of socialization as their preferences adapt to those of the other member states within a given organization (Finnemore, 1996).

In the case of China, many liberal scholars assumed that China's acceptance of the liberal order and its relationships with international governmental organizations would lead not only to China accepting the liberal economic order, but also eventually lead to the democratization of China itself (Lanteigne, 2005; Legro, 2007; Volgy and Bailin, 2003). The assumption was that China's acceptance of the liberal economic order would create wealth for the Chinese middle class, and that would have a democratizing effect. Further, they expected that Beijing's preferences would become aligned with the other members of the liberal economic order due to interconnectedness through IGOs (Abbott and Snidal, 1998; Acharya and Johnston, 2007; Bearce and Bondanella, 2007). Finally, it was expected that China would undergo socialization once it fully accepted the liberal economic order and fully engaged liberal IGOs, which would have a dramatic effect on the domestic preferences of China (Kent, 2002).

Ultimately, much of the scholarship has focused on Beijing's acceptance of the liberal economic order and the fact that it would be assimilated into the order. This is in stark contrast to the realists who believe that China will directly challenge the global order established by the United States. The problem with both the realist and liberal approach to China's engagement in the liberal economic order is that it examines China's relations from the perspective of the hegemonic power. Both theoretical approaches assume that China will either change or challenge based on the liberal order. At a fundamental level, China's acceptance of the liberal order is a continuing process of negotiation between organizations and Beijing. It is incorrect to assume that as China's power increases, that the liberal order can just assimilate China, but it is also incorrect to assume that China will directly challenge the liberal order. Instead, the liberal order is adapting to China and vice versa. However, to understand this process, it is necessary to understand China's relations with various international governmental organizations and its engagement of the liberal order. I now turn to an examination of first China's relations with global international organizations, and then will examine how Beijing interacts with regional international organizations.

CHINESE RELATIONS WITH GLOBAL INTERNATIONAL GOVERNMENTAL ORGANIZATIONS

As China has increasingly become engaged in the liberal economic order, its relations with IGOs has taken on two forms. The first form is an increase in cooperative behavior from Beijing toward these organizations. Beijing has become more open and cooperative in its negotiations and interactions with the IGOs, especially by stressing that the way that cooperation should occur is through multilateralism (Hempson-Jones, 2005; Kent, 2002). Beijing understood that as the world's most populous country, that it needed to become engaged and could add a necessary dynamic to liberal IGOs (Kim, 1992).

A more open and cooperative policy toward IGOs was not easy for Beijing to achieve. Traditionally, Chinese policy making had not been transparent, and decisions were closely shrouded in secrecy. This was especially true for negotiations, as negotiations were often viewed as more of a zero-sum game, and liberal global IGOs valued a more transparent negotiation process that believed in a positive-sum game. However, as Beijing began to engage with global IGOs, it was forced to adapt to many of the norms of the liberal IGOs. While Beijing's dealings with the International Monetary Fund (IMF) and the World Bank were motivated by self-interest and direct economic benefit, the process of adopting the policies of the World Trade Organization (WTO) prior to gaining membership was not an easy process and required a profound shift in Chinese foreign and domestic policy (Fewsmith, 2001; Hempson-Jones, 2005). For example, the WTO framework had profound effects on employment in China (Zhu and Warner, 2005) as well as domestic laws and regulations (Potter, 2001).

One of the most important changes to the global system and China's relations to the WTO was that any trade dispute would now be handled through the WTO dispute settlement mechanism. Prior to Chinese ascension to the

WTO, any disputes were handled through negotiations and threats of trade wars, especially between the United States and China. This was especially true of disputes involving intellectual property rights. For many years prior to joining the WTO, the US and China would argue about intellectual property rights and move to the brink of a trade war before both sides would back down at the eleventh hour to resume negotiations. The WTO ensured that there would be a dispute settlement mechanism and that trade disputes would thus be settled by the WTO instead of between the two states directly (Yu, 2006). The problem with this mechanism is that neither state might like the outcome of the settlement, however, the dispute settlement would be binding and would try to prevent future conflict between the disputants.

China not only actively engaged the WTO, but also began to engage more within the structure of the United Nations. Prior to the end of the Cold War, China was extremely protective of national sovereignty and was very reluctant to allow any action that might affect another state's sovereignty. This was especially evident in agreeing to UN peacekeeping missions in Cambodia, Somalia and East Timor, in which a "hard-line defense of absolute sovereignty has given way to a more pragmatic stance that sanctions a certain level of interference into another state's affairs" (Hempson-Jones, 2005, p. 704).

China's multilateral approach to relations with liberal IGOs has evolved into two distinct categories, economic and security (Wang, 2000). It has actively engaged global liberal IGOs especially in the economic category. Beijing has become immersed in these global liberal IGOs and has absorbed values such as common security interests and free market economics. It has engaged these global organizations in issues as varied from terrorism to intellectual property rights.

Despite Beijing's openness to engage in relations with liberal global IGOs, Beijing has been very wary of becoming too interdependent. Beijing had very serious concerns that globalization (quanqihua) and modernization (xiandaihua) would create a trap for its internal politics and lead down to a path of forced democratic changes (Kent, 2002; Zhang and Austin, 2014). Therefore, Beijing developed a strategy to counter such socialization forces. First, Beijing realized that it needed to develop good relations with the liberal IGOs, but it also realized that it was gaining power. By 2012, China had the world's second largest economy, which meant that negotiations with liberal IGOs were begun from a position of strength and not weakness. The other member states of the liberal IGOs needed Beijing's membership as much as Beijing needed the liberal IGOs.

Second, Beijing realized that it was mainly interested in engaging with global liberal IGOs on economic issues. While security concerns were of great concern to Beijing, it mainly addressed economic issues multilaterally through relations with global liberal IGOs, and addressed security issues either multilaterally through regional IGOs or bilaterally with individual states. For example, while China actively engaged the European Union (EU)[3] on economic issues, it remained wary of the EU's concerns in regard to human rights protection and activism in climate change (Pan, 2010; Zhimin, 2012). Thus, it negotiated economic treaties with the EU, but moderated those treaties with bilateral treaties with the EU member states to ensure that the EU did not become an overly powerful player and force China to adopt the same norms as the EU (Fox and Godement, 2009). For example, Fox and Godement (2009) argue that prior to the Czech Republic's ascension into the EU, it tried to reach out to China to cooperate bilaterally. Beijing was not interested at the time. However, once the Czech Republic became a member state, Beijing actively engaged the Czech Republic in bilateral cooperation to ensure that it had some protection and insurance in cooperating with the EU directly.

It should be noted that Beijing has always held the EU in high regard. Beijing believes strongly in a policy of multilateralism, and believes that the EU is an effective balance against US unilateralism even if the US and the EU agree on many different policies. Therefore, Beijing has developed a very close relationship with the EU while still balancing that relationship with bilateral relationships with the EU member states (Zhimin, 2012). In contrast, the EU has understood the importance of China as a global partner, and has worked to steady their relationship and not to disrupt relations by pushing China too hard on human rights or other issues of importance to the EU (Gottwald, 2010; Pan, 2012). Washington and Brussels understand that they must work to keep China's cooperation to maintain the global order while Beijing believes that the future global order will transform from the current unipolar system to a multilateral system in which the US, the EU, and China will be the main players (Ross et al., 2010). For this reason, relations between Beijing and Brussels are of strategic importance to maintain in the future.

To better understand the relationship between Beijing and Brussels, it is important to analyze the specific treaties between the EU and China. However, not all bilateral or multilateral treaties are equal. Slobodchikoff (2014, 2013) developed a method for analyzing bilateral and multilateral relationships using treaties and network analysis. What he found was that some relationships used treaties to resolve single issues in a very ad hoc manner, while other relationships used treaties to institutionalize and build more cooperative relationships. He discovered that many treaties specifically mention other treaties within the text of the treaty. This ties the treaties together and means that network analysis should be used to examine how treaties are linked. Thus, individual treaties are attempts at cooperation, whereas treaties that specifically mention other treaties, better known as nested treaties, are attempts at institutionalizing a relationship.

Examining treaties using network analysis allows scholars to determine whether a relationship is cooperative or noncooperative, and whether there is a higher likelihood of militarized conflict between states (Slobodchikoff, 2013). Further, treaty networks show how regional order is built and how tied a specific state is tied to the global or regional order (Slobodchikoff, 2014). Slobodchikoff (2014) has also examined Russia's relations with the regional IGOs in the post-Soviet space to determine how Russia built its regional order. More recent use of network analysis in examining treaties has examined China's relationship with Russia and the Shanghai Cooperation Organization (SCO) as well as identifying the most important issues of cooperation between Russia and China (Ambrosio, 2017).

Much like in previous studies, it is possible to examine the treaty network between China and the EU to determine China's approach to the liberal order that is personified by the EU. An examination of the Chinese-EU treaty network shows that Beijing has actively engaged the EU and indeed the liberal order (See Figure 11.1).[4] As Figure 11.1 shows, the GATT treaty, located in the upper center of Figure 11.1, is extremely central to the relationship between China and the EU. It should be noted that the individual treaty nodes' size is representative of the degree centrality. Thus, the larger the treaty is, the more central that treaty is to the overall relationship.

While the GATT treaty is central to the Sino-EU relationship, several other treaties are also central to the relationship. For example, the Trade and Economic Cooperation Agreement (9/16/1985) and the Agreement on Trade in Textile Products (12/9/1988) are both extremely important to the relationship. In fact, of the three most central treaties to the relationship between China

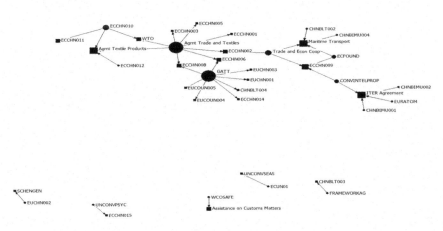

Figure 11.1   China-EU Treaty Network.

and the EU, two of the three address trade in textile products. Specifically, the Trade and Economic Cooperation Agreement (9/16/1985) provided a very broad set of standards with which to build an economic relationship. The EU and China both agreed to provide each other with Most Favored Nation (MFN) status, and to work toward limiting tariffs. Further, both parties agree that they will attempt to resolve any dispute through peaceful consultations without involving any other party. Finally, the agreement seeks to set a very broad set of issue areas in which cooperation and trade will be sought between the two parties, in the hopes that the agreement will serve as a basis for further and expanded cooperation.

In contrast to the Trade and Economic Cooperation Agreement (9/16/1985), the Agreement on Trade in Textile Products (12/9/1988) specifically defines which textiles are allowable to be imported to the EU and in what amounts. The agreement works to very clearly define the exact circumstances under which trade in these textiles is possible. Interestingly, both of the most central treaties are opposite in their approaches. One is extremely broad, used as a building block for future cooperation, while the other is a very specific set of regulations defining what items and quantities can be traded.

Figure 11.1 also shows that there is one major network at the top, and several treaties below that are more ad hoc and less institutionalized. The major network at the top shows that the relationship is relatively institutionalized. Interestingly, most of the treaties in the top of Figure 11.1 have to do with economics and trade. There are very few treaties related to security issues. The vast majority of the treaties in the top of the figure 11.1 have to do with GATT and ensuring that the proper amount of Chinese goods are imported into the EU.

One important issue that is addressed in the top right of Figure 11.1 that does not have to do with trade is the ITER Agreement. The ITER Agreement is an agreement among advanced industrial nations to develop fusion energy for peaceful purposes. Coming from the 1985 Geneva Superpower Summit between the United States and the Soviet Union, the ITER project was conceived as a way to increase cooperation among various advanced countries in developing new sources of energy production. While the ITER Agreement is not trade per se, it is peaceful cooperation among scientists to develop fusion energy, so it cannot be considered a security treaty either. It is instead to be considered as an integrative treaty designed to increase multilateral cooperation.

It is extremely important to note that the ITER Agreement is linked to the Agreement for Scientific and Technical Cooperation between the European Community and the People's Republic of China (ECCHN009—Signed 12/12/1998). This agreement set the stage for scientific cooperation between Beijing and the EU. However, one of the fundamental aspects of scientific cooperation within the liberal order is the requirement that states recognize intellectual property and do not violate that right. Thus, the Agreement for Scientific and Technical Cooperation had to be nested within the 1967 Convention Establishing the World Intellectual Property Organization. By nesting the Agreement on Scientific and Technical Cooperation within this 1967 Convention, Beijing was signaling its intent to abide by the rules of intellectual property, which in turn reinforces its acceptance of GATT, the WTO, and the liberal order.

It is very important to note that treaties dealing with security issues are totally absent from the top part of the network. All of those treaties have to do with trade or energy. Instead, there are a couple of security treaties that are dealt with in an ad hoc manner at the bottom of Figure 11.1. For example, there are two treaties that deal with customs and immigration, an agreement that allows the EU diplomatic passport holders to enter China on a visa-waiver program (EUCHN002), and the Agreement on Assistance in Customs Matters. Both of these treaties are nested within either the EU treaties such as the Schengen agreement related to diplomatic passports, and the Safe Framework of Standards established by the World Customs Organization. However, these treaties are not linked to each other, nor are they connected to the larger network at the top of Figure 11.1. Again, this indicates a rather ad hoc approach to solving a short-term problem or issue rather than institutionalizing cooperation in these security matters within the larger relationship. Further evidence of this ad hoc approach can be found by the fact that the Agreement between the European Community and the Government of the People's Republic of China on Drug Precursors and Substances Frequently used in the Illicit Manufacture of Narcotic Drugs or Psychotropic Substances is nested within the UN Convention on Psychotropic Substances (signed 12/12/1988) and not tied to any other treaties or the network at large.

Ultimately, China's approach to the EU has been to fully embrace the liberal order through trade and scientific cooperation. However, it has been very standoffish with the EU when it comes to security issues, preferring to handle these issues in more of an ad hoc manner, addressing issues as it becomes apparent that they need to be addressed. Beijing is very wary of the trap placed by many liberal organizations of requiring domestic political changes. Thus, it remains very careful in how it engages with the EU and other liberal global IGOs.

While I have focused on China's relationship with the EU in this analysis, China's approach to other global IGOs is similar. There is a distinct pattern in China's relations with liberal global IGOs. China actively engages in relations with them, especially cooperating on economic issues. However, Beijing has been much more reticent in cooperating with liberal global IGOs in security fearing that it will be forced to adapt and find itself trapped. Beijing has been more open to relations within the BRICS structure to try to alleviate that concern (Armijo, 2007; Ban and Blyth, 2013). For example, in 2014, at the BRICS Summit, plans were introduced for a new BRICS Development Bank. This bank was designed to counter the IMF in that it would grant loans to states without the necessary structural changes required by the IMF (Abdenur, 2014; Chin, 2014; Tierney, 2014).

Beijing continues to value multilateralism, and the BRICS structure allows for this preference. The problem is that while the BRICS countries had a long period of rapid economic growth, the 2008 financial crisis had a negative effect on their economies. Thus, while the BRICS structure is very beneficial to Beijing, it is much too early to deem it a viable alternative to the other liberal economic IGOs. Instead, the BRICS organization is complimentary to the other liberal economic IGOs in that China receives benefits and can actively engage both groups of IGOs without having to choose one set over the other.

Ultimately, while wary of the traps of the liberal IGOs, Beijing has actively engaged the liberal IGOs. However, Beijing has developed a complex strategy of engaging the IGOs while balancing those IGOs against bilateral agreements. The bilateral agreements help to mitigate any requirements that Beijing must adhere to in order to be in compliance with the negotiated agreements with the liberal IGOs. Complicating matters further is that Beijing has developed a very robust strategy in engaging regional IGOs within Asia to further balance the effects of the liberal global IGOs.

Beijing's relations with global IGOs have proved a conundrum for most international relations theorists. While realists point to Beijing's careful relationship with the IGOs and its wariness to be socialized as evidence that it is in fact opposed to the current global order, liberals point to the fact that Beijing does fully cooperate with these organizations as evidence that Beijing is satisfied with the current global order and will eventually be socialized and become more of a liberal democracy. The truth is more complex than either theoretical perspective allows. In truth, the evidence shows that Beijing is not wholly opposed to the global order in its current form. The problem is when the global order tries to directly change China. Then, Beijing is opposed to the order. In other words, Beijing is cautiously accepting of the global order, and is looking to create a positive-sum game in its relations with other states. It is not actively trying to challenge the global order, nor is it an acolyte of the global order. Beijing is a major player within the global order, trying to discover how best to navigate complex relationships within the global order. It seeks to combine a nuanced approach at several different levels to ensure not only that it remains an important player, but that it continues to benefit from the current order.

By focusing on economic issues and trade while not cooperating in security matters, Beijing is showing other states that states do not have to fully adopt the liberal global order. Instead they can adopt a more à la carte approach to the liberal global order. While embracing the global liberal economic order and reaping the benefits of the order, it is still possible to keep the transformative domestic political aspects of the liberal order at arm's length. Even though the United States wants China to be more open to the transformative aspects of the liberal order, Beijing has made it clear that is not an option. Because the United States needs China, Beijing is allowed to keep pursuing this strategy despite the fact that it supplies a unique blueprint for the approach that states that are apprehensive of the global liberal order should take. With the forecast that China will become more powerful than the United States in the near future, China's approach to the liberal economic order may yet become the new global order in the future.

APPENDIX

Table 11.1   List of China's Treaties with the EU

Treaty Code	Title	Date
ECFOUND	Treaty Establishing European Community	3/25/1957
EURATOM	Treaty Establishing EURATOM	3/25/1957
CONVINTELPROP	Convention on Establishing World Intellectual Property Organization	7/14/1967
UNCONVSEAS	UN Convention on Law of the Sea	12/10/1982
ECCHNTrade1	Agreement on trade and economic cooperation between the European Economic Community and the People's Republic of China	5/21/1985
SCHENGEN	Schengen Acquis	6/14/1985
ECCHNPre2	Trade and Economic Cooperation Agreement between the Community and China	9/16/1985
ECCHNPre1	Agreement between the European Economic Community and the People's Republic of China on trade in textile products	12/9/1988
UNCONVPSYCH	UN Convention on Psychotropic Substances	12/12/1988
ECCHN001	Agreed Minute amending the Agreement between the European Economic Community and the people's Republic of China on trade in textile products	4/2/1990
ECCHN002	Agreement between the European Economic Community and the People's Republic of China on trade in textile products - Protocol A - Protocol B - Protocol C - Protocol D - Protocole E - Agreed Minutes - Exchange of Notes	9/24/1990

(Continued)

Table 11.1 *(Continued)*

Treaty Code	Title	Date
ECCHN003	Agreement in the form of an exchange of letters amending the Agreement between the European Economic Community and the People' s Republic of China on trade in textile products - Agreed Minutes - Notes verbale - Exchanges of notes	12/2/1993
GATT	GATT	3/21/1994
WTO	WTO	4/1/1994
ECCHN004	Agreement in the form of an Exchange of Letters between the European Community and the People's Republic of China amending the 1988 MFA Agreement between the European Economic Community and the People's Republic of China on trade in textile products to take into account the expected accession of the Republic of Austria, the Republic of Finland and the Kingdom of Sweden to the European Union - Exchange of Notes	2/20/1995
ECCHN005	Agreement between the European Community and the People's Republic of China on trade in textile products not covered by the MFA bilateral Agreement on Trade in Textile Products initialed on 9 December 1988 as extended and modified by the exchange of letters initialed on December 8, 1992 - Protocol A - Protocol B - Protocol of Understanding concerning the implementation of Article 12 of the Agreement - Agreed Minute	4/10/1995
ECCHN006	Agreement on the modification of certain provisions of the 1988 MFA bilateral Agreement on Trade in Textile Products between the European Community and the People's Republic of China	6/13/1995
ECCHN008	Agreement in the form of an Exchange of Letters between the European Community and the People's Republic of China amending the Agreement between the European Economic Community and the People's Republic of China on trade in textile products as last amended by Agreements initialed on 14 December 1994 - Agreed Minute	12/22/1995
ECCHN009	Agreement for scientific and technological cooperation between the European Community and the Government of the People's Republic of China	12/22/1998

Table 11.1 *(Continued)*

Treaty Code	Title	Date
ECCHN010	Agreement in the form of an Exchange of Letters between the European Community and the People's Republic of China initialed in Beijing on 19 May 2000 amending the Agreement between them on trade in textile products and amending the Agreement between them initialed on 19 January 1995 on trade in textile products not covered by the MFA bilateral Agreement - Protocol A	5/19/2000
ECUN01	CONVENTION ON THE CONSERVATION AND MANAGEMENT OF HIGHLY MIGRATORY FISH STOCKS IN THE WESTERN AND CENTRAL PACIFIC OCEAN	9/5/2000
CHNBLT001	Agreement on maritime transport between the European Community and its Member States, of the one part, and the government of the People's Republic of China, of the other part	12/6/2002
ECCHN011	Agreement in the form of exchange of letters between the European Community and the People's Republic of China initialed in Beijing on 6 December 1999 amending the Agreement between the European Economic Community and the People's Republic of China on trade in textile products as last amended by an agreement initialed on 20 November 1999 and amending the Agreement between the European Community and the People's Republic of China initialed on 19 January 1995 on trade in textile products not covered by the MFA bilateral Agreement	3/3/2003
ECCHN012	Agreement in the form of an exchange of letters between the European Community and the People's Republic of China amending the Agreement between the European Economic Community and the People's Republic of China on trade in textile products as last amended by Agreements initialed on 13 December 1995 - Agreed Minutes	3/3/2003
ECCHN013	Memorandum of Understanding between the European Community and the National Tourism Administration of the People's Republic of China, on visa and related issues concerning tourist groups from the People's Republic of China (ADS) - PROTOCOL ON THE NEW MEMBER STATES - Declarations	2/12/2004

(Continued)

Table 11.1 *(Continued)*

Treaty Code	Title	Date
EUCOUN001	Information on the entry into force of the Agreement between the European Community and the Government of the Hong Kong Special Administrative Region of the People's Republic of China on the readmission of persons residing without authorization	3/2/2004
EUCOUN002	Information concerning the entry into force of the Agreement between the European Community and the Macao Special Administrative Region of the People's Republic of China on the readmission of persons residing without authorization	8/5/2004
ECCHN014	Agreement between the European Community and the Government of the People's Republic of China on cooperation and mutual administrative assistance in customs matters	12/8/2004
FRAMEWORKAG	Framework Agreement for International Collaboration on Research and Development of Generation IV Nuclear Energy Systems	2/28/2005
Bilat002	Information relating to the entry into force of the Agreement between the European Community and the Government of the People's Republic of China and on cooperation and mutual administrative assistance in customs matters	4/30/2005
WCOSAFE	SAFE Standards WCO	6/1/2005
CHNBLT002	Protocol amending the Agreement on maritime transport between the European Community and its Member States, of the one part, and the Government of the People's Republic of China, of the other part	9/5/2005
ECCHN014	Agreement in the form of an Exchange of Letters between the European Community and the People's Republic of China pursuant to Article XXIV:6 and Article XXVIII of the General Agreement on Tariffs and Trade (GATT) 1994 relating to the modification of concessions in the schedules of the Czech Republic, the Republic of Estonia, the Republic of Cyprus, the Republic of Latvia, the Republic of Lithuania, the Republic of Hungary, the Republic of Malta, the Republic of Poland, the Republic of Slovenia and the Slovak Republic in the course of their accession to the European Union	4/3/2006
CHNBIMU001	Agreement on the privileges and immunities of the ITER International Fusion Energy Organization for the Joint Implementation of the ITER Project	11/21/2006

Table 11.1 *(Continued)*

Treaty Code	Title	Date
CHNBIMU002	Arrangement on Provisional Application of the Agreement on the Establishment of the ITER International Fusion Energy Organization for the Joint Implementation of the ITER Project	11/21/2006
CHNBIMU003	Agreement on the Establishment of the ITER International Fusion Energy Organization for the Joint Implementation of the ITER Project	11/21/2006
EUCOUN003	Information relating to the entry into force of the Agreement in the form of an Exchange of Letters between the European Community and the People's Republic of China pursuant to Article XXIV:6 and Article XXVIII of the General Agreement on Tariffs and Trade (GATT) 1994	3/30/2007
ECCHN015	Agreement between the European Community and the Government of the People's Republic of China on drug precursors and substances frequently used in the illicit manufacture of narcotic drugs or psychotropic substances	11/27/2008
CHNBIMU004	Protocol amending the Agreement on maritime transport between the European Community and its Member States, of the one part, and the Government of the People's Republic of China, of the other part	3/31/2009
ECCHN016	Information relating to the entry into force of the Agreement between the European Community and the Government of the People's Republic of China on drug precursors and substances frequently used in the illicit manufacture of narcotic drugs or psychotropic substances	7/8/2009
EUCHN001	Agreement in the form of an Exchange of Letters between the European Union and the People's Republic of China pursuant to Article XXIV:6 and Article XXVIII of the General Agreement on Tariffs and Trade (GATT) 1994 relating to the modification of concessions in the schedules of the Republic of Bulgaria and Romania in the course of their accession to the European Union	9/9/2013
CHNCCC001	2014/772/EU: Decision of the Joint Customs Cooperation Committee established under the Agreement between the European Community and the Government of the People's Republic of China on cooperation and mutual administrative assistance in customs matters of 16 May 2014 regarding mutual recognition of the Authorised Economic Operator program in the European Union and the Measures on Classified Management of Enterprises Program in the People's Republic of China	5/16/2014

(Continued)

Table 11.1 *(Continued)*

Treaty Code	Title	Date
EUCOUN004	Notice concerning the entry into force of the Agreement in the form of an Exchange of Letters between the European Union and the People's Republic of China pursuant to Article XXIV:6 and Article XXVIII of the General Agreement on Tariffs and Trade (GATT) 1994 relating to the modification of concessions in the schedules of the Republic of Bulgaria and Romania in the course of their accession to the European Union	6/28/2014
CHNBLT003	Agreement extending the Framework Agreement for International Collaboration on Research and Development of Generation IV nuclearenergy systems	2/26/2015
CHNBLT004	Declaration on the Expansion of Trade in Information Technology Products	7/28/2015
EUCHN002	Agreement between the European Union and the People's Republic of China on the short-stay visa-waiver for holders of diplomatic passports	2/29/2016
EUCHN003	Agreement in the form of an Exchange of Letters between the European Union and the People's Republic of China pursuant to Article XXIV:6 and Article XXVIII of the General Agreement on Tariffs and Trade (GATT) 1994 relating to the modification of concessions in the Schedule of the Republic of Croatia in the course of its accession to the European Union	4/19/2016
EUCOUN005	Notice concerning the entry into force of the Agreement in the form of an Exchange of Letters between the European Union and the People's Republic of China pursuant to Article XXIV:6 and Article XXVIII of the General Agreement on Tariffs and Trade (GATT) 1994 relating to the modification of concessions in the schedule of the Republic of Croatia in the course of its accession to the European Union	12/24/2016
EUCOUN006	Information relating to the entry into force of the Agreement between the European Union and the People's Republic of China on the short-stay visa-waiver for holders of diplomatic passports	12/29/2016

NOTES

1. As quoted in *The Economist* ("Shades of Grey," 2011).
2. Data obtained from World Bank Accounts Data.
3. While the EU is a regional organization, it has a global reach, and Beijing treats the EU as a global player as opposed to a regional one.
4. Treaties analyzed between 1990 and 2016. 1990 is the end of the Cold War and the triumph of the liberal order, so was the logical starting point to see whether or not China has embraced the liberal order. While the beginning of the analysis is 1990, if a treaty specifically mentions a treaty signed prior to 1990 such as the GATT treaty, then that treaty is included in the analysis. Thus, the later treaty is considered to be nested within the earlier treaty, and will be used in the network analysis.

REFERENCES

Abbott, K.W., Snidal, D., 1998. Why States Act through Formal International Organizations. *J. Confl. Resolut.* 42, 3–32.

Abdenur, A.E., 2014. China and the BRICS Development Bank: Legitimacy and Multilateralism in South–South Cooperation. *IDS Bull.* 45, 85–101. doi:10.1111/1759-5436.12095

Acharya, A., Johnston, A.I., 2007. Crafting Cooperation: Regional International Institutions in Comparative Perspective. Cambridge, UK: Cambridge University Press.

Almond, G.A., 1991. Capitalism and Democracy. *PS Polit. Sci. Amp Polit.* 24, 467–474. doi:10.2307/420091

Ambrosio, T., 2017. The Architecture of Alignment: The Russia–China Relationship and International Agreements. *Eur.-Asia Stud.* 69, 110–156. doi:10.1080/09668136.2016.1273318

Arat, Z.F., 1988. Democracy and economic development: Modernization theory revisited. *Comp. Polit.* 21, 21–36.

Armijo, L.E., 2007. The BRICs Countries (Brazil, Russia, India, and China) as Analytical Category: Mirage or Insight? *Asian Perspect.* 31, 7–42.

Ban, C., Blyth, M., 2013. The BRICs and the Washington Consensus: An introduction. *Rev. Int. Polit. Econ.* 20, 241–255. doi:10.1080/09692290.2013.779374

Bearce, D.H., Bondanella, S., 2007. Intergovernmental Organizations, Socialization, and Member-State Interest Convergence. *Int. Organ.* 61, 703–733. doi:10.1017/S0020818307070245

Brzezinski, Z., Mearsheimer, J.J., others, 2005. Clash of the Titans. *Foreign Policy* 146, 46–49.

Chin, G.T., 2014. The BRICS-led Development Bank: Purpose and Politics beyond the G20. *Glob. Policy* 5, 366–373. doi:10.1111/1758-5899.12167

DiCicco, J.M., Levy, J.S., 1999. Power Shifts and Problem Shifts: The Evolution of the Power Transition Research Program. *J. Confl. Resolut.* 43, 675–704.

Doyle, M.W., 1986. Liberalism and World Politics. *Am. Polit. Sci. Rev.* 80, 1151–1169.

Doyle, M.W., 1983. Kant, Liberal Legacies, and Foreign Affairs. *Philos. Public Aff.* 12, 205–235.

Fewsmith, J., 2001. The Political and Social Implications of China's Accession to the WTO. *China Q.* 167, 573–591. doi:10.1017/S0009443901000328

Finnemore, M., 1996. National Interests in International Society. Ithaca, NY: Cornell University Press.

Fox, J., Godement, F., 2009. A power audit of EU-China relations. European Council of Foreign Relations.

Fukuyama, F., 1989. The End of History? *The National Interest*, (16), 3–18. Retrieved from http://www.jstor.org/stable/24027184

Glaser, C., 2011. Will China's Rise Lead to War? Why Realism Does Not Mean Pessimism. *Foreign Aff.* 90, 80–91.

Gottwald, J.-C., 2010. Europe and China: Convergence, Politicization and Assertiveness. *East Asia* 27, 79–97. doi:10.1007/s12140–009–9103–2

Hempson-Jones, J.S., 2005. The Evolution of China's Engagement with International Governmental Organizations: Toward a Liberal Foreign Policy? *Asian Surv.* 45, 702–721. doi:10.1525/as.2005.45.5.702

Heo, U., Tan, A.C., 2001. Democracy and Economic Growth: A Causal Analysis. *Comp. Polit.* 463–473.

Huntington, S.P., 1993. The Third Wave: Democratization in the Late Twentieth Century. Norman, OK: Univ. of Oklahoma Pr.

Ikenberry, G.J., 2008. The Rise of China and the Future of the West: Can the Liberal System Survive? *Foreign Aff.* 87, 23–37.

Ingram, P., Robinson, J., Busch, M.L., 2005. The Intergovernmental Network of World Trade: IGO Connectedness, Governance, and Embeddedness. *Am. J. Sociol.* 111, 824–858. doi:10.1086/497350

Kent, A., 2002. China's international socialization: the role of international organizations. *Glob. Gov.* 8, 343–364.

Kim, S.S., 1992. International organizations in Chinese foreign policy. *Ann. Am. Acad. Pol. Soc. Sci.* 519, 140–157.

Kim, W., 2002. Power Parity, Alliance, Dissatisfaction, and Wars in East Asia, 1860–1993. *J. Confl. Resolut.* 46, 654–671. doi:10.1177/002200202236168

Kirshner, J., 2012. The Tragedy of Offensive Realism: Classical Realism and the Rise of China. *Eur. J. Int. Relat.* 18, 53–75. doi:10.1177/1354066110373949

Kugler, J., Organski, A.F.K., 1989. The Power Transition: A Retrospective and Prospective Evaluation, in: Midlarsky, M. (Ed.), *Handbook of War Studies*. University of Michigan Press, Ann Arbor.

Lanteigne, M., 2005. *China and International Institutions: Alternate Paths to Global Power*. London and New York: Routledge.

Legro, J.W., 2007. What China Will Want: The Future Intentions of a Rising Power. *Perspect. Polit.* 5, 515–534. doi:10.1017/S1537592707071526

Lemke, D., Werner, S., 1996. Power Parity, Commitment to Change, and War. *Int. Stud. Q.* 40, 235–260.

Levy, J.S., 1998. The Causes of War and the Conditions of Peace. *Annu. Rev. Polit. Sci.* 1, 139–165. doi:10.1146/annurev.polisci.1.1.139

Lipset, S.M., 1959. Some Social Requisites of Democracy: Economic Development and Political Legitimacy. *Am. Polit. Sci. Rev.* 53, 69–105.

Mearsheimer, J.J., 2014. Can China Rise Peacefully? *Natl. Interest* 25, 23–37.

Mearsheimer, J.J., 2006. China's Unpeaceful Rise. *Curr. Hist.* 105, 160.

Mearsheimer, J.J., 2003. *The Tragedy of Great Power Politics.* New York, NY: WW Norton & Company.

Pan, Z., 2012. *Conceptual Gaps in China-EU Relations: Global Governance, Human Rights and Strategic Partnerships.* New York, NY: Palgrave Macmillan.

Pan, Z., 2010. Managing the Conceptual Gap on Sovereignty in China–EU Relations. *Asia Eur. J.* 8, 227–243. doi:10.1007/s10308–010–0263-x

Potter, P.B., 2001. The Legal Implications of China's Accession to the WTO. *China Q.* 167, 592–609. doi:10.1017/S000944390100033X

Ross, R., Tunsjø, Ø., Tuosheng, Z., 2010. *US-China-EU Relations: Managing the New World Order.* London, UK: Routledge.

Russett, B.R., Oneal, J.R., Davis, D., 1998. The Third Leg of the Kantian Tripod for Peace: International Organizations and Militarized Disputes, 1950–85. *Int. Organ.* 52, 441–467. doi:10.1162/002081898550626

Shades of Grey, 2011. Dec. 10, 2011; The Economist.

Slobodchikoff, M.O., 2014. *Building Hegemonic Order Russia's Way: Order, Stability, and Predictability in the Post-Soviet Space.* Lexington Books, Lanham, MD.

Slobodchikoff, M.O., 2013. *Strategic Cooperation: Overcoming the Barriers of Global Anarchy.* Lanham, MD: Lexington Books.

Tammen, R.L., Kugler, J., 2006. Power Transition and China-US Conflicts. *Chin. J. Int. Polit.* 1, 35–55. doi:10.1093/cjip/pol003

Tierney, M.J., 2014. Rising Powers and the Regime for Development Finance. *Int. Stud. Rev.* 16, 452–455. doi:10.1111/misr.12153

Volgy, T.J., Bailin, A., 2003. *International Politics & State Strength.* London, UK: Lynne Rienner Pub.

Wang, H., 2000. Multilateralism in Chinese Foreign Policy: The Limits of Socialization. *Asian Surv.* 40, 475–491. doi:10.2307/3021157

Yu, P.K., 2006. From Pirates to Partners (Episode II): Protecting Intellectual Property in Post-WTO China. *Am. Univ. Law Rev.* 55, 901–1000.

Zhang, Y., Austin, G., 2014. *Power and Responsibility in Chinese Foreign Policy.* Canberra, Australia: ANU E Press.

Zhimin, C., 2012. Europe as a Global Player: A View from China. *Perspectives : review of Central European affairs*, 20(2), 7–29.

Zhu, Y., Warner, M., 2005. Changing Chinese Employment Relations since WTO Accession. *Pers. Rev.* 34, 354–369. doi:10.1108/00483480510591471

Chapter 12

Comparative Analysis of China's Policies toward Integrated Organizations

Zhigao He

With the evolution of domestic political and social structure and international society, it exerted significant influences on China's role and perception toward international society, thereby formulating and developing China's foreign policy. In order to fulfill their national interests, it is important for major powers, including China, to rely on various platforms (regional, international and global) to carry out foreign policies. For instance, China stressed bilateral relations with other major powers, including Russia and the United States, while China actively exerted influences on international organizations, including International Monetary Fund and the World Bank. Nevertheless, China has increasingly paid attention to integrated (regional) organizations. China could make use of integrated organizations as leverage, improving the efficiency, legitimacy and reputation of China's policies in global governance. In other words, region (and integrated organization) is one platform of China to integrate and influence international society and cultivate international order.

Interactions between China and international organizations have been a hot topic in international relations. On the one hand, China's policies toward international organizations have changed a lot, from negative participation to positive participation, from xenophobic and reject attitude to engagement and compliment (Kent, 2007). On the other hand, it strengthened the legitimacy of international organization, because of China's full integration and active cultivation in relations with international organizations, thereby consolidating the role of international organization in global and regional governance. Interactions between China and international organizations, to some extent, not only constitute significant component of China's foreign policy, but also become an indispensable approach of international society's engagement with China.

When it refers to interactions between China and international organizations, they not only consist of changes of perceptions and attitudes, but also comprise China's understanding, recognition, compliance and reform of international organizations as well as international rules. Specifically, with the rise of China, the role of China in international organizations has changed from passive compliance with international organizations to initiative cultivation of international organizations. Main research objects are about the development and alternation of China's policy toward international organizations (Johnston, AI. 2003; 2008). Furthermore, we would figure out different variables for explaining changes of China's perceptions and policies, including interests proposition, domestic legitimacy, international reputation, and audience costs. With the development of constructivism, socialization and internalization of international norms would contribute to explain interactions between China and international organizations.

With regard to interactions between China and international organizations, there are six phases of China's policy toward international organizations: resistance (1949–1971), preliminary engagement (1971–1979), comprehensive engagement (1979–1989), full integration (1989–2002), initiative cultivation (2003–2008), and active cultivation (2008–). It is the historical dimension of China's policy toward international organizations that relies on variations of China's status and international society. Regarding for horizontal comparison, there are at least five differences between China and Western countries' policies toward international organizations. Number one, China stressed informal agreements, while Western countries preferred to formal institutions. Number two, China's policies emphasized process dimension, while Western countries stressed rules and regulations. Number three, China preferred to soft constraints, while Western countries preferred to rigid restrictions. Number four, when it comes to relationship between China and international organization, China advocated for openness and inclusiveness of international organizations, Western countries maintained closure and exclusiveness of international organizations. Number five, regarding for patterns of operation, China proposed task-oriented cooperation based on multiple values, Western countries stressed for burden-sharing based on common values.

Nowadays, China's interaction with international organizations has reached an unprecedented height. On the one hand, China is a highly compliance power in the international society, strictly abiding, to some extent, by the rules and regulations of international organizations. On the other hand, in the face of the emerging global issues and changes of international norms, China tries to put forward the proposition of China's governance scheme, set up the international agenda, and render some alternative governance norms and ideas. For example, China has increasingly proposed some initiatives, including initiating the establishment of the Asian infrastructure investment bank (hereinafter referred to as the "Asian investment bank"), the new BRICS Development Bank, Silk Road Fund, etc. These not only reflect China's compliance and defenders of the international order, but also highlight the image of China as a responsible major power. These also manifest that the legitimacy of international organizations are too small for the stakeholders. Therefore, China put forward new norms and ideas about international organizations on the one hand, China stressed the role of integrated organizations and regional platform on the other. It not only safeguards China's own interests, but also belongs to the connotation of community of common destiny, especially with developing countries.

There are two categories of China's interactions with regional organizations. The first one is that China actively integrated in regional organizations. For example, Asia-Pacific Economic Cooperation (APEC), ASEAN Regional Forum (ARF). The second one is China actively participated with regional organizations. For example, China-Arab States Cooperation Forum, Shanghai Cooperation Organization, China and ASEAN Free Trade Area (CAFTA) are the platform of China's policies toward integrated organizations. China has a respect for diversity, people's livelihood-oriented, open regionalism, partnership but nonalignment, in terms of policies towards integrated organizations. This paper intends to explain why China stress the regional platform, and pick up three cases to analyze China's policies toward integrated organizations, and lastly address possible approaches for China toward integrated organizations.

THEORETICAL FRAMEWORK

Mao Zedong has put forward the theory of "Three Worlds"(Dirlik, 2014) and regarded China as a member of the Third World, which has been the foothold of China's foreign policies toward other international actors during a long period. It is the main path for China to maximize national interests

Table 12.1   Patterns of China's Policies Towards International Organizations

	Participation	*Cooperation*
Regional level	Asian Infrastructure Investment Bank, BRICS Development Bank, Silk Road Fund, SCO, ASEAN+3 (CEPT)	Forum on China- Africa Cooperation, China-Arab States Cooperation Forum
Global level	WTO, World Bank	International Labour Organization (ILO), UN Committee against Torture

Source: Ministry of Foreign Affairs of the People's Republic of China.
Available from: http://www.fmprc.gov.cn/web/gjhdq_676201/gjhdqzz_681964/ (Accessed 18 December 2016).

based on the strategic platform of Third World. However, with the evolution of international society (or the international system and order) as well as the domestic political and social structure, it is not enough to fulfill the orientation and development of China's international strategy, if China still exclusively stress the role of Third World. Consequently, China put forward comprehensive strategic configuration, which is "major power relations are critical, the surrounding areas are the policy priorities, developing countries are the foundation, and the multilateral relations are important arena." (Jin, C., Duan, H., and Hong, J., 2013, p. 24). Nevertheless, there is not a clarified or published regional strategy or Asian strategy.

International actors' participation in international society is based on the objective assessment of its domestic and international circumstances, thereby realizing the organic integration of subjective willing and objective circumstances. There are three variables for explaining China's regional strategies and policies toward integrated organizations, the decisiveness of national power, the role of international society, and the importance of regional politics. More specifically, the former two variables are the necessaries for China's policies toward integrated organizations, while the latter one is the possibility for China's policies toward integrated organizations. We could assume that the world is composed of regions. Based on China's domestic considerations and international circumstances, China's international strategy might focus at the regional level, East Asia and Central Asia might be the first platform of China's policy toward integrated organization. Subsequently, China-European Union and China-Africa could be another dimension of China's policies toward integrated organization, in terms of inter-regional connection and strategic partnership construction. This strategic thinking may be more likely in line with the Chinese nation's thinking habits, which will effectively practice this strategic orientation.

First, national power highlights domestic dimension of nation state, based on an inward perspective, it is composed of three parts, which are the country's substantive basis, institutional framework and idea aggregation. Substantive basis is an objective existence of one international actor. Institutional framework connects substantive basis with idea aggregation of international actor. Idea aggregation distinguished substantive basis from institutional framework, which, to some extent, replaced or complemented with institutional framework. The substantive basis of the state, mainly refers to territory, population, natural resources and wealth. The institutional framework of state includes bonding framework between the government and society, and the state machine, which is composed of formal and informal rules. The idea or norms of state aggregation problem, is the core of the deep, abstract, more reflected in the national characteristics, namely, the legitimacy dimension. Specifically the relationship between state and nation and supporting the ideology cover the country's main idea of aggregation problem.

Second, macro-oriented international system cultivates and shapes the orientation of national foreign policy. An international society refers to "a group of states which not merely form a system, in the sense that the behavior of each is necessary factor in the calculations of the others, but also have established by dialogue and consent common rules and institutions for the conduct of their relations, and recognize their common interest in maintaining these arrangements" (Bull, H. and Watson, A., p.1). China's strategic choice will be, to a large extent, shaped by the international society, as it is largely determined by China's domestic situation and by its own intentions. International society is a mixer, including the transitions of the system structure, transformation of interaction and process, and the reconstructing of norms. More specifically, the transition of international system or structure is due to significant changes in the international order, which is the shift of international actors or shift among international actors (upward or downward), distribution of powers, and polar of international order.

Firstly, with the deepening of globalization, interdependence and the enhancement of interactive density, international society also provides a significant strategic opportunity for China, historical window or time window. Secondly, process dimension refers to the model and pattern of interaction between international actors, and contains not only material dimension but also normative dimension. In this part, members of the international society adjust their interests and strategic intention based on the interaction and communication process. Thirdly, even though the international society is still under the discourse of Western countries, it has been improved since transition and development of international pattern and international process, thereby bringing variations of discourse and ideas of international actors. Therefore, changes of this dimension are the slowest, but harbor the most profound influences.

Third, regional studies, like foreign policy analysis, have been at the edge of international relations. However, mainstream international relations theories have not paid enough attention to region studies. The region is one concept in terms of geopolitics, which refers to similarity of geographical proximity and circumstances. Moreover, the region is one comprehensive concept in terms of social and political culture, which refers to mutually constructed, inter-constructed, and cultivated among different actors. According to Barry Buzan, region is with a common identity and internal interaction and collective action within a geographical region. (Buzan, B., 1998, P.73)

When it comes to region evolution, it is coincident that the deepening of globalization is accompanied by regional integration. It is the region that becomes one of the important dimensions of international society. Some scholars viewed that the world is composed of regions, which is "a world of regions" (Katzenstein, 2005), "a more regional world system" (Acharya, 2007). It has been a norm status of international order since the end of cold war, which has been viewed region as an analysis level and analysis variable. On the one hand, region itself has the characteristics, structure, system, process and environment of the region. The interactions of international actors mainly settled at the regional level, "interactions of major powers and international affairs fundamentally occurred and conducted in the specific regional framework" (Wang, X., 2000, p.39). The importance of regional level challenged the assumption of traditional international theories, which is the homogeneity of international actors. It put forward the assumption that the world is composed of heterogeneous and complicated regions. Therefore, it is sufficient to say that region could be an analysis variable and policy platform. On the other hand, it is globalization that highlights the role of regional cooperation. For instance, European integration still keeps moving even though there are multiple crises challenging the role of regional governance structure. Besides, Asia regional cooperation and Africa regional cooperation are also experiencing slow but continuous development. Therefore, integrated organizations or regional governance provides another option for world peace, prevention of war, and economy prosperity and social stability. It further strengthened the evidence that region is a new analysis level and new area of international relations and world society.

Cooperation is one complicated and difficult issue. There are different perspectives to understand cooperation and solutions to reach cooperation. More specifically, if we talk about cooperation, there could be at least four dimensions: for instances, sphere of cooperation, degree of cooperation, effectiveness and target of cooperation. Regarding independent variables, factors

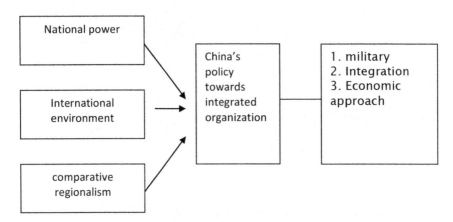

Figure 12.1   Mechanism of China's Policies Towards Regional Organizations.

such as perceptions of security, foundations for cooperation, mechanism of cooperation, approach of actions, capability of building and rule-making could exert influence on variations of cooperation. When we talk about China's policies toward integrated organizations, it is essential to figure out variations of cooperation. Therefore, the following part touches upon three regional organizations, that is, Shanghai Security Cooperation, Association of Southeast Asian Nations, and China-Arab States Cooperation Forum.

CHINA'S POLICIES TOWARD INTEGRATED ORGANIZATIONS

Integrated organizations not only provide space dimension of international studies, in terms of dynamics, structure, process and consequences, but also render the platform for other variables embedded in regional dimension with specific meaning. Integrated organizations could exert intermediary and filtering influence on the relationship between global system and circumstance and national foreign policies, which is more local and specific. China could maintain a certain distance from the Western countries, if China's strategic priority is at the regional level, thereby to some extent reducing the resistance from the Western countries. Besides, there are higher culture inter-connections, economic ties, close strategic connections with periphery regions. China could exert more feasible and influenced role at the regional level. And those countries might easier accept the norms rendered by China. If China continues its combination of national culture, political nationalism and economic liberalism, it is the regional level rather than the global level that serves the ideal platform where China conducted its foreign policies.

NON-ALIGNED COOPERATION: CHINA AND SHANGHAI COOPERATION ORGANIZATION

When it refers to the role of North Atlantic Treaty Organization (NATO), we would view it as the product of the Cold War, and a tool for political conflict. However, Shanghai Cooperation Organization (SCO) is neither for military confrontation with other countries or international organizations, nor solving conflicts and disputes of member states or other countries with use of force. It is the fundamental difference between NATO and SCO. There is a dimension regarding external threats in security cooperation of SCO, but it not explicitly mentioned the object of prevention in the treaty of SCO. For more than ten years, the SCO members have carried on intimately security cooperation in response to nontraditional security threats, thereby cultivating cooperation partnership of non-aligned rather than alliance. In July 2015, Ufa summit adopted a resolution to embrace India and Pakistan as members of SCO. Besides, Afghanistan, Belarus, Iran, Mongolia currently are the observers. Meanwhile, Azerbaijan, Armenia, Cambodia, Nepal, Turkey, Sri Lanka are dialogue partners. In this sense, the SCO has become a significant security cooperation platform of countries from East Asia, South Asia, Central Asia, the Middle East, Europe and Russia.

There are at least three features of Shanghai Cooperation Organization, based on the rule of non-aligned cooperation. Number one is soft balance in issue of security. SCO is not the counterpart of NATO. It is one approach to urge the West to balance the core concerns of developing countries, stressed political communication and policy coordination, as well as soft balance of the US-led NATO and US-Japan alliances under the political and security framework. Number two is ambiguity of strategy. Under the framework of the SCO, China's foreign policy endeavors to develop and cultivate partnership with other countries, as well as develop comprehensive national power. Meanwhile, China seeks a middle way between bandwagon strategy and neutral strategy, and avoids provocative consequences of hegemony strategy or balancing strategy. Number three is concert of powers. China's diplomacy not only emphasizes peace and development, but also emphasizes cooperation and coordination among major powers. It is not necessary for conflict among great powers, but also cooperation even with the United States. The SCO is expected to coordinate with Russia and the United States, Japan and Europe, India and other powers. Therefore, it could go beyond the "enemy's enemy is my friend," "friend's enemy is my enemy," which is black and white, zero-sum logic. For example, China stressed that "Belt and Road Initiative" could fit with Russia's initiative of the "Eurasian Economic Union" strategy. Meanwhile, under these two frameworks, it is necessary to strengthen coordination and communication with China and Russia, Iran and Turkey and other countries of Eurasia.

OPENNESS REGIONALISM: CHINA AND ASSOCIATION OF SOUTHEAST ASIAN NATIONS

When it comes to relationship between China and ASEAN countries, there is a huge difference, in terms of the political system, ideology, development path, as well as the difference of religious belief. Besides, there is the reality of territorial disputes, including China, Vietnam, Malaysia and the Philippines and other countries around the Nansha and Xisha islands ownership disputes, territorial disputes between Singapore, Malaysia and Indonesia, Thailand and Cambodia's territorial disputes, etc. Therefore, relationship between China and ASEAN is different from the trans-Pacific Partnership Agreement (the TPP). More specifically, the latter is a kind of exclusive regional cooperation, while the former is respecting for the diversity of the ASEAN member countries, establishing the multiple strategic cooperative relations with external powers, and advocating open regionalism in this region.

According to former Malaysian prime minister Mahathir Mohamad's initiative in 1990, East Asia Economic Caucus or East Asian community aims to bring together ASEAN countries with China, Japan and South Korea. Therefore, major cities like Beijing, Seoul, Tokyo, Hong Kong, Shanghai, Taipei, Bangkok, Manila and Hanoi, Singapore, Kuala Lumpur, Jakarta and other big cities in East Asia will be connected as a whole, and become the urban agglomeration. Furthermore, Northeast Asian community (including China, Japan and South Korea), Greater China Community (including mainland China, Taiwan, Hong Kong and Macau), and ASEAN countries form a "Dumbbell Structure" (Sun, H., and Ren Y., 2011). It could be the third largest economic community in the world, in terms of tranquility, peace and prosperity, in line with the European Union and North American Free Trade Area. In the construction of East Asia community, China's local government is playing a positive role, especially provincial units such as the Tumen river area cooperation, greater Mekong sub-regional cooperation, etc.

In terms of relationship between major powers and ASEAN countries, the United States had established hub-and-spoke system, with the United States as the center while Southeastern Asian countries as the peripheral in military, political and economic issues. In 1980s, Japan proposed Flying Geese Model, with Japan as the leader while other others as the follower. However, hub-and-spoke system and flying geese model (Zha, D. And Hu, W., 2006) are established on the basis of asymmetric relationship, because Southeast Asian countries are subsidiary to the leadership and dominant position of the United States and Japan separately.

Admittedly, China and ASEAN countries are quite asymmetric in terms of economic scale, geographical area, military strength, population and other aspects. (Ahn, B., 2004). But China proposes for open regionalism on the basis of sovereign equality, thereby achieving comprehensive openness, less powerful institution and limited binding. China's blueprint of East Asia cooperation focuses on intra-regional cooperation, and inter-regional cooperation including international organizations and extra-regional countries, based on equality, mutual trust, cooperation and development. It manifests that China and ASEAN countries seek common ground while putting differences aside. Moreover, it emphasizes functional and pragmatic cooperation between China and ASEAN countries, laying foundations for economic and political communities of East Asia, in terms of economy, mechanism and ideas. In November 2015, Chinese prime minister Li Keqiang presented on the eighteenth of China-ASEAN (10+1) leaders summit, pointed out that "both sides need to stick to the general direction of enhancing political mutual trust in order to strengthen the foundation for cooperation, promoting integrated development, thereby achieving common prosperity and win-win cooperation." China and ASEAN countries expand common interests and seek common ground while set aside differences, thereby narrowing gaps and seizing the opportunities. Both sides dovetail their development advantages to elevate overall development of 11 countries, aiming to complete the East Asia Economic Community by 2020 and promote sustainable peace and prosperity in East Asia. (Li, K. 2015).

RESPECTING DIVERSITY AND EQUALITY: CHINA-ARAB STATES COOPERATION FORUM

When it comes to cooperation with China and Arab states, it might view China as the representative of Eastern Confucian civilization, while the Arabia world is the representative of Islamic civilization. The former is a sovereign state, the latter is a political alliance composed of 22 Arabia countries (Wang, Z., 2015; Polk, A., 2014). There are huge differences between those countries and the Western countries, even China, in terms of political system, ideology, religious beliefs, and economic development stage. Nevertheless, China has established strategic relations with Arabian countries on the basis of fully respecting the diversity of the Arabian world. In 2004, the relationship between China and Arab countries has developed rapidly since the establishment of China-Arab States Cooperation Forum in 2004. In 2016, China became the second largest trading partner of all Arab states, and the largest trading partner of nine Arab states.

On June 5, 2014, President Xi Jinping mentioned in the sixth ministerial conference of the China-Arab States Cooperation Forum that the two sides should hold a broader vision and down-to-earth attitude to establish a "1+2+3" cooperation pattern, namely, to take energy cooperation as the core, infrastructure construction and trade and investment facilitation as two wings, and three high and new tech fields of nuclear energy, space satellite and new energy as new breakthroughs (Xi, 2014).

It is difficult to figure out the role and intention of China policy in the Middle East, for the sake of energy security or acting as a strategic rival or a supplement to the United States. However, China's policy in this area has been regarded as successful, because China kept friendly relationship with all countries in this region. For example, even though the relationship between Saudi Arabia and Iran is not so good, China cooperated with Saudi Arabia, Iran, irrespectively, to build railway line. More importantly, China "has no alliance anywhere whose economic or other interests it must defend on the battlefield or in the international fora" (Freeman, C., 2015). It is, to a large extent, different from perceptions of the United States, because the United States was viewed as an imperial power in this region. Take Asian Infrastructure Investment Bank (AIIB) for example, Israel, Jordan, and Turkey have joined in this China-initiated institution, and even Iran and Saudi Arab were founding members of the AIIB. One Belt, One Road (OBOR) initiative required China to pay attention to the Middle East, besides Central Asia areas. 'OBOR' initiative was regarded as one way to construct a comprehensive cultural, economic and political network, connecting with states, regions and cities along the OBOR. Meanwhile, OBOR initiative is also flexible, inclusive and open, because OBOR is neither a regime nor an organization, instead of cooperation among varieties of actors.

The American security architecture left room for China, especially from which the strategic (political and security) vacuum in the Middle East after the withdrawal of theUnited States. Even so, there are no indications that China is willing or able to replace the United States as the main security guarantor in the Middle East. Furthermore, regarding for the major powers in the Middle East, both Iran and Saudi Arabia own ambitions to become a regional hegemon, which caused more potential to conflict (Reardon, M., 2015). The United States has tried to keep the balance of power in the Middle East (Cooper, A., 2012). Saudi Arabia has acted as an informal alliance with the United States. For example, "oil explorations and developments in Saudi Arabia have been carried out almost entirely by American companies" (Bahgat, G., 2016). Both the United States and Saudi Arabia have shared mutual interest rather than shared values since the Charter Doctrine in the late 1970s. On the contrary, the relationship between Iran and Western energy consumers is not so friendly because of history and religion. For example, Gulf Co-operation Council (GCC) security framework is an extension of the North Atlantic Treaty Organization (NATO), which exacerbated the balance of power in this region (Mansour, I., 2015). Because members of GCC are Bahrain, Kuwait, Oman, Qatar, Saudi Arabia, and the United Arab Emirates. In other words, the security architecture is under the unstable and deteriorating conditions, which is one indicator for China's policies toward this region.

Through platforms such as China-Arab States Cooperation Forum, SCO, 10+1 cooperation between China and the Association of Southeast Asian Nations, China could render a series of ideas on China-integrated organizations cooperation and South-South cooperation. There are other platforms including 16+1 cooperation between China and the Central and Eastern Europe, and Forum on China-Africa Cooperation, which might also draw previous tangible experience from cooperation mentioned above. Therefore, China's polices toward integrated organizations might win positive evaluation from the developing countries and fulfill China's strategic interests.

APPROACHES FOR CHINA'S STRATEGY
TOWARD INTEGRATED ORGANIZATIONS

China's regional strategy is one of the contents of China's foreign policy. And the goal is to enhance China's authority and influence in different regions, like Asia and the Western Pacific, Europe and Central Asia. However, the foremost region is Asia, especially East Asia. Regarding China's strategy toward integrated organizations, there are three approaches for China' regional strategy, specifically is moderate military strategy, regional path, and economic integration.

First, moderate military strategy is the basic condition for China to carry out regional strategy. From the general trend of international development and Chinese domestic situation, Chinese adhere to the path of peaceful development, pursue an independent foreign policy of peace and a national defense policy; on the other hand, emphasizing the construction of national defense and military modernization is a strategic task and a guarantee for the peaceful development of the country. This requires China to achieve the great rejuvenation of the Chinese dream, while China will work with the rest of the world to safeguard peace, seek development and share prosperity. China neither take the Western powers once traversed the road, increase military spending, challenge the existing international order, nor walk alliance strategic path, with other countries to deal with the alliance, the United States military pressure.

The essence of active defense is "defense," the meaning of active defense is "actively." In the military issue, China adheres to comprehensive security, cooperative security, common security, sustainable security, in order to develop nonaligned, non-confrontational, military relations with third parties. By reviewing the history, China's military strategy could be divided into three stages: 1) active defense strategy, from 1949 to mid1960s, since the establishment of the new China, China has established to safeguard national security and defense against imperialist aggression; 2) active defense strategy, from mid 1960s to early 1980s, based on the formation of "early hit a big war, and nuclear war" thought; and 3) active defense strategy, from the middle of 80s to the beginning of twenty-first Century, the military strategy aims to win the local war with high technology. In May 26, 2015, Chinese government issued the first "China military strategy" white paper, stressed that under the new situation, China should implement the military strategy of active defense, accelerate the modernization of national defense and the army, and resolutely safeguard national sovereignty, security and development interests.

Second, regional path is China's guiding strategy to carry out security strategy in the surrounding areas. It is impossible for an area to develop and integrate without the participation, recognition and mutual support of the regional members. China's strategy to carry out the surrounding areas in the economic integration, but economic security, public safety and environmental security is inseparable.

As part of a China global strategy, regional strategy could be conducted under the strategic goal of national strategic objectives, as a starting point, thereby serving the relationship between regional strategy and wholesome strategy, coping with the relation between regional strategy and parts of global strategy (mainly referring to major power strategies). It refers to the relationship between whole and parts, relationship between parts and parts. Especially in the historical stage, the rise of China, regional strategy will provide a platform for the peaceful rise of China and the peaceful transformation of the international community.

Third, economic integration is the specific practice of China's security strategy in the periphery regions. Regional or sub-regional path selection and implementation strategy of the surrounding China starting point. Economic integration is a specific policy. It is essential for China to develop and promote economic ties with integrated regions. The rapid growth of economic strength and the increase in the density of foreign economic exchanges not only provide impetus for China's domestic reform and development, but also enhance China's political influence in the region. Under the impetus of the "economy first," China increasingly strengthened relationship with integrated organizations, integrated into the regional system, from a "out of the country" into a "region of the country," resulting in spillover effects.

The Asia-Pacific should boost economic integration and build open economy. Openness is vital for Asia-Pacific regional economy. "We need to promote inter-connectivity and realize collaborative development. Inter-connectivity is an important way to unleash development potential and serves as a basic premise for the realization of collaborative development."(Xi, 2016) The Asia-Pacific region became the main engine for the growth of the world economy. The center of gravity in the international geopolitical balance of forces continued to shift toward this region. All major powers pooled more strategic input into the region. The security situation in the region as a whole was stable, but there were increased instabilities and uncertainties (Yang, J., 2014).

China's international strategy, especially the dimension of economy strategy, need consider the closer relationship between China and neighboring countries in terms of economy and trade. It is prerequisite for China's international strategy that military strategy is the bottom line. Without defense and military strength, it is impossible to talk about other foreign policy tools. However, the military strategy is not an offensive military strategy of the Western hegemonic countries, but an active defensive and moderate military strategy. After fulfilling the basic military and national defense capabilities, we will focus on the regional level, emphasizing the integrity of the region, rather than just concentrating on specific bilateral relationship.

CONCLUSION

At the moment, we are in a somewhat uncertain situation. With the com-
plexities of globalization, anti-globalization, de-globalization, regional-
oriented foreign policy and behavior is to some extent a Pareto sub-optimal
choice. Regional platform, in terms of coordination and cooperation, not
only renders certain structure embedded with governments, but also ensures
equal participation and mutual benefit of the relevant countries. It means all
participants could be possible for accepting a unified standards and regulations, and supporting, to some extent, regional governance mechanism and
institutions. It is the most conducive to promote the process of globalization and its challenges, if we solve global problems at the regional level, or
implement regional standards and measures to achieve global standards. It is
certain regions that understand and appreciate the influence of globalization
and the importance of globalization. Meanwhile, it is more hypersensitive for
international actors to react with and response to the balance of interests and
motivations, not global level but regional level.

At the same time, international actors' response will firstly exert a direct
impact on the region. China has developed significantly, in sphere of materials,
economy and military. China's political influence is also expanding, and China
has been increasingly involved in multilateral platform in terms of identity,
other countries in the regions have altered their perceptions for the rise of the
China, because the countries in the region used to view China as the "threat,"
now they regard China as "good neighbors," "constructive partners," and non-
threatening regional powers. With the rise of China and the changes of neighboring countries' recognition of China, they adjust their relations with China
and expect China to play an increasingly important role in regional affairs.

The main point of this paper is that military strategy is the bottom line of
China's international strategy, including policies toward integrated organizations. Without defense and military strength, it is impossible to talk about other
foreign policy tools. However, the military strategy is not an offensive military
strategy of the Western hegemonic countries, but an active defensive and moderate military strategy. After fulfilling the basic military and national defense
capabilities, we will focus on the regional level, emphasizing the integrity of
the region, rather than just concentrating on specific bilateral relationship. It is
the starting point and platform for China's international strategy to concentrate
on regional or sub-regional level. Specifically, economic integration is China's
concrete policy to conduct international strategy. Based on the logic of economic integration, China conducted economic integration with regional or sub-
regional level, including Southeast Asia, Northeast Asia, South Asia and Central
Asia. Besides that China concentrate on the importance of military security and
economic integration, China might strengthen its cultural exchanges, via of
public diplomacy, people-to-people exchanges, with neighboring countries,

thereby improving China's international image and creating a friendly, peaceful and cooperative international image. It is also possible for China to expand Chinese language, Chinese culture, technology, to train foreign political and technical elites, thereby consolidating and developing relationship between China and neighboring countries, not only government level, but also social and public level. It is not paradox for China's military strategy and economy strategy, however, it is parallel with the idea of community of common density with integrated organizations as well as their members.

REFERENCES

A. Dirlik (2014), Mao Zedong Thought and the Third World/Global South, *Interventions*, Vol.16, No.2, pp.233–256.

Amitav Acharya (2007), The Emerging Regional Architecture of World Politics, *World Politics*, Vol.59, No.4, pp.629–652.

Andy Polk (2014), China: A Major Power in the Middle East? April 01, 2014, Available: HYPERLINK "http://thediplomat.com/2014/04/china-a-major-power-in-the-middle-east/" http://thediplomat.com/2014/04/china-a-major-power-in-the-middle-east/. [Accessed 17 October, 2016]

Andrew Scott Cooper (2012), *The Oil Kings: How the US, Iran and Saudi Arabia Changed the Balance of Power in the Middle East*, London: Oneworld Publications.

Ann Kent (2007), *Beyond Compliance: China, International Organizations, and Global Security*, Stanford: Stanford University Press.

Barry Buzan (1998), The Asia-Pacific: What Sort of Region in What Sort of World? In: A. Mc Grew and C. Brook, (Eds), *"Asia-Pacific in the New World Order,"* London and New York: Routledge, pp.70–74

Barry Buzan and Ole Waever (2003), *Regions and Powers: The Structure of International Security*, Cambridge: Cambridge University Press.

Byung-Joon Ahn (2004), "The Rise of China and the Future of East Asian Integration," *Asia-Pacific Review*, Vol. 11, No. 2, p.34.

Chas W. Freeman (2015), The Middle East and China, Middle East Policy Council, February 17, 2015. Available: http://chasfreeman.net/the-middle-east-and-china-2/ [Accessed 17 October, 2016]

Gawdat Bahgat (2016), Chinese and US Energy Policy in the Middle East, In Niv Horesh (Eds), *Toward Well-Oiled Relations? China's Presence in the Middle East Following the Arab Spring*, New York: Palgrave Macmillan, p.117.

Hedley Bull and Adam Watson (1984), *The Expansion of International Society*, London: Oxford University Press, p.1.

Imad Mansour (2015), The GCC States and the Viability of a Strategic Military Partnership with China, Middle East Institute, March 17, 2015. Available: http://www.mei.edu/content/map/gcc-states-and-viability-strategic-military-partnership-china. [Accessed 14 November, 2016]

Jin, C., Duan, H., and Hong, J., New Features of the Surrounding International Environment and China's Response, Contemporary International Relations, 2013, Vol.23, No.6, pp.24–30.

Johnston AI. (2003), Zhongguo yu guoji zuzhi: lai zi waibu de guancha [China and international organizations: perspectives from outside China]. In: Yizhou W Mohe zhong de jiangou: Zhongguo yu guoji zuzhi guanxi de duoshijiao toushi [Construction in contradiction: multi-dimensioned perspectives on China's relations with international organizations]. Beijing: China Development Press.

Johnston AI. (2008), *Social States: China in International Institutions, 1980–2000,* Princeton: Princeton University Press.

Li Keqiang (2015), 18th China-ASEAN (10+1) Summit, Dock Development Strategies, Elevate Development Level and Promote Enduring Peace and Prosperity in East Asia, 2015/11/12, Available: http://www.fmprc.gov.cn/mfa_eng/topics_665678/lkqcxdyhzldrxlhybdmlxyjxzsfw/t1317768.shtml. [Accessed 27 October, 2016]

Louis J. Cantori and Steven L. Spiegel (1970), The International Relations of Regions, *Polity*, Vol.2, No.4, pp.397–425.

Martin Reardon (2015), Saudi Arabia, Iran and the Great Game in Yemen, Al Jazeera, March 26, 2015. Available: http://www.aljazeera.com/indepth/opinion/2014/09/saudi-arabia-iran-great-game-ye-201492984846324440.html. [Accessed 7 November, 2016]

Ministry of National Defense of the People's Republic of China (2015), China's Military Strategy, Available: http://www.mod.gov.cn/auth/2015–05/26/content_4586723.htm. [Accessed 14 October, 2016]

Peter J. Katzenstein. (2005), *A World of Regions: Asia and Europe in the American Imperium,* Cornell University.

Su Hao, Ren Yuan-zhe (2011), Making the rocks of dispute drown in the sea of cooperation: the role of the south China sea in the process of East Asian cooperation. In: Tran Truong Thuy (Ed), *The South China Sea: towards a Region of Peace, Security and Cooperation*, anoi, Vietnam Thế Giới Publishers, pp.16–30.

Walter Mattili (1999), *The Logic of Regional Integration: Europe and Beyond*, Cambridge: Cambridge University Press.

Xi Jinping (2014), Opening Ceremony of Sixth Ministerial Conference of China-Arab States Cooperation Forum and Delivers Important Speech Stressing to Promote Silk Road Spirit and Deepen China-Arab Cooperation. 2014/06/05. http://www.fmprc.gov.cn/mfa_eng/zxxx_662805/t1163554.shtml. [Accessed 11 October, 2016]

Xi Jinping (2016), Highlights of Xi's address at 2016 APEC CEO summit, 2016–11–20, http://news.xinhuanet.com/english/2016–11/20/c_135843072.htm. [Accessed 11 October, 2016]

Xueyu Wang (2000), Regional Politics and International Relations Studies, *Journal of World Economics and Politics*, No.4, p.39.

Yang Jiechi (2014), China's New Foreign Relations for a Complex World, *China International Studies*, No.1, pp.5–17.

Zha Daojiong and Hu Weixing (2006), *Building a Neighborly Community: Post-Cold War China, Japan and Southeast Asia*, Manchester: Manchester University Press, p.19.

Zheng Wang (2015), China's Alternative Diplomacy. *The Diplomat*, Available: http://thediplomat.com/2015/01/chinas-alternative-diplomacy/. [Accessed 6 December, 2016]

Chapter 13

The US Pivot to Asia

Implications for China and East Asia

Jeanne L. Wilson

The rise of China as a global economic power has been accompanied by a more assertive foreign policy presence. Since the launching of its economic reform movement in late 1978, the Chinese leadership has consistently subordinated its foreign policy to the goal of economic development, an approach encapsulated in Deng Xiaoping's alleged injunction to 'keep a low profile while bidding one's time' (tao guang yang hui). For a number of years, Chinese commentators have been urging the Chinese leadership to shed its deferential stance and assert China's rightful place as a major global player. In fact, the elevation of Xi Jinping to the Chinese presidency in 2012, replacing the cautious and risk averse Hu Jintao, has seen a marked change in Chinese international behavior. Xi signaled China's rise in a 2013 meeting with Barack Obama when he heralded a 'new type of great power relations' (xinxing daguo guanxi) between the United States and China. But the Xi leadership has selected to focus its predominant attention on East Asia, a process that has been accompanied by an implicit claim to regional hegemony.

This development sets China up for an intensifying competition with the United States. The policies adopted by the Obama administration were underpinned by a commitment to play a hegemonic role in the Asia-Pacific region. The adoption of the 2009 strategy known as the 'pivot to Asia' or later modified as the 'rebalance' to Asia set out a plan to bolster the US presence in East Asia. Both terms implied that the George W. Bush administration had neglected US interests in Asia, becoming overly involved in the broader Middle East, and that it was imperative to strengthen a network of economic, political, and military ties in the region. Although US participation in negotiations on the Trans Pacific Partnership (TPP) began in 2008 during the Bush administration, the Obama presidency eventually came to push for the implementation of the trade agreement as a cornerstone of its Asia policy.

The election of Hillary Clinton to the US presidency in November 2016 would presumably have indicated the continuation, in perhaps a modified format, of the approach to Asia adopted by the Obama administration. During her tenure as Secretary of State, Clinton was the standard bearer of the Obama policy to Asia (see Clinton, 2011). In fact, Clinton's electoral platform on foreign policy largely conformed to the policy preferences of a bipartisan political elite. The deterioration of political discourse in the United States in recent years has tended to obscure the high level of agreement among the political class on foreign policy issues. These include a commitment to the maintenance of multilateral and bilateral treaties born out of the Cold War era, as well as an affirmation of the neo-liberal economic precepts embodied in the Bretton Woods structures and the primacy of Western values and norms as a universal ideal. The specific approach to China has been an attempt at 'constructive engagement,' rooted in the assumption that China can be socialized into the Western-dominated international order as a 'responsible stakeholder' (see Zoellick, 2005).

Donald Trump's election as the US president calls into question the continued relevance of many of these long-held precepts. It is too early to assess with any certainty the overall trajectory of a Trump foreign policy toward Asia, which remains inchoate. Trump has repudiated, as his campaign promised, US participation in the TPP. But he has also been compelled to reaffirm the US commitment to a one-China policy. Trump's campaign slogan 'to make America great again' obviously signals that the United States is in a state of decline, but it does not provide detailed guidelines as to the means to national renewal, especially in the foreign policy sphere.

It is also the case that a Trump presidency simultaneously provides a series of challenges and opportunities to China. But his election also injects a great deal of uncertainty into the future evolution of the Sino-American relationship, as well as the United States' global role. It is ironic that China, still ostensibly a Marxist-Leninist state, has emerged as the leading defender of globalization and the legitimacy of the Bretton Woods financial system. This is a reflection in part of China's deep integration into the global economic system, and the costs that would be incurred as a consequence of its dissolution or partial restructuring (although this potential development would reverberate throughout the entire system, including, of course, in the United States). On the other hand, the US withdrawal from the TPP leaves the United States with a reduced ability to use economic levers as a means of influence in the East Asian region, while enlarging the economic opportunities available to China.

This chapter is primarily concerned with examining the regional power transition that is currently underway in East Asia, which is to say the means by which China seeks to consolidate its status as a regional power and the

United States' reaction to this effort. At this point, the Trump administration is still in the process of formulating a policy toward East Asia. To date, Trump has seemed more focused on military rather than economic means of projecting power, more interested in bilateral compared to multilateral forms of interaction, and largely inattentive to the regional initiatives undertaken by China, which were watched closely—and with apprehension—by the Obama administration. Realist theory posits the persistence of timeless and immutable structural conditions that shape the foreign policy behavior of states, as well as discounting the impact of individual personalities (Morgenthau, 1973; Waltz, 1979). Although presidential candidates have often been critical of China—most often due to perceived human rights abuses rather than trade policy—the continuity of US foreign policy that transcends presidential administrations suggests the enduring importance of fundamental interests in negotiating the Sino-US relationship. In this sense, the Trump presidency provides an interesting test case to gage the extent to which realist assumptions retain a contemporary significance.

It further raises the question, given Trump's divergence from the largely consensual assumptions that have permeated the US foreign policy establishment, of the role of individual agency, here embodied in the leadership role of Donald Trump, in the foreign policy behavior of a hegemonic state.

Although leadership perceptions of national interest have evolved over time, US foreign policy toward China since the Nixon era can largely be viewed through the lens of political realism. Richard Nixon's overture to China was an explicit attempt to counterbalance the Soviet Union (a movement that met with Mao Zedong's approval).

For all its embrace of principles of liberal internationalism, the Obama administration was surprisingly candid in its realpolitik appraisal of Chinese intentions. What is unfolding is a form of great power competition between a rising state and the long dominant hegemon in the region. This is a complex process that is further complicated by the high degree of economic interdependence between China and the United States. As Ikenberry (2015) notes, both states simultaneously engage in efforts at liberal engagement as well as a competitive jousting for power. There is a lack of transparency between means and ends. Economic policies are simultaneously advanced as a reflection of norms and values while also being deployed to serve political goals. The first section of this paper discusses China's recent attempts to expand its regional role as well as an examination of the US reaction. Specifically, the leadership's unveiling of its Silk Road project is examined, as well as its concurrent program to establish the Asian Infrastructure Investment Bank (AIIB). The second part of this paper shifts to an investigation of the Obama administration's pivot to Asia in the context of its implications for China. This involves a focus on the United States' promotion of the TPP, as well as its attempts to consolidate relationships with the smaller states in the region so as to impede their economic, or even more worrisome, political drift to China. The final section speculates as to the future evolution of this rivalry in the Trump administration.

CHINA'S EMERGENT REGIONAL STRATEGY

The decision of the Xi leadership to direct its attention to East Asia was signaled by a working conference held in October 2013 on diplomacy with neighboring states. This convocation was the highest-level meeting on foreign affairs to be held since 1949 and the first to be attended by all of the members of the Standing Committee of the Politburo (Yan, 2014). Roughly concurrently, Xi introduced the pair of initiatives that collectively form OBOR (also known as yi dai yi lu [One Belt, One Road] or the Silk Road projects). In a speech at Nazarbaev University in Kazakhstan in September 2013, he proposed that China and the states of Central Asia cooperate to establish trade and economic linkages as a means of promoting regional cooperation. During a visit to Indonesia the following month, Xi unveiled the maritime aspect of the project, envisioning the establishment of a series of transportation corridors, accompanied by the promotion of trade and development projects, focused on East Asia in its first stages. The AIIB was conceived to be the financial arm of this arrangement, serving as the source for infrastructure loans, as a means to the goal of promoting 'interconnectivity and economic integration in the region' (AIIB). The Chinese leadership has offered several rationales for OBOR, all of which, taken on their own terms, are persuasive and consistent with China's development goals. The land based component of OBOR, which looks to Central Asia and beyond, is explained as aiding in the development of China's less prosperous Western provinces—specifically Xinjiang and Tibet—with their large potentially restive minority populations.[1] OBOR further provides an outlet for China's huge foreign exchange reserves and is perceived to serve as a stimulus to economic growth within the Chinese domestic economy.

The Chinese leadership has formally sought to play down the obvious geopolitical implications of OBOR. This has not been the case with Chinese commentators, the boldest (and most politically well connected) of whom have identified OBOR's strategic goal as contesting American power in a drive to assume regional hegemony (see Yan, 2015). Nonetheless, the government has proved itself quite willing to promote OBOR as a civilizational construct. Chinese officials have advocated OBOR as a means, in the words of the Minister of Commerce Guo Hucheng (2015), 'to learn about Chinese civilization that has a long history and profound culture.' In his speech in Indonesia introducing the Maritime Silk Road, Xi made reference (as he has subsequently) to the creation of a 'community of common destiny' (mingyun gongtongti) (Arase, 2015; Xi, 2013). At the 2014 APEC summit, Xi (2014) took this concept a step further, evoking the idea of the Asia-Pacific Dream, which he specifically related to his domestic promotion of the Chinese Dream. Although the Chinese Dream is a contentious concept, it appears that Xi identifies its realization with the emergence of a prosperous and self-confident China (see Callahan 2015; Wang 2013a; 2013b). This mode of discourse is evocative of China's historical position as the dominant power in the region, to which its neighbors paid tribute in a hierarchical relationship of superior and subordinate (see Deng, 2015). In this vision, what the Chinese leadership contemplates as a win-win partnership could also be re-cast as the construction of a Sinocentric order in which China is the dominant economic and civilizational partner.

THE UNITED STATES AND CHINA'S SILK ROAD AMBITIONS

The US response to OBOR has ranged from a deliberate disregard to outright hostility. In 2015, Xi raised the topic of OBOR in remarks made at a White House press conference describing the project as a 'means to expand mutual and beneficial cooperation with other countries,' a measure that he considered to be in the interests of the US. Obama, in contrast, was silent on the topic (Joint Press Conference, 2015) As Gal Luft (2016, p. 71) has noted, US and Chinese officials detailed more than 100 areas of potential cooperation at the 2015 and 2016 meetings of the US-China Strategic and Economic Dialogue without any mention of OBOR. Washington, however, adopted a different tactic with regard to Chinese plans to establish the AIIB, seeking to dissuade states from seeking membership in the bank. Despite the strenuous objections of the United States, this effort largely ended in failure, as even its closest allies chose to jump on the Chinese bandwagon.

The US reaction to the AIIB focused on the threat that it provided to the existing international economic institutions, and its presumed lack of conformance to transparency and time-tested best practices developed over time. Washington insisted that any newly established financial institutions—specifically the AIIB and the BRICs New Development Bank—must incorporate the same operative principles as the Bretton Woods Structures or the Asian Development Bank. (see Harris, 2015; Sheets, 2015). The Obama administration portrayed the bank as a danger because it was viewed as potentially operating according to lower standards. As least equally importantly, Washington feared the challenge that the AIIB posed to the US-led economic system forged in the post–World War II era. As Larry Summers, Obama's former economic advisor, noted: the establishment of the AIIB might be remembered as 'the moment the United States lost its role as the underwriter of the global economic system' (Summers, 2015).

Originally, the Chinese conceived of the AIIB as a regional structure that would provide infrastructure loans to OBOR initiatives. The leadership assumed that many states would be unsupportive of the bank given Washington's clear opposition to the project (Sun, 2015). The receptivity of European states—which saw large potential business opportunities in Asia—to membership came as a welcome surprise to China. The United States sought to use its powers of persuasion to prevent its allies from joining the AIIB, originally focusing on Australia and Canada. In March 2015, the United Kingdom broke ranks with the United States, announcing its decision to join the AIIB, which led to a number of other NATO states—including Germany and France—applying to join. In April, 2016, Jin Liqun, the president of the AIIB, announced that the AIIB would have 100 countries as members by the end of the year, making it a global institution (Li X., 2016) In August 2015, Canada applied to join the bank, leaving Japan the sole major ally that has remained aligned with the United States. Although there is considerable speculation that Japan will be compelled eventually to apply for membership, the Japanese leadership remains highly wary of China and suspicious, as with the United States, that the bank serves as a means for China to expand its strategic and economic power (Kawai, 2015). In sum, the unforeseen success of the AIIB in attracting members (although its long-term performance remains unproven) was a major diplomatic triumph for China and a humiliating defeat for the United States.

Washington's position that it was serving as a gatekeeper to maintain the integrity of global norms and standards was not considered credible. On the one hand, China insisted that it was not challenging the global status quo and proved amenable to making changes to the bank's architecture. Beijing, for example, gave up its original plans for veto power over loans to be granted, and proved amenable to working with the World Bank and the Asian Development Bank for guidance and technical assistance in drafting plans to operate as a Multilateral Development Bank. On the other hand, it was widely acknowledged that the Bretton Woods structures were badly in need of structural reforms to reflect the rising economic power of the developing states, foremost among them China. The repeated failure of the US Congress to sanction agreements that would adjust voting shares in the IMF was but one example of this structural inequity (deLisle, 2016, p. 172; Sun, 2015).

THE UNITED STATES, CHINA, AND THE TPP

The TPP is an outgrowth of the Transpacific Strategic Economic Partnership (comprised of Chile, New Zealand, Singapore and Brunei), which was concluded in 2005. The Bush administration announced its intention to join negotiations in 2008 and a larger group of states, including the United States in the Obama presidency, began negotiations on the TPP in 2010. A finalized proposal was signed by 12 states of the Asian-Pacific Rim in February 2016. The TPP is a preferential trade agreement that goes beyond the current standards of the WTO with regard to trade liberalization, in addition to addressing such issues as international investment, intellectual property, labor rights, and environmental protection. Although the TPP (if ratified) is claimed to include 800 million people and almost 40 percent of global GDP, it excludes China, which was not invited to participate in the TPP negotiations (Aggarwal, 2016).

The coincidence of the Obama administration's pivot to Asia in 2011 and its participation in the TPP negotiations reinforced the widespread perception that the United States was seeking to employ the TPP as a means to achieve its security interests in Asia through the encirclement of China. Despite periodic efforts to dispel this view, White House statements were explicit in their identification of the TPP as a means to maintain US hegemony in the region. As Obama (2015) noted in a 2015 statement on the TPP: 'we can't let countries like China write the rules of the global economy.' Secretary of Defence Ashton Carter (2015) reinforced this idea even more graphically: 'In terms of our rebalance in the broadest sense, passing TPP is an important to me as another aircraft carrier' (also see Rice, 2015; Rhodes, 2016). As Capling and Ravenhill (2013, p. 190) have noted, once the United States entered the TPP negotiations, it was inevitable that the most powerful actor would seek to impose its preferred template on the proceedings, dictating standards that were difficult for many of the less developed states to attain. These demands, moreover, ensured that China, with its large number of state-owned enterprises and lax labor and environmental standards, would not be able to meet the criteria to apply for membership.

The Chinese reaction to the TPP has been multifaceted. As is typical, the leadership has refrained from commentary that would identify the TPP as a geopolitical instrument wielded by the United States. This assessment, however, is widely distributed in the Chinese media. A number of commentators have stressed that the United States has sought to employ the TPP as a means of isolating China and choking off its trade relationships. The high bar set by the United States with respect to requirements for membership has similarly been perceived as a means of justifying China's exclusion from the agreement (although there is some bitterness that Vietnam, with its high proportion of state-owned enterprises and semi-reformed economy, was accepted for membership) (TPP, 2015a). At the same time, Chinese analysts, including members of the Chinese government, have often been positive toward the TPP, which is seen as providing an external impetus (somewhat akin to China's entrance into the WTO in 2001) to compel domestic reforms in the face of internal opposition. In this scenario, the Chinese government has not excluded the prospect of eventually joining the TPP. Tso (2016) notes that the Commerce Ministry has been investigating the issues involved regarding a serious bid for TPP membership, while Premier Li Keqiang has been a robust proponent of China's continued openness in the global market.

Beijing, however, has also responded to the TPP by advocating for the implementation of alternative multilateral regional trade partnerships as a means of counterbalance. This has mostly focused on the Regional Comprehensive Economic Partnership (RCEP). The RCEP initiative was developed at the 2011 summit of ASEAN and is formally an ASEAN project. Yet, as with the United States and the TPP, China has assumed a leading role in promoting the venture, which was formally launched in November 2012 with the 10 member states of ASEAN and six regional partners. The RCEP conforms more to the stature of a traditional free trade agreement; it does not go nearly as far as the TPP in seeking the liberalization of domestic economies. If instituted (negotiations are on-going), it would function as a largest free trade area in the world (Aggrawal, 2016; TPP, 2015b). In addition to the RCEP, Beijing has also sought to resurrect the Free Trade Agreement of the Asia-Pacific (FTAAP) as a regional trade association. The summary document of the 2014 APEC summit in Beijing called for the initiation of a feasibility study, a move reluctantly acceded to by the United States. With the TPP's long-term viability in doubt, Chinese president Xi Jinping returned to this theme in his keynote speech at the APEC summit in Peru in November 2016 calling the FTAAP 'a strategic initiative critical for the long-term prosperity of the Asia-Pacific' (Xi, 2016; Li, B., 2016).

True to his campaign promise, Donald Trump signed an executive order withdrawing US participation in the TPP shortly after assuming office, a move that has elicited mixed emotions in China. It is ironic that China, ostensibly still a Marxist-Leninist state, appears as one of the most enthusiastic, if not the most enthusiastic, proponents of neo-liberal economic precepts in the international system. Through the fall of 2016, Xi continuously reiterated his support for economic globalization in keynote speeches at global fora, not only at the APEC summit, but also at the BRICS and G20 meetings (Xi, 2016). Xi's message has been unequivocal and solidly neo-liberal in asserting that a free trade agenda is beneficial to all participants. Nonetheless, there is an acknowledgment that if the TPP fails, the RCEP will likely emerge as the default free trade structure in the Asian-Pacific region, with China replacing the United States as the leader, not only of the region, but eventually of the global financial order (see RCEP, 2016; Yang, 2017). In the short run, this is seen as a geopolitical advantage for China. At the same time, the CCP leadership views its economic achievements in the reform era as a consequence of its global economic integration. In this sense, the TTP's lack of success in verification is not a cause for celebration, but can be seen as potentially indicating a major reversal of globalization, signaling a more fragmented global economy (Xu, 2016). This message was reiterated by Xi in a forceful defense of globalization at the 2017 Davos World Economic Forum in which he pointedly noted that 'pursuing protectionism is like locking oneself in a dark room' while proclaiming that 'no one will emerge as a winner in a trade war' (Xi, 2017a).

THE US PIVOT TO ASIA: ECONOMIC, POLITICAL AND MILITARY DIMENSIONS

Although the Obama administration came to focus on the TPP as the centerpiece of its Asia policy, a large component of the pivot to Asia consisted of strengthening already existent ties with the region. This policy, partly seen as an effort to reorient the United States away from an excessive preoccupation with events in Iraq and Afghanistan, further reflected the understanding that the global center of economic and geopolitical gravity was shifting to East Asia. It is difficult to separate the economic from the political and military components of the Obama policy: they were interrelated, inasmuch as the administration emphasized that it could not sustain its hegemony in East Asia unless it remained the major state orchestrating the rules that govern the global economic system. To these ends, the TPP was explicitly framed as a national security issue (see Rhodes, 2016; Rice, 2015). But the Obama presidency has also signaled its attention to East Asia through a host of military and diplomatic measures: these included an increased diplomatic presence as seen in repeated visits by high-ranking officials to the area, the strengthening of military ties, the courting of previously ignored—and often maligned—states, and a heightened involvement in multilateral structures in the region.

The US pivot concentrated in particular on cultivating links with the ASEAN states both bilaterally and multilaterally.[2] The United States engages with the ASEAN states multilaterally through participation in the East Asia Summit (comprised of the ten members of ASEAN plus the United States, Russia, and India) and the ASEAN Regional Forum (a larger dialogue body that includes most states in East Asia as well as the European Union). The ASEAN-US Summit is an annual meeting between ASEAN leaders and the US president. In 2009 the United States was the first non-ASEAN country to appoint a resident ambassador to ASEAN, as well as signing the Treaty of Amity and Cooperation in Southeast Asia, the founding document of ASEAN. In 2015 ASEAN and the United States elevated their relationship to that of a strategic partnership. An action plan (2016–2020) lays out priority areas of cooperation, which include a commitment to maritime security in the South China Sea and forms of economic cooperation. Obama further signaled the importance he accorded to ASEAN by hosting a diplomatic summit with ASEAN leaders in February 2016, the first meeting of this sort to be held in the United States.

On a bilateral basis, the United States significantly improved its relationship with Myanmar, Laos, and Vietnam. The increasingly close ties between Vietnam and the United States are indicated by a seven fold increase in trade since 2009, the establishment a US-Vietnamese Comprehensive Partnership in 2013, the admittance of Vietnam to membership in the TPP, and the strengthening of military ties, including the lifting of the embargo on US arms sales to Vietnam (Fact Sheet: United States-Vietnam Relations, 2016; Nakamura, 2016). Following the transition from military rule in Myanmar in 2010, the United States restored full diplomatic relations with Myanmar, as well as resuming forms of development and humanitarian aid. Obama became the first US president to visit Myanmar in 2012, another tangible symbol of the upgrade to the relationship. A similar pattern of engagement pertains to US relations with Laos. A comprehensive partnership was established during Obama's 2016 visit (the first by a sitting president) that provides for various forms of development and humanitarian aid (as well as the resources to clear land mines and search for the remains of Americans unaccounted for since the end of the Vietnam War).

The Obama presidency also focused increased attention on Malaysia, Singapore, and Indonesia, states that were relabeled 'emerging partners' in the US pivot. In addition to the TPP, Washington was concerned to strengthen defense and security ties, an endeavor that also included dealing with insurgency and counterterrorism measures. In contrast, the Obama administration faced considerable challenges in defining its relations with Thailand and the Philippines, historically its two most stalwart allies in the region who are connected to the United States through mutual defense treaties. Thai relations with the United States became strained as a consequence of the 2014 military coup. Even before the coup, Thailand tended to view China as a positive force for development in the region, rather than a potential strategic threat. China's indifference to military rule, moreover, contrasted with the moralistic efforts of the Obama administration to compel a restoration of democratic elections. Shortly after assuming office in June 2016, Philippine president Roberto Duterte became involved in a conflict with the United States that apparently arose as a consequence of American criticism over his handling of a crackdown on drugs during which over 2000 people were killed. His response was to tilt toward China, announcing a 'separation' from the United States.

In a broader context, the pivot sought to reaffirm, deepen and expand US traditional security arrangements in the region. This was largely a military endeavor, concentrating on the enhancement of the United States' military force posture. In addition to the defense treaties with Thailand and the Philippines, the United States has longstanding defense treaties with Japan, South Korea, and Australia. The Pentagon was assigned the task of updating and modernizing its bases in Japan and South Korea, while moving US marines to Australia (as well as Guam and Hawaii) (Carter, 2016). In addition, the United States resumed defense cooperation with New Zealand in 2013 after a thirty-year hiatus.

Statements from the Obama White House about the rebalance to Asia were clearly oriented toward the development of a network of ties and relationships within the states that surround China on its periphery. China was perceived as a challenge to be managed rather than a peer partner. The distinctive feature of the pivot lay in its emphasis on building relationships with ASEAN, which was envisioned to a far greater extent than in previous administrations, as a multilateral regime. The political roots of ASEAN can be traced to its founding in 1967 by a group of states (Thailand, the Philippines, Indonesia, Malaysia, and Singapore) motivated by a fear of domino-style Communist infiltration, set against the backdrop of the Vietnam war. It is a testimony to the vastly changed landscape in Southeast Asia over the last thirty years that ASEAN incorporated Laos, Vietnam and Cambodia as members, and that the United States sought to set aside former animosities and build cordial ties with these states.

The US rivalry with China in the Obama years was intensified by their coincident interest in expanding their influence among the ASEAN community. The ASEAN states, moreover, were not passive actors but possessed their own sense of agency motivated by perceptions of self-interest. Generally speaking, the ASEAN states have welcomed forms of economic cooperation with China, while looking to the United States as a guarantor of their security interests. There are degrees of variation in this relationship, however, that reflect a host of intervening historical, economic, and political factors. Vietnam is far more wary, for example, of China than is Thailand.

A key aspect of the US-Chinese rivalry is being played out as an economic competition in the ASEAN states. At present, both the United States and China are important but not dominant players in the ASEAN economies. Table 13.1 lists the top ten sources of foreign direct investment (FDI) in ASEAN from 2013–2015. The United States was the fourth and China the fifth largest source of FDI in 2015. However, if Hong Kong's contribution to FDI is added to that of China, the United States' FDI at 13.645 billion

Table 13.1   Top Ten Sources of Foreign Direct Investment Inflows in ASEAN 2013–2015, Value in US Billions. Share in Total Percent

| | 2013 | | 2014 | | 2015 | |
	US bil.	*%*	*US bil.*	*%*	*US bil.*	*%*
ASEAN	19.562	15.7	22.134	17.0	22.232	18.4
European Union	24.511	19.6	24.989	19.2	20.127	16.7
Japan	24.750	19.8	15.705	12.1	17.559	14.5
US	7.157	5.7	14.748	11.3	13.645	11.3
China	6.426	5.1	6.990	5.4	8.256	6.8
S. Korea	4.303	3.4	5.750	4.4	4.542	4.7
Australia	2.587	2.1	6.281	4.8	5.246	4.3
Hong Kong	5.251	4.2	9.813	7.5	4.542	3.8
Taiwan	1.381	1.1	3.253	2.5	2.807	2.3
N. Zealand	.336	.3	.550	.4	2.241	1.9
Total	124.864	100	129.995	100	120.818	100

Data for Laos is not available.
Source: ASEAN.
Available from http://asean.org/storage/2015/09/Table-27_oct2016.pdf
(Accessed November 29, 2016).

dollars, and China/Hong Kong's FDI at 12.798 billion dollars are close to equivalent, comprising 11.37 percent and 10.6 percent of FDI respectively. Table 13.2 compares the volume of China/Hong Kong and US imports and exports for ASEAN states in 2015, and their proportional share of trade. The data indicate that the ASEAN states all imported a higher percentage of goods from China than the United States (although the difference between the United States [9.02 percent] and China [9.94 percent] with respect to Brunei is minimal). This disparity is accentuated when imports from Hong Kong are included in the data for China, a situation that is most sharply revealed in the case of Cambodia where China/Hong Kong is the source of 48.11 percent of total imports compared with 2.51 percent for the United States. A similar pattern prevails with respect to ASEAN exports to the United States and China/Hong Kong. In the case of Cambodia, exports to Hong Kong exceed those to China, while Philippine exports to Hong Kong (10.57 percent) are almost as high as those to China (10.9 percent). Vietnam is the only state in the region, which has a higher volume of exports to the United States than to China and Hong Kong, with 19.07 percent of its exports directed to the United States, compared with 9.94 percent for China, and 3.50 percent to Hong Kong.

The trade patterns indicate—especially for imports—the geographical advantages that accrue to China as a regional actor, and the dispersed nature of exports for the ASEAN economies, which are also an important source of manufactured products for Japan, and the European Union. But this development also reflects China's targeted goal of increasing its economic interactions in the Asia-Pacific region, a pattern that will likely be intensified

Table 13.2 China, Hong Kong, and US Export and Imports to ASEAN States 2015, Volume of Trade and Percentage Share, US Billions

	Imports						Exports					
	From China		From Hong Kong		From United States		To China		To Hong Kong		To United States	
Country	Billions $	%	Billion $	%	Billions $	%	Billions $	%	Billions $	%	Billions $	%
Brunei	0.358	9.94	0.026	0.79	0.325	9.02	0.0954	0.91	0.006	C.06	0.0198	0.19
Cambodia	7.457	39.3	1.670	8.81	485.6	2.51	358.9	3.34	2.327	21.8	2.000	18.7
Indonesia	30.624	17.2	1.848	1.04	8.188	4.6	17.610	10	2.780	1.6	16.560	9.41
Malaysia	33.242	18.9	2.962	1.68	14.226	8.1	26.062	13.0	9.459	4.72	18.947	9.46
Myanmar	1.128	27.1	507	0.12	0.0245	0.59	0.476	6.25	1.611	21.14	0.002	0.02
Singapore	42.124	14.2	2.653	.89	33.072	11.14	47.724	13.76	39.678	11.44	23.211	6.69
Philippines	11.977	19.4	1.900	2.71	7.629	10.88	6.393	10.9	6.199	1C.57	8.811	15.02
Thailand	40.919	20.25	1.567	0.76	13.923	6.89	23.31	11.05	11.64	5.52	23.717	11.25
Vietnam	43.647	29.52	1.03	0.70	6.286	4.25	14.928	9.94	5.264	3.50	28.649	19.07

Data for Laos is not available; Data for Myanmar is from 2010.
Source: World Bank; World Integrated Trade Solution.
Available from http://wits.worldbank.org/ (Accessed December 8, 2016).

through Chinese promotion of OBOR in both its land and maritime versions. All ten ASEAN states are founding members of the AIIB. In comparison, the US strategy to ensure its economic presence in Asia has been explicitly linked to the TPP, which is now moribund, at least for the United States.

Despite China's military modernization in recent years, the United States maintains an overwhelming position of military superiority in the Asia-Pacific region. For the most part, the American military presence has been welcomed by East Asian states, where it has been seen as a hedge against Beijing's economic rise. In this bifurcated arrangement, as detailed by Ikenberry (2016, p.13), the states of the region look to China for economic gain and to the United States for security. A certain ambivalence toward US military dominance exists even within the Chinese leadership that views the American treaty relationship with Japan as a means of constraining Japanese regional ambitions. Nonetheless, although the United States traditionally has not taken a position on the sovereignty disputes regarding the contested islands in the South China Sea, the Obama presidency insisted that it expected this issue to be handled peacefully and in accordance with international law (see deLisle, 2016). This position, articulated most forcefully by Hillary Clinton during her term as Secretary of State, was positively received in South East Asia especially among the disputants (Brunei, Malaysia, Philippines, Vietnam, and Taiwan), but largely rejected by China. In recent years, the Chinese leadership has seemingly come to expand its territorial interpretation of its 'core' (hexin liyi) interests (which previously focused on Tibet, Xinjiang, and Taiwan) to include the contested islands and waters of the South China Sea as well as the Senkaku/Diaoyu islands, jointly claimed by China and Japan (see Christensen, 2015, pp. 253–255; Wong, 2015). The White Paper on China's Military Strategy (China's Military Strategy, 2015) reaffirmed this interpretation, noting that some of its offshore neighbors had illegally occupied China's reefs and islands. More pointedly, the paper further indicated that 'some external countries are also busy meddling in South China Sea affairs,' an implicit reference to the United States.

Beijing's claim to sovereignty over the contested island chains has been accompanied by ambitious construction projects of dredging and land reclamation to expand its defense capabilities in the area. Fiery Cross Reef, for example, is home to a 3000-meter airstrip, in addition to a port that can receive tanks and surface combat ships (see Marcias and Bender, 2016). The 2016 decision by an international tribunal in the Hague brought by the Philippines against China ruled against China on almost all points, condemning its construction of artificial islands and dismissing its sovereignty claims as illegal and lacking in historical basis. In the wake of the decision, China released a lengthy White Paper that reaffirmed its position that the disputed areas between China and the Philippines were China's 'inherent territory' and that the Philippines' 'illegal claim' had no 'historical or legal basis' (State Council, 2016). The magnitude of the ruling, however, was mitigated by Duterte's subsequent tilt to Beijing, as a rebuke to the United States. Duterte downplayed the decision in favor of an agreement with China that allowed Filipino fisherman to return to contested waters. There is no doubt, however, that the Chinese claim to sovereignty over much of the South China Sea was, in the words of Secretary of Defence Ashton Carter (2015), 'out of step' with the Obama administration's perception of the United States as the principle security power in the Asia-Pacific, a position that was envisioned to include the enforcement of maritime traffic throughout the region.

THE TRUMP PRESIDENCY: PRELIMINARY IMPLICATIONS FOR CHINA AND EAST ASIA

As of this writing, an assessment of the Trump administration's policy toward Asia is highly tentative. Trump did not present anything in the manner of a coherent overall strategy toward Asia in his presidential campaign, and a number of his remarks challenged the bipartisan framework of internationalism that has characterized US policy in the post–World War II era. Several points, nonetheless, can be guardedly set forth.

First, it seems unlikely that a Trump administration will retain much of the substantive framework of the Obama pivot to Asia. To a large extent, this assessment is self-evident, inasmuch as the TPP served as the conceptual underpinning of the policy. But Trump has shown little interest in ASEAN (he never mentioned the topic during his campaign) as a multilateral organization, and in fact, has largely ignored its individual members as well (see Velloor, 2017). The Obama's presidency's deliberate—and largely appreciated—recognition of the ASEAN states is unlikely to be duplicated. Trump has shown a clear preference for engaging in bilateral rather than multilateral interactions, as well as a general distaste for free trade arrangements, which he perceives as inimical to US interests.

Secondly, the Trump administration appears committed to strengthening the US military presence globally, including in the Asia-Pacific region. Trump has moderated his campaign rhetoric that was highly critical of a perceived unequal defense burden born by the United States in his bilateral and multilateral treaty agreements. His February 2017 meeting with Japanese Prime Minister Shinzo Abe followed upon conventional lines in praising the alliance between the two states as the 'cornerstone of peace and stability in the Pacific region' (Nakamura and Philip, 2017). Nonetheless, Trump's proclivities appear to be more inclined toward a unilateralist projection of hard power, including in the Asian-Pacific region. His February 2017 proposal to increase military spending by 54 billion dollars evoked consternation in the Congress but was consistent with his campaign message that the United States military was chronically underfunded (Shear and Steinhauer, 2017). This includes proposals to expand the US navy to 350 ships, a measure that if enacted would greatly bolster the navy's fleet presence in the Pacific region.

The Trump administration to date has shown little interest in the use of soft power measures. Rather, the emerging doctrine appears to be rooted in the assumption that US power can be demonstrated as an expression of military capabilities, a process that will simultaneously serve to achieve policy goals. This strategy—articulated as 'peace through strength'—strongly contrasts with the measures of the Obama pivot to Asia which, although not disavowing the security dimension, relied on diplomacy and the strengthening of economic ties as a means of influence. Internationalist rhetoric aside, the Obama approach was solidly realist in its efforts to constrain China's goal of achieving a regional hegemony. The withdrawal of US participation in the TPP (as well as the presumed disinclination of the Trump administration to engage in extensive forms of diplomacy) leaves a power vacuum in the region that China will move to fill. Even longstanding allies such as Australia are rethinking their relationship with the United States, largely because of the overwhelming importance of their economic relationship with China (White, 2017). The smaller ASEAN states find themselves similarly compelled to tilt toward China. As former Singapore Prime Minister Lee Kuan Yew noted in a 2013 interview, without Free Trade Agreements [with the US], 'Korea, Japan, Taiwan, and the ASEAN countries will be integrated into China's economy' (Allison and Blackwill, 2013).

Throughout his campaign, Trump was highly critical of China. He accused China of unfair trade practices and currency manipulation, promising to place a 45 percent tariff on all Chinese imports to the United States. He further outraged the Chinese after his election by taking a phone call from Taiwanese president Tsai Ing-wen, followed by various twitter suggestions that he would use the one-China policy as a bargaining chip in dealing with China. Trump, however, discovered that the issue was non-negotiable to the CCP leadership, and was eventually compelled to issue a statement upholding the US adherence to the one-China policy before Xi would take his phone call (Landler and Forsythe, 2017). In the first months of his presidency, moreover, Trump adopted a more restrained position on China. After meeting with Xi at his Palm Beach, Florida residence in April 2017, Trump announced that the two presidents 'had a great chemistry. I liked him and he liked me a lot' (Buckley, 2017). A few days later, Trump further acknowledged that China was not currently manipulating its currency. Although the White House portrayed a May 2017 trade deal with China as an 'herculean accomplishment,' trade analysts largely concurred that the agreement was underwhelming in its scope, focused on increasing US agricultural and energy exports to China, as well as approving the incremental implementation of previously pending financial services and regulatory standards (Hsu, 2017; Worstall, 2017). In contrast, moreover, to the Obama administration, the trade agreement noted that the United States recognized the importance of China's OBOR initiative, agreeing to send representatives to China's Belt and Road Forum held in Beijing in May 2017. The Forum, which brought together over 1000 participants including 30 world leaders, promoted OBOR as a trillion-dollar project with a global reach, thus showcasing China's continued emergence on the world stage as an economic superpower. The Trump administration's endorsement of OBOR appears to be rooted in the desire (also seen in the appraisal of European leaders) to gain advantages for US firms to participate in vast infrastructure projects, but there is no doubt that this is an endeavor in which the United States appears more as a supplicant than a leader as a driver of global economic growth.

To a certain extent, it seems that the White House has sought to improve ties with China as a means of leveraging Chinese support in pressuring North Korea to halt its nuclear and missile programs. This is hardly a novel approach, inasmuch as it has been an established strategy of previous presidential administrations. The success of this effort, which might overestimate China's leverage on North Korea as well as China's calculus of its own interests, is also complicated by the Trump administration's simultaneous criticism of China's territorial claims in the South China Sea. During Abe's February 2017 visit, Trump indicated that the mutual defense treaty between the United States and Japan included the disputed Senkaku (Diaoyutai for the Chinese) islands, a claim also backed by Secretary of Defence James Mattis. This commitment, in fact, is not a departure from that of previous administrations (see Christensen, 2015, pp. 111–112). More provocative, however, have been the comments of Secretary of State Rex Tillerson, who called, in his Senate confirmation hearings for China to be denied access to its artificial islands in the South China Sea, labeling China's behavior as 'akin to Russia's taking of Crimea' (Forsythe, 2017). Sean Spicer, the White House press secretary backed up these remarks when questioned, but Mattis did not collaborate this position, hinting that the White House had yet to develop a coherent policy on the matter. Nor did Tillerson address the question as to how the United States would block Chinese activity, although most analysts speculated that this would involve, as a matter of course, a military blockade (see Simon, 2017). In June 2017, moreover, Mattis sharply criticized Beijing for its disregard of international law and 'indisputable militarization' of artificial islands in the South China Sea (Mattis, 2017).

These inchoate comments do not indicate a policy, but they do reflect an increased militancy, relate to past administrations, regarding China's sovereignty claims in the region. The Chinese reaction to these statements was formally dismissive, although more nationalistic publications reacted with outrage (see Dreyer, 2017; Global Times, 2017). In any case, the Chinese leadership is not averse to engaging in its own form of saber rattling. The Chinese deployment of an aircraft carrier to the South China Sea in late December 2016 was interpreted by some as a challenge to US military dominance in the Pacific (Hernendez, 2016).

CONCLUSION

In the post–World War II era, US foreign policy has conformed to broadly realist precepts, first in its bipolar competition with the Soviet Union, and since 1991, as the dominant global hegemon.[3] The US power capabilities have been diminished and there has been an increase in regional centers of power, which is reflected in the rhetoric—especially as voiced by Russia—that the world is moving toward multipolarity. However, it is the rise of China that provides, seen through the lens of realist analysis, the most substantive challenge to the US predominance. The Obama administration rightly identified the Asian-Pacific region as the most dynamic (and emergent) region of the globe, and signaled through the pivot to Asia, a commitment to strengthen its foothold in the region as a matter of national security.

The Trump presidency, at least at its onset, has challenged the largely consensual assumptions of the US political class. Trump is often perceived as having realist proclivities, but his world view is heavily oriented toward a traditional emphasis on military capabilities as a measure of power. Trump, however, unlike many prominent neorealists (see Mearsheimer 2001) shows little interest in or understanding of the structural impact of the international system on global outcomes. His offhand campaign remarks, for example, that Japan and South Korea could acquire nuclear weapons, seemed to be a remedy to lower the US defense burden, absent a consideration of its systemic effects. Trump, moreover, differs from his post-war predecessors in showing little interest in promoting the United States as the global standard bearer of norms and values (portrayed as universal) upheld by the United States and the other Western states.

Trump's election to the US presidency bespeaks a populist dissatisfaction with the forces unleashed by globalization, the loss of domestic jobs, the challenges to traditional concepts of national identity, and rising income inequalities. The Trump victory, largely unanticipated by the political classes, was an indication of the growth of anti-globalist sentiment in the West, also seen in the rise of right-wing parties in the European Union, and an unanticipated Brexit vote in the United Kingdom. This development indicates considerable popular dissatisfaction with the Bretton Woods system, which has been constructed on the edifice of free trade and neo-liberal economics. In the aftermath of the election, Eric Li (2016), writing in *Foreign Affairs*, the flagship journal—and voice—of the American foreign policy establishment, declared that 'globalism has committed suicide.' It is too early to say, however, that the world is on the cusp of an impending paradigm shift that marks the end of neoliberalism as the prevailing global economic orthodoxy.

One reason for hesitation is that, in the economic sense at least, East Asia is home to what Daniel Drezner (2016) has described as the 'last great liberals in the world.' The Chinese leadership, along with other political elites in the region, remains committed to free trade and global integration as an economic strategy. In his January 2017 speech at Davos, Xi Jinping (2017a) implicitly claimed the mantle of global leadership in asserting the benefits of economic globalization. Xi acknowledged the defects of globalization (which he saw as remediable), but concluded that its benefits outweighed its costs. Xi's speech (his first at Davos) was both lauded and disparaged by those who noted that the Chinese embrace of liberalism rejected its political components (see *Economy*, 2017; Roy, 2017). Xi expanded upon these themes a few months later in his keynote speech at the Road and Belt Forum in Beijing, where he labeled the OBOR initiative the 'project of the century' (Xi, 2017b). Trump's decision in June 2017 to pull the United States out of the Paris climate accord provided China—somewhat ironically since China is by far the largest carbon emitter—yet another opportunity to assume a position of global leadership.

The Chinese, moreover, did not waste any time in making common cause with European leaders—many of whom already felt disenchanted with Trump's reluctance to endorse NATO as a security guarantor—in pledging to maintain a commitment to the climate accords.

The interdependence of the economic relationship between China and the United States means that a trade war would have detrimental outcomes for both sides. It is uncertain to what extent the United States will seek to check China's behavior in the South China Seas. But in a geopolitical sense, the Trump administration—assuming that it continues on its current course—provides notable opportunities for China. The United States' withdrawal from the TPP, the disinclination of the Trump White House to defend the global economic system, as well as the United States' withdrawal from the Paris climate accords leave a sort of power void at both the regional and global levels, that China has aspirations to fill. The Trump administration's conception of 'America First' has, moreover, to date been starkly detached from a sense of responsibility for global leadership. Nonetheless, just as it is premature to proclaim the death of neoliberalism, it is too soon to forecast the imminent geopolitical transformation of the international system. Chinese ambitions to hegemony are for the time being most apparent in East Asia. While the evolving tendency of the United States in the Trump administration has been to perceive of its security interests in East Asia in military terms, the Xi leadership has adopted an alternative strategy that seeks to expand its influence by economic means. In this sense, OBOR serves as an implicit challenge to US hegemony in the Asia-Pacific region, and more broadly signals Xi's intention to assert China's great power status in the global arena.

NOTES

1. Meeting with Wang Yiwei, Senior Fellow, Chongyang Institute for Financial Studies, Renmin University, Beijing, May 13, 2015.
2. The ten member states of ASEAN are Brunei, Singapore, Malaysia, Thailand, Indonesia, Philippines, Vietnam, Laos, Cambodia, and Myanmar.
3. This view is rejected by John Mearsheimer, who argues that the United States is not a global hegemon but only a regional hegemon in the Americas. Nonetheless, Mearsheimer is also a prime advocate of the view that the United States needs to do as much as possible to contain China and prevent its assertion of regional hegemony in East Asia. See Mearsheimer 2001, 2006.

REFERENCES

Aggarwal, V. (2016) 'Mega-FTAs and the Trade-Security Nexus: The Trans Pacific Partnership (TPP) and Regional Comprehensive Economic Partnership (RCEP),' Asia-Pacific Issues, March, 123, pp. 1–8.

AIIB. Available at http://euweb.aiib.org/html/aboutus/introduction/history/?show=0 [Accessed November 20, 2016].

Allison, G. and Blackwill, R. (2013) 'Interview: Lee Kuan Yew on the Future of U.S.–China Relations,' The Atlantic, 5 March.

Arase, D. (2015). 'China's Two Silk Roads Initiative: What It Means for Southeast Asia,' Southeast Asian Affairs, 2015, pp. 25–45.

Buckley, C. (2017) 'A Spring Thaw? Trump Now Has "Very Good Words for China's Leader,' New York Times, 20 April.

Callahan, W. (2015) 'Identity and Security in China: The Negative Soft Power of the China Dream, *Politics*, 35(3–4), pp. 216–229. doi:10.1111/1467–9256.12088.

Carter, Ashton (2016) 'The Rebalance and Asia-Pacific Security,' *Foreign Affairs*, 95, 6, pp. 65–75.

Capling, A.and Ravenhill, J. (2013) 'Symposium: Australia-US Economic Relations and the Regional Balance of Power. Australia, The United States and the Trans-Pacific Partnership: Diverging Interests and Unintended Consequences,' *Australian Journal of Political Science*, 48, 2, pp. 184–196. http://dx.doi.org/10.1050/10 361146.2013.786677.

Carter, A. (2015), 'Remarks on the Next Phase of the U.S. Rebalance to the Asia Pacific (McCain Institute, Arizona State University),' 6 April, Available from http://www.defense.gov/News/Speeches/Speech-View/Article/60666. [Accessed November 25, 2016].

China's Military Strategy (2015) Information Office of the State Council. 5 May. Available from http://www.chinadaily.com.cn/china/2015-05/26/content_20820628.htm. [Accessed June 15, 2015).

Christensen, T. (2015) *The China Challenge* (New York: W.W. Norton).

Clinton, H. (2011) 'America's Pacific Century,' Foreign Policy, 11 October. Available from http://foreignpolicy.com/2011/10/11/americas-pacific-century/ [Accessed July 10, 2016]

deLisle, J. (2016) 'International Law in the Obama Administration's Pivot to Asia: The China Seas Disputes, the Trans-Pacific Partnership Rivalry with the PRC, and Status Quo Legal Norms in U.S. Foreign Policy,' *Case Western Reserve Journal of International Law,* 48, pp. 143–176.

Deng, Y. (2015) 'China: The Post-Responsible Power.' *Washington Quarterly,* 37(4), pp. 117–143.

Drezner, D. (2016) 'Five Things I Learned About Russia Last Week,' *The Washington Post,* 31 October. Available from: https://www.washingtonpost.com/posteverything/wp/2016/10/31/five-things-i-learned-about-russia-last-week/?utm_term=.a82ba744e33e. [Accessed December 9, 2016].

Economy, E. (2017) 'Beijing is No Champion of Globalization,' Foreign Affairs 22 January. Available from https://www.foreignaffairs.com/articles/china/2017–01–22/beijing-no-champion-globalization [Accessed January 23, 2017]

Fact Sheet: United States-Vietnam Relations (2016) The White House, 23 May, Available from: https://www.whitehouse.gov/the-press-office/2016/05/23/fact-sheet-united-states-vietnam-relations; [Accessed December 4, 2016].

Forsythe, M. (2017) Rex Tillerson's South China Sea Remarks Foreshadow Possible Foreign Policy Crisis,' New York Times, 12 January.

Global Times (2017) 'Is Tillerson's Bluster Just a Bluff for Senate?,' 13 January. Available from http://www.globaltimes.cn/content/1028568.shtml [Accessed March 4, 2017).

Guo, H. (2015,) 'Belt and Road' Initiatives Follows the Trend of Peace and Development, Cooperation, and Win-Win Ideas, a Chinese Plan to Promote Global Development and Cooperation.21 September. Available from http://english.mofcom.gov.cn/sys/print.shtml [Accessed November 5, 2015)

Harris, T. (2015) 'The U.S. Response to the Asian Infrastructure Investment Bank,' in Daniel, B. ed., Asian Infrastructure Investment Bank: China as Responsible Stakeholder? Sasakawa Peace Foundation, USA, pp. 43–52.

Hernendex, J. (2016) 'China Deploys Aircraft Carrier to Disputed South China Sea,' New York Times, 27 December.

Hsu, S. (2017) 'Trump's Trade Deal "Win" With China: Fake News?,' Forbes, 14 May. Available from https://www.forbes.com/sites/sarahsu/2017/05/14/trumps-initial-trade-win-on-china-fake-news/#1533cbc34303 . [Accessed June 9, 2017].

Ikenberry, G.J. (2015) 'Between the Eagle and the Dragon: America, China and Middle State Strategies in East Asia,' *Political Science Quarterly,* 20, 20, pp. 1–35.

Joint Press Conference (2015) 'Remarks by President Obama and President Xi of the People's Republic of China in Joint Press Conference,' September 25, 2015. Available from www.whitehouse.gov/the-press-office/2015/09/25/remarks-president-obama-and-president-xi-peoples-republic-china-joint [accessed October 24, 2016].

Kawai, M. (2015) 'Asian Infrastructure Investment Bank in the Evolving International Financial Order,' in. Daniel, B., Asian Infrastructure Investment Bank: China as Responsible Stakeholder? Sasakawa Peace Foundation, USA, pp. 5–26.

Landler, M. and Forsythe, M. (2017) 'Trump Tells Xi Jinping U.S. Will Honor "One-China" Policy,' New York Times, 9 February.

Li, B. (2016) 'China's President Xi Jinping's Opening Address of G20 Summit: A New Blueprint for Global Economic Growth,' Global Research ,4 September. Available from: http://www.globalresearch.ca/chinas-president-xi-jinpings-opening-address-of-g20-summit-a-new-blueprint-for-global-economic-growth/5543895 [Accessed December 3, 2016].

Li, E. (2016) 'The End of Globalism: Where China and the United States Go From Here,' Foreign Affairs, 9 December. Available from: https://www.foreignaffairs.com/print/1118897/ [Accessed December 9, 2016]

Li, X. (2016) 'AIIB Will have 100 Countries as Members by Year-End: Jin Liqun,' China Daily, 31 May. Available at http://www.chinadaily.com.cn/bizchina/2016–05/31/content_25555337.htm [Accessed November 25, 2016].

Luft, G. (2016) 'China's Infrastructure Play: Why Washington Should Accept the New Silk Road,' *Foreign Affairs,* 95, 5, pp. 68–75.

Marcias, A. and Bender, J. (2016) 'These Images Might Just be the Clearest Signs of China's Expansion in the Disputed South China Sea,' Business Insider, 20 March. Available from: http://www.businessinsider.com/images-chinas-expansion-in-the-disputed-south-china-sea-2016–3. [Accessed October 27, 2016].

Mattis, J. (2017) 'Remarks by Secretary Mattis at Shangri-La Dialogue,' News Transcript US Department of Defense, 3 June. Available from https://www.defense.gov/News/Transcripts/Transcript-View/Article/1201780/remarks-by-secretary-mattis-at-shangri-la-dialogue/. [Accessed June 10, 2017].

Mearsheimer, J. (2001) *The Tragedy of Great Power Politics* (New York: W.W. Norton).

Mearsheimer, J. (2006) 'China's Unpeaceful Rise,' *Current History*, 105, 690 (April) pp. 160–162.

Morgenthau, H. (1973). *Power Among Nations*. 5th Edition (New York. Alfred A. Knopf).

Nakamura, D. (2016) 'In Historical Move, US Lifts Embargo on Arms Sales to Vietnam,' The Washington Post, 23 May. Available from https://www.washingtonpost.com/news/post-politics/wp/2016/05/23/in-historic-move-u-s-lifts-arms-sales-embargo-to-vietnam/?utm_term=.5d93ae3e9dfc [Accessed December 4, 2016].

Nakamura, D. and Phillip, A. (2017) 'Trump Reaffirms Security Alliance in Bid to Soothe Fears in Japan,' The Washington Post, 11 February. Available from https://www.washingtonpost.com/politics/japanese-prime-minister-visits-white-house-but-trumps-travel-ban-dominates-event/2017/02/10/95ad4b2a-efa6–11e6–9662–6eedf1627882_story.html?utm_term=.080b21467ea7 [Accessed March 2, 2017]

Obama, B. (2015) 'Statement by the President on the Trans-Pacific Partnership,' 5 October, The White House. Available from: https://www.whitehouse.gov/the-press-office/2015/10/05/statement-president-trans-pacific-partnership.[Accessed October 24, 2016].

RCEP (2016) 'RCEP keneng chaoqian TPP luodi, Zhongguo youwang qudai Meiguo zhudao guoli maoyi zhixu' [The RCEP may have surpassed the TPP: China is expected to replace the US led economic order],18 August. Available from http://www.jiemain.com/article/804437.html; [Accessed November 2, 2016].

Rice, S. (2015) 'Remarks as Prepared for Delivery by National Security Advisor Susan E. Rice at the Export-Import Bank's Annual Conference,' 24 April. Available from https://www.whitehouse.gov/the-press-office/2015/04/24/remarks-prepared-delivery-national-security-advisor-susan-e-rice-export- [Accessed November 5, 2016].

Rhodes, B. (2016) 'Why President Obama's Trade Deal Matters to U.S. National Security,' 4 May, The White House Available from: https://www.whitehouse.gov/blog/2016/05/04/why-president-obamas-trade-deal-matters-us-national-security [Accessed October 24, 2016].

Roy, D. (2017) 'Look at China's Reality, Not Xi's Rhetoric,' *Pacific Forum CSIS*, 11, 2 February.

Shear, M. and Steinhauer, J. (2017) 'Trump to Seek $54 Billion Increase in Military Spending,' New York Times, 27 February.

Sheets, N. (2015) 'Building a Global Infrastructure for Growth, 7 January. Available from http://www.cnbc.com/2015/01/07/building-a-global-infrastructure-for-growth-commentary.html [Accessed November 23, 2016].

Simon, D. (2017) 'Is Trump Ready for War in the South China Sea, or Is His Team Just Not Being Clear?,' Washington Post, 24 January.

State Council (2016) 'Full Text: China Adheres to the Position of Settling Through Negotiation the Relevant Disputes Between China and the Philippines in the South China Sea,' State Council Information Office, 13 July. Available from http://news.xinhuanet.com/english/china/2016–07/13/c_135509153.htm. [Accessed December 9, 2016].

Summers, L. (2015) 'A Global Wake-Up Call for the U.S?.' Washington Post, 5 April. Available at https://www.washingtonpost.com/opinions/a-global-wake-up-call-for-the-us/2015/04/05/6f847ca4-da34–11e4-b3f2–607bd612aeac_story.html?utm_term=.81d86f916beb [Accessed November 23, 2016].

Sun, Y. (2015) 'China and the Evolving Asian Infrastructure Investment Bank,' in B. Daniel, B (ed) Asian Infrastructure Investment Bank: China as Responsible Stakeholder? Saskawa Peace Foundation, USA, pp. 27–42.

TPP (2015a) 'TPP daodi ruhe yingxiang zhongguo yidai yilu ruhe duikang TPP,' [How the TPP affects China's OBOR and how to combat it] 14 November. Available from http://www.minnanwang.cn/news/20151114/c_157440.html [Accessed October 20, 2016].

TPP (2015b) 'TPP zhihou you lai RCEP, Zhongguo ne?' [After the TPP, then the RCEP, China?], 23 November; Available from http://wallstreetcn.com/node/226451 [Accessed November 2, 2016].

Tso, C. (2016) 'China's About-Face to the TPP: Economic and Security Accounts Compared,' *Journal of Contemporary China*, 25, 100, pp. 613–627; DOI: 10.1080/10670564.2015.1132960.

Velloor, R (2017) 'A Trump Hammer on Asian Nails," The Straits Times, January 27. Available from http://www.straitstimes.com/opinion/a-trump-hammer-on-asian-nails [Accessed March 3, 2017]

Waltz, K. (1979) *Theory of International Politics* (New York: McGraw Hill).

Waltz, K. (1999*)* 'Globalization and Governance,*'* PS: Political Science and Politics, 32, 4 (December), pp. 693–700.

Wang, Y. (2013a,). 'Zhongguo meng de sanchong neihan' [Three connotations of the China dream]. Pinglun, 29 January. Available from http://opinion.huanqiu.com/thought/2013–01/ 3592579.html [Accessed October 10, 2015).

Wang, Y. (2013b) 'Waijie dui "zhongguo meng" de shida wujie' [Ten misperceptions Held by Foreigners about the China dream]. Pinglun, 16 April. Available from http://opinion. huanqiu.com/opinion_world/2013–04/3833876.html [Accessed October 10, 2015].

White, H. (2017) 'Trump Pushes Australia Toward China,' New York Times, 9 February.

Wong, E. (2015) 'Security Law Suggests a Broadening of China's "Core Interest," New York Times, 2 July.

Worstall, T. (2017) 'Trump's China Trade Strategy Becomes Clearer—Concessions on Beef, Win Bigly, Do Victory Lap,' Forbes, 13 May. Available from http://www.forbes.com/sites/timworstall/2017/05/13/trumps-china-trade-strategy-becomes-clearer-concessions-on-beef-win-bigly-do-victory-lap/#3fa07970337d [Accessed June 9, 2017]

Xi, J. (2013) 'Let the Sense of Community of Common Destiny Take Deep Root in Neighbouring Countries,' 25 October. Available from http://www.fmprc.gov.cn/mfa_eng/wjb_663308.[Accessed November 5, 2015].

Xi, J. (2014). 'Chinese President Proposes Asia-Pacific Dream.' Available from http: www.Apec-china.org.cn/41/2014/11/09/3@2418.htm. [Accessed November 14, 2015].

Xi, J. (2016) 'China Renews Call for FTAAP as Economic Globalization Falters, Xi Warns BRICS Summit Globalization Backlash,' 16 October, Asia Times, Available from: http://www.atimes.com/article/xi-warns-brics-summit-globalization-backlash/ [Accessed December 3, 2016

Xi, J. (2017a) 'President Xi's Speech to Davos in Full.' Available from https://www.weforum.org/agenda/2017/01/full-text-of-xi-jinping-keynote-at-the-world-economic-forum) Accessed February 28, 2017].

Xi, J. (2017b) 'Full Text of President Xi's Speech at Belt and Road Forum,' Xinhua, 14 May. Available from http://news.xinhuanet.com/english/2017-05/14/c_136282982.htm. [Accessed 25 May, 2017].

Xu, X. (2016) 'Women huo jiang mian dui yige gengjia suipian hau de shijie' [We will face a more fragmented world], 28 September. Available from http:finance. sina.com.cn/roll/2016–09–28/doc-ifxwermp4068698 [Accessed October 13, 2016.

Yan, X. (2014) 'Silk Road economic belt shows China's new strategic direction: Promoting integration with its neighbors,' Carnegie-Tsinghua Center for Global Policy, 27 February. Available from http://carnegietsinghua.org/2014/02/27/ silk-road-economic-belt-shows-china-s-new- strategic-direction-promoting-integration-with-its-neighbors [Accessed December 9, 2015].

Yan, X. (2015). 'Yan Xuetong: Yatai yi xingcheng zhong mei liangji geju (tu),' [Yan Xuetong: The Asian-Pacific region has become a bipolar structure with China and the United States]. International Herald Tribune. Available from http://news.163. com/15/0205/ 20/AHNH024U00014AED.html. [Accessed November 6, 2015].

Yang, M (2017) 'Aodaliyi bei zhuanxing Zhongguo?' [Is Australia forced to turn to China?], Global Times, 8 February. Available at http://news.163.com/17/0208/18/ CCPA41N6000187V9.html [Accessed February 17, 2017].

Zoellick, R. (2005). 'Whither China: From Membership to Responsibility?' US Department of State Archive, 21 September. Available from http://2001–2009. state.gov/s/d/former/zoellick/ rem/53682.htm. [Accessed January 13, 2016].

Chapter 14

Can China's Rise Continue without Conflict?

Kees van der Pijl

The rise of China that constitutes the central topic of this collection is hardly a contested theme today. It becomes a different matter when we ask the question, *what sort of challenge* does it pose to the existing, liberal international order. Various features of China's political economy, such as the continuing prominence of the state in guiding social and economic development, or a long-term investment project such as its One Belt, One Road scheme, seem to depart from the format of capital accumulation currently prevailing in the West, which since at least the 1990s revolves primarily around speculative finance. This difference also applies, to varying degrees, to some of China's neighbors.

This chapter proposes to view the development pattern of twenty-first-century China, Russia, and the other members of the BRICS bloc (Brazil, India, and South Africa) in the broader historic framework of a struggle of state-oligarchic rivals to the liberal West, or *contender states*. Several of the chapters in this collection emphasize the peaceful intentions accompanying the rise of China, but the historical experience suggests that past contender states challenging Western hegemony also went through a benign phase of their ascent and yet later slipped into armed conflict with the Atlantic heartland of globalizing capital. In the case of the BRICS, too, what emerged as a seemingly innocuous banker's gimmick referring to the 'emerging market' potential of the economies thus thrown together, is meanwhile attracting a less benevolent response; in some cases, straightforward economic warfare. Since this is most evident in the case of Russia, I will concentrate on it here, albeit in light of what appears to be the shape of things to come also for China.

THE EURASIAN/BRICS CONTENDER BLOC
FACING A CAPITALIST HEARTLAND

The Western, liberal political economy historically crystallized in the First British Empire and has retained its North Atlantic geo-economic center ever since. Here for the first time, the diverse elements of a capitalist social order (long-distance trade for profit, notably the slave trade; the privatization of feudal land expelling a surplus humanity as free labor power; various financial practices) were synthesized into a single process. In the English Civil War, a class compromise was forged between the commercializing, enclosing landlord class and the ascendant bourgeoisie no longer dependent on royal monopolies, sealed in the Glorious Revolution of 1688. John Locke in the *Two Treatises of Government* provided the ideological justification of this compromise. Thus, the first state-society configuration centring on the protection of private property was created, defining the role of the state in the British Isles and the North American colonies. Henceforth a transatlantic 'Lockean heartland' came to occupy the commanding heights of the global political economy. On the basis of the free circulation of capital within its own confines, this enabled the industrial revolution that made Britain the workshop of the world until the late nineteenth century, before passing on the leading role to the United States in the twentieth (Van der Pijl, 1998, 2006).

Historically only a limited number of states and social formations have been able to hold their own against liberal Western pre-eminence. In these contender states, the social roles of a propertied ruling class, fractions of capital and managerial and governing cadre, and the organization of military power are condensed into a single *state class*. The term highlights the subsumption of these social categories under the state apparatus, rather than being distributed around it as in the Lockean setting (where a distinct, hereditary ruling class is in command). France in the long eighteenth century, Germany and Japan from their unification and accelerated modernization from the late nineteenth through the first half of the twentieth century, are the main examples of contender states; the state socialism of the Soviet Union represents its ultimate historical form. In the slipstream of the primary contenders, which to varying degrees relied on a strong state confiscating its social sphere, a long tail of other states have borrowed aspects of the different contender state/society complexes. This would include Turkey and Iran, the large states of Latin America, and in a sense all Third World states until the late 1970s.

The Chinese state class, although formed under comparable auspices, can no longer be reduced to the contender role because it would seem today as if the entire heartland/contender structure is unravelling in the wake of the 2008 crisis. As the West is slowly being dislodged from the commanding heights of the global political economy, losing its inner cohesion in the process, its rivals, having nominally converted to capitalism but refusing to bow to Western global governance, are becoming contenders for primacy almost against their own preferences. Hence the inadvertent, and to some extent incoherent contender formations such as the Eurasian Union, the BRICS, and the Shanghai Cooperation Organisation are emerging. In what follows I will argue that the West has responded to these formations with economic warfare and various forms of interference including violence.

The inherent logic of capital is to become global (Pradella, 2015). Hence the state system, the system of multiple sovereignties, clashes with the immanent, overarching sovereignty of capital (if we take sovereignty to mean that the sovereign entity recognizes no authority above itself). Capital is not global yet, if it ever will be (the fate of comprehensive treaties intended to codify its sovereignty, such as TTIP, TPP, CETA, etc. will be an indicator); it is necessarily *transnational*. As it originated and was codified in the Lockean heartland, capital enjoyed such transnationality as a constitutional principle. Yet even here, in the original English-speaking West, states retain a distinct 'nationality' as a result of cumulative class compromises which are necessarily different (the United States from Britain, Canada from the United States, etc.), although they share the Lockean, property-centered constitutionality.

Outside the Atlantic West, 'nationality' (in a civic, not ethnic sense; ethnically most states are multi-national) is even more pronounced; whilst capital is correspondingly weaker. In the process of globalisation of capital, the political-economic power of the Western states must be mobilised to ensure the 'Open Door'. This produces imperialism, the competitive effort of opening up all states for commodification and exploitation, in order to 'introduce and intensify ... "the silent compulsion of the market" across political jurisdictions sheltered from the complete instantiation of market imperatives' (Di Muzio, 2007, p. 519). Regime change is the ultimate consequence of this imperative. For even though the profits made in the newly opened world economy continue to flow overwhelmingly to the West (Starrs, 2014), this cannot be taken for granted as long as state sovereignty persists. Hence, in the words of Claude Serfati, 'the defense of "globalisation" against those who would threaten it should ... be placed, along with military threats properly speaking, at the top of the security agenda' (Serfati, 2001, p. 12).

Contender states epitomize *the defense of state sovereignty against the sovereignty of transnational capital championed by the West*. After the state-capitalist turn in China and collapse of the Soviet bloc and the USSR, the BRICS represent the key contender formation today, albeit a fractious and involuntary one, since the oligarchic- capitalist strand within the state class wants nothing more than being included into the Atlantic ruling class. Comprising half the world's population, the BRICS bloc on the eve of the financial crisis of 2008 was closing in on the West. In Purchasing Power Parity (PPP) terms, China's GDP was three-quarters the size of the US economy, and India no. 4 behind Japan, while Brazil and Russia were catching up with the main EU states (Armijo 2007, p. 12).

THE DEFENSE OF GLOBALIZATION AGAINST THE EURASIAN/BRICS CONTENDER BLOC

When China made its turn to (state) capitalism and the Soviet Union collapsed, the ideological motif of the Cold War (the fight against communism as illiberal, undemocratic, godless, etc.) evaporated and the defense of globalisation had to be formulated anew to justify forcibly opening up states and subordinate their sovereignty to that of transnational capital. 'The defence of globalisation' in other words required express articulation. Hence, right from 1991, several strategic doctrines were being formulated to cover the unexpected ideological void.

This centrally concerned the Wolfowitz Doctrine, named after Paul Wolfowitz, undersecretary of defense in the Bush Sr. administration. Wolfowitz signed for the *Defence Planning Guidance for Fiscal 1994-'99* of 1992, which proclaims the United States the world's sole superpower. The United States should remain ahead of all possible contenders in terms of arms technology and no longer accept a situation of military parity, as with the USSR during the original Cold War (in fact, two Cold Wars: the first ending in 1970s détente, the second launched by the Reagan administration and ending with the Soviet demise, Halliday, 1986). To rein in the new-found self-confidence of the European Union after 1991, it too was obliquely warned that the United States alone would handle global policing (Mann, 2004, pp. 209–15; *Defence Planning Guidance, FY 1994–1999,* April 16, 1992).

The Clinton administration did not take exception to the assumptions of the Wolfowitz Doctrine, including the principle of 'unilateral use of force' (Van Apeldoorn and De Graaff, 2016, p. 133). Yet the blatant reference to the United States as the one 'indispensable nation' (a phrase attributed to Clinton's second secretary of state, Madeleine Albright) would not be sufficient in the longer run. The fundamental principle of the Wolfowitz Doctrine, which remains the bottom line of the West's global strategy under US leadership, was elaborated into at least four further doctrines. These each in their own way advocate opening up other states by subverting non-pliant governments, waging war including economic warfare, and providing the ideological cover for it. In this respect Fukuyama's *End of History* thesis, while gaining wide resonance as a celebration of the West's victory in the Cold War, provided little in the way of justifying further intervention in illiberal capitalist state/society complexes, apart from declaring them illegitimate (Fukuyama, 1989).

The other doctrines, then, are:

1. *The Abramowitz Doctrine.* Former US ambassador Morton Abramowitz, the president of the Carnegie Endowment for International Peace, at the time of the Soviet collapse assembled a working group to study regime change and/or war in the new circumstances. It recommended framing US intervention as intended to support 'groups within states... staking claims to independence, greater autonomy, or the overthrow of an existing government' and who by doing so, risk becoming exposed to 'humanitarian calamities' (cited in Johnstone, 2016, pp. 43–4). The Abramowitz report was published in 1992 as *Self-Determination in the New World Order* and provides a moral justification for 'humanitarian intervention'. It would be applied in Yugoslavia and remains in reserve for future regime changes, certainly in the former Soviet space. One of the members of the Abramowitz team, the investment banker and diplomat, Richard Holbrooke, was entrusted with the Yugoslavia portfolio in the State Department. In a 1995 article in *Foreign Affairs*, entitled 'America, a European Power', he argued the rationale of US intervention in shaping the post-Soviet order when he wrote, 'the West must expand to central Europe as fast as possible in fact as well as in spirit, and the United States is ready to lead the way' (Holbrooke, 1995, p. 42).

2. *The 'War on Terror' Doctrine.* We tend to associate this notion with the attacks on the Twin Towers on September 11, 2001. In fact, the concept was elaborated already in a series of conferences between 1979 and 1984 at the initiative of Israeli Likud politicians, and with high-level Anglo-American neoconservatives in attendance. The restriction of civil liberties at home and 'going after terrorists' in 'countries supporting terror' are all elaborated on at length in the printed papers (e.g., Netanyahu, 1986). Intended to make Israel's occupation policy of Palestine and the incursion into Lebanon of 1982 part of the Reagan Cold War drive, the unexpected demise of the USSR temporarily eclipsed the concept. However, Samuel Huntington in his *Clash of Civilizations* argument of 1993 revived its key theses. It provided a narrative both for a War on Terror (as a substitute for Third World counterinsurgency) and for Western military pre-eminence in the post-Soviet inter-state arena. By placing Russia and China outside the boundary of Western civilisation along with 'Islam', Huntington restores a comprehensive 'logic of encounter' to the overly optimistic End of History thesis (Huntington, 1993; Coward 2005, p. 868) and warrants regime change, to protect against alleged terrorists or illiberal states accused of harboring weapons of mass destruction.

3. *The Brzezinski Doctrine*. Zbigniew Brzezinski in *The Grand Chessboard* of 1997 gave a new version of the classical thesis of Eurasia becoming the dominant 'world island' marginalizing the Anglophone insular outer ring (also including Japan). This was first formulated when Tsarist Russia was threatening the British Empire in south Asia in 'the Great Game' (Mackinder, 1904). Brzezinski is not content with the break-up of the USSR into fifteen separate states; he also proposes to cut up Russia proper into three separate republics (Brzezinski, 1997, p. 202). In addition he proposes to combine France, Germany, his native Poland, and Ukraine into a 'critical core of European security' to overcome the advantage of strategic depth that allowed Russia and the USSR to absorb foreign invasions by Napoleon and Hitler (Ibid., pp. 84–5). In an update for the Obama administration, Brzezinski added the aspect of actual intervention, reminding his readers how he himself, as Carter's National Security Adviser, in the late 1970s had proposed to organize covert support for the aspirations of the non-Russian nationalities in the USSR, just as he had recommended luring Moscow into Afghanistan by supporting the Islamist *mujahedeen* resistance against the communist regime in Kabul (Brzezinski, 2008, pp. 60–61; Tripathi, 2013, pp. 44–5). The ultimate aim was to cut off Russia from Europe, so that it would become 'Asianised' (Brzezinski, 1997, p. 113).

4. *The Krasner-Pascual Doctrine*. The doctrine associated with Stanford International Relations scholar Stephen Krasner and the Cuban-American career diplomat, Carlos Pascual, formerly US ambassador in Kiev, was formulated in 2005. In the wake of the Iraq invasion of 2003 Bush's secretary of state, Condoleezza Rice, wanted a more aggressive doctrine of regime change. Krasner, a long-time critic of the (ab)uses of sovereignty by weak states (such as their joining forces in the United Nations to achieve a New International Economic Order in the 1970s, Krasner, 1985) was made policy planning director. With Pascual (credited with having convinced Ukraine to join in the Iraq invasion, and appointed as Coordinator for Reconstruction and Stabilization) he elaborated a doctrine of preventive intervention in weak states ('weakness' including ethnic or religious divisions), to be followed by the introduction of a stabilization and reconstruction rulebook prescribing 'market democracy'. Here the subsumption of state sovereignty to the sovereignty of capital is made explicit. A list of countries liable to breaking up (something Pascual argued might be precipitated to allow market democracy to be introduced more effectively; cited in Klein, 2005) was drawn up. The new authorities in 'failed states', reconstructed along lines dictated by the United States and IMF, would then be invited to sign contracts in which elements of their sovereignty would be alienated, 'shared' (Krasner, 2005; Krasner and Pascual, 2005).

From these one-plus-four doctrines (more could be adduced, but these are the most pertinent ones) we may conclude that after 1991, Western intervention to ensure the priority of the sovereignty of capital over national states, was not left to chance. How, then, have these doctrines affected actual Western policy if we keep in mind the eventually resurgent contender states, Russia and China?

ALTERNATING EMPHASES IN THE WESTERN ADVANCE INTO THE POST-COLD WAR WORLD

Although the West has consistently sought to occupy new space in the post-Cold War world along the lines of the Wolfowitz Doctrine, it would appear that Democratic administrations have focused primarily on Europe, seeking to push back Russia (in the spirit of Brzezinski). Republicans primarily sought to confront the rise of China and 'Islamic terrorism' (between quotation marks because the response largely preceded the emergence of a real threat). The latter theme as we saw was prepared in the Reagan period and updated by Huntington. The regime change doctrine of Krasner and Pascual would again be largely a bipartisan doctrine, albeit that the new US president, Donald Trump, in his campaign spoke out against it on several occasions.

The collapse of the USSR left NATO without a mission, as no credible threat existed any longer. Secretary of State James Baker promised to Gorbachev that the eastern part of Germany would not become militarized after a united Germany would join NATO, and that once Russia pulled out its 24 divisions from the east, the alliance would not advance *one inch* (this and comparable assurances cited in *House of Lords*, 2015, pp. 44–5). However, this was soon reneged on. Already in November 1991, NATO countries signed up to the principle of out-of-area operations (Fouskas and Gökay 2005, pp. 61–2). French proposals to revive the idea of a European defense in mid-1991, as well as the precipitate recognition by Germany of the secession from federal Yugoslavia of Croatia and Slovenia, were aggressively responded to by the United States (S. Woodward, 1995, pp. 174, 159–60, respectively). The First Gulf War to expel Iraq from Kuwait, still in 1991, in addition signaled that Washington no longer considered the Middle East an area where its influence was balanced by the USSR's, let alone Russia's.

In January 1994, the North Atlantic Council in Brussels took the decision to expand the alliance to include Poland, Hungary and the Czech Republic, and in the break-up of Yugoslavia NATO undertook its first actual out-of-area operation against the Bosnian Serbs later in the year. Probing deeper into the former USSR, NATO invited Ukraine and other former Soviet republics in the same year to join the Partnership for Peace, the newly created waiting room for NATO membership. In 1997, jointly with Georgia, Azerbaijan, and Moldova, Ukraine joined a low-key organization of former Soviet republics (after the initials, GUAM) under the auspices of the United States, the United Kingdom and Turkey. To quell Russian concerns, the NATO-Russia Founding Act in the same year laid down that no NATO nuclear weapons and permanent troop deployments would take place in the new member states. The United States democracy promotion apparatus meanwhile was seeking to capitalize on the new Atlantic bond by sponsoring 'colour revolutions' that brought pro-Western governments to power, 'Rose' in Georgia in 2003 and 'Orange' in Ukraine in 2004. Uzbekistan, which had joined the GUAM group in 1999, adding one U to the acronym, actually left again in 2005 in the wake of a color revolution that failed (Nazemroaya, 2012, p. 166). During the NATO intervention over Kosovo in 1999, the GUAM states demonstrated their new Atlantic loyalty by preventing Russia from supplying the Serbian army and even Russia's own peacekeeping units at Priština airport (van der Pijl, 2006, p. 281).

The main axis of Western expansion then shifted. In 2000, the first intelligence memo to president-elect George W. Bush, Jr., identified three strategic threats: 1) al-Qaeda terrorism, 2) the proliferation of weapons of mass destruction, and 3) the rise of China as a military power—but third only because it still 'was 5 to 15 or more years away.' Yet Paul Wolfowitz also stated that 'over the long run the Chinese political system is going to have to change' (cited in B. Woodward, 2004, p. 12), an echo of the statements on the USSR made by Richard Pipes and others in Reagan's days. The September 11 attacks on the Twin Towers in 2001 then led to the proclamation of the War on Terror; NATO was enlisted in the invasion of Afghanistan. Russia showed its readiness to facilitate the Afghan intervention, but the United States in 2002 nevertheless withdrew, over Moscow's objections, from the Anti-Ballistic Missile Treaty to allow a missile defense system to be deployed in new and prospective NATO member states, the Czech Republic, Poland, and Rumania (Van Apeldoorn and De Graaff, 2016, pp. 179–80). The Anglo-American invasion of Iraq in 2003 then saw the first stirrings of discontent among large countries not willing to submit to the whims of the United States and Britain, with France and Germany (briefly, as it turned out) siding with Russia and China against the invasion.

Under Obama, the United States would redirect the thrust of expansion against Russia again. Moscow was superficially cultivated by a 're-set' under Obama's first-term secretary of state, Hillary Clinton. In one of her last statements as secretary of state, however, she called Russia's Eurasian development plans an attempt to re-'Sovietise' the region, which the United States should try to slow down or better, prevent altogether (cited in Clover, 2012). By 2012, the hopes pinned on Dmitry Medvedev as caretaker president proved unfounded except that under the former chairman of Gazprom, the European Union's dependence on Russian gas had in fact deepened (Lyne, 2015, p. 9). In July, the first meeting of the 'Friends of Syria' followed on the refusal of Russia and China to allow the UN Security Council to mandate another regime change operation as in Libya. Hillary Clinton warned them that they were going to pay a price for their obstinacy (cited in Johnstone, 2016, p. 75).

Obama did not go along with calls to intervene in Syria, but the mood against Russia hardened further after his re-election in November, especially once Putin returned to the Kremlin. In December 2012, work began on the compressor station at the Russian end of South Stream, a new pipeline across the Black Sea to supply gas to Bulgaria and on to Austria. No wonder Hillary Clinton in hindsight considered the re-set with Moscow a sign of weakness, as Russia was not only deepening energy links with the European Union, but also 'worked to expand its own military footprint across Central Asia.... *It was like a modern-day version of the "Great Game"'* (cited in Johnstone, 2016, p. 133, emphasis added). In the Clinton state department, Victoria Nuland, the assistant secretary of state for European and Eurasian Affairs, would take it upon herself to execute such a policy in line with the neoconservative agenda drawn up by Krasner and Pascual, Wolfowitz, et al. She stayed on when John Kerry became secretary of state in Obama's second term. Signs are that a Trump presidency, although far from a regular Republican administration, will shift the emphasis back against China and notably, Iran, which plays an important part in the contender posture of the BRICS bloc (Sit et al., 2017, pp. 37–8).

THE DEFENSE OF GLOBALIZATION IN THE CRISIS

Globalizing capital is not an unchanging phenomenon. The task of 'introducing and intensifying the silent compulsion of the market', as Di Muzio phrases it, falls on changing constellations of capitalist interests. Capital is composed of different 'fractions' (productive, money, or commercial capital, mainly), and is subject to recurrent reconfigurations, affecting the direction of state policy at home and abroad. Thus we often hear that here or there, a new 'Marshall Plan' would be desirable. But the particular composition of the capitalist class that from 1947 directed the industrial reconstruction of Western Europe to bolster a mass consumption capitalism against Soviet state socialism, has long since dissolved. At the time, productive capital was the dominant fraction, money capital was still repressed under the New Deal regime imposed by the 1933 Glass-Steagall act, in line with the recommendations of J.M. Keynes for a 'euthanasia of the *rentier*, the functionless investor' (Keynes, 1970, p. 376).

It took until the 1970s before this regime was rescinded and finance was allowed to becoming the directive fraction again, inaugurating the process of a global redistribution of production. First, this occurred under inflationary conditions following the abandoning of the Bretton Woods gold-dollar standard and fixed exchange rates. From 1979, with the 'Volcker shock', real interest rates forced the discipline of capital back on credit-financed industrialization programs of the Third World and the Soviet bloc, including Yugoslavia. Indebted countries found themselves forced to export to the West to earn the hard currency for debt service henceforth. Initially the money capital perspective guiding the West in the assault on class compromise in production, state socialism, and national liberation, was 'systemic', that is, aimed a restructuring a global capitalist productive economy (Greider, 1989, pp. 75, 101). But with the lifting of the repressive Keynesian regime, a second form of money capital, 'money-dealing capital' also resurfaced (i.e., the 'rentier' variety Keynes had railed against). Especially after the collapse of state socialism, this particular form of money capital, actually a form of commercial capital, began to sideline the systemic guidance of global restructuring and replace it with a quest for short-term profit opportunities (Naylor, 1987, p. 13).

Unlike investment money with its systemic view of the accumulation cycle (the Volcker perspective of 1979), money-dealing capital, or in contemporary lingo, 'trade in financial services', has no long-term vision of a social order. It is only marginally connected to the production of surplus value, on which it preys from the outside, via the profit distribution process. As a result, issues other than buying cheap and selling dear (such as research and development, long-term investment, and the social stability required for it to mature) are secondary to its mode of operation and class perspective. Peter Gowan captures the shift when he writes that 'trading activity here does not mean long-term investment . . . in this or that security, but buying and selling financial and real assets *to exploit—not least by generating—price differences and price shifts*' ('speculative arbitrage') (Gowan, 2009, p. 9, emphasis added).

Hence, the raids on companies, pension funds, etc. and the use of credit derivatives as collateral for increased borrowing. Banks, increasingly submerged in a universe of 'shadow banking' outside the regulatory authority of central banks, gained ever-greater leverage on economic and social policy. 'Proprietary trading' (speculating not just on commission but also with a bank's own or leveraged money and deposit base) was pioneered by John Meriwether at Salomon Brothers. In 1994, Meriwether set up his own hedge fund, Long Term Capital Management (LTCM), with two 'Nobel' (Swedish central bank) laureates in economics, supposedly a fail-safe operation based on hard science. Risk-taking and manipulating the chances of coming out on top by complex insurance schemes are at the heart of the mental and moral universe this fraction of money capital inhabits and the values it propagates (Gowan, 2009). State classes wary of this type of operations, and unwilling to be the target of them as 'emerging markets', on the other hand were less and less willing to expose their societies to such speculative practices.

As in every reconfiguration of the fraction structure of capital, a key moment for the ascendant bloc is the capture of the state. Only thus can it subordinate public policy to its logic and interests. So when Meriwether's LTCM crashed in 1998, it was bailed out by the head of the Federal Reserve, former JP Morgan banker Alan Greenspan, with $3.6 billion; a pattern to be repeated in the across-the-board banking crisis of 2008, also precipitated by the 'trading desks' (Johnson, 2002, p. 216; Gowan, 2009). Amidst the high-velocity movement of funds, flowing through offshore jurisdictions, asset bubbles became a regular feature of post-1990s capitalism. The predatory raid on Asian 'emerging markets' in 1997–98 had momentous consequences for the countries affected (South Korea, Thailand, and Indonesia, notably). China was able to shield itself from the ravages of the Asian crisis, but Russia, which defaulted on its $183 billion foreign debt in 1998, and Brazil in the same year, was jolted around by short-term capital movements (Nesvetailova, 2002). The lesson the state classes in these countries learned was that the defense of sovereignty cannot be taken for granted. Yet soon after, a new round of investment opportunities in 'emerging markets' led bankers in Goldman Sachs, one of the pivots of this sort of speculative operations, to coin the notion of the BRICs (initially still without South Africa, Armijo 2007, pp. 10–11). As long as the Anglophone centers of finance were in charge, the handling of the crises following short-term capital movements only 'allowed the financial turmoil to transmute into yet another stock market/housing bubble' (Rude, 2008, p. 211).

State capture by speculative finance also includes securing the leading role of the United States in neoliberal global governance. Thus, in the midst of the storm, Japanese financial authorities proposed an Asian Monetary Fund to stabilize the situation (not unlike the currency fund of the BRICS Bank signed off on July 16, 2014). However, the United States immediately vetoed the idea, and the proposal was killed off so that 'the IMF [remained] at the forefront of the bailout' (*Financial Times* cited in Van der Pijl, 2006, pp. 319–20). This apparently technical financial governance, as Christopher Rude comments, is 'as important in maintaining global capitalism under US domination as the role played by . . . the US military in Kosovo, Afghanistan, Iraq and elsewhere' (Rude, 2008, p. 199). With the crisis of 2008, actual violence would again move into the foreground and the BRICS by then had become the target of Western aggression.

THE CRISIS OF SPECULATIVE GLOBALIZATION
AND THE TURN TO VIOLENT CONFRONTATION

The crisis of 2007–08 was the result of speculative capital movements having completely run out of control. The fact that the management of the economy, and of social and international relations as a whole, since the 1990s had increasingly been conducted from the perspective of this particular fraction of capital, also preordained the response to the crisis (Mirowski, 2013). Of course, one can abstract from real power relations and ideological tendencies and for instance regret that the incoming Obama administration did not exploit the crisis in order to restructure capitalism on an ecologically sustainable basis. The bankruptcy of General Motors might have been an excellent opportunity to do just that. In fact, Obama instructed Larry Fink, the founder of an up-and-coming investment company, BlackRock, to organize the recapitalization of financial institutions bankrupted by speculative defaults, thus bolstering the very sort of companies that had caused the crisis (Rügemer, 2016, p. 75; Fichtner et al., 2016). This serves to indicate how a particular class configuration, inspired by a particular, 'fractional' viewpoint (in this case, speculative risk-taking, which means not only financial speculation but also risk-taking in every other arena of public affairs, including foreign relations) remains the prisoner of such a mindset even when things go wrong.

2008, then, marks an epochal rupture, without a 'moderate' way out. All attempts by Western governments to cover their eroding legitimacy by throwing money into the breaches now came to an end (Streeck, 2013). As to the centrality of the United States in the global political economy, its role as the destination of the world's surpluses of money and products was reduced to a mere haven for flight capital, leaving only one leg of what Yanis Varoufakis calls the 'Global Minotaur' standing (the foreign purchase of US Treasury Bonds and other assets, Varoufakis, 2013). In the circumstances, global governance by the West has become increasingly dependent on force, the 'defence of globalisation'. Russia was now the primary target, and right in 2008, the US moved to capitalize on its political investments in, notably, Georgia and Ukraine (through the color revolutions of 2003 and 2004, respectively).

Indeed, in spite of Russian warnings it would no longer tolerate NATO adventures on its borders, GUAM members Georgia and Ukraine were told they were candidates for NATO membership at the Bucharest summit in April 2008, and it was only thanks to French and German objections that the Bush administration did not yet initiate the NATO membership process (Sakwa, 2015, p. 55). After the color revolution of 2003, the Saakashvili government had been armed by Israel on US account, partly in exchange for the use of airfields by Israel for a possible attack on Iran. In the second half of July 2008, 1,000 US military personnel conducted joint war games with the Georgian army, while an assistant of Vice President Dick Cheney, Joseph R. Wood, visited Tbilisi briefly before the attack. The attack, for which the opening day of the Beijing Olympics, 8 August, had been chosen, ended in a humiliating defeat for Georgia (De Borchgrave, 2008; Hyland and Marsden, 2008). Moscow, meanwhile, viewed Western support for Georgia and also the provision of shelter for Chechen terror suspects by the West as aimed at 'the destruction of Russia and the filling of its huge area with numerous dysfunctional quasi-state formations' (Vladislav Surkov cited in Lyne, 2015, p. 6).

This can be read as a reference to Brzezinski's ideas about cutting up Russia proper, but Moscow also saw the war as a dangerous gamble. In an interview with CNN on 28 August, president Putin accused the outgoing Bush administration of having instigated the Georgian adventure with an eye to stirring up an international crisis intended to pay off for John McCain ('create a competitive advantage for one of the candidates fighting for the post of US president'). (Hyland and Marsden, 2008). The gamble behind the Georgian assault is best understood as a corollary of the speculative mindset inherent in the primacy of money-dealing capital; the recourse to violence becomes a substitute for economic globalization through productive investment. Economic risk translates into political risk (Nederveen Pieterse, 2007). The same goes for NATO: 'Since 1989 the Alliance has attempted to institutionalize a new set of norms and to create a new identity. As in its early days, NATO today is working to create a new "social reality"—this time a reality that reinforces the *Zeitgeist* of the risk society' (Williams, 2009, p. 25. Williams sees the origins of risk society in 'a new kind of capitalism' and 'rampant globalization', pp. 5, 11).

THE BRICS DEFENSE LINE AND RENEWED WESTERN PRESSURE—TARGET RUSSIA

The 2008 collapse hit the BRICS countries hard, too. It forced China, the bloc's locomotive, to leave the fast track for a slower lane. 'As growth slows in China and in the advanced industrial world,' wrote Morgan Stanley economist Ruchir Sharma in 2012, 'these countries will buy less from their export-driven counterparts, such as Brazil, Malaysia, Mexico, Russia, and Taiwan'. These countries' export performance had risen to around 6 percent of GDP in the boom period, but now subsided again to below two percent, heralding hard times (Sharma, 2012, p. 6). However, the two most populous BRICS economies, China and India, recovered to surpass the United States and Japan, respectively. In 2015, China's GDP (PPP) stood at $ 19,731.4, the

United States at $ 18,496.0; India stood at $ 7,905.6 , well before Japan ($ 4,934.4). Russia and Brazil trailed just behind Germany (*World Bank,* 2016).

The solution to the 2008 crisis was unpalatable to the BRICS economies, though. As state-oligarchic capitalist formations, they rely on finance in a qualitatively different way from the liberal heartland. Unlike Western finance (or the patrimonial sovereign wealth funds of the Gulf monarchies), they continue to mobilize money capital for infrastructural development first, as the investment banks in late-industrializing contender states such as France or Germany did in the past (Schwartz, 2012, pp. 523–4). So when the United States and the EU countries responded to the crisis by bailing out the banks and supplying them with new money ('quantitative easing') to resume the predatory financial practices that had caused the crisis, the BRICS could not but try and shield their investment funds from it.

Private finance for infrastructure fell sharply after the crisis and banks' lending capacity was obviously reduced (and further diminished by Basle III capital requirements. Sovereign wealth funds and pension funds spend relatively little on infrastructure (Chin, 2014, p. 367–8). A BRICS development bank was to fill the gap. Its blueprint was worked out at meetings in Delhi and Durban in 2012–13, prompting Radhika Desai to write that 'Not since the days of the Non-Aligned Movement and its demand for a New International Economic Order in the 1970s has the world seen such a co-ordinated challenge to western supremacy in the world economy from developing countries' (Desai, 2013).

The key state in the involuntary contender bloc of the BRICS, the Eurasian Union, and the Shanghai Cooperation Organisation is Russia. Because it was election year in the United States, a 'Baltic bloc' of militant Atlanticist, anti-Russian states (Poland, Sweden, and the Baltic countries properly speaking) temporarily led the effort of thwarting Moscow's Eurasian economic project through an 'Eastern Partnership'. Under the Partnership, Ukraine, Georgia, and other post-Soviet states not yet incorporated into NATO and the European Union, would be invited to sign up to an Association Agreement with the European Union (Korosteleva, 2016). The Agreement, in combination with the Deep and Comprehensive Free Trade Agreement (DCFTA), is best understood as a market democracy contract in the sense of the Krasner-Pascual Doctrine, including regime change in Kiev, the chief prize.

The Association Agreement/DCFTA offer was not just an economic project. In articles 4, 7 and 10 it also included a reorientation of the country's military-political position toward the West. When Ukraine's president, Viktor Yanukovych, in November 2013 refused to sign it in spite of tremendous pressure of both the European Union and the United States (through Victoria Nuland, assistant secretary of state for European and Eurasian

Affairs, and the US ambassador in Kiev, Geoffrey Pyatt), demonstrations erupted against the kleptocracy that had distributed the country's wealth among themselves since the mid-1990s, and of which the Yanukovych family were the latest recruits. Lacking a clear set of political demands, however, the demonstrations were soon transformed into an armed insurrection by far right ethnic-Ukrainian nationalists, who chased away Yanukovych in February 2014. Western commentators did not hide their relief that Ukraine's adhesion to the Eurasian bloc had been prevented. In the words of a Chatham House author, 'Had Ukraine joined, the Eurasian Union would have extended west-wards right up to the European Union's borders. But this key element—and probably the whole enterprise—is stalled at best because the Ukrainians have created new facts on the ground' (Nixey, 2014, p. 36).

After the ultra-nationalist government in Kiev issued a law restricting the use of Russian (rescinded under Western pressure, but resumed later through separate measures) and while armed gangs were roaming the country to remove Yanukovych allies from the administration, the judiciary, and the media, Crimea seceded from Ukraine and two Russia-oriented provinces in the east, Donetsk and Lugansk, revolted in turn. The new rulers in Kiev, who had been warned not to respond with violence against the Crimean secession because of the danger that Russia would intervene to save its crucial Black Sea naval base at Sebastopol, now hesitated to respond with force against the Donbass revolt. However, their US advisers urged them to overcome their hesitations. Thanks to the hacking of the e-mail traffic of NATO commander General Philip Breedlove and his circle, we can reconstruct how this encouragement fits into a broader offensive against the Eurasian/BRICS contender bloc.

Breedlove's predecessor at the time of the Yugoslavia intervention, Wesley Clark, played a prominent role in this correspondence, since he was already active as an adviser in eastern Ukraine before the first occupations in the Donbass occurred. In an e-mail to Nuland of 12 April, Clark suggests that the United States should make a statement supporting a military operation to regain control of the east, urging her to ignore possible German objections. Still on the 12th, he asked Breedlove whether the NATO commander was willing to arrange a statement blaming Moscow for the violence, because 'if the Ukrainians lose control of the narrative, the Russians will see it as an open door' (Clark e-mails to Nuland and Breedlove, April 12, 2014; original mails on the DCLeaks website).

Clark then expands on the general geopolitical situation, another important insight into why the war party in the United States believed that Ukraine was to be 'held' and chosen as a battle ground to confront Russia and China. Claiming that 'Putin has read US inaction in Georgia and Syria as US "weak-ness",' Clark goes on to explain that

China is watching closely. China will have four aircraft carriers and airspace dominance in the Western Pacific within 5 years, if current trends continue. And if we let Ukraine slide away, it definitely raises the risks of conflict in the Pacific. For, China will ask, would the US then assert itself for Japan, Korea, Taiwan, the Philippines, the South China Sea? . . . *If Russia takes Ukraine, Belarus will join the Eurasian Union, and, presto, the Soviet Union (in another name) will be back.* . . . Neither the Baltics nor the Balkans will easily resist the political disruptions empowered by a resurgent Russia. And what good is a NATO "security guarantee" against internal subversion? . . . And then the US will face a much stronger Russia, a crumbling NATO, and [a] major challenge in the Western Pacific. *Far easier to [hold] the line now, in Ukraine than elsewhere, later* (Clark e-mail to Breedlove, April 13, 2014, emphasis added).

Thus the trope of a 'Russian invasion' served to legitimate a military strategy directed ultimately against the emerging Eurasian/BRICS contender bloc. This reading of the civil war in Ukraine contributed to widespread anti-Russian sentiment, notably in Europe. The civil war broke out in earnest in mid-April, followed by massacres by ultra-nationalists in Odessa and Mariupol in early May. A large-scale military offensive to recapture the insurgent eastern provinces, coordinated with NATO maneuvers in the Black Sea, began on 1 July. Events then took a dramatic turn when a Malaysian Airlines Boeing en route from Amsterdam to Kuala Lumpur was brought down on 17 July, in the midst of heavy fighting. Although many thousands of casualties had been made and more than a million refugees had sought a safe haven notably in Russia, this incident, in which all on board perished, was seized on to intensify the anti-Putin campaign in the West.

There was a subtext to the incident, less often noted, and related to developments surrounding the establishment of the BRICS bank. As their calls for a rupture with austerity and a more development-oriented regime at the IMF and World Bank kept being rebuffed, the BRICS countries fast-forwarded the development bank plans at a meeting in Fortaleza, Brazil, in mid-July. The 'long-term implications for global order and development' were not lost on those watching this event. The intended creation of an equivalent of the World Bank with a capital of $100 billion, with a reserve currency pool of the same size (an equivalent of the IMF), was meant to lay the groundwork of a contender pole in the global political economy challenging the West's austerity regime frontally (Chen, 2014; Pilling, 2014).

Today, with little realized of the project so far, we may dismiss the project as bluff. But on July 16, 2014, the day the BRICS leaders met in Fortaleza, the United States, in a sign of real concern about a challenge far bigger than the Japanese-sponsored AMF in 1998, imposed new, biting sanctions on Russia for aiding the Donbass revolt. These sanctions were all the more hurtful to the European Union because they were aimed at disrupting energy dependence on Russian gas, and more specifically, prevent the Black Sea pipeline, South Stream, from being realized (*Stratfor*, 2015; Venturini, 2015). The European Union, certainly the large continental EU member states, had an urgent interest in settling the Ukrainian conflict; if only to secure their gas supply, which still for the greater part passed through Ukraine. With German chancellor Merkel, who happened to be in Brazil for the world football championship finals, Putin agreed to work for a comprehensive solution that would grant federalism to the Russia-oriented provinces and legitimate the return of Crimea into the Russian Federation, in exchange for a massive economic rehabilitation plan including a rebate on the gas price for Ukraine ('Land for gas', Pagano, 2014). All this went down with Malaysia Airlines Flight MH17—the European Union dropped its hesitations concerning the new round of sanctions, and the Land for gas negotiations were suspended indefinitely. Who actually shot down the Boeing may be obscured by the propaganda war that followed, but there is no doubt about the consequences of the event.

The next step in the economic warfare program unleashed by the West was the strategic lowering of the oil price, to hit Russia directly. As argued in a *World Economic Forum* report of January 2015, 'the US and EU in recent months have come up with new forms of sanctions (e.g., the Treasury Department's Sectoral Sanctions Identifications or "SSI" list)'. The authors suggest Washington sees sanctions 'as the drones of the future—highly targeted weapons that can be deployed to devastating effect' (Bhatia and Trenin, 2015, p. 5; Crozet and Hinz, 2016, pp. 8–9). Oil prices dropped from $115 a barrel in June 2014 to around $60 by December, although the excess of supply over demand was small (Levi, 2015). One explanation is offered by investment banks speculating against the oil price on the basis of their own (oil) reserves. As Eric Draitser has reported, a US Senate hearing in July 2013 revealed that major Wall Street banks were holding physical oil assets giving them the ability to manipulate oil prices. In a Senate report focusing on Morgan Stanley, it was noted that by 2012 this bank alone had 'operating leases on over 100 oil storage tank fields with 58 million barrels of storage capacity globally' (cited in Draitser, 2016).

Since the price collapse was not remotely proportional to the market situation, the banks obviously had moved into the geopolitical domain in line with US foreign policy. The reason they and other large business would do this is what Karan Bhatia and Dmitri Trenin call, the process of 'de-globalization'. This means that 'companies are increasingly forced to think of themselves as tied to their home governments' (Bhatia and Trenin, 2015, p. 5). After the US government has defined Russia and the different contender blocs it is part of, as the enemy, the banks too have aligned themselves on this policy. This would be another example of how risk-seeking foreign policy and speculative capital have become entwined. Surveillance by heartland intelligence, the 'Five Eyes' (NSA, GCHQ, etc.) specifically targets certain BRICS embassies and companies such as Gazprom or Aeroflot, or Brazil's Petrobras (Canada's CSEC targets the Brazilian ministry of Mines and Energy (Greenwald 2014, pp. 119, 135). As Draitser concludes,

> Russia is the target of a multi-faceted, asymmetric campaign of destabilization that has employed economic, political, and psychological forms of warfare, each of which has been specifically designed to inflict maximum damage on the Kremlin. While the results of this multi-pronged assault have been mixed, and their ultimate effect being the subject of much debate, *Moscow is, without a doubt, ground zero in a global assault against the BRICS nations* (Draitser, 2016, emphasis added).

The European Union meanwhile is paying a heavy price for its Atlantic loyalty. Of the overall costs of Western sanctions and Russian countermeasures to mid 2015 of around $60 billion, 76.7 percent was incurred by EU countries, with Poland, Lithuania, Germany and the Netherlands hit hardest (Crozet and Hinz, 2016, pp. 3, 5; Kyselchuk, 2015, p. 10).

At this point the fragility of the Eurasian alternative revealed itself when Russia's closest partners, Belarus and Kazakhstan, did not wish to join Moscow's retaliatory import ban of food imports from countries sanctioning Russia. The ensuing trade frictions to prevent disguised EU food imports entering Russia highlight to what extent the contender bloc of Eurasian Union, BRICS and SCO, is an involuntary response to Western pressure. Neither do the BRICS offer the prospect of a replacement market any time soon. To China, Russia only exports 10 percent of the total, one-fifth of trade with the European Union (Sakwa, 2016, p. 13; Marioni, 2015, p. 18).

In the course of 2015, the BRICS contender bloc suffered a further setback when one of the signatories of the BRICS bank charter, Brazilian president Dilma Rousseff, was demoted from the presidency in August. She was replaced by her vice-president, Temer, a representative of the corrupt bloc dominating parliament and the media, and whose antecedents can be traced back to the military dictatorship that ruled Brazil from 1964 to 1985 (Vieira Santana, 2016). While South Africa was rocked by a corruption scandal involving another signatory, president Jacob Zuma, India under prime minister Narendra Modi was being courted by the United States with arms and other deals. Thus between 2014 and 2017, it would seem that the Eurasian/ BRICS contender bloc has been effectively reduced to China's continuing ascent as the main challenger of Western neoliberal pre-eminence. The Asian Infrastructure Investment Bank (AIIB) and the OBOR in the process have largely eclipsed the BRICS bank as a consequence (Sit et al. 2017).

How the West and pro-Western forces have succeeded in narrowing down the Eurasian/BRICS/SCO challenge to China, is an important indicator of what may well await the main contender itself.

REFERENCES

Armijo, L. E. 2007. 'The BRICs Countries (Brazil, Russia, India, And China). As Analytical Category: Mirage Or Insight? *Asian Perspective*, 31(4) 7–42.
Bhatia, K., and Trenin, D. 2015. 'Challenge Two: Economic Warfare'. In *World Economic Forum* (January), *Geo-Economics: Seven Challenges to Globalization*. Accessible through https://www.weforum.org/agenda/2015/03/why-the-oil-price-drop-matters/ (last accessed July 23, 2016).
Brzezinski, Z. 1997. *The Grand Chessboard. American Primacy and its Geostrategic Imperatives*. New York: Basic Books.
Brzezinski, Z. 2008. *Second Chance. Three Presidents and the Crisis of American Superpower*. New York: Basic Books.
Chen, D. 2014. '3 Reasons the BRICS' New Development Bank Matters'. *TheDiplomat.com* (23 July) http://thediplomat.com/2014/07/3-reasons-the-brics-new-development-bank-matters/ (last accessed June 3, 2016)
Chin, G. T. 2014. 'The BRICS-led Development Bank: Purpose and Politics beyond the G20'. *Global Policy*, 5 (3) 366–373.
Clover, C. 2012. 'Clinton vows to thwart new Soviet Union'. *Financial Times*, 6 December.
Coward, M. 2005. 'The Globalization of Enclosure: interrogating the geopolitics of empire'. *Third World Quarterly*, 26 (6) 855–871.
Crozet, M., and Hinz, J. 2016. *Collateral Damage. The Impact of the Russia Sanctions on the Economies of Sanctioning Countries' Exports*. [CPII Working Paper 16]. Paris: Centre d'Etudes Prospectives et d'Informations Internationales.
De Borchgrave, A. 2008. 'Commentary: Israel of the Caucasus', *Middle East Times* online ed., 2 September. Here accessed through http://thesaker.is/israel-of-the-caucasus/ (last accessed October 22, 2016)
Defence Planning Guidance, FY 1994–1999 (April 16, 1992, declassified 2008). Original photocopy.
Desai, R. 2013. 'The Brics are building a challenge to western economic supremacy'. *The Guardian*. 2 April http://www.theguardian.com/commentisfree/2013/apr/02/brics-challenge-western-supremacy (last accessed June 3, 2016)
Di Muzio, T. 2007. 'The "Art" of Colonisation: Capitalising Sovereign Power and the Ongoing Nature of Primitive Accumulation'. *New Political Economy*, 12 (4) 517–539.
Draitser, E. 2016. 'BRICS Under Attack: Western Banks, Governments Launch Full-Spectrum Assault On Russia'. *Russia Insider*. 21 April [reprinted from MintPress News] http://russia-insider.com/en/politics/brics-under-attack-western-banks-governments-launch-full-spectrum-assault-russia/ri14006 (last accessed April 24, 2016).

Fichtner, J.; Heemskerk, E. M., and Garcia-Bernardo, J. 2016. *Hidden power of the Big Three? Passive index funds, re-concentration of corporate ownership, and new financial risk*. Working Paper, CORPNET (University of Amsterdam. October).

Fouskas, V. K., and Gökay, B. 2005. *The New American Imperialism, Bush's War on Terror and Blood for Oil* [foreword, Peter Gowan]. Westport, Connecticut: Praeger.

Fukuyama, F. 1989. 'The End of History?' *The National Interest*, 16, 3–18.

Gowan, P. 2009. 'Crisis in the Heartland. Consequences of the New Wall Street System'. *New Left Review*, 2nd series (55) 5–29.

Greenwald, G. 2014. *No Place to Hide. Edward Snowden, the NSA and the Surveillance State*. London: Hamish Hamilton.

Greider, William. 1989 [1987]. *Secrets of the Temple. How the Federal Reserve Runs the Country*. New York: Simon and Schuster Touchstone.

Halliday, F. 1986 [1983]. *The Making of the Second Cold War*, 2nd ed. London: Verso.

Holbrooke, R. 1995. 'America, A European Power', *Foreign Affairs*, 74 (2) 38–51.

House of Lords. 2015. *The EU and Russia: Before and Beyond the Crisis in Ukraine*. EU Committee, 6th Report of Session 2014–2015.

Huntington, S. P. 1993. 'The Clash of Civilizations?', *Foreign Affairs*, 72 (3) 22–49.

Hyland, J., and Marsden, C. 2008. ´Danger grows of NATO-Russian clash in Black Sea´. *World Socialist Website* (September 1). https://www.wsws.org/en/articles/2008/09/bsea-s01.html (last accessed May 5, 2016).

Johnson, C. 2002 [2000]. *Blowback. The Costs and Consequences of American Empire*, rev. ed. London: TimeWarner.

Johnstone, D. 2016. *Queen of Chaos. The Misadventures of Hillary Clinton*. Petrolia, Cal.: CounterPunch Books.

Keynes, J. M. 1970 [1936]. *The General Theory of Employment, Interest and Money*. Basingstoke: Macmillan.

Klein, N. 2005. 'The Rise of Disaster Capitalism. Rebuilding is no longer the primary purpose of the reconstruction industry.' *The Nation* (14 April). http://www.thenation.com/article/rise-disaster-capitalism/ (last accessed May 22, 2016)

Korosteleva, E. A. 2016. 'Eastern partnership and the Eurasian Union: bringing "the political" back in the eastern region'. *European Politics and Society*, 17 (sup1) 67–81.

Krasner, S. D. 1985. *Structural Conflict. The Third World Against Global Liberalism*. Berkeley, Cal.: University of California Press.

Krasner, S. D. 2005. 'The Case for Shared Sovereignty'. *Journal of Democracy*, 16 (1) 69–83.

Krasner, S. D., and Pascual, C. 2005. 'Addressing State Failure'. *Foreign Affairs*, 84 (4) 153–163.

Kyselchuk, E. 2015. 'What effect have sanctions had so far?' In Adriel Kasonta, ed. *The Sanctions on Russia*. Bow Group Research Paper, August. www.bowgroup.org.uk (last accessed July 7, 2016).

Levi, M. A. 2015. 'Why the oil price drop matters'. *World Economic Forum* (2 March). https://www.weforum.org/agenda/2015/03/why-the-oil-price-drop-matters/ (last accessed July 23, 2016)

Lyne, R. 2015. 'Russia's Changed Outlook on the West: From Convergence to Confrontation'. In K. Giles et al., *The Russian Challenge*. [Chatham House Report, June]. London: The Institute of International Affairs.

Mackinder, H. J. 1904. 'The Geographical Pivot of History'. *The Geographical Journal*, 23 (4) 421–437.

Mann, J. 2004. *Rise of the Vulcans. The History of Bush's War Cabinet*. New York: Penguin.

Marioni, M. 2015. 'The cost of Russian sanctions on Western economies'. In Adriel Kasonta, ed. *The Sanctions on Russia*. Bow Group Research Paper, August. www.bowgroup.org.uk (last accessed July 7, 2016).

Mirowski, P. 2013. *Never Let A Serious Crisis Go to Waste. How Neoliberalism Survived the Financial Meltdown*. London: Verso.

Naylor, R.T. 1987. *Hot Money and the Politics of Debt*. London: Unwin Hyman.

Nazemroaya, M. D. 2012. *The Globalization of NATO* [foreword Denis J. Halliday]. Atlanta, Georgia: Clarity Press.

Nederveen Pieterse, J. P. 2007. 'Political and economic brinkmanship'. *Review of International Political Economy*, 14 (3) 467–486.

Nesvetailova, Anastasia. 2002. 'Asian Tigers, Russian Bear and International Vets? An Excursion in the 1997–98 Financial Crises'. *Competition and Change*, 6 (3) 251–267.

Netanyahu, B., ed. 1986. *Terrorism. How the West Can Win*. London: Weidenfeld & Nicolson.

Nixey, J. 2015. 'Russian Foreign Policy Towards the West and Western Responses'. In K. Giles et al., *The Russian Challenge*. [Chatham House Report, June]. London: The Institute of International Affairs.

Pagano, M. 2014. 'Land for gas: Merkel and Putin discussed secret deal could end Ukraine crisis'. *The Independent* (31 July). http://www.independent.co.uk/news/world/europe/land-for-gas-secret-german-deal-could-end-ukraine-crisis-9638764.html (last accessed February 2, 2016).

Petro, N. 2016. 'Why Ukraine needs Russia more than ever. With country at risk of becoming a failed state, Kiev must recognise that economic survival depends on Moscow not the west.' *The Guardian* (9 March). http://www.theguardian.com/world/2016/mar/09/ukraine-needs-russia-nicolai-petro (last accessed March 10, 2016).

Pilling, D. 2014. 'The BRICS Bank is a Glimpse of the Future'. *Financial Times* (4 August).

Pradella, L. 2015. *Globalisation and the Critique of Political Economy. New Insights from Marx's Writings*. London: Routledge.

Rude, C. 2008. 'The Role of Financial Discipline in Imperial Strategy'. In L. Panitch and M. Konings, eds. *American Empire and the Political Economy of Global Finance*. Basingstoke: Palgrave Macmillan.

Rügemer, W. 2016. 'Blackrock-Kapitalismus. Das neue transatlantische Financkartell'. *Blätter für deutsche und internationale Politik*, 61 (10) 75–84.

Sakwa, R. 2015. *Frontline Ukraine. Crisis in the Borderlands*. London: IB Tauris.

Sakwa, R. 2016. 'How the Eurasian elites envisage the rôle of the EEU in global perspective.' *European Politics and Society*, 17 (sup 1) 4–22.

Schwartz, H. 2012. 'Political Capitalism and the Rise of Sovereign Wealth Funds'. *Globalizations*, 9 (4) 517–530.

Serfati, Claude. 2001. *La mondialisation armée. Le déséquilibre de la terreur.* Paris : Textuel.

Sharma, R. 2012. 'Broken BRICs. Why the Rest Stopped Rising'. *Foreign Affairs*, 91 (6) 2–7.

Sit T.; Wong, E.; Lau, K. C., and Wen, T. J. 2017. 'One Belt, One Road. China's Strategy for a New Global Financial Order'. *Monthly Review*, 68 (8) 36–45.

Starrs, S. 2014. 'The Chimera of Convergence'. *New Left Review*, 2nd series (87) 81–96.

Stratfor. 2015. 'How the Game is Played: The Life and Death of South Stream' (17 September). https://www.stratfor.com/sample/analysis/how-game-played-life-and-death-south-stream (last accessed November 2, 2016)

Streeck, W. 2013. *Gekaufte Zeit. Die vertagte Krise des demokratischen Kapitalismus* [Frankfurter Adorno-Vorlesungen 2012]. Frankfurt: Suhrkamp.

Tripathi, D. 2013. *Imperial Designs. War, Humiliation and the Making of History* [foreword J. Galtung]. Washington, DC: Potomac Books.

Van Apeldoorn, B., and De Graaff, N. 2016. *American Grand Strategy and Corporate Elite Networks. The Open Door since the end of the Cold War*. London: Routledge.

Van der Pijl, K. 1998. *Transnational Classes and International Relations*. London: Routledge.

Van der Pijl, K. 2006. *Global Rivalries from the Cold War to Iraq*. London: Pluto and New Delhi: Sage Vistaar.

Varoufakis, Y. 2013 [2011]. *The Global Minotaur. America, Europe and the Future of the Global Economy* [rev. ed]. London: Zed Books.

Venturini, G. 2015. 'Pipeline Geopolitics: From South Stream To Blue Stream.' *Countercurrents.org* (7 March). http://www.countercurrents.org/venturini070315.htm (last accessed November 7, 2016)

Vieira Santana, C. H. 2016. ‚Der Zusammenbruch der brasilianischen Demokratie.' *KoBra* (Kooperation Brasilien) December. http://www.kooperation-brasilien.org/de/themen/politik-wirtschaft/der-zusammenbruch-der-brasilianischen-demokratie (last accessed February 12, 2017).

Williams, M. J. 2009. *NATO, Security and Risk Management: From Kosovo to Kandahar*. Abingdon, Oxon: Routledge.

Woodward, B. 2004. *Plan of Attack*. New York: Simon & Schuster.

Woodward, S. L. 1995. *Balkan Tragedy. Chaos and Dissolution After the Cold War*. Washington, D.C.: The Brookings Institution.

World Bank. World Development Indicators: Size of the economy http://wdi.worldbank.org/table/1.1 (last accessed December 27, 2016).

Index

Index

Xi'an, 92

Xi Jinping, 37, 43, 47, 66, 69, 70,
   77, 79, 81, 85, 88, 94, 101, 104,
   119, 121, 126, 137, 138, 142, 147,
   199, 210

Xinjiang, 67, 85, 92, 93, 94, 95, 97,
   101, 102, 103, 105, 106, 112, 134,
   206, 214

Xi-Putin summit, 212

Yanykovych, Viktor, 304
Yarkant, 93
Yugoslavia, 14, 204, 295, 297, 300, 305

Zhang Qian, 48
Zuma, Jacob, 308

About the Contributors

Richard T. Griffiths graduated from Swansea University and obtained his PhD from Cambridge University (UK). He has been professor at the Free University, Amsterdam and the European University Institute, Florence before being appointed at Leiden University. He is currently emeritus professor of economic history and of international studies. He has published widely on nineteenth- and twentieth-century economic development. He has also taught courses in Canada, China, Denmark, Italy, Portugal, Turkey, Thailand and the UK. His recent publications include *Configuring the World. A Critical Political Economy Approach* (HIPE Publications, Leiden, 2016) and *Revitalising the Silk Road. China's Belt and Road Initiative* (HIPE Publications, Leiden, 2017).

Zhigao He is assistant professor at the institute of European Studies of Chinese Academy of Social Sciences. He received his PhD from Free University of Berlin in 2015. Now he is in charge of the project supported by National Social Science Foundation of China (16CGJ017), China's foreign policies towards integrated organizations under the circumstances of OBOR initiative. Recent publications include legitimacy and legitimization of the European Union, World Economics and Politics (Chinese), No. 2, 2016; The analysis of influence of Brexit on EU actorness, International Forum (Chinese), No. 6, 2016.

Shigehisa Kasahara was a staff member (an economist affairs office) of the United Nations Conference on Trade and Development (UNCTAD) (1987–2013), and presently a researcher at the International Institute of Social Studies (ISS), the Hague, of Erasmus University Rotterdam, the Netherlands. His intellectual interests lie mainly in development research, including East Asian development. He co-edited the 2004 publication of Beyond the Conventional Wisdom: An intellectual history of UNCTAD. He has delivered presentations on development diplomacy, UNCTAD, East Asian development, etc., as a visiting lecturer at veracious academic institutes in Europe and Asia. Presently, his research focuses on East Asian development, particularly industrial relocations in the region.

Mohammad Razaul Karim is an assistant professor of the Department of Public Administration at Comilla University in Bangladesh. He is currently a PhD candidate in International Politics under School of Political Science and Public Administration at Shandong University of P.R. China. His research interests are in South Asia, Bangladesh foreign policy, urban local government of Bangladesh. He has published several articles in various national and international research journals.

David Lane is a fellow of the Academy of Social Sciences. He is currently emeritus fellow of Emmanuel College and previously Professor of Sociology at Birmingham University. Recent publications include: The Eurasian Project in Global Perspective (2016); (With V. Samokhvalov) The Eurasian Project and Europe (2015); Elites and Identity in the Transformation of State Socialism (2014); The Capitalist Transformation of State Socialism (2014); Elites and Classes in the Transformation of State Socialism, 2011; (With Stephen White) Rethinking the 'Coloured Revolutions', (2010).

Mikhail A. Molchanov is an independent researcher and international relations scholar based in Canada. He has worked as senior policy analyst for the government of Canada, and as professor of political science at several Canadian universities. His research focuses on international relations in Eurasia. He was the recipient of E.S. Muskie Fellowship, the United Nations University Institute of Advanced Studies PhD. Fellowship, and the NATO-EAPC Research Fellowship. In 2011, he was awarded the Japan Foundation's prestigious Japanese Studies Fellowship, and in 2012, elected Foreign Member of the National Academy of Educational Sciences of Ukraine. He is the winner of the inaugural Robert H. Donaldson prize of the International Studies Association for best paper written on the postcommunist region. His research has been supported by the Social Sciences and Humanities Research Council of Canada, the New Brunswick Innovation Foundation, the United States Institute of Peace and the United Nations University Institute of Comparative Regional Integration Studies. He has authored and co-authored 7 books and nearly 120 articles and book chapters, including, most recently, *Eurasian Regionalisms and Russian Foreign Policy* (Routledge, 2015). Dr. Molchanov is section program chair with the International Studies Association.

Kees van der Pijl is emeritus professor in the School of Global of Studies and fellow of the Centre for Global Political Economy of the University of Sussex. Before moving to the UK he taught at the University of Amsterdam. His work deals with transnational classes, global political economy, and the history of ideas. His writings include *The Making of an Atlantic Ruling Class* (1984, republished 2012), *Transnational Classes and International Relations* (1998), *Global Rivalries from the Cold War to Iraq* (2006), and a trilogy, *Modes of Foreign Relations and Political Economy* (2007–2010–2014) of which volume 1, *Nomads, Empires, States*, was awarded the Deutscher Memorial Prize for 2007.

Harry Roberts has a BA in War, Peace and International Relations from the University of Reading. He completed his first MA at UCL at the School of Slavonic and Eastern European Studies (SSEES), focusing on domestic and regional political issues affecting former Soviet Central Asia. He have recently finished his second MA at the OSCE Academy in Bishkek, Kyrgyzstan, studying China's role in the Central Asia region. His current research interests are the Silk Road Economic Belt and China Pakistani Economic Corridor.

Kaneshko Sangar is a PhD candidate at the UCL School of Slavonic and East European Studies. Previously he worked on various projects and assignments in Afghanistan, Russia, Central Asian states and Ukraine, followed by stints in Britain and the Netherlands. Kaneshko's research interests orbit around topics such as Russia's relationships with key players in Eurasia, followed by Russian foreign policies and defence strategies in Afghanistan and Central Asian region. His work has been featured in peer-reviewed journals, including "Afghanistan's significance for Russia in the 21st Century: Interests, Perceptions and Perspectives" (2016), "Russia and China in the Age of Grand Eurasian Projects: Prospects for Integration Between the Silk Road Economic Belt and the EEU" (2017). He co-founded the UCL-based Platform Ukraine / Eastern Platform in 2013, continuing to coordinate them. Email: k.sangar.12@ucl.ac.uk.

Carlos Henrique Santana is a fellow at the Capes/Humboldt Foundation and postdoctoral researcher at the Department of Political Science, TU Darmstadt. He has research expertise on comparative political economy, especially on industrial policy, financial systems, state-owned public banks, and energy policy. His main works have focused on South America, relations between South America and Central-Eastern Europe, and BRIC countries. He obtained his PhD in Political Science at Instituto de EstudosSociais e Políticos (IESP-UERJ), spent a year as visiting researcher at UC Berkeley, and since then worked with a large interdisciplinary network called Brazilian National Institute of Science and Technology (INCT-PPED). With his colleagues from the Institute for Applied Economic Research (IPEA) he also was engaged in comparative analysis of state capacity in BRIC countries. In addition, he is trying to articulate analyzes about EU external energy and resource policy. Currently, Dr. Santana is developing a comparative analysis of energy infrastructure policies adopted by Brazil, Russia, India and China in the last twenty years. The project analyzes three aspects: the federative dilemmas in coordinating policies, public financing instruments in long-term credit, and bureaucratic cohesion as the mainstay of policy implementation.

Stefan Schmalz is a senior lecturer in sociology at Friedrich-Schiller-University Jena. His research centers on global economy, development and labor relations in Europe and China. His most recent book is on China's rise in the capitalist world-system (forthcoming in 2017).

Michael O. Slobodchikoff has published several peer-reviewed articles. He has published two books, the first book, *Strategic Cooperation: Overcoming the Barriers of Global Anarchy* was published in 2013, while his most recent book, *Building Hegemonic Order Russia's Way: Rules, Stability and Predictability in the Post-Soviet Space* was published in 2014. He has another book, *Russian and Western Soft Power in Eastern Europe: Cultural Imperialism*, which is currently in press with Routledge. He is an assistant professor of political science at Troy University, and the Director of the Master's in International Relations Program. He specializes in relations between Russia and the former Soviet states, international conflict and peace, and comparative politics. He is a regular contributor to Russia Direct, and has often served as an analyst on Russian relations with Ukraine for BBC World News as well as Voice of Russia Radio.

Akram Umarov is a senior research fellow at the University of World Economy and Diplomacy (Tashkent, Uzbekistan). His field of research includes regional political processes, security and development problems in Central Asia, Russia, Post-Soviet states, Iran and Afghanistan, at the same time their relations with China, the USA, the EU, Canada, Pakistan, India, etc. The author can be reached by email at akram.umarov@gmail.com.

Jeanne L. Wilson is the Shelby Cullom Davis Professor of Russian Studies and a professor of political science at Wheaton College in Norton, MA, USA. She is also a research associate at the Davis Center for Russian and Eurasian Studies, at Harvard University. Her research interests focus on comparing Russian and Chinese foreign policy both with respect to their efforts to construct a national identity and their status as relative outliers in the international system. To these end, she is interested in interpreting their behaviour through the conceptual lens of both realism and constructivism. Her recent publications include articles in Problems of Post-Communism, European Politics and Society, Politics, and Europe-Asia Studies dealing with the topics of soft power, cultural statecraft, and the Eurasian Economic Union and China's Silk Road projects. Currently, she is involved in a collaborative project that compares Russia and China's search for status in the international system.

Xueyu Wang is professor in international relations and director of the Centre for European studies at Shandong University of China. His research interest includes regional politics theory and comparative studies, regional security, European integration, Chinese relations with its periphery regions, and China-EU relations within international organizations. Presently, his research focuses on EU and its member states' security policies toward East Asia.

Guichang Zhu is professor of international studies of Shandong University and a research fellow of the Center for European studies at Shandong University. His research interests focus on European integration and European governance. His most recent book, the *Interaction between European Supranational Governance and Member States' Governance* (in Chinese) was published in 2016.